A General
Theory of
Bureaucracy

Heinemann Educational Books, Inc.
70 Court Street, Portsmouth, New Hampshire 03801 USA

Gower Publishing Company Ltd.
Gower House, Croft Road, Aldershot, Hampshire, GU113HR, England

ISBN 0-435-82478-3 (Heinemann)
ISBN 0 566 05302 0 (Gower)
©Elliott Jaques 1976
First published 1976
Reprinted 1977, 1981, 1983, 1986

Library of Congress Cataloging in Publication Data
Jaques, Elliott.
A general theory of bureaucracy.

1. Bureaucracy. 2. Community. 3. Decentralization in government.
4. Pluralism (Social sciences).
5. Political participation. 5. Work. I. Title.
JS113.J35   1976   301.18'32   76–7380
ISBN 0-435-82478-3

Printed in the United States of America

A General Theory of Bureaucracy

ELLIOTT JAQUES

HEINEMANN

GOWER

Contents

Preface

For the past twenty-five years in the course of professional work with social institutions as a social analyst[1] and with individuals as a psycho-analyst, I have had the opportunity and the privilege to be granted that access to the inner regions of social and personal life which professional consulting relationships often make possible. That opportunity has provided a running encounter with a rich kaleidoscope of interactions between individuals within social systems. My aim in this book is to relate this experience to the work and theories of others, and to build a general theoretical construction of how social institutions and human nature affect each other, with special reference to bureaucracy.

This social-analytic work has not been pursued in any spirit of raw empiricism. I have, however, always had a liking for seeking ideas and information from the observation and teasing out of real-life situations and from involvement in social change rather than from systematic experimental work. Since I shall be basing my arguments upon the richness of qualitative data from single cases rather than upon controlled comparative studies, let me set out what these cases have been. This display of sources of data may be taken as a presentation of credentials, as evidence of relevance of background and seriousness of intent, and as a statement of entitlement to a point of view.

The Glacier Project and the Seven-year Test

The main source of data has been an extraordinary opportunity offered by the Glacier Project. I have been able to work with The Glacier Metal Company in an independent social-analytic role continuously since 1948, when the project began. The project is thus, at the time of writing, in its twenty-eighth year. For better or worse, it is possibly the longest continuous engagement of one social scientist in a social research project in connection with the growth and development of one institution. The chance to maintain what may perhaps be regarded as an exceedingly fruitful collaboration with a single institution seemed to me to be one that it

---

[1] See E. Jaques (1965), 'Social-Analysis and the Glacier Project', and R. W. Rowbottom *et al.* (1973), *Hospital Organization* (Appendix).

would be professionally and scientifically irresponsible not to take part in to the full. I have accordingly tried to do so.[2]

Nearly every area of the organization and policy of this industrial concern has been examined. New concepts and methods have been introduced on the basis of intensive analysis involving discussions with many hundreds of employees at all levels. These concepts and methods have been tested in practice not over the months but over the years, and with continual changes in the personnel involved, including four managing directors.

As a result of this long-term experience I have come to apply what I think of as the seven-year test: that is to say, I have little confidence in the validity of any new development until it has been in force for seven years. I have seen — in various institutions — too many new methods tried, such as the introduction of piecework, or of job evaluation schemes, or of co-operative systems, or of group methods, for which claims are made on the basis of follow-up studies carried out for months or perhaps a year to two years after. Every bit of my experience suggests that these periods of time are too short. The consequential effects and difficulties associated with any one change or with any shortcoming in the change itself may not necessarily begin to show for some years. They take time to work into the system.

Other Experiences

Since 1965 my experience has widened out considerably from the Glacier Metal Company, although I have actively continued my work there. Mention of these new projects may be of interest.

When Wilfred Brown became Minister of State at the Board of Trade, I had the opportunity of working with him between 1965 and 1970 as adviser on the organization of export marketing. This experience was my first direct contact with governmental organization. It gave me the chance to be

---

[2] The results of work done have been presented in a number of publications, not only by myself but also by a number of members of the company itself.

Wilfred Brown (now Lord Brown) was Managing Director and Chairman of the company from 1937 to 1965, and has written: (1960) *Exploration in Management*; (1962) *Piecework Abandoned*; (1971) *Organization*; (1973) *The Earnings Conflict*; and, jointly with myself, (1964) *Product Analysis Pricing*, and (1965) *Glacier Project Papers*.

John Collyear was Managing Director and Chairman from 1972 to the present, and has recently been appointed Managing Director of the Associated Engineering Group of which Glacier is one subsidiary company; he has written (1975) *Management Precepts*.

Derek Newman, Ralph Rowbottom, and John Evans were on the staff of the Glacier Institute of Management (GIM) for varying periods. The first two wrote (1968) *Organization Analysis*, and Evans has written (1976) *The Management of Human Capacity*.

My own books arising from the Glacier Project are (1951) *The Changing Culture of a Factory*; (1956) *Measurement of Responsibility*; (1961) *Equitable Payment*; (1964) *Time-Span Handbook*; (1968) *Progression Handbook*.

involved at first hand in the interaction between a government minister and civil servants, and to work with the civil servants themselves.[3]

During this period I was also retained by the Permanent Secretary to the Board of Trade to work on an organization analysis of the Export Services Branch of the Board. This analysis went on over a year and led to an extensive reorganization. It gave me access to a civil service organization at all levels from cabinet minister and permanent secretary to junior administrative and clerical staff.[4]

In 1965 I became Head of the School of Social Sciences at Brunel University and learned, by making many mistakes, that universities were decidedly different from industrial companies. The discovery that the bureaucratic hierarchy is an inappropriate form of organization for academic staff in a true university was a moment of illumination for me, and is reflected in the sections of this book dealing with the unfortunate tendency of industrial societies to bureaucratize everything. It is a notion that I have had the opportunity to test in other universities in England and in the United States, and as a member of the Consultative Committee of the Nuffield Foundation's Group for Research and Innovation in Higher Education.

At Brunel I have had the opportunity to take part in the development of the Brunel Institute of Organization and Social Studies (BIOSS). Through my work in the Institute I have become involved in a series of long-term consultancy research projects. The most extensive of these is the work of the Institute's Health Services Organization Research Unit, whose work began in 1966 and is contracted to continue until at least 1979.[5] This project has come at a time when the National Health Service is being reorganized as a whole after its first twenty-five years of existence. The work on the project ranges from collaboration within the Department of Health and Social Security with respect to the organization of the NHS as a total system, to collaboration at the level of the hospital ward and the general practitioner's surgery. The NHS is a vast and complex organization with national, regional, and local authorities, giving a total range of family, community, and hospital services. It is one of the largest and most complex bureaucratic systems in the world, employing about 850,000 people – including medical and dental consultants and general practitioners, nurses, administrators, architects, engineers and works staff, physiotherapists, oc-

---

[3] Some of the results of this work were published in A. Duguid and E. Jaques (1971), *Case Studies in Export Organisation*.

[4] E. Jaques (1972), 'Grading and Management Organisation in the Civil Service'; and Hansard (1969), House of Lords Official Report.

[5] Some of this work has been published in: M. Kogan *et al.* (1971), *Working Relationships Within the British Hospital Service*; R. Rowbottom *et al.* (1973), *Hospital Organization*; and Health Services Organization Research Unit (1973), *Working Papers on the Reorganisation of the National Health Service*.

cupational therapists, some twenty other kinds of professional therapist, radiographers, pathology technicians, biochemists, and some ten or more other kinds of scientist and technician.

The NHS project has pitched the Research Unit into collaborative work in a large-scale and long-term organizational change concerned with problems of organization of large and complex social systems; with questions of professionalization and of professionals in bureaucracy, of semi-professions and emerging professions, and of professional independence and clinical autonomy; with the political organization of national government services; with community participation in policy-making for public services; and much else besides. The date of implementation of change was April 1st, 1974, and the Unit is now engaged in collaborative social analytic work following up the effects of implementation. It is hoped that by the end of the 1970s a great deal will have been learned.

At the same time I have been involved as supervisor of the Social Services Organization Research Unit – sister unit in BIOSS to that working on health services organization – which is engaged in social analysis within the personal social services provided by Social Services Departments of local authorities. Here again is long time-scale consultancy research involved with large-scale bureaucracy giving professional services, with problems similar to those in the health services. Moreover, the two projects together are now giving the opportunity for work with the development of institutions which will mediate working relationships between the health and social services both at local governmental level and at the level of the home and the clinic.

On a smaller scale there has been equally interesting collaboration in work concerned with the organization of the Church of England, Civil Service Departments, and industrial, commercial and public organizations in Holland, Switzerland, Scandinavia, the United States, and Canada.

Along with these projects with which I have been directly involved, there are and have been other connected projects with which I have some association as Director of BIOSS and which have helped to widen the scope of experience – into educational policy and school systems, community and family organization, the organization of youth services, and the administration of the police and the courts.

There has also been some opportunity to back up these field studies by more systematic research studies, including a three-year study of the relationship between time-span and felt-fair pay, carried out in twelve different organizations;[6] and more recently a developing research into

---

[6] J. S. Evans: (1970) 'Time-Span: The Neglected Tool'; (1970) 'Tracing Salary Patterns'; (1971) 'Salary Patterns and the Language of Responsibility'; (1971) 'Con-

what I have termed work-capacity,[7] and a study of normal personality related to the problem of defining requisite organization.[8]

These experiences have made it possible for me to compare industrial, commercial, civil service, local government, hospital, social service, educational, university, and church organization. The comparisons have given insight into the so-called professional occupations – doctors, nurses, teachers, paramedical workers – the civil service groupings, managers, and manual workers. The involvement in these comparisons has been salutary. The discovery of differences and of similarities has led to refinements in conceptualization.

Finally, I must mention the fact that during this period I have been engaged in the practice of psycho-analysis with adults and with children. I have been engrossed in particular with the developments in psycho-analysis associated with Melanie Klein, and have found in her theories about object relations in early infancy, about the internal world, and about the nature of anxiety, some of the deeper links between the individual and his social world.

trasting Task Analysis Procedures in Consultancy-Based and Survey-Based Research'; (1971) 'Responsibility: Can We Talk It?'; G. E. Krimpas (1975), *Labour Input and the Theory of the Labour Market*.

[7] Sponsored by The Glacier Metal Company Limited and Richard Baxendale & Sons Limited.

[8] Sponsored by The Melanie Klein Trust.

To Gemma

Acknowledgments

It may be clear from this account that acknowledgments are peculiarly difficult. Gratitude for stimulation and help during more than twenty-five years of activity is not easy to record briefly. I have therefore decided to note my debt to those institutions in which I have worked intensively, or which have sponsored this work, and to some few individuals in those institutions as representative of the much wider group to whom my thanks are due. In the Glacier Metal Company I am indebted to Lord Brown (Wilfred Brown), R. L. Barnes, J. G. Collyear, P. P. Love, all the members over the years of the London Factories Works Council, and through them to the hundreds of managers, employee representatives, and employees with whom I have worked directly. On the National Health Service project I have had extensive working relationships with Mrs A. S. Blofeld, Dr D. Burbridge, J. B. Cornish, R. P. MacMahon, Sir Richard Meyjes, F. J. Short, G. H. Weston, H. I. Wickings, and F. D. Williams. J. B. Heath, W. Nicoll, and Sir Antony Part were deeply involved in the Board of Trade project. K. Adams, Canon E. James, The Reverend P. Pavey, and Canon S. Verney have initiated me into the intricacies of church organization. P. S. Baxendale of Richard Baxendale and Sons has contributed to the support of work on measurement of capacity. Wilfred Brown, Professor Keith Hopkins, Professor Maurice Kogan, Professor Dan Miller, J. A. Morris, Dr R. W. Rowbottom, Professor John Vaizey, and Professor W. Westley have made helpful criticisms of the text. I must of course acknowledge my indebtedness to all my colleagues in the School of Social Sciences and the Institute of Organization and Social Studies at Brunel University. My secretary, Miss R. Fowler, has worked with me practically from the beginning of these researches; she not only prepares the index and types the manuscript for my books, but contributes to improving the text itself.

Prolegomenon: Metamorphosis of Bureaucracy and the Question of Values

Social and political thought in industrial societies remains polarized between two conflicting ideologies: that of the centralized State and that of the pluralist society. Centralization, in the tradition of the Encyclopaedists, Rousseau and Marx, emphasizes the interaction between rational man – the individualist freed from the bonds of traditional authority – and the centralized state controlled by public opinion. Pluralism, in the sociological tradition[1] of de Tocqueville, Weber, Durkheim, Simmel, Tonnies, with an equal concern for the growth of industrial democracy, sees the need, if individual freedom is genuinely to be preserved, for the power of the central State to be balanced by an authority sub-structure in society distributed in true communities in the intermediate zone between the individual and the State.

Of the two points of view, centralization – in spite of its superficial attractiveness – leads, as bitter experience has shown, to the totalitarian State with bureaucratic domination. Pluralism, on the other hand, with a *prima facie* strong case in its favour, has been the harder view to argue. For it is difficult to discover where substantial and effective intermediate institutions, capable of supporting a sense of *gemeinschaft* or immediate community, are to be found under the conditions of urbanized industrialism which are an integral part of modern life. Durkheim's vision of corporations based upon occupational community has never come to pass. Neither have new ways readily been found of reviving or strengthening the authority of the family, the Church, the local community, the co-operative association, the trade union or professional association, without somehow regressing to outmoded and archaic social forms at best served up in a new guise.

In the controversy between centralism and pluralism, the rise of bureaucracy has almost invariably been seen as the handmaiden of autocratic centralized governmental power, and, indeed, as continually threatening to arrogate that power to itself as in the final stages of the autocratic coup or revolution. There is thus a strong tendency for most writers on bureaucracy to end up with a pessimistic view of bureaucracy's eventual effects upon democratic society. This pessimism is forcefully illustrated by Michels, for example, who wrote that 'bureaucracy is the

---

[1] Described by R. A. Nisbet (1966) in his scholarly *The Sociological Tradition*.

sworn enemy of individual liberty, and of all bold initiative in matters of internal policy. The dependence upon superior authorities characteristic of the average employee suppresses individuality and gives to the society in which employees predominate a narrow petty-bourgeois and philistine stamp. The bureaucratic spirit corrupts character and engenders moral poverty.'[2] And the question as Weber saw it was whether democratic institutions would be able to contain and constrain their bureaucratic instruments, or whether the bureaucracies would succeed in dehumanizing the democratic world.

The argument I shall pursue is that, contrary to general opinion, bureaucracies *per se* are neither centralizing nor localizing powers, neither humanizing nor dehumanizing. They are dependent institutions, social instruments, taking their initial objectives and characteristics from the associations which employ them. The powers of central government of any society should never be handed over to its bureaucrats. Those powers must remain in the hands of the governmental and other employing associations in the society. It is essential that this distinction between bureaucrats and the associations which employ them be widely understood in all industrial democracies.

The bureaucracies which dehumanize are those which have outgrown their organization structure or have never had an adequate structure, and which are too rigidly controlled from the centre: it is such bureaucracies which become monolithic in nature and ripe for abuse. It may well be, however, that in a society determined to avoid the false attractions of artificial rationalism with its dehumanized core and pseudo-democratic centralization, there is hope that bureaucracies themselves can be transformed to become agents of human feeling, pluralism, and community. If designed and managed with due regard both for the constructive qualities of human beings and for the necessary societal foundations of a liberal democracy, they could be spread out through the local community to take up their proper place as intermediate institutions serving not only local needs but central ones as well.

I will argue that under conditions of urban industrialism in which the great majority of people come to work in bureaucracies, these selfsame institutions which seem to stultify so many lives can be made to offer at least one sanctioned source of authority at community level. In factories, in offices, in schools, in government departments, in hospitals, and in social services, representatives of each employing association can interact with elected representatives of their employees, locally as well as centrally, to find policies and on-going modifications to policy which have a sufficient consensus to be acceptable.

[2] R. Michels (1949), *Political Parties*, p. 191.

Through this constitutional process of interactive participation and sanctioning, bureaucratic power can be harnessed. It can then be transmuted into the legitimated managerial authority necessary for the bureaucracy to work in a humanizing way. If bureaucracies are made more human, then their adverse effects upon those employed within them – in factories, schools or other institutions – can be alleviated, and strain removed from the families and communities to which those employees belong and in which they live. It will help these institutions to strengthen local community bonds and to reinforce the family as a source of constructive authority. I shall furthermore propose that bureaucracy metamorphosed can not only provide the motive power for social mobility in an open society, but may thus also hold the key to the prevention of the differentiation of societies into disruptive classes with rigid and nearly impermeable boundaries.

There is, of course, far more involved than participation. Bureaucracies are complex institutions, and a thorough-going change both inside and out will be required if their transformation is to be achieved. There will be required, for example, abundance of employment with opportunity for all to exercise their natural abilities to the full; a framework for the equitable distribution of economic rewards; safeguards for individual justice; linkages of public bodies with local community through consumer representatives; elimination of inappropriate bureaucratization of universities and religious institutions; provision of requisite organization for the full employment of professional skills and talents.

These aspects and many others besides must be dealt with for bureaucracy to be reunited with community, and for enrichment of human relationships to replace the alienation of institutions and individuals which has become such a feature of our time. It may then be possible to resolve the centralist-pluralist antinomy in a dialectical way by a living interaction – an intermeshing or *engrenage* – between local and central power.

I believe, in short, that the organization and control of bureaucracy can be designed so as to ensure that the consequential effects on behaviour are in accord with the needs of an open democratic society, and can serve to strengthen such a society. Whether the political will can ever exist to do so is another question. Nevertheless, the exposition of the theory and design of such institutions is my present theme and my endeavour.

The Concept of Requisite Social Institutions

The design of institutions of course implies design for some specified social object, and that object must always in the end be value-laden and political. This problem of values will be tackled in sociological terms at two levels – at the surface and in depth. At the surface it will be treated as a matter of professional sociological ethic; that is to say, society determines the social policies by its normal political means. The professional sociologist can then help to formulate and develop the types of institution which can best effect the implementation of those policies. Bureaucratic institutions are one type of such design. Such professional work in itself demands an ethical code of professional conduct. That question I have touched upon elsewhere.[3]

In depth, however, two further problems arise. The first problem is that of the values implicit in the social policies themselves. The professional sociologist must have views about those values as a sociologist and not just as a political citizen, before allowing himself to be embroiled in the design of institutions to implement the policies. The second problem is that even if the value system underlying the policies is accepted, the design of institutions must take into account and satisfy the nature of man, and not be limited to satisfying the non-human criterion of technical efficiency of output. To overlook or to avoid the question of man's nature in relation to his institutions is to reduce professional sociology to a thin and worthless social technocracy. Both these problems are inherent and inescapable parts of the professional work of institutional design. I shall consider them briefly in order to set out the criteria to be used in assessing what kinds of bureaucratic organization might contribute to the development of a socially healthy industrial society.[4]

[3] See, for example, my paper (1965) 'Social-Analysis and the Glacier Project'.

[4] How active is the value debate in sociology is attested in the proceedings of the special meeting of the German Sociological Society in 1964, in celebration of the Weber centenary. The issues raised by Weber in his 'The Meaning of "Value-Free" in the Sociological and Economic Sciences' are as live today as when he wrote in 1917, or as he stated in his 'Science and Vocation' (1918), p. 145: 'To take a practical political stand is one thing, and to analyse political structures and party positions is another. When speaking in a political meeting . . . one does not hide one's personal viewpoint . . . But the true teacher will beware of imposing from the platform any political position upon the student.'

Opinions ranging from the political activism of Habermas and the Frankfurt School, to the sober recognition by Popper that all scientific descriptions of facts are highly selective and inevitably imply values, to the widespread criticism of the conservative values implicitly taken for granted in functionalism, ensure that the dispute will continue. And so it must: for as sociological knowledge comes increasingly to be applied, Dahrendorf's admonition becomes more pressing: 'Our responsibility as sociologists does not end when we complete the process of scientific enquiry. . . . It requires no less than the unceasing examination of the political and moral consequences of our scholarly activity. It commits us, therefore, to professing our value convictions in our writings and in the lecture hall as well'. ('Values and Social Science' (1968), p. 18.)

Eric Voegelin has made one of the most telling critiques of raw value-free positivism in *The New Science of Politics* (1952), where, in his sympathetic and understanding evaluation of Max Weber's dilemma, he writes: 'When Weber built the great edifice of his "sociology" (i.e., the positivistic escape from the science of order), he did not seriously consider all "values" as equal. He did not indulge in a worthless trash collection but displayed quite sensible preference for phenomena that were "important" in the history of mankind;

The view to be adopted[5] takes as its starting point the fact that man is a species of animal which has survived and developed through the possession of certain main characteristics.[6] These characteristics include: a reliance upon living in human societies – the societal embeddedness giving man his human characteristics; a dominating will to live, to reproduce, and to maintain his society; the ability for reciprocal interaction with others, including the ability to communicate and to establish relationships based upon trust, confidence, and love; and the ability to collaborate in primary activities such as family formation and the production of the goods and services essential to survival.

It need not be assumed or argued that there is anything inherently good or bad in any of these qualities, or indeed in human survival itself. But it is self-evident that mankind believes that such qualities are good – because mankind believes that it is fundamentally good that man should survive. If it did not believe so, man would not be here to hold views and possess values. Species survival calls for the greatest tenacity or 'will to live'. It is only the species with such qualities which could possibly survive. And the will itself is not enough: there must be over-generous provision of the mechanisms of species survival such as, for example, the enormous overprovision for reproduction which characterizes all species of plants and animals.

It may come as no surprise, therefore, that what men have held to be moral or ethical or good since time immemorial are precisely those modes of behaviour which are best calculated to enhance the survival of one's own society; and at a deeper level and in more general terms, the survival of the human race. The reasonable man of the lawyers; the ethical or moral man of the philosophers; the good or godly man of the great religions; the normal man of the psychologists and psycho-analysts; the satisfied man of the utilitarians; all these men appear to conform to what might be called the sociological imperative that men must behave in such a way as to ensure that society can survive.[7] The general feature of normal behaviour is that it reinforces collaborative interaction between people – interaction of a type which includes all people or which at least does not reject anyone in

---

he could distinguish quite well between major civilizations and less important side developments and equally well between "world religions" and unimportant religious phenomena. In the absence of a reasoned principle of theorization he let himself be guided not by "values" but by the *auctoritas majorum* of his own sensitiveness for excellence.'

[5] Elaborated in work on the meaning of the normal personality, on which Professor Dan Miller and I are engaged under a grant from The Melanie Klein Trust. I have set out earlier formulation of these views in (1970) 'The Human Consequences of Industrialisation', and in (1972) 'What is The Normal Personality?'

[6] A related view is that pursued by Pepper (1970) in 'Survival Value'.

[7] As Moritz Schlick has written, 'The same moral act that makes for the happiness of persons also makes for the survival or enhancement of society.' (1939) *Problems of Ethics*.

the sense of denying their right to life and to social relationships also. Along that route seems to lie the greatest likelihood of social cohesion and in-dividual peace of mind.

The particular characteristics in individuals which are required for social interaction include at least: an awareness of self and of the self of others; the ability to communicate — with words, gesture, expression — and to comprehend the communication of others; capacity to co-operate with another in paying attention to the same subject; and the capacity for social and economic exchange relationships. It is these characteristics which I would argue are central to so-called normality.

These psychological values have their counterpart in the structure and design of social institutions. Some types of structure facilitate these normal relationships between individuals, make it easy for them to link into im-mediate social relationships, and through these into the larger network of institutions which lies beyond, with feelings of trust and confidence. I would call such institutions requisite or socially connecting: requisite in the sense of being called for by the nature of things including man's nature; and socially connecting in the sense of linking man to his society and giving him a hold upon it.

Other types of structure make it difficult or impossible for individuals to have normal relationships of confidence and trust. They force social in-teractions into a mould calling for forms of behaviour which arouse suspi-cion, envy, hostile rivalry, and anxiety, and put brakes on social relationships, regardless of how much individual goodwill there might be. Mutually antagonistic groups and societies form, the survival of one seeming to threaten the survival of the other. I would call such institutions anti-requisite or alienating — they run counter to man's normal nature, and split individuals off from their society. They are paranoiagenic institutions in the sense that in place of confidence and trust they breed mistrust and weaken social bonds.[8] They cause men of good will to despair about the

---

[8] Alan Fox explores this same field in terms of the distinction he draws between 'high-trust' and 'low-trust' societies: (1974) *Beyond Contract: Work, Power and Trust Relations*. This view of the importance of trust and of the elimination of paranoiagenesis was strongly expressed by John Stuart Mill in his analysis of the social foundations of representative government. He emphasized the importance of 'Progress' which in turn required 'Order', and it was the main function of 'Order to diminish men's suspicion of one another'. 'Yet if it is effectual to promote Order, that is, if it replaces crime, and enables everyone to feel his person and property secure, can any state of things be more conducive to progress? . . . The release of the individual from the cares and anxieties of a state of imperfect protection, sets his faculties free to be employed in any new effort for improving his own state and that of others: while the same cause, by attaching him to social existence, and making him no longer see present or prospective enemies in his fellow creatures, fosters all those feelings of kindness and fellowship towards others, and interest in the general well-being of the com-munity, which are such important parts of social improvement.' ((1861) *Representative Government*, p. 162.)

duplicity of human nature without seeing the extent to which social institutions are calling forth the worst in men and suppressing the good.

Requisite societies are open societies in the systems theory sense. So too are requisite institutions. In requisite institutions, work can be done and energy created and stored in the form of physical and cultural objects and knowledge and information. Requisite institutions and societies are thus negatively entropic. By contrast, anti-requisite institutions are entropic: suspicion and mistrust undermine collaborative interaction and work: man's relation to his physical and social environment becomes increasingly closed. Xenophobia is the social paradigm and social life runs down.

I shall try to show that some institutions are patently anti-requisite – alienating, paranoiagenic, entropic. To take but one example, collective bargaining procedures all depend upon dissembling, concealment of real attitudes, manipulation, the seeking of any advantages fair or unfair – and in the end the powerful emerge on top regardless of the justice of their case. Or to take other examples, in most bureaucratic systems people are required to do things without being consulted, and to be under the influence of one person's judgement without appeal.

There are yet other institutions which by contrast are less obviously requisite or anti-requisite. Judgement has to be exercised as to whether they will strengthen or weaken social bonds, and the judgment will depend upon the social and cultural circumstances obtaining at the time. Thus, for example, types of authority and power are accepted in social systems in time of war which would be unthinkable in time of peace.

The peculiar significance of anti-requisite institutions lies in the fact that they influence the behaviour of so many people at once. They have a double effect. There are the primary effects already described – the real weakening of social bonds, the undermining of confidence and trust, the spread of alienation and social insecurity. Then there are the secondary and more subjective effects consequent upon the first. When the institutions in a society breed objectively valid suspicion, they also stimulate the primitive irrational and pathological roots of anxiety and dread at the unconscious level in each member of that society. These invalid pathological anxieties – akin to psychotic processes – enter into and distort the judgements men make about the motives and behaviour of others – reinforcing and magnifying the objectively arguable suspicions, and enormously increasing the difficulty of achieving even that degree of mutual confidence which the real situation in a society might warrant.

It is not my intention, however, to suggest that social tension and mistrust are merely psycho-pathological phenomena, and that if everyone were psycho-analysed then social disruption and destructive conflict would disappear. The quality of social relationships is determined by much more than the sum of the psychological make-up of the individuals involved. However free from psycho-pathological suspicion the members of a society might be, they will still have to discover how to design their social institutions to enable individual constructiveness to express itself.

It is also important for purposes of sociological analysis to note the relationship between individual anxiety and the requisiteness of social institutions. And not just because of the 'angst' which is so typical of modern industrial societies! Anxiety is the state of irrational dread of being destroyed by forces outside the self, associated with the transfer into current relationships of unresolved infantile conflict and phantasized catastrophe from the social relationships of earliest infancy. As Melanie Klein has pointed out, anxiety is persecutory – the irrational dread of being harmed, damaged, destroyed by others. Suspicion, mistrust, threat – these are the unconscious phantasies at the root of anxiety.[9]

The point of my argument is that it is precisely in the area of trust, confidence, and love, as against suspicion, hostility, and mistrust, that the concepts of normality and abnormality in personality functioning meet directly with those of the requisiteness and anti-requisiteness of social institutions, each illuminating and defining the other.[10] The growth of human societies as open systems upon which the survival of the human species depends requires a sufficient number of individuals who are free enough from persecutory anxiety to be able to take part in requisite social relationships, given the opportunity and the social setting necessary to do so: society already tends to call such individuals normal. But it also requires social institutions in which it is possible for individuals to relate to one another with enough confidence for reciprocal social interaction and negatively entropic work to occur – I am calling such institutions *requisite*.

The usual situation, of course, is one in which the social institutions of a society depart to greater or lesser degree from the requisite, and the individuals making up that society range from those who are only infrequently subject to the disruptive play of anxiety to those who are so affected as to be hardly able to take part in social relationships at all – the psychologically alienated. The constant threat, however, is that the social institutions become so anti-requisite and so seriously alienating as to create a descending spiral: anti-requisite institutions arousing objective suspicion

[9] I am here using Melanie Klein's concept of persecutory or paranoid anxiety. She uses, in addition, a second concept, that of depressive anxiety, but careful study of her writings reveals that she is in fact not describing a second type of anxiety but rather the occurrence of the primitive persecutory anxiety at a more advanced level of infant development. See, for example, her very detailed accounts of the occurrence of anxiety and its theoretical formulation: Melanie Klein (1948), *Contributions to Psycho-Analysis*.

[10] It is useful to note that the term *alienation* has a psychiatric as well as a sociological and psychological meaning. Etymologically it derives from L. *alius* – other – and carries the sense of stranger, foreigner, alien. In the nineteenth century it carried the common meaning of mad or insane, and the common term for psychiatrist was alienist.

with its resonating persecutory anxiety; the anxiety in its turn disrupting individual functioning and social relationships, making the social institutions function worse.

In these latter circumstances a society will become increasingly alienating and its members increasingly alienated – a process difficult to stop. It is a process which threatens our so-called most advanced industrial nations. A split and fragmented society results. At that point rational and effective solutions become more and more difficult to achieve, because the value of rational argument has been diminished by the combination of anti-requisite institutions and of widespread suspicion floating on persecutory anxiety.

It is alienation under such conditions which contributes to violence in society. It contributes also to that particular kind of violent revolution which destroys institutions and human beings but without bringing any noticeably more requisite social institutions into existence.

In short, then, I shall take as a prime and central value that of social institutions – including social policies and procedures – which function as open systems and enhance societal survival. This same value applied to individual behaviour identifies as normal that behaviour which makes reciprocal social activity and collaborative work possible, and as abnormal that which makes them impossible. Any other value assumption would in any case imply the more or less rapid disappearance of the human race, and with it the disappearance of the problem of values. I shall illustrate in detail the many ways in which bureaucratic systems are structured and used so as to make them into anti-requisite paranoiagenic institutions. I shall hope, equally, to show how they may be requisitely organized as open systems for the benefit of society.

In adopting this point of view I must also make it clear that there is no automatic way, or 'scientific' or 'objective' way of applying the criteria of requisiteness, of openness, of species survival under particular conditions. Whether at any given point in time – immediate or historical – a particular set of values or a particular type of institution will act in the direction of the open society and enhance species survival must always be problematic. It must be decided by argument and debate, supported as much as possible by experience and knowledge. But having the criteria of openness and of species survival at least takes the debate out of the frame of reference of inherent or metaphysical or absolute values, and substitutes a question of human judgment and debate. The relationship between those criteria and pluralism in society is one which I shall hope to demonstrate.

PART ONE

INTRODUCTION AND DEFINITIONS

1

Bureaucracy in Industrial Society

One of the outstanding features of twentieth-century industrial societies is the concentration of nearly all the working population into employment in bureaucratic organizations for a wage or salary. There is little purpose in arguing in favour of this process of bureaucratization, or in decrying it. For bureaucracy is merely the instrument of a deeper social process. It is one of the primary social institutions for any society which seeks the democratic enrichment and economic security which large-scale social, political, educational and production technologies seem at their best to be able to provide. The simple fact is that *if* we decide to proceed with the development of industrialized societies, then bureaucracies on a large scale are here to stay.

The general evidence and the most widely held opinion are of course in favour of the view that bureaucracy, in spite of its practical value, tends to become socially and psychologically stultifying. This view is not difficult to understand. A pathological condition has come to dominate our bureaucratic institutions to such an extent that the democratic foundations of society are seriously threatened. But this pathology is not necessarily inherent in bureaucracy *per se*. Bureaucracy is not only a rational and efficient type of human organization, as Weber emphasized, but it has the potential to provide the setting both for constructive human relationships and for individual creative expression and satisfaction. To gain this creative setting, however, requires that we learn enough about the properties of bureaucratic organization to use and control these institutions and to avoid being controlled by them.

The particular theme of bureaucracy is merely one aspect of the more general theme of how the social institutions of any society incisively influence and channel not just the outlook and the aspirations of its citizens but their behaviour also — what they do and how they do it. Fortunately for mankind, the progress of civilization does not depend upon changing the nature of people; there is more than enough goodness in human nature to make a better society possible. Progress depends upon civilizing the social institutions which set the context within which human nature is expressed. If further progress is to be made it will be because of the discovery and creation of more humane institutions — institutions which guide and encourage the actual behaviour of people increasingly in accord with our universal sense and feelings of the normal, the reasonable, the ethical, the moral, and the good.

The effects of institutions upon behaviour are not the result of our individual personalities being changed overnight – individual personalities are hardier than that. The effects are brought about by the complex web of role relationships in which we are all enmeshed. The boundaries established by these roles play an important part in delineating the particular parts of each person's total personality which it becomes appropriate and even possible to express: allowing, encouraging, or demanding the expression of some characteristics by rewarding them; and restricting, inhibiting, or suppressing others by penalizing them. The structure of relationships between roles has a decisive effect upon the inter-subjective experience of the people who occupy them, and upon the quality of their social interactions.

It is because of the continuous and pervasive way in which role relationships set the context and limits within which people can think and act – and because the effect is largely covert and unrecognized – that the design of social institutions is important. The well- or ill-functioning of an institution is not just a matter of 'personalities'. Its primary source lies buried in the structure of the institution itself. Change the nature of this structure of social relationships and you change behaviour and the quality of social life. The same people act and go about life differently. Patterns of human relations can be critically modified. Psychic integration can be reinforced, or disintegration and confusion can be induced. In short, social institutions produce powerful effects on human behaviour and relationships: they are never neutral or innocent.[1]

The importance of the interaction between people and social institutions has had explicit recognition for thousands of years in the attempts of societies to design political institutions so as to raise the level of political responsibility and behaviour in the State. We shall explore what professional sociology could do about this same issue of institutional design in relation to the bureaucratic institutions in industrial society.

For bureaucratic institutions are ubiquitous in industrial society. By exerting a powerful influence upon the attitudes and acts of their members, bureaucracies exert a powerful influence upon the way a society functions and holds together; indeed, even whether it can survive in democratic

---

[1] I do not, however, mean to imply in any way that individual behaviour can be explained simply in sociological terms. As I shall argue in the next chapter, the issue is to understand how individual personalities express themselves within social constraints. This connection is one with which writers such as Argyris, Bennis, and Levinson, for example, have been so much concerned. C. Argyris (1957), *Personality and the Organisation* and (1960) *Understanding Organizational Behaviour*; W. G. Bennis (1966), *Changing Organizations*; and H. Levinson (1972), *Organizational Diagnosis*.

form. The possible forms of organization of bureaucratic institutions are thus a matter of importance to the establishment of the good society. These forms cannot be left to chance; nor can they be left to changing individual talent or taste, or to the interest or lack of interest of employers and administrators. And the efficiency of one or other form of organization cannot be assessed merely in terms of economic or material outcomes: it must be considered in the fullness of its impact on human feelings, on community, and on social relationships and the quality of life in society.

Phenomenology of Work

This study, then, is about democracy and the bureaucratic sector of modern industrial societies. It was very early recognized in sociological theory that this sector holds a position of special importance in such societies. Even before the present total industrialization of nations, sociologists such as de Tocqueville, Durkheim, Tonnies and Weber were well aware that industrialization makes a man's work role one of the main roles through which he experiences not only the quality of his society but his own identity as well. Bureaucracy, constituting as it does the main workplace, thus carries much of the function in modern industrialized society that was carried by the extended family, the village and the surrounding community before the industrial revolution.[2]

The particular significance of bureaucracy as the central workplace derives from the psychological importance of work itself. It is through his work that a person maintains his primary sense of reality. His work is his prime contact with the external world, and with the relationship between his own mental processes and the external world. In work, he tests the relevance of his planning and judgment by observing the actual outcome of his actions which stem from that judgment. He can match what he really produces against what he intended to produce: or in more general terms, he can check his picture of the physical and social world by trying to transform that world.

This view of the significance of work coincides with the view of reality expressed by G. H. Mead's idea that the 'I' can appear in experience as a part of the 'Me' only after it has carried out the act by means of work. In his

---

[2] As Talcott Parsons wrote: 'The dominant feature of the kinship system of modern Western urban and industrial society is the relatively isolated conjugal family which is primarily dependent for its status and income on the occupational status of one member, the husband and father. This role, however, is segregated from the family structure itself, unlike the role of the peasant father. Work is normally done in separate premises, other members of the family do not co-operate in the work process and, above all, status is based on individual qualities and achievements which specifically cannot be shared by other members of the family unit.' (T. Parsons (1949), *Essays in Sociological Theory, Pure and Applied*, p. 256.)

analysis, the core of reality lies in the actual manipulation of objects with the hands, lies in the 'manipulatory area'. It is through what he calls the 'resistance' experienced when physical things are manipulated that the basic test of reality can occur.[3] This manipulation takes place in its most effective form in work.

This view of G. H. Mead's has been greatly extended by Schutz in his analysis of the various planes of reality. Taking up Bergson's analysis of reality into a number of planes ranging from the plane of action to the plane of dreams, he gives primacy to the world of work. 'For our purposes', he writes, 'we suggest calling the stratum of the world of working which the individual experiences as the kernel of his reality, the *world within his reach*. This world of his includes not only Mead's manipulatory area but also things within the scope of his view and the range of his hearing, moreover not only the realm of the world open to his actual but also the adjacent ones of his potential working.'[4] Later in the same paper he powerfully elaborates this idea: 'The world of working as a whole stands out as paramount over against the many other sub-universes of reality. It is the world of physical things, including my body; it is the realm of my locomotions and bodily operations; it offers resistances which require effort to overcome; it places tasks before me, permits me to carry through my plans, and enables me to succeed or to fail in my attempt to attain my purposes. By my working acts I gear into the outer world, I change it; and these changes, although proved by my working, can be experienced and tested both by myself and others, as occurrences within this world independently of my working acts in which they originated. I share this world and its objects with Others; with Others, I have ends and means in common; I work with them in manifold social acts and relationships, checking the Others and checked by them. And the world of working is the reality within which communication and the interplay of mutual motivation becomes effective.'[5]

The Marxist analysis of the development of consciousness in man also takes its point of departure from work. The particular outlook of man, and indeed the major factor separating man from animal, is seen as stemming from the organization of labour. Thus, Marx and Engels write: 'They [men] begin to distinguish themselves from animals as soon as they begin to *produce* their means of subsistence, a step which is conditioned by their physical organization. By producing their means of subsistence men are indirectly producing their actual material life.'[6] They link this effect of

---

[3] G. H. Mead (1932), *The Philosophy of the Present*, pp. 124ff. See also (1934) *Mind, Self and Society*, and (1938) *The Philosophy of the Act*.
[4] A. Schutz (1967), *Collected Papers I: The Problem of Social Reality*, p. 224.
[5] ibid., pp. 226–7.
[6] (1939) *The German Ideology*, p. 7.

material production with the production of ideas and the nature of consciousness. 'Men are the producers of their conceptions, ideas, etc. – real, active men, as they are conditioned by a definite development of their productive forces and of the intercourse leading up to these, up to its furthest forms. Consciousness can never be anything else than conscious existence, and the existence of men is their actual life-process.'[7]

But perhaps the main point they make is that it is with increase in population and what they refer to as the 'true' division of labour based upon a division between material and mental labour that a significant change occurs in man's consciousness. For 'from this moment onwards consciousness *can* really flatter itself that it is something other than consciousness of existing practice', and it is this development to which they attribute the growth of sterile idealist ' "pure" theory, theology, philosophy, ethics, etc.'[8]

These ideas are systematically set out in Marx's *Theses on Feuerbach*.[9] In the first thesis he argues that 'the chief defect of all materialism up to now is, that the object, reality, what we apprehend through our senses, is understood only in the form of the *object* or *contemplation*; but not as *sensuous human activity*, as *practice*; not subjectively.'[10] It is this theme which is very close to the argument to be pursued about the significance of work as the activity by means of which reality is most fundamentally tested.

Work may thus be regarded as a critical area of human activity. To emphasize its importance is not to adopt a puritan or protestant ethical point of view. As I have pointed out previously, it is by their work that people reinforce their sanity and keep it under review.[11] It need occasion no surprise, therefore, if the bureaucratic institutions are subject to particularly intense strain: they are, after all, *the* institution by means of which industrial societies provide work roles and working relationships.

Background to Bureaucracy

Although bureaucratic hierarchies have existed as work systems at least since the Chinese and Assyrian cultures of some five thousand years ago, the dominant position of the bureaucratic hierarchy as the means by which

---

[7] ibid., p. 14.
[8] ibid., p. 20.
[9] Reprinted in (1939) *The German Ideology*, pp. 197–9.
[10] ibid., p. 197.
[11] 'Working for a living is one of the basic activities in a man's life. By forcing him to come to grips with his environment, with his livelihood at stake, it confronts him with the actuality of his personal capactiy – to exercise judgment, to carry responsibility, to achieve concrete and specific results. It gives him a continuous account of the correspondence between outside reality and his inner perception of that reality, as well as an account of the accuracy of his appraisal and evaluation of himself (even though he may not always desire

society gets its work done is a modern phenomenon. Until the onset of the industrial revolution the bureaucratic hierarchy was almost exclusively confined to the governmental and religious sector of society – to the organization of government administration, armies, and the administrative arm of the church. Even in mercantile states, no more than twenty per cent of the population were likely to have gained their livelihood through such employment.

There are a number of reasons for this fact. The first is that church and government have had sufficient capital accumulation to afford the investment necessary to provide contracts of employment and the required capital goods and equipment. But possession of capital is not enough – after all, many individuals, families and partnerships in agricultural and mercantile nations also had capital. A second factor is that a society must have become sufficiently removed from the ideology of slavery and of serfdom to make it possible for employee status – other than that of soldier, civil servant or servant of the church – in which a person works for another who is not of his own family, to be dissociated and differentiated from the status of slave or serf.[12] A third factor is that there must also be sufficient pressure from technological advance – both scientific and commercial technology – and a free market to stimulate the need for large-scale production and trading institutions. There have always been wealthy families and individuals in society, but they did not assume the position of heads of governing bodies of great managerial hierarchies of wage and salary employees. The non-governmental economic sector of society constituted self-employed traders, large and small landowners, and craftsmen. Only in exceptional circumstances did any of these permanently employ large enough numbers to warrant the establishment of even a two-level hierarchy with an employed manager in charge. The colleges of artisans and the guilds were associations of craftsmen – they were not bureaucratic employment organizations.

From the sociological point of view, a significant factor in the development of capitalism as a social and economic system was the creation of a new social institution, the limited liability company. The partnership had been the common form of private enterprise throughout economic history.[13] The company, especially the company as a large-scale employer,

---

to observe the account). And more, in the quality of enthusiasm or apathy which he brings to his work, he is faced with the state of the balance between the forces of life and the forces of death within him. In short, a man's work does not satisfy his material needs alone. In a very deep sense, it gives him a measure of his sanity.' (1961) *Equitable Payment*, p. 25.

[12] An observation for which I am indebted to my colleague Professor Keith Hopkins.

[13] A. Schlemenson (1971), unpublished M. Tech. thesis, Brunel University: 'Professional Work in Organizations, with Special Reference to Partnership as an Organizational Model.'

is a comparatively recent feature of society. Its development has been fostered nationally and deliberately by legislation on limited liability. Using Britain as an example, the acts bringing companies with limited liability into being date from the middle of the nineteenth century.[14] The change in the existing law was recognized at the time as being a profound one, and it has proved to be so.

Companies are associations of investors who take part by purchasing shares in an enterprise. Their return is in the form of dividends paid out of profits, if any, and of enhancement of the value of shares. It becomes possible for such a company of persons to get together without having to work together, indeed without even having to know one another, and to put up the investment resource necessary to launch an economic enterprise. The limited liability institution allows the risk attaching to private enterprise to become more tolerable: the investment may be lost, but family possessions are not forfeit, as they once were.

It is through the limited liability company that the use of bureaucracy comes fully into its own in industrial societies. These institutions protected the investment capital in private hands and thereby enabled the bureaucratic system to be adapted to the private economic sector of society. And once the process of industrialization gets under way it brings in its wake the full burgeoning of bureaucratic institutions for every purpose – as companies take over the main weight of production and trading activities, the public and social services grow to serve the new economy, until almost the whole of the work system of society is transformed into a bureaucratic work system. It is this development in industrial societies which in turn both facilitates and is facilitated by the rapid movement towards urbanization and the emergence of the conception of the socially mobile individual on employment contract.

The proportion of the working population employed in bureaucracies has increased rapidly until in the United States and Great Britain, for example, it is now of the order of 90 per cent,[15] and this proportion is rapidly being approached in France, Italy, Germany, Russia, and the Central European nations. With full industrialization only some ten to fifteen per cent of the working population are left who gain their livelihood as self-employed persons – including all self-employed professionals, owners of

[14] Legislation over the period 1825–56 gradually granted limited liability to most types of company. The great debate on the subject was at its height during the late 1830s, the time of the railway boom. There was initially bitter opposition from many quarters on the grounds that such an innovation would encourage rash speculation and fraudulent promotions. Eventually, the Limited Liability Act of 1855 and the Joint-Stock Companies Act of 1856 established most of the present-day practice in the United Kingdom.

[15] United Nations *Statistical Yearbook* (1955), table of 'Wage and Salary Earners as Proportion of Economically Active Males, Various Countries Around 1950'; quoted by Wilbert E. Moore (1966), 'Changes in Occupational Structures'.

small and large businesses, shops and farms, other entrepreneurs and ren-
tiers, and itinerant labour. It is useful to recognize that this development is
a nineteenth- and twentieth-century phenomenon. Until the industrial
revolution began in England, no country had more than 20 per cent of the
adult population working in bureaucratic systems.

Bureaucratic Sector of Intermediate Zone

It is this drift from the individual capitalist entrepreneur or partnership to
the dominance of the large-scale bureaucratic economic enterprise that
gives to modern industrial societies — whether capitalist or socialist or
welfare states — one of their main sociological characteristics. As these
employment hierarchies have grown both in size and in number they have
generated a new and distinct bureaucratic sector of the intermediate
zone in industrial societies. It is essential to note that this bureaucratic sector includes not just manual workers: it includes *all* employees from the
very top executives through all levels of managers, technologists, accountants and other specialists, all office staff and shop-floor production
workers.

The situation affects everyone who is employed. It is the same whether a
person is an industrial manager, senior or junior civil servant, production
engineer, secretary, toolmaker, nurse, working director, schoolteacher, airline pilot, assembly-line worker, invoice clerk, research worker, sales
representative, social worker, or belongs to any of thousands of occupations. Each one is an employee. Each is subject to the same type of
employment conditions and to similar forces and pressures. Each is dependent for his livelihood upon finding and holding a job. Each is dependent
for his progress upon an employing organization. Each is deeply rooted
socially and economically in the intermediate zone.

De Tocqueville, with his characteristically shrewd insight, foresaw this
situation. Referring to all kinds of civil association between government
and the individual as 'intermediate associations', he held them to be essential to protect the individual from being lost in the mass, and to prevent
governmental participation and centralization from dominating society.[16]

Durkheim writes in similar terms of what he calls the *corps in-
termediaries*, the associations lying midway between man and the State;
but he notably points to the occupational association as the crucial intermediate social institution upon which industrial societies must depend
to avoid disintegration. However hard it might be to conceive of corporations 'being elevated to the dignity of moral powers', he nevertheless
believed that 'sentiments of solidarity as yet unknown will spring up, and

---

[16] A. de Tocqueville (1952), *Democracy in America*, Vol. II, p. 115.

the present cold moral temperature of this occupational environment, still so exterior to its members, would necessarily rise . . . Thus the social fabric, the meshes of which are so dangerously relaxed, would tighten and be strengthened throughout its entire extent.'[17] Even though Durkheim's predictions remain unfulfilled after some eighty years, his diagnosis of what is required remains as cogent as ever. It is a view reflected in many subsequent writers, the most recent expression of it being Daniel Bell's analysis of the possible impact of professionalism and service provision in what he terms post-industrial society.[18]

The bureaucratic sector of the intermediate zone is then one of the critical regions of industrial societies, since the individual's most direct experience of the nature of himself and of his society is in the reflection of society in his place of work. In agricultural societies, the place of work overlaps his participation with his family in local community affairs. In industrial societies with developed intermediate zones, the experience of most will come from participation, away from family and local community, in the affairs of the employing organization in which they work. How the institutions in the bureaucratic sector of the intermediate zone are managed thus strongly affects the very being of citizens and their attitude towards their society and its form of government.

Whether they like it or not, and whether or not they care to recognize the fact, those who manage employment organizations bear a heavy responsibility for the well-being of the nation. By the same token, one of the critical political tasks of any democratic industrial society must be to ensure that the institutions of the intermediate zone are managed in such a way as to strengthen its democratic spirit and sense of community and not to undermine them. An explicit and accepted framework is required which will ensure that each and every bureaucratic institution will conform in its management to proper social standards while effectively carrying out its work competitively. That is the pluralist solution. It is a constitutional solution. It calls for a constitutional base for bureaucracy in the same way that we have established our political institutions on a constitutional base.

[17] E. Durkheim (1952), *Suicide*, p. 381.
[18] D. Bell (1973), *The Coming of Post-Industrial Society*.

2

Role, Social Structure, and Certain Other Social Things[1] Defined

In this chapter a number of concepts will be defined which are needed for the analysis which follows. Additional concepts will be defined as they arise in later chapters. The concepts to be defined at this stage are:

1. role, role relationships, social structure, and the nature of the social context of behaviour;
2. the differences between organization structure as manifest in charts, as assumed by the participants, as the structure can be shown *de facto* to exist, and as it ought requisitely to be;
3. public and private identities of the individual, and their connection with roles;
4. interaction between systems of roles, and role conflict and role consistency;
5. conflict between individuals and between social groups, including both consensual and dissensual conflict;
6. power and its relation to authority seen as the legitimating context of power;
7. social class as distinct from social status; status congruence and discrepancy; social inequality and social stratification;
8. social structure seen as surface phenomenon and as depth phenomenon (depth structures).

It is fortunately no longer necessary to argue the case for rigorous definition of concepts in sociology. Weber and Durkheim were masters of definition, and many authors have pointed out the great difficulties which have arisen through others' not always having followed this lead. Dahrendorf, for example, illustrates the point very well. He lists a selection of definitions of the concept of class, and describes the dilution of the concept as a result of variation in definition: 'Whoever reads these definitions may well be tempted to regard sociology as a rather frivolous discipline. Indeed, theories can neither be formulated nor refuted on the basis of these definitions, some of which are plainly bare of substance, others too

---

[1] E. Durkheim (1964), 'The Determination of Moral Facts'.

profuse, and all far removed from the original concept of class.'[2]

It is useful, indeed essential, to recognize two different types of definition, and to use them both. The first is that of *boundary definition*: the definition of physical, social or psychological things by means of categorization and the setting of boundary limits. Thus, the concepts 'chair' or 'social class' would be defined in terms of those characteristics which would be included within the boundaries of these categories: legs, backs, seats, etc., in the case of a chair; aggregates of people with common interests seeking power, etc., in the case of a social class.

The second type of definition is *operational definition*: the definition not of things but of *dimensions* or *qualities* of things by means of a description of the operations necessary to measure those dimensions or qualities.[3] Thus, the concepts of redness or of temperature of physical bodies would be defined in terms of the operations involved in constructing and using a spectrometer or a thermometer. I shall illustrate how operational definition may apply to the definition of level of work, and its significance for the definition of such important qualities as degrees of power, degrees of authority, violence of conflict, etc.

Role, Role Relationships, and Social Structure

The concepts of role relationships and social structure are completely central to my argument. The design of institutions is the theme; and roles and role relationships are the building blocks of which the institutions are to be constructed. The definition of role and of social structure, however, presents a problem of the same order as the definition of bureaucracy (a problem to which we shall turn in the next chapter). The terms are used in many different senses. And even the usefulness of the concepts themselves

---

[2] R. Dahrendorf (1959), *Class and Class Conflict in an Industrial Society*, p. 75. Dahrendorf's comments are reminiscent of Francis Bacon and John Hobbes, both of whom were so punctilious over questions of clear definition. One of Hobbes' comments has always seemed to me especially acute – 'Errors of definitions multiply themselves according as the reckoning proceeds ... in the right definition of names lies the first use of speech; which is the acquisition of science; and in wrong, or in no definitions, lies the first abuse; from which proceed all false and senseless tenets; ... for words are wise men's counters, they do but reckon by them; but they are the money of fools, that value them by the authority of an Aristotle, a Cicero, or a Thomas, or any other doctor whatsoever, if but a man.' (1962) *Leviathan*.

[3] As defined originally by P. W. Bridgman (1927) in *The Logic of Modern Physics*. There has been a tendency to lose sight of this definition in the social sciences and replace it by an incorrect and less useful notion of operational definition as meaning definition of a thing in terms of what it can do. The importance of keeping to Bridgman's definition is that it lays a necessary foundation for the development of measurement and measuring instruments. For it is the properties of things which are measurable, not the things themselves.

has been called into question by the phenomenologists[4] on the grounds that it is difficult if not impossible for the scientific observer, a third person, to envisage with any accuracy the meanings of a given relationship to those immediately involved in it.

The difficulty can be illustrated in the most common usage of the term *role* as established by Ralph Linton who defined it as the dynamic aspect of status. This usage, firmly established in sociology by Merton, has also become the standard social psychological usage. By the dynamic aspect of status is meant what the person does, how he behaves as a result of social position or status. Indeed, the term role used in this way is completely interchangeable with the term behaviour, but behaviour seen as determined by social structure. The analogy with the stage – rightly criticized by the phenomenologists – is used to illustrate that the actor's role is what he does, how he acts, as determined by his part. What is less explicitly acknowledged is the extent to which this definition has led in the direction of seeing all social interactive behaviour as a function to be explained simply by external social forces, leaving practically nothing to be explained by personality factors and inter-subjective interaction.

By contrast, Simmel, Goffman and his co-workers, and Garfinkel and the ethno-methodologists[5] are inclined towards a definition in terms of behaviour alone, without reference to status in Linton's terms. They are more concerned with socialization processes, spontaneous social interactions, and the general cultural background of behaviour. Social interaction is to be seen largely in terms of the free and mutually adjusting behaviours of the individuals immediately concerned, within spontaneously assumed roles arising in the immediate situation.

The central issue, of course, is how social behaviour – that is to say, social interaction as against subjective phantasy or reverie – is to be explained. How much is this interaction determined by the interactions of socialized personalities, and how much by the roles in which those personalities are placed? How much of behaviour is idiosyncratic, psychologically determined from within the individual; and how much is generalized, externally determined by forces in the social situation in which the individuals find themselves? Some sociologists such as Brim[6] would argue that if the sociological content of roles were sufficiently described, then all aspects of behaviour would be satisfactorily explained. Some social psychologists such as Katz and Kahn and Rommetveit[7] would tend

---

[4] See, for example,: A. V. Cicourel (1973), *Cognitive Sociology*; A. Schutz (1972), *The Phenomenology of the Social World.*

[5] E. Goffman (1961), *Encounters* and (1970), *Strategic Interaction*; G. Simmel (1950), *The Sociology of Georg Simmel*; H. Garfinkel (1967), *Studies in Ethnomethodology.*

[6] O. G. Brim (1960), 'Personality Development as Role Learning', pp. 127–59.

[7] D. Katz and R. L. Kahn (1966); *The Social Psychology of Organizations*; and R. Rommetveit (1955), *Social Norms and Roles.*

towards the opposite view.

Parsons and the structure-functionalists have tried to resolve the issue by laying emphasis upon the conception of the individual and his personality meshing into the role he occupies and emerging as the actor, the person-in-role. Role here is taken as a normative concept, influencing the behaviour of the individual by setting social norms within which he should act. The difficulty, however, has been that in application the personality factors have tended to be overlooked, social interaction has been seen largely in terms of dominating social forces, with the result that the actor has tended to become something of a sociological robot.[8]

These difficulties may be overcome by *defining a role as the sociological context of individual behaviour*. Roles are not separate social entities but always parts of role relationships, the relationship between roles being an integral part of the definition of role itself. Role relationships in turn have to do with the setting of the social context (including both boundaries and direction) within which those taking part in the relationship will constrain or limit their idiosyncratic behaviours so that a mutually adaptive interaction may occur. In phenomenological terms, the role relationship is a typification of boundaries or limits; these define the social accord with respect to the areas of relevance within which the persons involved agree to act and thus to have some hope of achieving an inter-subjective relationship.

Dynamic Boundaries of Role Relationships

In its most general sense a *role* may be defined as a knot in a social net of role relationships. No role can exist by itself. A role stands not on its own feet but only in relation to other roles with a connection between them. The *social net* describes the array in which the roles are set out in relation to one another. *Social structure* refers to particular patterns of role relationships in social nets; for example, hierarchical, circular, etc.

The concepts of role and role relations will be used not to refer to required behaviours but rather to the ruling out or exclusion of behaviours, to the setting of the general direction or goals of behaviour, and the boundaries within which the individuals involved may behave. Within those boundaries, behaviour is free; it is for the individuals to behave as they will, to decide what to do, to assess the meaning of one another's behaviour, and

---

[8] How easy it is for this result to occur can be seen in Talcott Parsons and in Kingsley Davis (1949), *Human Society*, p. 26. Both make provision for the individual, but fail in their writings to follow through to actual individual differences. This present book also will be seen to be open to some extent to this same criticism. I have not included much in the way of individual case material, but have concentrated upon bureaucracy as social institution.

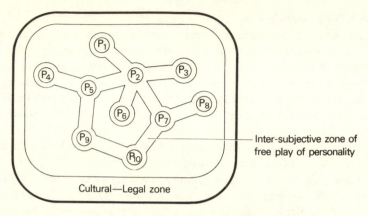

Inter-subjective zone of free play of personality

Cultural—Legal zone

Figure 2.1

to judge how to respond to one another, so long as they do not move outside the boundaries of their role relationship.

Figure 2.1 illustrates a network of roles. The role relationships are drawn as boundaries setting up channels within which the incumbents P_1, P_2, P_3, etc. may act towards one another at their own discretion. The boundaries are shown as having thickness and as irregular in outline. They are social constructions.

Looking at the field in more detail, we can examine the interaction between, say, P_1 and P_2, as illustrated in Figure 2.2. The interaction is

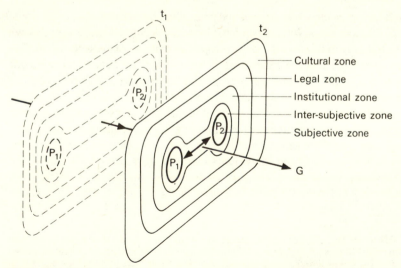

Cultural zone
Legal zone
Institutional zone
Inter-subjective zone
Subjective zone

Figure 2.2   Field of behavioural interaction (P_1 and P_2 moving together towards a cooperative goal, G)

shown as a cross-section in time, in which the two persons are working together to achieve a common objective, O. The *objective* sets the direction for the behaviour of P_1, and P_2. The persons may not necessarily be in full co-operation, or may even be in conflict, with respect to the direction in which they are moving. The direction may have been set for them, or agreed between them. But there must be a direction of some kind for a social interaction to continue, even if it is only that each person is trying to use the other for his own ends.

This overall socially determined direction is one of the two main dimensions of the social context of their behaviour. The second dimension comprises the social boundaries within which the behaviour is channelled. In general, the structure of social boundaries may be conceived of as composed of layers or zones, the outer layers constraining the inner, as illustrated in the diagram.

The three outer layers are culturally or socially determined, and envelop the individuals concerned. They exist in social reality, independently of particular individuals. They constitute a broad background of social interaction.

The first of these outer layers, the *cultural zone*, is the most pervasive. It contains all the implicit cultural constraints which individuals pick up in the course of socialization and which make up the folkways; for example, the boundaries of appropriate behaviour in ordinary social greetings, in deference to age, and in any of a wide variety of different manners and customs on which the functioning of a society depends.

The next layer, the *legal zone*, contains the framework of laws within which everyone is legally required to constrain his behaviour.

There may then be an *institutional zone* in those cases where the interaction is taking place within an institutionalized setting, such as, for example, in the bureaucratic systems we shall be considering, or in a professional association.[9]

There are then two inner zones, constructed by the actual persons concerned in the interaction, which last only so long as the interaction is taking place. These two zones give the fine tuning, so to speak, to any social interaction. They give the particular quality to the interaction set by the sub-identities of the individuals themselves, within the broader background set by the three outer zones.

[9] I am indebted to Professor D. Miller for the observation that a further elaboration of this analysis would include another zone; namely a *social network zone*. This zone would be composed of the implicit constraints set by the non-institutionalized social networks to which people belong. As these networks become explicitly organized, with established rules governing the members, they become part of the institutional zone. Towards the more personal side, they interact with the inter-subjective zone, helping to establish the public identities of the individuals involved.

The first of these two inner zones may be termed the *inter-subjective zone*. It is the zone of mutual arrangement by the participants of the special limits or rules of their relationship. It is an arrangement which flows, fibrillates, readjusts, as their perceptions of each other influence their interacting behaviours. It is as in a card game where the players not only agree on certain special rules but adjust to each other in terms of how quickly they play, how forcefully they put the cards down, whether they use facial expressions to mislead the other, how and whether they speak — in short, how by expressive movement, tone of voice, and other non-verbal indicators, they carry on the style and tone of the on-going interaction.

The second of the two inner zones concerns each person separately. It consists of the boundaries which each one sets for his own behaviour, and may be termed the subjective zone of the behavioural context. This *subjective zone* is in constant interplay with the inter-subjective zone, and gives the colouring of the personality of each participant to the interaction. Internally — that is to say, within the person — the subjective zone forms part of each individual's public identity (q.v. later in this chapter). It is thus through the subjective zone and its link with the subjective interaction that role becomes linked to public identity to self-identity and core personality. Role and personality are zones in a continuous field.

It is within these boundaries that P_1, P_2, P_3 ... will constrain their behaviour. In order to do so, they have to be able to recognize the locus of the boundaries, either by long socialization as in family role relationships, or by special training as in the case of some occupational roles. Processes of attention enable the individuals to keep note of the location of the boundaries, and (if they wish to remain in role) to inhibit inappropriate behaviours — the process referred to as keeping control of oneself. Attention is thus also a boundary process. It is concerned with the screening out of parts of the field, leaving the rest in sharper focus for the free play of perceptual searching.[10] This process of inhibition in relation to the limits and direction set by the social context is precisely the process of self-control.

The various layers composing the boundaries setting the field of role relationships are not necessarily sharply demarcated, nor are they fixed and immutable. They may range from boundaries which have relatively sharp outlines and are relatively fixed — as in the case of some highly institutionalized and specified offices or caste relationships — to boundaries which have only the sketchiest outline and are continually changing — as in the case, for example, of role relationships between new neighbours, where most of the detail of the social constraints remains to be established and

---

[10] This view of attention as a process of inhibition restricting a field is one which has been well described by E. G. Schachtel (1963), *Metamorphosis*.

filled in by the particular persons concerned in their own way as part of the inter-subjective zone.

Role relationships thus constitute a field within which behaviour occurs. The persons occupying the roles are part of the total field. The actual behaviour at any given point in time will be a resultant of the personalities of those persons, their perception and understanding of one another, their attitudes to the behavioural constraints imposed by the role relationships setting their social field or areas of relevance, their degree of socialization with repect to those constraints, and their ability to inhibit and control their flow of behaviour so as to keep it within the field. The social field of role relationships serves to reduce the areas of relevance and thus to decrease the areas of possible uncertainty in inter-subjectivity to manageable proportions.

It will be apparent from the foregoing that in the delineation of the field each role has a position in relation to other roles. The *position* is the particular location of each knot in the net. It establishes the structurally given connections between roles – which roles are immediately connected and which are more distant and connected only through other roles. If the social net is a hierarchical one, the description of the position of a role may also require a statement of its level in the hierarchy, an aspect of position for which I shall use the term *status*.[11]

This conception of role and role relationships fits readily into the everyday use of the terms. It gives, for example, a more precise concept of role in a play than does the pure structural definition. An acting role is seen as setting boundaries: the role relationships are given; certain sounds must be made within the context set by written words; the general objectives are set out; the sequence of lines is prescribed. The actors must stay within these boundaries. But so long as they do so, the actors must judge how to speak the words, how to stand, how to move, what inflections to give, how to interact with other actors, what pace to use, when to pause, what gestures to use; that is to say, how to bring to each role that personal and idiosyncratic individuality in actual behaviour known as an interpretation, within the personally coloured subjective and inter-subjective contexts.

The network of connections has characteristics depending on the type of institution. Defining with precision the various contents of these connections in terms of role relationships will be one major part of my analysis. It will take us into the establishment of role specifications for a family of some fifteen or more main types of role relationship to be found in bureaucratic systems. It is upon the elaboration of these roles and role relationships that the development of the design of sound institutions will depend.

[11] In contrast to Linton and others who use *status* to refer to the elements of social structure.

Detachability and Permanence of Roles

What then of offices as compared with status or roles? I would suggest that these distinctions – including Parsons' structuralist concept of role, Weber's offices, Linton and Merton's status, and the Simmel and Goffman type of situated role – can be seen as different types of role and generalized into a single conceptual framework by taking account of two major properties of roles (defined in relational terms as knots in a social net). These properties are: first, the *detachability* of the role from the person who occupies it – the extent to which it can be institutionalized so as to be able to exist as an explicit vacancy in a social net for which an occupant can be sought, or contrariwise the extent to which it is attached to a particular person and will cease to exist when that person gives it up; second, the *permanence* of the role – the extent to which it is evanescent, existing for the moment while a particular group of people happen to be together, or long-lasting because it has been institutionalized and detached, or has become attached to a person perhaps for life.

Different roles and role systems will vary in their degree of detachability and permanence: for both these properties are quantitative continua. There are three particular combinations of these two properties, giving three special sets of role which I shall require for my analysis. I am extracting these sets of role from these two scales in a rough and ready way as first approximations, and not in any way to set up an artificial typology.

First are those roles – the offices – such as employment roles, or elective roles in associations – which are towards the permanent and the detachable end of the spectrum. They tend to be established independently of specific individuals, they remain permanently in existence unless explicitly modified or terminated, and become vacant any time the current incumbent leaves.

Second, there are roles which tend to be attached to a specific individual and which are associated with him permanently or nearly permanently. The individual always carries the role regardless of immediate circumstances, and the role ceases to exist only with his death or by some legal process of alteration or severely penalizing process of disqualification – such as the role of father of the X family or the role of the qualified Doctor Y. Their most extreme forms would be roles determined by sex, age or colour.

Third, there are those roles which are evanescent, situational in the Simmel and Goffman sense, and which are created by individuals who have come together or have been thrown together by circumstances, whether in pairs, triads, or small or large groups. Being evanescent they are inevitably attached to individuals, although they have a general existence in the cultural role repertoire described by Goffman. Such roles are the roles occupied by acquaintances out for a walk or having a drink together; or even more to the extreme end of the spectrum, by the individuals involved in an accidental gathering.

Since both offices and kinship roles are relatively permanent, the systems composed of nets of those roles form stable social institutions such as bureaucracies, families, professional associations. Since situational roles are evanescent, the social systems composed of nets of these roles form evanescent gatherings or social networks.

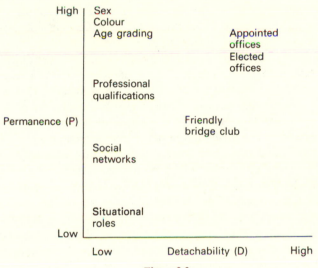

Figure 2.3

It is those systems whose roles are relatively permanent and relatively detached – the high-P-high-D role systems – which are often referred to as 'formal organizations', and those systems whose roles are relatively permanent and relatively undetachable – the high-P-low-D role systems – which are often referred to as informal organizations acting usually within the framework of the formal. I find the formal-informal dichotomy a weak one, however, obscuring or missing the richness of the plurality of different organizational systems. Thus, for example, I have referred to three different sets of roles based upon the combination of different degrees of detachability and permanence. Many other combinations are possible, such as, for example, the moderately permanent and moderately detachable roles of a small friendly bridge club, or the absolutely attached roles (with therefore a degree of permanence dictated by the lifetime of the occupants) of the 'broken plate' situation.[12] I believe it important to try to give as precise content as possible to the properties of each of the multiplicity of structures shown by sociological analysis to merit attention.

Manifest, Assumed, Extant and Requisite Social Structure

The phenomenologists such as Schutz and Cicourel[13] have of course cast doubt upon the value of this type of definition of role. They have reasonably raised the question of whose description of a role or role relationships is to be taken – the actor's, those with whom the actor is in role relationship, or the outside observer's? This problem need not raise insurmountable difficulties. It certainly does not require the simple so-called commonsense description of everyday life in which Garfinkel and the ethnomethodologists seem to have trapped themselves.[14]

This problem can never be completely resolved, any more than can the general epistemological problem of the existence or non-existence of an external world. The method we have been using, however – that of social analysis[15] – does, I believe, go some way towards a resolution. All the data about role relationships and social structure which I shall be using have been processed meticulously and in detail in a particular way. The data have been collected at the invitation of those directly involved in the role relationship. The social analyst analyses each role in discussion with the incumbent to the point where a statement has been created which seems correct to that incumbent. The description of each of the roles in the relationship is then, with the agreement of each individual, reported to the others. Each participant's view of the nature of the role relationship is publicly shared. Any discrepancies in perception can then be analysed and discussed with them all, until an agreed analysis is achieved.[16]

This process of analysis may sometimes take weeks or months before an

---

[12] A situation described by G. Simmel in his *Soziologie*, and referred to by R. M. MacIver and C. H. Page (1960) in *Society: An Introductory Analysis*, in the following footnote on page 44: 'A group of industrialists were seated at a banquet when a plate was dropped and shattered into fragments. It was observed that the number of pieces correspondended to the number of those present. Each received one fragment, and the group swore that at the death of any member his fragment was to be returned, the plate thus being gradually pieced together until the last surviving member fitted in the last fragment and shattered again the whole plate.'

[13] See supra, n. 4, p. 24.

[14] H. Garfinkel, see supra, n. 5, p. 24.

[15] See E. Jaques (1965), 'Social-Analysis and the Glacier Project', and R. W. Rowbottom (1973), *Hospital Organization*, Appendix B.

[16] Experience shows that people do not lightly agree to a given analysis. There is too much at stake: accountability, authority, degrees of freedom, field of action. Feelings run high, and agreement is achieved only at that stage where the incumbents feel comfortable with the analysis. Even so, subsequent experiences may throw doubt upon the agreed formulation, and the process of analysis is taken up again.

agreed description of the role relationship and social structure is obtained. Often no definition of the role relationship has been in existence, so that new role relationships have had to be formulated and defined. It is by this means that a number of new types of role relationship have been discovered, as described in Chapter 17. As with any process of discovery, the time required is unpredictable.

The description of a role relationship can thus never be more than a process of successive approximation. But with careful and continuing research and testing, an increasingly close approximation may be gained. The start of the process is always to some extent confusing. On the one hand, there are the role relationships as set out in the organization chart – what might be termed the *manifest social structure*. The role relationships thus publicly described are rarely correctly defined, and are certainly not to be taken at face value even if they can be understood.

On the other hand, there are the role relationships as understood by each of the participants – what might be termed the *assumed social structure*. The structure as assumed by one participant will differ to greater or lesser extent from that assumed by any of the others, and some or all may differ from the organization as manifest.

One of the main difficulties in sorting out and comparing these different views of the role relationships in which the participants are ensconced is the absence of sufficiently elaborated and precisely defined concepts, the absence of even the beginnings of a serviceable language.

The object of analysis and research is thus a twofold one. The first part of the object is to progress by successive approximation to an increasingly precise conception of the 'actual' nature of the role relationship, the 'actual' nature of the context within which the participants are behaving – what might be termed the *extant structure*. This extant structure may be complex and shifting when the areas of relevance of the participants are different. In the case of bureaucratic systems, the extant situation will be influenced by the limits set for the roles which the incumbents have been employed to take up.

The second part of the object, carried out in concert with the first, is to develop an adequate language in which to formulate the findings of the research into role relationships. As the contents of role relationships are analysed they can be named, and the process of further analysis and research is facilitated.

Thus, we shall require the concepts of manifest, assumed, and extant social structure, the last being always an approximation to the actual situation as revealed by analysis and research and as confirmed by the participants. There is a fourth perspective on role relationships. It is a normative one. It is concerned with what a given role relationship ought to be. It will be referred to as the *requisite social structure*: requisite in the dictionary sense of required by the nature of things. A preliminary formulation of requisiteness was presented in the Prolegomenon. It will not be defined further at this stage, however. In one sense, the completion of the definition is what this book is about.

The proposed resolution of the phenomenological problem of the meaning of role relationships to the participants, is much more readily applied to relatively high-P-high-D bureaucratic social systems. Precisely because the role relationships are detachable from their incumbents and are relatively permanent, they can be held up by their incumbents and looked at in the light of day, considered at leisure and at a distance, *in abstracto*. The role relationships can be described and written up as though the roles were vacant. Under such conditions it becomes possible for the third-person observer to assist the incumbents to clarify the nature of their extant role relationship, of the institutionalized limits within which they have been behaving towards each other; that is to say, the institutional context of the area of freedom of inter-subjectivity.

It is then possible, in addition, for such analyses to be offered up to the decision-making centre of the system – higher up the bureaucratic system or to a policy-making council. At this point decisions can be taken as to what the role boundaries *shall* be – shall, in the sense that a condition of the employment contract is that the incumbents of the role can be held accountable for constraining their behaviour within the explicitly institutionalized context: that is the meaning of an office in a bureaucracy.

This kind of analysis becomes less possible the less permanent are the role relationships and the less detachable are the roles from their incumbents. Thus, for example, in the evanescent occasions, or situational role relationships, to which Goffman has devoted such intensive study, the meaning of the relationship to the actors becomes far more difficult to establish, and the phenomenological critique of much of the analysis of social structure becomes more apposite. Where role relationships are fleeting, and determined by personally established inter-subjective contact of the moment within more or less overlapping fields of relevance (or indeed, by varying degrees of lack of contact), then the analysis of role relationships must either be based upon the pure conjecture of the observer or else reconstructed afterwards *in vitro* out of the memories of the participants. Such *post hoc* analysis can provide only an approximation to the nature of each role relationship as it was. The accumulation of such approximations in the hands of Goffman and others has, of course, illuminated the nature of the cultural repertoire of role relationships, the unconscious role boundaries that are part of the folkways of a society.

With respect to the actual inter-subjective relationships between people acting within these role-relational boundaries, that analysis must always be either conjecture or *post hoc* as in the case of the analysis of evanescent role relationships themselves. The clarification of on-going inter-subjectivity is a delicate and subtle matter of psychological analysis. The sociological analysis of the boundaries of interpersonal relations, with which this book is concerned, however, is an essential frame for the understanding of the meanings to actors of their inter-subjective play.

Public and Self Identity of Individuals

If social interaction is to be understood in terms of the interplay between a definable social context and the personal peculiarities of the particular persons involved, then it must be possible to link our concepts of social structure with a related conceptualization of personality. We have already indicated how this interplay might occur at the juncture between the subjective zone of the behavioural context and the public identity of the individual. This concept of public identity, and the related concept of self-identity, are taken from an analysis of personality made by Professor Daniel Miller.[17] His concepts interlock with our conceptualization of social structure like the pieces of a jigsaw puzzle.

Miller defines a person's *identity* as the 'pattern of observable or inferable attributes [which] "identifies" a person to himself and others; . . . [it] is a socially labelled object which is . . . frequently re-evaluated both by the person and others in groups in which he is a member. . . . In time, the members of a social group develop a detailed picture of each individual, his *public identity*. They conceive of this identity in terms of the characteristics which are most relevant to the group's norms and which therefore have the greatest effect on his relationships with others. . . . The *objective public identity* is a person's pattern of traits as they appear to members of the groups; *subjective public identity* is his perception of his appearance to the group. *Self-identity*, the person's private version of his pattern of traits is similar to the more common "self-concept" — except that self-concept sometimes lacks the connnotation that the self is a social object. Subjective public identity exerts a considerable influence on self-identity.'[18]

The particular viewpoint adopted is close to that of sociologists like Mead, Cooley and Goffman. Miller quotes from Mead to the effect that in great part 'the individual experiences himself as such, not directly, but . . . indirectly, from the particular standpoints of other individual members of the same social group, or from the generalized standpoint of the social group as a whole to which he belongs.'[19]

[17] D. Miller (1963), 'The Study of Social Relationships: Situation, Identity and Social Interaction'.
[18] ibid., p. 673.
[19] G. M. Mead (1956), *The Social Psychology of George Herbert Mead*, p. 215.

Miller then divides the total identity, both public and self, into three spatially connected regions: core, peripheral region, and intermediate sub-identities. The *core* is the most central part of the identity, comprising the most basic traits, those formed earliest and which 'involve his body and its sensations, his awareness and evaluation of self, his feelings of intentionality and control, and his sense of responsibility.'[20] The *peripheral region* is that part of identity which is idealized and presented to the world. Between these two regions are found the *sub-identities* which have to do with the particular characteristics of his personality which a person brings to bear in the way he carries particular roles: how he personally behaves as a father, or a lawyer, or a manager, or a friend. Each person will thus have as many subidentities as the number of different roles he occupies.

Interaction Between Systems of Roles (Role Conflict)

Because the present study is concerned with institutionalized structures of the bureaucratic type, it will be strongly oriented towards roles of the high-P-high-D type. But it will be necessary also to consider two related role systems: the high-P-low-D roles of the non-hierarchical professional institutions in connection with the employment of the professions in bureaucratic hierarchies; and the low-P-low-D situational roles in connection with those gatherings of individuals which are the necessary precursors of the formation of institutionalized associations, as well as in connection with the behaviour of the particular individuals involved in any given bureaucratic event.[21]

There is another reason why it will be necessary to take at least these two types of role into account. Every person's behaviour is influenced, bounded, pressed into place, not solely by whichever role he happens most immediately to be occupying but by his full complement of roles – one or more active, others latent, some overt, some covert, some consistent and some in conflict.

Systems of roles do not interact directly upon one another – if the roles are connected they become part of the same social structure. Systems of roles interact only indirectly, by acting through individuals who occupy roles in the different systems. Two social nets do not touch each other: they communicate only if there is an individual who occupies a knot in each net, or if there are individuals from each net in personal relationship with one another. Two social systems interact with each other through the agency of

---

[20] ibid., p. 674.

[21] Goffman's analysis of the behaviour of members of a team of surgeons, junior doctors, nurses, during the course of an operation illustrates the interaction between the boundaries of behaviour in the various offices, and the boundaries of behaviour in the situational roles selected from the cultural role repertoire by the particular individuals: (1961) *Encounters.*

persons occupying roles in both. In doing so they exert stress in varying degree upon those persons.

Role conflict is that state where an individual occupying roles in two or more social systems is subject to inconsistent boundaries limiting his behaviour in the different roles, so that to the extent that he remains within the boundaries of the one, he will be falling outside the boundaries of the other. *Role consistency* is the opposite state, where the various behavioural boundaries are congruent and mutually reinforcing.

The design of any social institution must therefore take into account the nature of other established institutions in society. If it does so, it may gain in functional competence through mutually reinforcing interaction with other institutions. If it does not do so, it risks functional distortion or paralysis through the inhibiting effect of role conflict upon its members. We shall have cause to consider such interactions between bureaucratic systems, political systems, professional associations and trade union associations.

Individuals and Conflict Between Social Groups

No two individuals or groups in interaction are ever likely to desire to move in precisely the same direction, any more than any two forces are likely to by found in nature acting in precisely the same direction. Conflict is as much an ordinary and inevitable feature of social interaction as opposing forces are an inevitable feature of fields of force in the physical world.

In the social world, conflict may exist at three different levels. *Intra-psychic conflict* is the situation within the individual seeking two or more incompatible goals at the same time. *Interpersonal conflict* arises wherever two individuals interact in seeking to fulfil incompatible goals. Such conflict may occur, for example, when two people seek to possess the same object; competition consists of just such conflict. Or it may arise as a result of two people in role relationship being determined to go in different directions but required by the role relationship to find a common direction.

Social group conflict arises whenever two or more institutionalized groups (associations or nations) find themselves involved in interaction with respect to incompatible objectives as formulated by their governing bodies. As with interpersonal conflict, so in social conflict the incompatibility of objective may arise in attempts to possess the same object (conflict over pay or over territory, for example); or as a result of differences between power groups within the same social system desiring to go in different directions (espousing incompatible policies, for example).

The distinction is made between interpersonal conflict and social conflict for the following reason. In any social system it is inevitable that all kinds of interpersonal conflicts will continually occur. There will also continually be individuals within the system who are dissatisfied to greater or lesser degree with its policies, its functioning, its value to them. But these individual dissatisfactions and interpersonal conflicts within a social system do not singly or in aggregate constitute social conflict. For social conflict to occur there must be a confluence of dissatisfactions around which groups associate with the common aim of taking action as a group to mitigate the problem. It is when organized group acts against organized group that social conflict may be said to exist.

It will serve my purpose to distinguish between two categories of conflict. First, varying degrees of *consensual conflict*, in which each of the contenders aims to achieve as much of his objective as possible, but within an overall live-and-let-live framework and ending with mutual accommodation if not full-scale resolution of differences. Interactive or consensual conflict requires, and indeed thrives upon, debate, argument, reasoning, discussion, persuasion. It is among the most constructive of all social activities. It leads to the precipitation of possible decisions or policies and their formulation so that they can be considered, possibly accepted or even endorsed – ranging from mundane family discussions and decisions through to far-reaching decisions of state. To move from conflict to discussion to *pro tem* resolution of conflict is a vivid enriching human experience, at the absolute core of democratic life. It acts as a centripetal force binding society together.[22]

The second type of conflict is a very different matter. It is that conflict which has passed the point of no return; that is to say, irreconcilable or *dissensual conflict*, in which the contenders cannot conceive of co-existence without sacrificing integrity, and the aim of each is either to get the other to submit completely to coercion or else to break the relationship by banishing the other or in the final analysis by annihilating him. Here we are dealing with social breakdown or potential breakdown, with an absence of the kind of dialogue which might lead to resolution. At best there may be truce for a time, but it is an uneasy truce likely to explode and disintegrate at any moment. Such conflicts act as a centrifugal force, tearing social systems apart.

Consensual conflict would fall into the category of what Dahrendorf calls regulated conflict. 'For effective conflict regulation to be possible, both parties to a conflict have to recognize the necessity and reality of the conflict situation and in this sense the fundamental justice of the cause of the opponent ... Wherever the attempt is made to dispute the case of the opponent by calling it "unrealistic" or denying the opponent the right to

---

[22] Consensual conflict is consistent with the Zen concept of the dilemma, as against the tendency to regard conflict in terms of antinomies. This point is developed in an interesting manner by A. Low (1976) in *Zen and Creative Management*.

make a case at all, effective regulation is not possible.'[23]

For consensual conflict to occur there must be institutionalized procedures for the regulation of conflict. These procedures must be agreed upon by the potential parties to a conflict *before* the conflict occurs. That is to say, consensual conflict includes the mechanisms by which the conflict is to be regulated.

By contrast, dissensual conflict cannot be regulated. As Dahrendorf puts it,[24] it is dealt with by the suppression of one of the conflicting parties by the other. Where there is no agreement on the mode of regulating conflict, suppression by coercive power is the only possible outcome. The coercive force may be manifestly physical as in the case of police or military suppression. Or it may be indirectly physical, as in the case of the threat of unemployment to a group of strikers during an economic depression.

Power and Authority

I shall employ the terms *power* and *authority* in what is their common current usage in sociology. *Power* is the rate of the induction of behaviour in others. It is the quality of an individual (or a group) which enables him to influence other individuals either singly or collectively by channelling and directing their behaviour in such a way as to help him to fulfil his aims. It is that quality which gets others to act, to work, to do things on one's behalf. The power of individuals or groups may derive from many sources, physical strength, psychological ability, social prestige, collective action, economic wealth. *Coercive power* is that power deriving from the ability to force another to carry out instructions, by physically constraining and directing him or by physically detaining him.

Authority is an attribute of a role which gives the incumbent the right to exercise power within socially established limits, and to apply to others positive or negative sanctions (rewards or punishment) depending upon the quality of their behaviour. It is thus the exercise of power in a manner which others have said is allowable and are prepared to support. Authority is therefore the institutional transformation of power channelled and limited within a social system.

So defined, power may be authorized by anything from one other person to a whole nation through its government. The *strength of authority* will rest upon the power of the authorizing group. The greatest authority is that vested in a role by government on the part of the State, since to the State is reserved the right *in extremis* to exercise coercion, even to the point of deciding life or death.

[23] R. Dahrendorf (1959), *Class and Class Conflict in Industrial Society*, p. 226.
[24] ibid., p. 225.

It may be noted that authorization of power may be given by two very different groups: by the group towards whom the power is being used; or by some other group which sanctions the exercise of power against a third party. The use of power in these two circumstances will be experienced as very different by those subject to its influence. In the first instance they will not be surprised, because they will have agreed in advance to be influenced and will have agreed the sanctions to be used against themselves if they fail to react satisfactorily to the authorized power stimulus. In the second instance they will feel resentful, or feel themselves being subjected to attempted coercion — the authority will not be acceptable to them.

The process by which those subjected to power may take part in setting its context and thereby authorizing it is the *legitimation of power*, and the resulting power is *legitimate or authorized power*. The governments of states have legitimate power in this sense towards all citizens, although those who would wish to overthrow the State would certainly not experience it as legitimate. It is in circumstances of deviance of this kind that governments may decide to exercise coercive power towards citizens who refuse to conform to legislated requirements.

Social systems on a smaller scale than the nation may contain roles which carry legitimate power — for example, bureaucracies. The question of the legitimacy of the power is simply a matter of determining to what extent those subjected to power are able to take part in authorizing its use, and in circumscribing or removing the power if the authorized limits are exceeded.

Multi-dimensional Analysis of Class and Status

A person's occupation and income are among the most powerful determinants of the class and status of himself and of his family. Since in industrial societies occupations and the distribution of income are provided mainly through the bureaucratic sector, the manner of functioning of bureaucracies is of considerable import in social class formation and the fixing of social status. At the same time the nature of class, status and power in a society are among the important external factors which influence the extent to which requisite bureaucratic organization is possible.

A *social class*, as in the original Marxian sense, is a group which through a common relationship to the means of production is led to organize to act to retain power or to seize it from some other group. In this sense 'the analysis of social class is concerned with an assessment of the chances that common economic conditions and common experiences of a group will lead to organized action.'[25]

[25] S. M. Lipset and R. Bendix (1951), 'Social Status and Social Structure'; B. Bernstein (1971), *Class, Codes and Control*, Vol. I, p. 45.

This definition of social class differs sharply from a usage which began to some extent with Weber and has become widespread in sociology, in which class is simply one type of stratified social status, as in, for example, Lloyd Warner's six-stratum classification. The difference is important. The present definition leaves the concept of social class intact as a major element in the analysis of social conflict. As Dahrendorf has put it, 'Class is a category for purposes of describing hierarchical systems at a given point in time.'[26]

Social status, by contrast with social class, I shall use in the multi-dimensional sense current in sociology, to refer to a person's position on any of a series of different social scales which rank people in society. Such statuses include: economic status, including income and wealth; social position (in the Lloyd Warner sense of social class) both of individuals and of families; occupational status, referring to the prestige attaching to occupation but not necessarily to the true level of work of occupation; true level-of-work status (as measured in time-span of discretion); prestige, honour and respect; caste. In addition, in certain circumstances, religion, ethnic group, race, kinship and nationality may confer social status.

Status congruency exists to the extent that all of a person's social statuses rank at the same level. To the extent that they do not, *status discrepancy* may be said to occur.

Some statuses are ranked in a continuum of *inequality*; for example, the scale of income runs continuously from very low to very high without being divided or divisible by definable boundaries into any identifiable groupings. Some statuses (and social class as well) are divided into *bounded groupings*; that is to say, there are identifiable separations between groupings, as in the case, for example, of castes in a caste system. As I have indicated in my definitions of role and social structure, these boundaries have form and are dynamic. To cross a boundary implies a qualitative change in state, and not just a movement from one point to the next on a continuous scale.

Some statuses are not only organized and structured by boundaries, but may also be *stratified*; that is to say, they are divided by horizontal boundaries into a hierarchy of strata or layers, the social status being given by

---

[26] R. Dahrendorf (1959), *Class and Class Conflict in Industrial Society*, p. 76. W. G. Runciman (1973) in *Relative Deprivation and Social Justice* has made a reasonable attempt to make sense out of Weber's definitions. He tries to clarify and use Weber's distinction between class and status, but succeeds only in demonstrating that it is not possible in doing so to keep a clear distinction between the two. 'To speak of a person's "class",' he writes, 'is to speak of his approximate, shared location in the economic hierarchy as opposed to the hierarchies of prestige or of power. "Status", by contrast, is concerned with social estimation and prestige, and although it is closely related to class, it is not synonymous with it (p. 39). I prefer, with Dahrendorf and with Lipset and Bendix, to include the Runciman type of definition under economic status.

position in one or other stratum, rather than in a continuum of inequality as in the case of income; organizational levels (as I shall describe them) are stratified in this sense, as is the Lloyd Warner six-'class' (or strata) system.

Social stratification is often loosely and incorrectly used to refer to any status hierarchy. I believe it is important to separate scales of inequality from bounded groups and from stratified groups, because the dynamics of the relationships are different. Thus the 'working class' is a grouping but not a stratum, although it is often referred to as though social stratification could be applied to the analysis of class structure. Or, to take another example, many so-called class studies in Great Britain[27] adopt the Registrar General's classification in terms of strata based upon the drawing of a number of artificial boundaries through the income continuum and the occupational status continuum: such studies have a certain descriptive value and can be used for rough comparative purposes and studies of gross social trends; but they are of limited value from the point of view of social dynamics, and they serve to weaken both the concept of class and the concept of social stratification and to diminish their value.

The essence of a bounded group or a stratum is that its boundaries are socially real. To traverse the boundary requires force and a definable change in quality. To move from an income of £40 a week to an income of £41 a week does not of necessity demand any reorganization of the person or his outlook. To move from the working class into the capitalist class does of necessity imply an observable qualitative shift.

Surface Structure and Depth Structure

There are two main levels at which the concept of social structure may be used.

The first level of social structure is that of the system or network of connected roles which can be deduced or abstracted by direct observation: it is a generalization from the properties of social phenomena. The product of this type of structural modelling at the surface of concrete social relations may be termed *surface structure*.

The second meaning is that of structure in the philosophical sense of analytic structuralism, as used in the social sciences, for example, by Piaget, Lévi-Strauss and Chomsky. It refers to the assumption that there exist underlying systems or wholes which can be discovered and which can give explanatory meaning to the world of observation. These systems are discovered not by the abstraction of common features from the properties of things, but by reflective abstraction from 'our ways of *acting on things*,

---

[27] M. Abrams (1968), 'Some Measurement of Social Stratification in Britain'.

the operations we perform on them.'[28] They are deductive structural models, the conceptual structures which lie in depth below the concrete observational social relations. The product of this type of structural modelling in depth by reflective abstraction can be termed *conceptual* or *depth structure*.

From these two definitions of structure come two of the features of this book. The first is the description of the main findings from a few long-term studies of bureaucratic social systems. These findings will be used to construct a systematic outline of requisite organization composed of the surface structure and some of the policies which appear to be a necessary condition for those bureaucratic hierarchies to function effectively.

The second feature is the consideration of the conditions which underlie requisite organization. What are the structures in depth, whose operations may be discerned, which act powerfully on bureaucratic organizations, influencing their surface structure and the way they function? A number of depth structures will be described. These conceptual structures have been derived by means of reflective abstraction from a few cases, and not from statistical or comparative studies.[29] And the data have been obtained not from things but certainly by 'acting on things' as Piaget would have it, in the consultancy research setting in which the work was done and in which institutional analysis and development were the goals.

Surface, Superficial, and Depth

In speaking about surface analysis and depth analysis I do not mean to imply that one is more worthy than the other; that one is somehow superficial and the other more substantial. Scientific development requires both the systematic description and the display of the surface and

---

[28] J. Piaget (1971), *Structuralism* p. 19. The italics are his. In describing how algebraic groups are obtained, he writes: 'The primary reason for the success of the group concept is the peculiar – mathematical or logical – form of abstraction by which it is obtained; an account of its formation goes far to explain the group concept's wide range of applicability. When a property is arrived at by abstraction in the ordinary sense of the word, "drawn out" from things which have the property, it does, of course tell us something about these things, but the more general the property, the thinner and less useful it usually is. Now the group concept or property is obtained, not by this sort of abstraction, but by a mode of thought characteristic of modern mathematics and logic – "reflective abstraction" – which does not derive properties from *things* but from our way of *acting on things*, the operations we perform on them; perhaps, rather, from the various fundamental ways of *co-ordinating* such acts or operations – "uniting", "ordering", "placing in one-one correspondence" and so on.'

[29] As Claude Lévi-Strauss has put it, 'it is not comparison that supports generalization, but the other way around . . . – it is necessary and sufficient to grasp the unconscious structure underlying each institution and each custom in order to obtain a principle of interpretation valid for other institutions and other customs, provided of course that the analysis is carried far enough' (*Structural Anthropology* (1963), p. 21).

relationships at the surface, and intuitive grasp of the deeper structures which illuminate the surface and make it more comprehensible and more amenable to human control.

T. S. Eliot argued in a telling manner the difference between superficial and surface, and in so doing saved the concept of surface for its proper use. In his essay on Ben Jonson[30] he contrasts Jonson and Shakespeare, describing Shakespeare as a writer of the depths as compared with Jonson whose 'poetry is of the surface ... but not "superficial" in a pejorative sense. ... We must look with eyes alert to the whole before we apprehend the sense of any part ... and the "world" of Jonson was sufficiently large to allow him to do so.' Jonson did not get the third dimension, but – as Eliot points out – in contrast to many of his contemporaries he was not trying to do so.

In organizational terms, it is the manifest and assumed pictures of organizational structure which are likely to be superficial. The manifest or publicly displayed organizational structure will very often be found to be well wide of what is happening in reality. And the structure as it is assumed to be by the participants will vary not only from what is really the case but also from individual to individual – the inconsistencies demonstrating the superficiality of each one's view.

The true elaboration of the surface requires work. It is not there for the asking. The extant or actual situation at the surface is usually buried beneath the superficial manifest picture and further obscured by a glut of incorrectly assumed pictures. It needs to be exposed carefully, piece by piece, so that a whole pattern may be displayed. That is what is meant by surface.

The analysis of the depth structure of social systems is another matter. Our conception of the depth structure of a particular institution – such as, for example, bureaucracy – will strongly colour our conception of how that institution ought to be constructed, just as our conception of molecular structure influences our design of physical things. It is the concept of requisite organization which thus links depth structure and function – which links with what the institution is for or ought to be for, as required by the nature of things. In the case of social institutions this not only means as required by the activities to be carried out, but at a greater depth it means as required by the nature of man himself.

---

[30] 'Ben Jonson' in T. S. Eliot (1951), *Selected Essays.*

PART TWO

BASIC FEATURES
OF BUREAUCRACY

3
Bureaucracy and the Employment Contract

The concept of bureaucracy has been omitted from the previous chapter on definitions for two reasons. The first reason is that the clarification of this concept is the central task of the book, and it therefore warrants special treatment. The second reason is that the existence of any bureaucracy depends upon the prior existence of an employing association (whether an individual or a small or large number of individuals). In order to clarify the meaning of *bureaucracy* it is absolutely essential to consider it simultaneously with the concept of *association*: in so doing, the two concepts can be contrasted, the fundamental differences between these two social institutions can be established, and, that being done, their fateful interdependence may be fully revealed.

The first chapter of this section of the book will briefly define how it is proposed to use the concepts of bureaucracy and association. Associations are primary independent institutions formed by individuals who come together to pursue a common object, and they therefore have an existence in their own right. Bureaucracies, by contrast, are secondary and dependent institutions – set up in the main by associations. Without an employing association (or an individual employer) bureaucracies can neither exist nor persist: that is what employment is about.

The employment contract by means of which bureaucratic systems are established and employees recruited is then considered. The employment contract fixes the central feature of bureaucratic roles; namely the accountability of employees for the work they are expected to do. This accountability is the starting point for the analysis of managerial roles and managerial authority. Accountability calls for human judgment as to whether assigned tasks have been satisfactorily discharged; judgment in turn calls for authority – the authority of one person to assess another's competence. These questions of accountability and authority set the limits to how many immediate subordinates it is possible for one manager to have.

How associations function is described, including how associations are formed, and the representative mechanisms by which they are governed. The objects of associations are particularly important, since it is these objects which set the tasks of the bureaucratic system they employ.

Definition of Association and Bureaucracy

An *association* is a group of individuals with a common goal who have come together and formed themselves into an institution with explicit rules and regulations governing membership. There are many different types of association. Some of them – as MacIver and Page have pointed out – take on the explicit and institutionalized form of the corporate type in which they become unlimited in time-span and become able to hold financial and other assets as a corporate body.[1] Such permanent associations include companies (in the legal sense), trade unions and staff associations, employers' associations, institutionalized clubs, churches, universities, co-operative societies, political parties, professional societies and institutions – any or all of which can and do employ staff.

MacIver and Page also include the nation as a type of association. Such a broad definition of association must be open to question, since there are such marked differences between a nation and any other association – as for example, in the very special powers possessed by governments over the lives of citizens on behalf of the nation. Nevertheless, for my present purposes I find it useful to treat them together in the manner suggested by MacIver and Page. I shall regard nations as non-voluntary associations, and shall consider the special consequences of this feature in relevant sections.

The permanence of voluntary associations is commonly expressed in the legal phraseology of a 'body corporate with perpetual succession of membership and with the common seal'. The perpetuity of succession describes the institutional permanence, and the common seal symbolizes the corporate 'I' of the association.

People may form themselves into associations with a variety of different objects. They may wish simply to work together in some common co-operative endeavour as in a professional partnership or in a co-operative to build themselves houses. Or they may wish to regulate their behaviour towards one another so that all may be relatively free, as in a nation. Or they may wish to arrange for some common service to be made available, as in a club, and to legislate appropriate modes of conduct. Or they may wish simply to join together to invest in the capitalization of some economic pursuit, as in a company. In order to pursue the objects of the association, they may co-operate to do the work on a voluntary basis, they may leave it to their governing body of elected officers to do on a voluntary basis, or they may authorize their governing body to employ outsiders to help. This last is the point at which bureaucracies arise (Figure 3.1, p. 50).

Bureaucracies are to be sharply distinguished from the associations

[1] R. H. MacIver and C. H. Page (1949), *Society: An Introductory Analysis*, p. 448.

which establish them; they are the means by which people are employed to carry out work for the association. One of the difficulties, of course, is that the term bureaucracy has collected to itself an even wider range of different meanings than the term association. As Mouzelis[2] and others have pointed out, there is a serious state of confusion and ambiguity about its use in modern social theory. Theoretical advance will be thwarted unless this unclarity is removed. The definition we shall use is a more limited one than the concept as originally propounded by Weber. It is consistent, however, with the more limited sense in which Weber was himself driven to use the term in practice, as for example in his distinction between political parties and bureaucracy.[3] This definition also has the additional advantage of identifying without ambiguity a social institution of great importance in industrial society.

Bureaucracy is defined for our purposes as a *hierarchically stratified managerial employment system in which people are employed to work for a wage or salary; that is to say, a stratified employment hierarchy with at least one manager who in turn has a staff of employed subordinates*. The concepts of manager and subordinate will be considered at length in the next chapter.

Bureaucratic systems are thus secondary and dependent institutions. They are secondary in the sense that they cannot be formed directly in their own right: there must first exist an employing body which decides to establish a bureaucracy in order to employ people to work for it. They are dependent in the sense that their continued existence depends upon the continued existence of the employing body. Their function is to get work done on behalf of this employing body.

Some Rejected Definitions of Bureaucracy

In order to define as sharply as possible the particular meaning to be attached to the term bureaucracy, let me indicate a number of current usages of the term which have been excluded.

First there is that usage in which bureaucratization is taken to refer to the degree of formality and explicitness of rules and procedures in any

[2] N. Mouzelis (1967), *Organisation and Bureaucracy*.
[3] Weber wrote, for example: 'Bureaucratic authority is carried out in its purest form where it is most clearly dominated by the principle of appointment. There is no such thing as a hierarchy of elected officials in the same sense as there is a hierarchical organization of appointed officials. In the first place, election makes it impossible to attain a stringency of discipline even approaching that in the appointed type. For it is open to a subordinate official to compete for elective honours on the same terms as his superiors, and his prospects are not dependent on the superior's judgment.' (1947) *The Theory of Social and Economic Organisation*, p. 335.

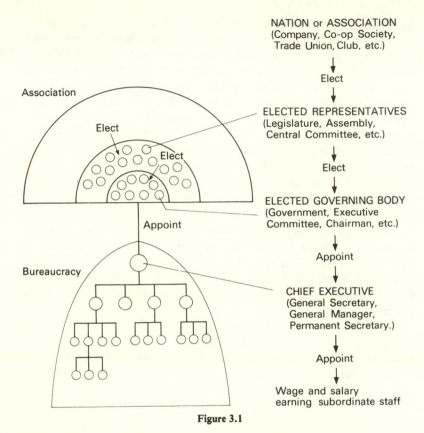

NATION or ASSOCIATION
(Company, Co-op Society,
Trade Union, Club, etc.)

↓

Elect

↓

ELECTED REPRESENTATIVES
(Legislature, Assembly,
Central Committee, etc.)

↓

Elect

↓

ELECTED GOVERNING BODY
(Government, Executive
Committee, Chairman, etc.)

↓

Appoint

↓

CHIEF EXECUTIVE
(General Secretary,
General Manager,
Permanent Secretary.)

↓

Appoint

↓

Wage and salary
earning subordinate staff

Figure 3.1

social institution whatever – the more formalized the more bureaucratic.[4] In this sense the term bureaucratic could be used to refer to employing associations as readily as to their employment systems; for example, to refer to a trade union organization which had developed rigid role specifications to govern its elected officers and comprehensive and mechanistic rules and procedures. In our usage, whereas the clerical and other staff *employed* by a trade union to work for it would be a bureaucracy, the trade union itself (that is to say, the union members and their elected officers) never can be, no matter how explicit and comprehensive its rules and regulations: it is a voluntary association. The 'bureaucratization' would refer only to the process whereby the union established a larger and larger employment organization of salaried staff (not

---

[4] A sense in which it is used by many sociologists, for example by T. Burns and G. M. Stalker (1961) in *The Management of Innovation*, in which 'bureaucratic' is used synonymously with 'mechanistic' and in contrast to 'organic' in which the definition of role is left more open. This usage can lead to the curious tautology 'the bureaucratization of a bureaucracy', although of course sociologists are careful to avoid such phraseology.

elective officers) to carry out its work for it. It is not that the trade union has been bureaucratized, it is rather that the trade union has set up a dependent bureaucracy.

This usage is in line with Weber's distinction between the corporate group and its administrative staff (its bureaucracy).[5] It leaves the term *bureaucratization* to be used to refer to one aspect of Weber's central concept of rationalization; namely, the establishment in society of more and larger bureaucracies, especially centralized bureaucracies, thereby increasing the number of role relationships governed by bureaucratic rules and regulations.

Second, our definition excludes that popular usage (which derives from the usage mentioned in the previous paragraph) which treats 'bureaucratic' as a pejorative term to be applied to any organization which has become monolithic, ensnared by its own regulations and hamstrung by red tape, or, as Crozier puts it, cannot learn from its own errors.[6] This distinction is important because of the fact – also to be discussed further – that the bureaucratic hierarchy has come into disrepute as impersonal, autocratic and dehumanizing, whereas it is potentially one of the most creative of all human institutions.

Third, it excludes that limitation on the term bureaucratic which would confine its use to the description of governmental departments – whether central or local government. It will be used here to apply to all employment hierarchies – whether employed by governments, or by commercial or industrial companies, or by trade unions, or by co-operative societies, or by any other type of association.

Finally, our definition excludes those systems of professional colleagues such as doctors in hospitals, teaching staff in universities, lawyers in partnerships. As Parsons points out in his introduction to *The Theory of Social and Economic Organisation*,[7] if Weber had recognized such systems as different it would have altered his perspective on several issues. Such systems will be dealt with separately from the bureaucratic

[5] M. Weber (1947), *Theory of Social and Economic Organisation*. It is also consistent with Sumner's distinction between crescive and enacted groups: W. G. Sumner (1959), *Folkways*, p. 54.

[6] Crozier's full definition is as follows: 'We shall describe as a "bureaucratic system of organisation" any system of organisation where the feedback process, error-information-correction, does not function well, and where consequently there cannot be any quick readjustment of the programmes of action in view of the errors committed. In other words, *a bureaucratic organisation is an organisation that cannot correct its behaviour by learning from its errors*. Bureaucratic patterns of action, such as the impersonality of rules and the centralisation of decision-making, have been so stabilised that they have become part of the organisation's self-reinforcing equilibria' [his italics]. M Crozier (1965), *The Bureaucratic Phenomenon*, p. 186.

[7] M. Weber (1947), *Theory of Social and Economic Organisation*, footnote starting on p. 58.

hierarchy (see Chapter 24).

This question of definition needs elaboration because many critical problems are being missed by sociologists today and many issues are being confused. The consequences of failure to tease out, define and differentiate significantly different social structures are serious. Thus, for example, many writers are led into treating the relationships between members of trade unions, between union members and their employed officials, between employees on the shop floor, and between managers and subordinates, as though they were all gripped within the same social structure – whereas in fact there are three very different systems of role relationships involved: those occurring among equals in associations (corporate or crescive); those occurring between superiors and subordinates within hierarchical employment systems; and those occurring between members of associations and their employed officials. This particular confusion is widespread in the sociological literature.[8] It makes rigorous formulation difficult and scientific communication almost impossible. Bureaucratic systems and associations are important enough institutions in their own right in industrial societies to warrant not being lumped together.

In short, the terms 'bureaucracy' or 'bureaucratic system' will be used to refer to all employment systems whether in the public or social services, in industry, in the armed services, in education, or in trade and commerce. They may range from the smallest with two levels consisting of a manager and his employed subordinates, to the largest composed of tens or hundreds of thousands of employees with many working levels ranging from the shop and office floor through first-line managers, departmental superintendents, general managers, to the chief executive at the top – be he permanent secretary, managing director, president, or the holder of some other title.

Differentiation of Bureaucratic Appointed Offices from Elected Offices

It may be noted that our definition of bureaucracy limits it to Weber's concept of the bureaucratic administrative staff, by which he refers to employ-

---

[8] The consequences can be illustrated, for example, in P. M. Blau and R. Scott's book *Formal Organizations* (1960). On page 1, the authors lump together trade unions, political parties, police forces and hospitals as formal organizations: as a result, a crucial difference is lost between trade unions and political parties as associations (Weber's corporate bodies, MacIver's associations, and Sumner's crescive groups), and police forces and hospitals as employment systems (or bureaucratic hierarchies) with hierarchical managerial structures employed by associations. Then, on page 7, they limit the concept of bureaucracy to administrative systems in the sense only of administrative departments within employment systems, failing to note that on page 32, in giving an outline summary of Weber's own view, they correctly describe his conception of the administrative organization as applying to the total employed system and not just to the administrative departments.

ment systems with appointed offices and not electoral systems. Although he begins with a general definition of bureaucracy as referring to any institution which contains roles explicitly established in the form of offices, he then in his description of the hierarchical structure of bureaucracy tends to limit the analysis to those *appointed* officers found in hierarchical employment systems. Although in his general definition Weber also included *elected* political officers such as heads of state and ministers, in his actual usage he excluded these particular offices on the grounds that they do not conform to the same hierarchical structure as do the administrative offices of the employment system.

I have given consideration to the possibility of including both the elected office-holders of the association and the appointed employees of the association within the same concept of bureaucracy. But that line of analysis places the elected representatives of associations in the same category of bureaucrat as the employed staff; such a conceptualization is a most unhappy one. It is essential to categorize the elected representatives acting for the association as a part of the association, and to separate them from the proper bureaucrats, the servants of the association. That keeps political and quasi-political associations and their elected representatives and governance separate from employment systems. It may help to prevent elected representatives from taking up the role of bureaucrat.

There is a world of difference between associations and their elected officers on the one hand and bureaucracies made up of appointed employees on the other – a world of difference between election by a group of voters and selection by a manager. The difference is important. For example, MacIver and Page[9] fail to make the distinction, and see one of the reasons for the persistence of associations in the 'organizational "will-to-live" [which] centres in the officials, in the occupants of the "bureaucratic structure".' I would want to distinguish between on the one hand the elected officials and on the other hand the employees in the bureaucratic structure where there is one. Recognition of the existence of two different groups allows the identification of two separate forces which may or may not act in the same direction with respect to persistence of association. As Michels, for instance, has argued, it is the elected representatives and not the bureaucratic employees who tend to become an oligarchic group and to whom he has applied his iron law of oligarchy.[10]

There is a further point of possible confusion to be noted. Some associations – for example, some political parties and some trade unions – appoint their salaried employed officers by means of election. These officers are called by some such title as party agent or union general

[9] R. M. MacIver and C. H. Page (1949), *Society, An Introductory Analysis*, p. 449.
[10] R. Michels (1949), *Political Parties*.

secretary. They are full-time employees, bureaucrats, despite their mode of selection and appointment. Their roles are to be distinguished from the chairman, or president, or treasurer, or other elected officials forming a central committee or governing body of the association. Just because both types of role are designated as officers or officials it does not make them all the same.[11]

To lump associations and bureaucracies together simply because each contains offices but to overlook the real differences which may exist in those offices, does not add to clarity and understanding. The concept of office will therefore be treated separately from the concept of bureaucracy. The concept of office merely defines that type of role which is highly detachable and has a relatively permanent existence (see previous chapter). This type of role is to be found in both associations and bureaucracies. The concept of bureaucracy can then be limited to the description of only one of the various kinds of institution which contain or establish offices. The alternative usage in which all institutions which happen to be composed of offices – or even to contain a small number of offices – are brought together into one category called bureaucracy (even taking into account the possible verbal argument that *bureau* is after all an office) is misleading because it puts associations and bureaucratic systems into the same analytic category: like grouping chalk with cheese because they start with the same two letters.

The Employment Contract and Human Judgment

Since bureaucratic systems are employment systems it is essential to consider the nature of the employment contract by means of which individuals become associated with a bureaucracy. The nature of this contract is of the greatest possible importance for our analysis. It will bear our most concentrated attention. From it stems not only the rationale for managerial authority, but also the foundation of legitimation of each bureaucratic system as a whole, and the absolute requirement for appeals systems, for employee participation, and for other mechanisms to ensure that social justice and equity in employment will be upheld.

The character of the employment contract can be illustrated by comparison with modes of joining an association. There are many methods of joining associations but only one way to join a bureaucracy. Thus, for example, the means of joining a company is to buy shares in it; to join a

[11] It should be noted, however, that appointment to a full-time administrative office by election subjects the incumbent to political pressures. Such officers have to attend to the need to be re-elected if they wish to continue. Thus, for example, chief executives in syndicalist organizations – as in Yugoslavia – have to become good politicians if they are to remain in their jobs.

trade union, you must apply for acceptance; to join some clubs you must be invited; and in every case you become a member. To join a bureaucratic system, however, you must apply for a job in it and be selected and appointed to that job. The mode of appointment is to be given a contract of employment. This contract need not be explicitly in writing but may be implicitly understood in terms of practice and precedent.

The employment contract is one of the most important social contracts in industrial societies. Its legal essence is still dominated by carry-overs from the old law of master and servant. It is a development area in law. It is concerned with the conditions under which people work for a wage or salary, their duties and entitlements, and raises all the vexed questions of security of employment, of hiring and firing, of redundancy, of transfer. The employment contract indicates – either explicitly or implicitly – the kind of work a person is expected to do, the role he will occupy to begin with, and the conditions of his employment, including his remuneration. The security of his employment will depend to a large degree upon the way the institution is financed.

When a governing body employs someone to do work for the association the two parties join together in an employment contract, in which the governing body agrees to pay the employee for his services while the employee agrees to carry out such work as the governing body might, within reasonable limits, decide to give him. Moreover – and here is the point of the very greatest emotional sensitivity in our whole construction, the central point around which all else revolves – *the employee agrees to be accountable to the governing body for the quality of his work, and to recognize that if the governing body is not satisfied it is entitled to dispense with his services.* The conditions under which this judgment of quality is made, and the safeguards for the employee, are among the most important questions of social justice in industrial societies.

Let me first emphasize one critical issue. It is concerned with human judgment. Such judgment, with all its frailties, is one of the cornerstones of the functioning of employment systems. It is revealed in its full significance in the fact that should there be a disagreement between the governing body and the employee about the adequacy of his work, then it is the *judgment* of the governing body which has the overriding force. That state of affairs continues to exist between governing bodies of all types of association and their employees, whether managing directors, civil service chiefs, directors of social services, or whatever. In the final analysis it is the judgment of the governing body that counts – objective indicators can be of some help in making these judgments, but there are no criteria by which the decisions can be made automatically. Human beings are always trying to substitute so-called objective indicators in place of the simple act of human judgment, and losing the essence of human ability in the process. This kind of technocracy is a prime enemy of humanity in industrial societies.

Thus, for example, it is often said that it is more difficult to assess the performance of the head of a government department or of a social service department than it is to assess that of the head of an industrial company, because the latter can be judged in terms of the profit or return on capital which he achieves. In fact one is no more difficult than the other. It is as easy to calculate how much service a department has provided as it is to maintain the accounting procedures necessary to calculate profit. But neither type of information can tell whether the chief executive has done good work under the conditions obtaining. Whether or not he might have made more profit or might perhaps have avoided even greater loss, remain matters of judgment and always will remain so; for it is impossible to know all the conditions at work in a complex field, or all the factors which might have been taken into account.

The competence of a person must always be judged in terms of how well or badly he did in the obtaining circumstances. There is no way of avoiding the exercise of judgment; and what is more, there never will be any way. All the computers in the world could not make the judgment. Indeed, if managerial judgment is rendered unnecessary by technology, then so is the subordinate's role – it will be possible to automate it. Managerial bureaucratic systems are not only accountability systems; they are systems of accountability built upon human judgment. The art is not to try to eliminate human judgment but to ensure that it is fully employed. The exercise of judgment is the greatest of human assets. One of the main features of requisitely organized bureaucracy is the opportunity it could provide for individuals to exercise in full their capacity to make judgments.

Security of Employment

The fact that an employee's economic security may depend upon the judgment of his employer raises sharply the question of the degree of security of employment given by the employment contract. In order to deal with this question it is necessary to distinguish between employment in the institution and assignment to a particular role. The process of appointment to a bureaucratic organization is in fact a two-stage process: first, appointment by employment contract between the employee and a senior executive acting on behalf of the governing body (and the association-employee contracts when written are often signed by an officer of the governing body, for example the secretary); and second, assignment to a particular role in the bureaucratic system. Security of appointment can thus be seen to be a twofold issue: security of appointment under contract with the governing body; and security of tenure in a particular role in the bureaucratic hierarchy.

The process of leaving an institution is also in principle a two-stage process. First, relinquishing a particular role within the bureaucratic hierarchy, without necessarily leaving employment with the governing body – which may be termed de-selection;[12] second, terminating the employment contract with the governing body.

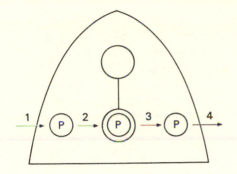

Figure 3.2

1. Appointment by employing association.
2. Assignment to a role.
3. Removal from role.
4. Termination of employment.

Examination of this two-phase process of joining and leaving a bureaucratic system reveals three possible degrees of security of tenure:

limited tenure in the sense that, within the period of notice prescribed by the employment contract, the individual may be removed from his role (de-selected) or dismissed from the enterprise;

institutional tenure, or the right to security of employment somewhere in the bureaucracy in a role which may be either at the level achieved by the individual or at a different level, but not in any particular role; the individual may be removed from his role and transferred to another, but in normal circumstances[13] will be entitled to retain a role somewhere in the enterprise;

role tenure, or the right to security of continued employment not only within the institution but in the particular role to which the individual has been appointed; individuals may not in normal circumstances be de-selected, transferred or dismissed.

What kind of employment contract and tenure any particular enterprise will be able to offer to its employees will be influenced strongly by the way it obtains its revenue finance, for that influences the security of continuation of the enterprise itself and therefore of its ability to offer employment security. I shall therefore turn to consider for a moment one particular feature of revenue finance in bureaucracies.

[12] Wilfred Brown (1971), *Organization*, pp. 72–7.
[13] By 'normal circumstances' are meant conditions other than a declared redundancy or summary dismissal for gross misconduct or gross negligence.

Grant Income and Earned Income

In order to create a bureaucratic system the governing body of an association will have to provide finance: capital for such plant, buildings and equipment as may be needed; and on-going revenue for running expenses including the wages and salaries of employees. It is not my intention here to consider the problems of capital finance.

Revenue for bureaucratic organizations can come from two main sources: first by means of grants from funds collected by the governing body and allocated to the bureaucratic organization; and second by means of funds which are in part raised by the governing body but mainly earned by the bureaucratic organization itself by selling the goods or services it produces, and which the governing body allows to remain available to defray its running expenses. I shall refer to these two types of revenue as *grant-income* and *earned-income*.

The largest grant-income institutions are central and local government departments and services. Other such institutions are charities and the Church. For the operation of government departments, money is raised by taxation and income is provided on a planned scale. The size of departments or service – civil service department, hospital service, educational system, army – is determined by the government, and that size may be counted on with only minor variations over a period of years. There may be changes in government policy leading to sudden drastic changes on a local scale – a department dropped or drastically reduced, or extended or newly created. But within the limits of major policy changes continuity is assumed, and continuity of income is not a problem for the employees. Not only capital but income also is provided by the governing institution.

Earned-income institutions may be either private enterprise or government-controlled. Their outstanding characteristic is that, whereas the governing institution is responsible directly for raising capital finance, the employee members in the bureaucratic hierarchy are responsible for earning that excess of income over expense which assures continuity of revenue finance and the survival of the executive establishment.

Thus, the main difference between grant-income and earned-income institutions is not simply that between government and private enterprise. It is a difference in immediacy of consumer effect upon the institution. Grant-income institutions are not subjected to direct consumer power. For example, in the case of government services, consumer power is expressed through governmental processes, the government standing between the consumer-electorate and the bureaucratic organizations. Reduced use of a government service does not necessarily have immediate effects upon the size of service provided.

Earned-income institutions are subjected directly and continuously to consumer pressure, whether they are in the public or private sector. Failure to satisfy a consumer need has immediate effects upon income through withdrawal of consumer support.

In short, in grant-income institutions the governing body provides the income and decides the size of establishment for which income is to be provided. In earned-income institutions, the governing body provides capital but not income (other than in exceptional circumstances); it is up to the employees to utilize that capital to achieve a profitable performance; the governing body sets limits on establishment by its control of capital; within capital limits the employees have security of establishment or growth only if they succeed in earning sufficient income.

The distinction between grant-income and earned-income institutions may be illustrated in the process sometimes referred to as 'hiving off', in which a government department or service is given quasi-independence under its own intermediate board. This process is in fact a change in which a grant-income institution is made into an earned-income institution. This change can be expected to arouse the anxieties of those concerned about the security of establishment of the bureaucratic system. Attempts to overcome these anxieties by continuing to provide the security of establishment that goes with being a grant-income institution will not be effective.

The decision as to whether a service should be established on a grant-income or earned-income basis depends on the extent to which it is considered that the satisfaction of consumer demand should impress directly upon those employed by the enterprise to provide the goods or services. Whereas consumers can make a direct impact upon earned-income institutions by purchasing or not purchasing the service offered, such an impact does not occur in the case of grant-income institutions. Special provision for consumer participation must therefore be provided in the case of those grant-income bureaucracies if they are to be safeguarded against becoming 'bureaucratic' in the pejorative sense of being unresponsive and monolithic.

Type of Income and Tenure

Because continuity of income in grant-income institutions is sufficiently secure, they are in a position to give greater security of appointment than earned-income institutions. They can offer *institutional tenure*. Employees may be transferred from one role to another, as opportunities arise, but unless either the department is subject to policy redundancy or the individual is found guilty of gross misconduct or incompetence, he will not be dismissed from the institution.

Earned-income institutions are in a position to give only *limited tenure* employment contracts. Even if an individual employee is not unsatisfactory, if the business of the enterprise falls away or requires to be changed in directions for which he is not suited, he may be de-selected and, if unacceptable elsewhere in the organization, may be made redundant. Special safeguards are required for the individual in such circumstances.

In order to round out the picture by contrast, the case of tenure in university teaching posts may be cited. What is meant by tenure here is *role tenure*, that is to say, the right to continued appointment as a lecturer in so-and-so or as a professor of such-and-such (again except in case of officially declared redundancy or gross misconduct or incompetence). This extreme type of tenure is the contractual means of creating the necessary conditions for intellectual freedom. But the tenure, note, is tenure not in a role in a bureaucratic hierarchy but as a direct appointee of the association. Those members of the teaching staff who have such tenure are usually statutory members of the association; that is to say, are members of the university. Granting of tenure is the mode of admission to the university association. Teaching staff without tenure will not be found to have the status of members of the university; they are its employees (perhaps on probation as association members) in the way that members of the administrative staff employed by the university are employees.

It is because of these contractual arrangements that being dismissed is a prime issue in earned-income organizations, being transferred is a prime issue in grant-income institutions, and gaining tenure is a prime issue in universities.

A number of important organizational characteristics flow from each kind of employment contract.

Their limited tenure contracts help to make the earned-income organizations the most readily sensitive and adaptive to fluctuations in consumer demand and to changes in consumer taste. Its employees, however, especially in a situation of less than full employment, tend to be resistant to the implementation of major policy changes which would lead to disbandment of departments and creation of new ones, since such changes might lead to the de-selection and dismissal of some of them.

The institutional tenure contracts of grant-income organizations act as a brake upon rapid oscillatory adjustments, because although individuals may be de-selected, it will be only for transfer to another role as opportunities arise and not for dismissal from the organization. The contracts therefore give a certain stability to organization; for example, in government departments they give such stability in the face of periodic rapid political and ministerial change. A paradoxical accompaniment of this brake upon change is that sudden wholesale reorganizations due to changes in policy are more readily accepted because there is institutional tenure security.

The role tenure contracts in universities tend to make these institutions react very slowly to change. Major adaptations may have to await changes in senior academic staff taking place by retirement over periods of many years.

4

Managerial Accountability, Authority, and Dependence

Bureaucracies are work systems in which people are responsible for using their judgment and discretion in carrying out tasks on behalf of a manager who is accountable for their work. In this chapter the nature of the relationship between manager and subordinate and its functioning will be considered.

The manager-subordinate relationship is one of the general class of relationships of superordination and subordination. It is undoubtedly among the most important of all two-person relationships in industrial societies – a relationship in which two people are thrown together for at least 35 to 40 waking hours each week, often for many years, with their ability to cope with working reality continually under test, and with the socio-economic status and security of themselves and their families at stake.

The accountability of the manager for the work of his subordinate is of central importance in the manager-subordinate relationship. It is that accountability which makes the manager so dependent upon his subordinate. It determines the precise quantity of authority to which he is legitimately entitled in relation to his subordinate.

The manager must maintain a running assessment of his subordinate's performance and competence. He is officially his subordinate's judge, fixing a most important aspect of the core area of his public identity. This reporting activity is a highly sensitive matter, concerned as it is with the subordinate's sense of reality, his livelihood, and his status. How it ought requisitely to be carried out will be outlined; and in later chapters (especially in Part Four) the conditions required to safeguard the human rights of subordinates if social justice is to be preserved will be considered.

Vertical and Horizontal Growth and Manager-subordinate Relationships

Given the necessary starting finance, the governing body of an association which wants to get work done can set up a bureaucratic employment system to employ people to work for it. There are two ways in which it may grow its bureaucratic system. First, it may set up one role, appoint someone to fill it, and then as work increases, simply increase the number of roles and fill these too: growth by *horizontal extension*. In so doing, the governing body is simply increasing the number of direct appointees; that is to say, employees directly appointed with no intermediate managers. Or, second, it may authorize its initial direct appointee to act as chief executive with a subordinate establishment into which he may appoint subordinates: growth by *vertical extension*. This process of vertical extension may be repeated at successive levels.

Growth by lateral extension of a governing body's direct appointees leads to the establishment of a group of colleagues in a *collegium*: it is a type of institution especially important in the organization, for example, of hospital consultant medical staff, and of the clergy in some churches.

Growth by vertical extension is the more common. It leads to the establishment of the bureaucratic hierarchy. When the process of vertical extension is combined with lateral extension at lower levels, it forms the familiar pyramid-shaped bureaucratic hierarchy with which we are mainly concerned.

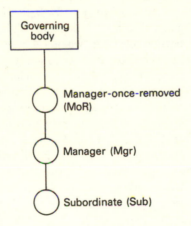

Figure 4.1

The process of vertical extension establishes the prime role relationship in bureaucratic systems – the *manager-subordinate role relationship*. It is the relationship upon which the bureaucratic hierarchy depends. It may be defined as that relationship in which one person – the manager – is held *accountable* not only for the quality of his own performance, but also for the quality of performance of others – his subordinates. It is this accountability which is the essence of the relationship.

The manager-subordinate relationship is but one type of the more general class of relationships of superordination and subordination. There is a wide array of other situations in which one person can be said to be superior in status to another. Superordination is a complex phenomenon with a variety of facets, as Georg Simmel so clearly described.[1] My analysis will, however, be a limited one. It will be confined to those superior-subordinate role relationships in which one role can be said to be higher than another role in the strict sense that the occupant of the higher role is held accountable for the performance of the occupant of the lower role, and carries the authority necessary to make that accountability a social fact.

Accountability of the Manager

The manager-subordinate role relationship is one of the most widespread and important of dyadic role relationships in industrial society.[2] To appreciate the saliency of this relationship it is necessary only to recognize that every bureaucratic hierarchy has at the very least only one less manager-subordinate pair than it has employees. That is to say, for every 1000 people employed in a bureaucratic organization there are at least 999 manager-subordinate pairs. It has become a critical issue for industrial societies to ensure that the relationships lived out by its citizens in manager-subordinate pairs should provide for individual satisfaction. For the manager-subordinate pair is the relationship within which most adults spend the greatest portion of their waking hours – each particular relationship lasting anywhere from months to many years.

The essence of the manager-subordinate relationship is that the manager, being assigned more work than he can do, is authorized to get some of that work done by others for whose work he is in turn accountable. For example, A is accountable to the governing body for B's work, and B is accountable to A for C's work. Indeed it is a *central feature of a bureaucratic hierarchy that it is an accountability system – one in which employees can get work done through other employees for whose work they remain accountable.* Unless this accountability can be clearly and directly ascribed, the bureaucratic hierarchy cannot function effectively. Moreover, there are certain minimum conditions that must be met for this accountability to be real. These conditions will be described in terms of the accountability of a manager for the work of a subordinate to his own superior, who is manager-once-removed. Any subordinate may or may not himself be a manager in charge of subordinate.

This point about accountability needs to be underscored, because bureaucratic hierarchies tend to be regarded primarily as systems of authority[3] or as systems of communications.[4] That the bureaucratic

---

[1] G. Simmel (1950), 'Superordination and subordination'.

[2] There are, for example, about three times as many manager-subordinate 'couples' in Britain – about 23 million – as there are married couples – about $7\frac{1}{2}$ million.

[3] Especially in sociological theory, following Weber.

[4] As for example, in the systems theory applications of D. Katz and R. L. Kahn (1966),

hierarchy and its manager-subordinate relationships are primarily concerned with accountability is a social fact. The object for which they were established was to achieve a situation in which one person could be held accountable for the doing of work by others: that is what the employment contract of a manager is about.

The Three-level Managerial Linkage

The manager-subordinate relationship is first fully realized where the chief executive has a subordinate, and the point is reached where he has more work to assign to his subordinate than the latter can possibly do. He may now cope with the situation either by lateral or by vertical extension. Without for the moment considering the factors leading to one course or to the other, we shall assume that the chief executive has decided in favour of vertical extension and has authorized his subordinate to have a subordinate.

It is this circumstance that gives rise to the three-level managerial linkage. This linkage constitutes an organizational molecule whose characteristics are of great importance: they may be stated in their most general form thus: the manager is accountable to the manager-once-removed for his own work and for the work of his subordinate, and he manages his subordinate within terms of reference set by the manager-once-removed.

Bureaucratic hierarchies are made up of overlapping chains of these three-level linkages. Because the roles in these chains are hierarchically structured, with authority operating from the top downwards, the chains have often been described – incorrectly – as one-way downward communication systems. This incorrect description has been a source of difficulty in sociological analyses. In particular, it is taken as the prototype of so-called formal organization,[5] while communication upwards or laterally has been taken as so-called informal organization.

The three-level linkage model represents only one part of bureaucratic organization – the manager-subordinate structure. It leaves out of account the many other types of role relationship which are a necessary part of bureaucratic systems, such as supervising, staff, monitoring and other types of lateral role relationship with weaker accountability and authority. But even in the manager-subordinate part of the total model, communication needs to be a responsive two-way up-and-down communication.

The Social Psychology of Organizations; and R. L. Ackoff and F. E. Emery (1972), *On Purposeful Systems.*

[5] As is the case for example in T. Burns and G. M. Stalker (1961), *The Management of Innovation*; P. M. Blau (1955), *The Dynamics of Bureaucracy*; A. Etzioni (1969), *Modern Organizations*, and R. Likert (1961), *New Patterns of Management.*

When this full picture is elaborated of two-way manager-subordinate communications plus a laterally organized support organization, as well as an interactive elected representative system, analysis in terms of formal and informal organization appears over-simplified and irrelevant. It is not a useful distinction.

Emotional Content of Manager-Subordinate Relationships

Given the establishment of the type of three-level manager-subordinate chain described, what then is the nature of the relationship between the manager and his subordinate? It has the following features:

the manager is authorized to give resources and to delegate tasks to his subordinate, within the policy the manager-once-removed has set in establishing the subordinate role; the subordinate has contracted to carry out these delegated tasks and must do so;

the manager is accountable for ensuring that his subordinate does carry out those delegated tasks, and that he carries them out in a manner acceptable to the manager; the subordinate is therefore vulnerable to the manager's assessment of his performance;

if the subordinate does not carry out his tasks in a manner acceptable to his manager, then the manager will have been let down and may not be able in his turn to discharge his accountability to his manager, the manager-once-removed; a manager is therefore vulnerable to the quality of his subordinate's performance.

Since the manager is vulnerable if his subordinate does not do his work properly, what authority must a manager have over a subordinate if he is to be able fairly to be held accountable for his subordinate's work? At the same time, since the subordinate is vulnerable to his manager's assessment of him, what safeguards must the subordinate have against unfair or unjust judgments?

Here is an intensely human situation founded upon a psychologically and emotionally subtle relationship. It is a social exchange, the outcome of which affects the future success and progress of both the manager and the subordinate. It is not a simple economic exchange relationship.[6] There is a complex underlay of hundreds of unspecified assumptions about appropriate modes of address and of speech, giving of praise and criticism, special concessions, time off, special effort. The rates of pay, holidays,

---

[6] I find Homans' and Blau's distinction between social and economic exchange relationships useful. Many economic theorists would like to think of bureaucratic systems as based upon a supply-and-demand economic exchange model. The relationships are in fact far too complex for such a model to describe. G. C. Homans (1961), *Social Behaviour*; P. M. Blau (1964), *Exchange and Power in Social Life*.

premium payments, and other negotiated and explicitly agreed conditions are only the manifest surface of the gamut of mores and customs learned as a result of normal socialization processes, upon which the ongoing subjective interactions rest.

These questions of accountability and authority in bureaucratic hierarchies, set in the uncertainties of social exchange, touch the deepest feelings of fairness, esteem and prestige in the human personality.[7] The work the manager gives his subordinate to do is a matter of very deep emotional importance to that subordinate. It is work for a living. It contains in one emotion-charged package a mixture of reality testing, future career, level of work allowed, uncertainty and judgment, skill and ability, recognition and reward, self-esteem. The manager can increase or decrease the subordinate's level of work. By assessing his performance as good or bad he enters helpfully or destructively into the subordinate's self-assessment. By giving or withholding an increase in pay, he affects directly the living his subordinate earns for his work – with the socio-economic status of his family at stake. It is a psychologically rich mixture that in the best of circumstances is supercharged. Given anti-requisite organization, or ineffectual management even within requisite organization, powerful trouble may be released. Every experienced manager will know what this trouble is like, and the amount of time that may have to be spent in sorting it out.

It is essential, therefore, that the content of accountability and authority in manager-subordinate role relationships should be specified correctly, precisely and explicitly. This content is a particularly important aspect of the immediate social context within which the subjective social interaction between managers and subordinates can take place. It gives the legitimate social setting within which individuals may personally legitimate each other's behaviour.

If the questions concerning accountability and authority are not satisfactorily answered they are a potential source of the accumulation of interpersonal stress and of personal malaise. They give rise to power which is not legitimate in the sense of being contained within a framework of authority which provides for proper public esteem. Whatever authority there has been tends to become dedifferentiated into an unstable state of delegitimated power. Delegitimated power of this kind becomes very difficult to relegitimate and authorize, however, since it is power which is expressed within breakdown of authority.[8] Such power constitutes a

---

[7] The importance of esteem in relation to a person's identity has been described by D. R. Miller (1963) in 'The Study of Social Relationships: Situation, Identity and Social Interaction'. Equally useful is E. Shils' (1965) analysis of prestige in J. A. Jackson (ed.), *Social Stratification*.

[8] As Kurt Lewin has shown in general for all dedifferentiation processes. (1936), *Principles of Topological Psychology*.

paranoiagenic situation par excellence. The subordinate is suspicious of what his manager might do to him, and the manager never knows when his authority might be undermined. If the situation becomes widespread it is a potential source of energy for social violence.

General Constraints Upon Managerial Roles

What then is the correct balance between the accountability of a manager and his authority over his subordinates? What is meant by the widely professed but seldom applied idea that the manager's authority must match his accountability? In order to consider this question, let us first examine the limits within which a role in a bureaucracy is established.

For a subordinate role to be established, a manager must get the necessary authority from his own manager and, in turn, must either already have establishment provision for it or must seek that provision. What is required for this decision is a specification or definition of what the subordinate role is to be. Such a specification or definition sets the institutional context of the role. This institutional context plays an important part in setting the contraints within which managers may act. It is the first step in the process of putting managerial power in a legitimate framework of authority. It is this institutional context also which makes bureaucratic systems into rational institutions – for it binds the institution into a coherent whole.

The institutional context must operate within the law. Both the employing association and the employee must work within its limits. Within the law there are numbers of other general constraints of a legal type which act from outside the employing institution. Among these are such things as national agreements with trade unions, stock exchange regulations, trade agreements, and the regulations of professional associations – associations sanctioned by society to impose regulations upon employing institutions as well as upon the members of the profession.

Within the institution, the governing body on behalf of the association sets the general context governing the functioning of the bureaucratic system. This context may comprise policies of various kinds, operational tasks, amounts and types of resource, directions of development. It will also comprise employment policies, including such conditions as hours of work, holidays, payment structure and payment methods, sickness benefits, career and progression policies, industrial relations systems. The employees can and ought to participate in fixing such policies and in their periodic modification if managerial authority is to be sufficiently sanctioned and legitimated.

These general contexts from outside and inside the institution set the framework within which managers establish roles. They constitute the outer limits of the roles.[9] Within these limits, a manger-once-removed will fix the more immediate and task-oriented context in terms of the type of activity to be carried out in the role-once-removed. He does so by determining the content of the role specification – the policy within which the immediate manager then manages his subordinate. The role specification sets out the main types of task to be undertaken in terms of the duties in the role; status and payment, and special conditions if any, are specified.

The limits on behaviour which constitute the boundaries of a role, and the specification of duties which set direction for behaviour in the role, are important sociological facts. Here are the realities of role theory exemplified in bureaucratic offices (detached roles). Nowhere can this theory be better displayed than in these systems. Every sociologist should have experience of role specification. Unfortunately the work of preparing role specifications has been relegated to rather low-level work or personnel work, and seems never to have become a part of sociology at all.

Minimum Requisite Managerial Authority

We may now return to consider in more detail the relationship between manager and subordinate, and in particular the stormy question of the authority which the manager requires if he is reasonably to be held accountable not only for the quality of his own work but for that of his subordinates as well. It is this managerial authority which gives rise to the incorrect notion that bureaucracies must inevitably be autocratic institutions creating an autocratic culture.

If the manager is to be held accountable by his own manager (the manager-once-removed) for the quality of the work done by the subordinate, then it can be demonstrated that the following two basic conditions must be met: first, the manager must be able to decide what tasks he will delegate to his subordinate, and what resources he will allocate to his subordinate to carry out those tasks; and second, he must have the authority to have a subordinate who is not unacceptable to him in relation to the work he is expected to do – or, to put it another way, he must not be forced to be accountable for the work of a subordinate who in his judgment is below the level of competence he is entitled to expect for getting his delegated work done.

The first proposition, then, is that the manager must requisitely have the authority to decide precisely what tasks he will assign to his subordinate and what resources he will make available to him up to the limit set by the manager-once-removed and by higher policy. If he is to be accountable for

[9] W. Brown (1971) has described how these policies are contained one within the other like the layers of an onion, in his book *Organization*, p. 42.

what he gives the subordinate to do, and if he is to be accountable for how he uses the total resources assigned to him, then he must be able to use his judgment about what he gives to the subordinate in the light of how he plans his work, what he judges the subordinate does well and what he does not do well, and what the subordinate needs in order to carry out particular tasks.

Indeed one of the central features of management lies in the authority of the manager to expand and to contract the discretion and resources of a subordinate, to make continual adjustments large or small depending upon his assessment of how competently the subordinate is using his own judgment.[10] It is by virtue of this authority, regardless of how much or how little, how frequently or infrequently, he requires to use it, that the manager is able to keep the continuity of control which he requires if he is to be held accountable for his work and the use of resources.

The alternative would be for the manager to be told by the manager-once-removed, or by someone else, what tasks he should give to his subordinate to carry out and what resources to give him. If the manager were not in agreement he would be caught in the managerial equivalent of the double bind.[11] On the one hand he is held accountable for what his subordinate does; on the other hand he is required to delegate to his subordinate tasks and resources which he judges to be beyond his capabilities, or to be in conflict with his own plans, or otherwise different from what he himself would have done. The manager is stuck. He is caught in inconsistent and contradictory instructions. If things go wrong he will be held accountable for a situation not necessarily of his own making; indeed, for a situation caused by someone else over whom he has no control.

Here is a recipe for confusion and for non-responsible behaviour. And if it is the manager-once-removed who has produced the manager's difficulty, the situation is at its worst: the manager-once-removed would be holding the manager accountable for the manger-once-removed's own shortcomings. The manager-once-removed would be manifestly saying that the manager is in a managerial role, but would be extantly behaving as though he were not.

The second proposition is that the manager must not be forced to be accountable for the work of subordinates whom he judges to be below the level of competence he is entitled to expect for getting his delegated work done. The manager must be able to exercise sanctions towards his subordinate that concern first the appointment of the subordinate to the role and his removal from that role, and second the manager's expression of his

[10] John Evans uses this criterion as the central feature of his definition of a manager: see J. S. Evans (1970). 'Time-Span: The Neglected Tool'.

[11] The double bind has been described by Gregory Bateson as a situation in which a child is subjected to mutually contradictory demands by its parents.

judgment by approval or disapproval of the subordinate's performance. The manager must requisitely have:

(a) the authority to veto the appointment of any applicant for the subordinate vacancy who is unacceptable to him; he cannot necessarily have anyone whom he wants, but may select only from among those screened by the manager-once-removed as acceptable in his command; but he cannot have anyone forced upon him by the manager-once-removed whom he has reason to judge as definitely unacceptable;

(b) the authority not only to assess the performance of his subordinate but to apply that assessment either by deciding his subordinate's level of earning within the payment bracket established for the post, or, if automatic annual increments are paid, to initiate action to stop an automatic increase, or to put on record his assessment of his subordinate's performance so as to influence his subsequent career;

(c) the authority to *decide* whether or not his subordinate has the necessary level of competence to carry out that minimal level of work which is established in the specification of the role and which the manager is therefore entitled to expect, and to report his decision to his own manager (who must then act).

De-selection of a Subordinate

These conditions take us into the vital subject of how power is transformed into authority by sanctioning, and of how to prevent managerial authority from degenerating into autocracy. Thus, with respect to the second and third conditions just outlined, the rights of the subordinate entitle him at least to know in advance about his manager's judgment and to have the right to try to do something about it. Thus he surely must be entitled to have had his manager inform him on at least two occasions that his performance was not acceptable; and not only to have informed him but also to have attempted to train him to do better. For only under such conditions could his manager judge that he was definitely unlikely to become acceptable even with training.

The last condition – (c) above – in particular raises some of the deepest questions of the rights of individuals – in this case, the rights of both the manager and the subordinate. Suppose the manager does decide that one of his subordinates is below the minimally required level of competence. What happens then? The first thing is for him to inform the manager-once-removed of his impending decision. That would give the manager-once-removed the opportunity to act in advance to readjust the manager's duties, if that were feasible and desirable, so as to enable the manager to try to get by with the subordinate. Such a move would of course imply the manager-once-removed's accepting a lower level of performance from the manager, and circumstances only occasionally allow for that.

But suppose, as is most likely, that it is not feasible for the manager-once-removed to readjust the manager's duties so as to make room for the subordinate, or that the manager opposes any curtailment of his duties. What is to happen then? In the answer to this question we come to one of the few differences between the earned-income and grant-income institutions. In the earned-income institutions, where the subordinate has limited tenure only, the manager must have the authority to decide that he will no longer keep his subordinate – to de-select him but not to dismiss him; that is to say, the manager must be able to remove the subordinate from the role, but does not need the authority to dismiss him from the institution. It is then up to the manager-once-removed to try to discover if there is any other suitable employment for the subordinate in the enterprise. If there is, then the subordinate is entitled to be tried out. It is only if there is not that the subordinate must then leave the enterprise. Without such conditions, a manager cannot requisitely be held accountable for his subordinate's work.

By contrast, in the grant-income institution, where the subordinate has security of tenure somewhere in the institution although not in any particular role, the manager might decide that the subordinate should be transferred to another role in the institution if someone else would have him; he must then wait until an opportunity for transfer arises. It is this difference in employment security that causes the question of dismissal, of the right to 'hire and fire', to come up as a critical problem in earned-income institutions, whereas the question of transfer comes up as an equally emotionally charged issue in grant-income institutions.

It is often thought that the institutional tenure in grant-income institutions makes the authority of managers weaker than in earned-income institutions where there is no security of tenure. There is an apparent paradox, however. Although in grant-income institutions the subordinate has institutional tenure and commonly the right to automatic annual pay increments, he is nevertheless subject to powerful sanctions through his manager's authority to record an assessment of performance and to initiate transfer. For the fact is that the only value to the subordinate of his institutional tenure is that it gives him a long-term career in that organization. His record therefore follows him about in a way that it does not do with individuals who change from one earned-income organization to another. What the manager decides to enter on that record may therefore enhance or inhibit the subordinate's chances of upgrading and promotion, and thereby can work as a very powerful sanction.

Without the authority to de-select or initiate transfer a manager could be asked to be accountable for the work of someone in whom he had no confidence. Acceptance of such a position would be quite typical behaviour in a masochist. Certainly the position is one calculated to arouse anxiety under normal psychological conditions.

It must be noted, and here is the rub, that if the manager is held accountable for his subordinate's work and is not given the authority to de-select or to initiate transfer, then his subordinates will be able to dismiss him. They can do so by a continuous just marginally sub-standard performance.[12] In the social reality of the manager-subordinate relationship it is not simply a question of deciding whether the manager should be authorized to de-select, or whether he should not. It is a question of deciding whether it is to be the manager who can de-select subordinates or subordinates who can de-select the manager. The accountability relationship makes it inevitable that one or the other condition must in fact apply.

Two Illustrations

Let me illustrate, by the following two actual cases, the potentialities of the manager-subordinate relationship for stirring the deepest human passions when accountability and authority are not requisitely matched.

First, consider the case where the manager was held accountable for his subordinate's work but his authority was less than the amount required and he was stuck with a subordinate who was less than acceptable to him; second, the case where the manager was accountable for his subordinate's work but had more than the authority he required and could autocratically dismiss his subordinate, without appeal, if he were dissatisfied with his work.

In the first case, the manger felt potentially persecuted by his subordinate. For his subordinate, by working just marginally badly so that it was not readily perceivable by the manager-once-removed, could at any time undermine his manager's performance without the manager's being able to do much about it. Even inadvertently sub-standard work by the subordinate could cause trouble for the manager and could lead to friction between the manager and the manager-once-removed. The manager came to realize how much a manager is dependent upon his subordinate; he relies upon him; he can be let down by him. He is in a chronically vulnerable position and is defenceless to the extent that his authority falls short of his accountability. In particular, the manager was placed in an im-

---

[12] If this point seems to be only a matter of academic analysis, I can report that I have been involved in working through just such problems between managers and immediate subordinates. My analysis stems from this experience rather than from *a priori* argument.

possible position when he was forced to retain a subordinate whom he judged not to be competent to do the work he required. The manager's position was threatened because his subordinates could get rid of him by continually doing sub-standard work. It is this vulnerable, dependent position that touches upon deeper-lying anxieties. Not that the manager is necessarily in a chronic state of nerves: but the deeper anxieties are there, maintained in a state of readiness to erupt by the continuous uncertainty of the reliance upon subordinates.

Thus it is that to have a group of immediate subordinates who are just not quite good enough is a managerial situation of some misery. By contrast, to have immediate subordinates who are co-operative, reliable, and well trained and competent, is a deeply satisfying experience.

In the second case, that of autocratic managerial authority, it was the subordinate who was in a state of continuous uncertainty. He worked inevitably under threat, even though his manager was in fact a fair-minded and reasonable person. The situation itself was a threatening one regardless of the personalities involved. If the subordinate did not work well there were insufficient external constraints to prevent the manager from behaving in an autocratic manner unless he took steps to constrain himself. Even though the manager was a lawful and reasonable person in himself, the situation was such that he did not have to pay as much attention to his subordinate's feelings as he might otherwise have done, even without his being consciously aware of his attitude. The subordinate was thrown too much upon his manager's personal goodwill.

In both these cases one person was too dependent upon the goodwill and integrity of another – too dependent upon another's personality. In the first case, the manager was dependent upon his subordinate's personal integrity as expressed in good performance; in the second case, the subordinate was dependent upon his manager's fair-mindedness and humanity. Because authority was greater or less than that needed for accountability, the managers and subordinates were thrown upon one another's good intentions and goodwill. The necessary external constraints were lacking – constraints that can not only support and reinforce good intentions and goodwill and preclude the play of malice and victimization, but can be seen to be doing so. It is not only in the courts that justice must not only be done but be seen to be done.

Every manager-subordinate relationship in the organization will be affected by the absence of an adequate context with requisite constraints. Therefore every single employee from chief executive downwards will be affected. No-one will be able to escape the arousal of unconscious feelings of anxiety.

The Advantage to Subordinates of Clearly-defined Managerial Authority

However paradoxical it may seem, subordinates also want to see their manager with the kind of minimum authority described. Otherwise they simply do not have a manager. I have been repeatedly struck in my Glacier Project experience by the disdain and scorn expressed by subordinates for a person who, while manifestly their manager, is extantly not so. They refer to him as a 'straw boss' or 'middleman', 'the person you have to go through in order to get to your real manager, the one whose decision really matters to you'. Subordinates want to be able to get directly to their real manager — not to an intermediary who has to go through the pretence of being a manager and then has to ask higher up for the decision which he then hands down. This view was dramatically expressed in the following document put forward by the Works Committee (the joint shop stewards' committee) to the Works Council:

Analysis of Workers' Requirements of Managers

1. The view which elected workers' representatives have of managerial organization at shop-floor level is very similar to the views held by supervisors.
2. Shop stewards urgently desire a clear and decisive managerial organization, for themselves as well as for the workers they represent. They do not wish to take over the jobs of managers (contrary to the view that 'the Works Committee runs the Company') — but feel required to take considerable initiative because of the unclarity surrounding managerial responsibility.
3. Difficulties experienced by shop stewards because of the unclarity of who is a manager, and what authority is carried at shop-floor level, are described as:
   (a) having a *'manager' and a 'middleman'*; i.e. being under an immediate superior — who allocates work, or supervises, or sets, but who does not have managerial authority — to whom you must first go before seeing your superior above that (or 'manager') who may have authority but is too far away;
   (b) inability to get decisions at shop-floor level means representatives having to 'do managers' jobs' by going from level to level up the executive system, having what feel like interminable meetings; representatives do not feel they have managers who know how to make effective use of representatives;
   (c) the Company feels to workers as though it is under-managed and over-supervised (a view consistent with that of supervisors, that

real managerial authority at supervisor level required
specifying);

(d) there is lack of clarity as to just what authority is carried by
whom, and representatives do not know whom they are entitled
to expect to give a decision

The Workers' Criteria of a Satisfactory Managerial Pattern

4. The following is an analysis of the views of shop stewards on
minimum conditions for effective leadership and direction of
workers; i.e. to create a situation where every member has an *effectively authorized immediate manager*:

(a) a manager who can take *necessary decisions* in connection with
work and work relationships, or else says, 'I can't do it, but I'll
get something done';

(b) a manager who is *sufficiently close* to be able himself to direct the
work of his subordinates (though not necessarily himself present
all the time); i.e. to be able himself to know and personally judge
the effectiveness of each of his immediate subordinates; and to be
able to anticipate needs of workers without having to be
reminded by shop stewards taking up grievances;

(c) non-separation of subordinates from manager by 'middlemen':
managerial assistants, specialists, auxiliaries, etc. should operate
as assistants and not in the direct line of command;

(d) creation of an atmosphere of positive direction and leadership;

(e) a manager who is secure enough and knows how to take initiative
in going to representatives, and who knows how to tell you
whether he thinks you are right or wrong.

Implications

5. To satisfy the above conditions would require:

(a) clarification of managerial structure at shop-floor level;

(b) clarification of other roles in the region between first-line management and operatives; e.g. work allocator, specialist assistants,
supervising assistants, setters, deputies, etc.

6. Basic to the clarification of policy in executive and representative
responsibilities are:

(a) clarification of managerial roles at shop-floor level, and at unit
level;

(b) clarification of reponsibilities in the working relationship between
representatives (and elected committees) and first-rank
managers, unit managers and general managers.[13]

---

[13] It was discussion around this and related documents that eventually led to a written

Judgments About Acceptability

The proposition about the minimal authority of the manager with respect to the acceptability of his subordinates is a double negative proposition. It is not simply that the manager must be able to have subordinates who are positively acceptable to him: such a proposition leaves too open the question of how acceptable, and allows for nepotism. What is required is a statement of the limiting case: if the manager is to get done the work for which the manager-once-removed is in turn holding him to account, then requisitely he cannot be forced to employ subordinates who are definitely unacceptable to him in the special sense that he judges he could not get the work done by them that he needs in order to discharge his own duties.

The concept of acceptability is not a question of whether or not a manager happens to like a subordinate or to be a friend of his. It is a question of whether he judges he can work with that subordinate, and the subordinate with him. Not all people can work together in a social exchange relationship as they should be able to do in an economic exchange relationship. It is possible for someone to be able to work quite satisfactorily for one person but not for another. If, however, a manager repeatedly found difficulties with subordinates who at face value seemed to have the necessary capacities for a subordinate post, the manager-once-removed would have to consider whether the manager himself had the necessary qualities to be a good manager. The safeguard against abuse by the manager, or his inadequacy, is for every subordinate to have the right to appeal to the manager-once-removed against the manager's judgment.

There is here a delicately balanced situation, one fraught with difficulty, relying upon subtle judgments within which there is much room for disagreement and argument. The manager-once-removed requires to achieve a given output from the manager's work. He judges what the manager ought to be able to accomplish with the aid of his subordinates. How much output ought to be achieved from work is always a matter of judgment, and must requisitely remain so. Therefore it is always potentially a matter of disagreement between the manager-once-removed and the manager. Similarly, how much output a subordinate ought to accomplish with the resources available is always potentially a matter of disagreement between him and the immediate manager.

Work study may help to reduce the area of disagreement between manager and subordinate with respect to the amount of output to be achieved. But even with work study the precise quantity of output to be achieved in the on-going situation must take into account the variations in conditions that inevitably occur in reality and can markedly influence out-

---

agreement between the company and the trades unions on the minimum authority of managers described on p. 71 above.

put on apparently identical tasks. These variations in conditions are one of the main reasons why payment-by-results systems can never be requisite.[14]

It follows, therefore, that a manager's judgment as to whether or not a subordinate is unacceptable to him is a matter that involves the manager-once-removed, the manager and the subordinate. The manager-once-removed's judgment of the manager is influenced by the extent to which he considers that the manager is idealizing or diminishing his subordinate or is realistically assessing him. The manager believes that the manager-once-removed is easy, or tough, or fair in judgment, to the extent that the manager-once-removed supports him in his judgment of his subordinate; and the subordinate considers that he is getting away with things, being fairly judged, or being victimized, to the extent that he considers that his manager's judgment of his output is based on a fair assessment of conditions or is biased by inappropriate personal issues.

It may be seen, then, that the manager-subordinate relationship is anything but impersonal. It is highly personal. It requires individuals to make exceedingly important judgments and decisions about other individuals. These judgments follow from the judgment that the employing association must make about the performance of its chief executive. He in turn must appraise his own subordinates, they theirs, and so on down the managerial lines. And it is not just a matter of one-way communication in which the manager-once-removed tells the manager and the manager tells the subordinate and so on. There must be the strongest two-way interaction beween manager and subordinate – interaction in which the manager can check his possible decisions by seeking his subordinate's views, and in which the subordinate can take up problems or challenge his manager's decisions, especially his manager's decisions about himself.

The essence of the requisite establishment of a manager-subordinate role relationship is to provide an adequate context setting realistic limits to managerial authority and to focus behaviour upon the tasks in hand. That is what distinguishes 'serious' relationships from 'social relationships or games' in Goffman's[15] sense: 'serious' means of sufficient importance to society to take the rules out of the hands of the immediate personalities, and thereby to socialize the relationships by institutionalizing them.

Appraisal and Reporting of Objective Results and of Personal Competence

Managers are accountable not only for assessing subordinates and their activities, but also for reporting upon them: whether they stay within

[14] See W. Brown (1962), *Piecework Abandoned*, and E. Jaques (1961), *Equitable Payment*.
[15] E. Goffman (1961), *Encounters*.

limits; how competent they are; whether they should be given an increase in pay and progressed in level of work; whether the objective results of their work should be reported. Such assessment and reporting is an important component of the intensity of authority, and hence of accountability, in any role. They are, however, matters about which people are understandably sensitive. Who assesses whom, and about what, are questions of obvious psychological importance in bureaucratic hierarchies. The status, careers and progress of individuals are at stake. To feel reported upon by people who have no business to report upon one has the quality of being spied upon and of tale-bearing.

At the same time it is essential both for the functioning of the system and for the proper recognition of individuals that there should be adequate reporting. Managers must have adequate feed-back on the outputs of the systems they control, and on the performance of their subordinates. The subordinates are entitled to expect that the results of their efforts will become known to those who make the decisions about their rewards and advancement.

It is important to distinguish between two main considerations. First, there is the objective assessment and reporting of results – of possible discrepancies between targeted and actual outputs, or between actions and policies. Second, there is the subjective appraisal of the personal competence of the individuals concerned in the activities. As I have already mentioned, I believe that it is not only important but essential to keep the authority to make and report objective assessment of results separate from the authority to make and report subjective appraisal of personal competence: the latter constitutes a much stronger and more emotion-provoking sanction.

A manager must be able to discuss a subordinate with his own manager (the manager-once-removed). But the manner in which that reporting is done must be handled with great care. It must be open to the individual so that he can know what is being said about him. Secrecy arouses all the deeper-lying feelings of alienation, of inferiority, of being left out, described so vividly by Simmel when he wrote of secrecy in terms of the strongly emphasized exclusion of all outsiders . . . 'From secrecy, which shades all that is profound and significant, grows the typical error according to which everything mysterious is important and essential. Before the unknown, man's natural impulse to idealize and his natural fearfulness co-operate towards the same goal: to intensify the unknown through imagination, and to pay attention to it with an emphasis that is not usually accorded to patent reality.'[16]

It is easy for managers to slip into the trap of half-consciously encouraging secret tale-bearing. Assessment of subordinates is always an

[16] G. Simmel (1950), 'Secrecy', pp. 332–3.

exceedingly difficult matter. It is at the same time utterly central to effective management. Any help with assessment seems so welcome, no matter how the information is obtained. When, however, the cost of secretly obtained information is coldly weighed against the apparent gains, the balance falls sharply and unequivocally towards setting out the conditions for reporting and adhering to these conditions rigorously and without exception.

If a manager wishes to stimulate mistrust and anxiety and to undermine confidence, he has only to say to his subordinate that he has heard that the subordinate has not done so-and-so (or in the case of the manager-once-removed, that one of the manager's subordinates has done something wrong) but without saying who has told him so. That kind of behaviour is infuriating. It arouses feelings of contempt towards the manager for listening to tales from others, and scorn for the unknown others. Such reactions are not surprising since secret tale-bearing is a very powerful paranoiagenic act. Any organization in which behaviour of this kind becomes rife is going to pieces: the behaviour is a powerful aid to the disintegration.

It is not sufficient merely not to encourage secret reporting. It must be actively discouraged. If it is not, then members of the hierarchy are tacitly accepting it. Any sign of tacit acceptance contributes to a sense that unfair judgment and victimization are always on the cards. Since secret reports cannot be mentioned to the individual reported upon without arousing in him the deepest resentment, he cannot be helped and the information itself cannot be checked. Moreover, if the secret reports are put in writing, then a prime condition of democracy itself is negated: that there should be no written records held secretly about members in such a society. Such secrecy is simply not acceptable.

We shall include an analysis of requisite reporting procedures for each of a wide variety of different role relationships in Chapter 17. Each needs to be seen against the background of requisite reporting in manager-subordinate relationships: the immediate manager is accountable for keeping each of his subordinates informed about his assessment of his performance and his competence, and for assisting and training him. He may discuss his judgments with his own manager, for it is up to the latter to decide the possibilities for each of his subordinates-once-removed to progress and to be promoted. Each subordinate should be entitled to hear periodically the nature of these judgments about him so that he can learn from them, query them, and know where he stands.

Reporting Concerns Individuals in Role Relationship

Reporting has to do with individuals and not with groups, for the fundamental reason that work is done by individuals and not by groups. Only the Board is accountable as a group. Employees in bureaucratic systems are always individually accountable.

Thus it is that if a group is reported upon unfavourably, anxiety and trouble will be stirred up. I have had experience of such reporting coming about, for example, as a result of the manager-once-removed's making it publicly known that he believed that the group of managers P, Q, R, was incompetent, or through the elected representatives of the subordinates of managers P, Q, R . . . reporting to the manager-once-removed that their constituents were dissatisfied with the behaviour of their immediate managers.

The non-requisiteness of this behaviour becomes apparent when it comes to deciding what is to be done about this information. Does it apply equally to all the managers P, Q, R. . .? Is none of them competent? Or does it not mean perhaps that subordinates are experiencing trouble in various degrees with each one?

The outcome is predictable. If the criticism is launched from above it will lead to resentment among managers P, Q, R . . . about the irresponsible behaviour of authority. Each manager will be left embarrassed, unable to handle such questions as 'Who does he mean?' 'Is he referring equally to all of us?' 'Where do I stand?' Any failure to advance in the future can always be blamed on the unfair shotgun assessment. If the criticism is launched from below, managers P, Q, R . . . feel that they are being got at by their subordinates and their subordinates' representatives. They may each demand of their subordinates, 'Do you mean me?' 'Why do you not say so?' 'Why did you not take your complaints up directly with me first in an above-board way?' 'Why go behind my back?'

To sort out the problem there will have to be direct discussions between each manager and his subordinates. If the subordinates are not satisfied they may then take the matter directly to the manager-once-removed. Whereas when he receives a complaint against a group of which he is a member, a manager can do nothing, when he receives a properly and openly conducted complaint against himself as an individual he can go into the matter and sort it out.

Every criticized individual is entitled to receive the criticism personally and to his face in the first instance, and to have the opportunity to rebut it or to modify his behaviour. Only after that step may complaints requisitely be lodged against him with his own manager. This principle is inviolate. Without its rigorous application everyone is potentially under fire without knowing about it.

Under this principle a manager who receives complaints or criticisms about a subordinate that have not been taken up first with that subordinate must requisitely refer the complaining member to the subordinate and must tell the subordinate what has happened. What has been said cannot be unsaid, and what has been heard cannot be obliterated from the mind; but the manager can make some amends by behaving requisitely, and he can thereby also reinforce the requisite operation of the system.

Appeal procedures may be viewed in terms of requisite reporting. They constitute in principle a report by a subordinate to his manager-once-removed on the performance of his manager. That is why appeal procedures must be institutionalized. They must provide the manager with the opportunity to hear the subordinate's report to the manager-once-removed and to comment on it from his own point of view. They must also call for the manager-once-removed to make public to the manager and subordinate his opinion about the manager's behaviour and the subordinate's report. That subject is discussed in Chapter 15.

How Many Subordinates Can a Manager Manage?

A question which has bedevilled the organization of manager-subordinate commands for the past fifty years is the question of how many immediate subordinates it is possible for a manager to have. The importance of getting the right number of subordinates for a manager, depending upon the conditions, is twofold. First, it provides for a realistic role for the manager, and for realistic manager-subordinate role relationships. But, second, it helps to prevent the development of too many management levels. For the common consequence of having too small commands is to spread out the manifest managerial organization vertically – a subject to which I shall return in Chapter 8 as a central aspect of my general theory. Thinking on this subject has been shaped by the so-called Graicunas theorem[17] which argues for six as the optimum. This notion has been persuasively argued by Urwick[18] on the grounds that in military organization the size of an officer's immediate command is usually around six subordinates. There is in fact, however, no evidence whatever to support the Graicunas view, as Blau and Scott, for example, have shown.[19] Even in military organization the first-line managers (the platoon commanders as shown in Chapter 8) have up to forty or more immediate subordinates. And James Worthy has argued the case for the 'flat organization' policy of Sears Roebuck – a policy which allows for immediate commands of thirty of more subordinates at any level in the organization.[20]

There is no uniformly optimum number of direct subordinates of a manager. It may range anywhere from one up to fifty of sixty or more depending upon the following factors.

[17] V. A. Graicunas (1937), 'Relationship in Organisation'.
[18] L. Urwick (1947), *Elements of Administration*.
[19] P. M Blau and R. Scott (1963). *Formal Organizations*, p. 168.
[20] J. Worthy (1950), 'Organizational Structure and Employee Morale'.

The first question is how many subordinates the manager requires. If he is a research investigator, or a salesman, or in some professional role, and requires only one or a few subordinates, then there is no managerial problem. Moreover, it is anti-requisite to give him more subordinates just because he could manage more: that would be to interfere with his operational work.

It is in the labour intensive situation that the problem of what is the maximum number of subordinates arises. Here – in offices, factories, hospital wards, building sites, and so on – it is often most efficient to arrange as large commands as possible under each manager. The limiting condition is that the manager must be able to be accountable for the work of each of his immediate subordinates. He must be able to know each of those subordinates in the sense of having sufficient first-hand contact with them and with their work to be able to make up his own mind about the quality of their performance. He must further be available to them as needed to help to overcome difficulties they may encounter, to carry out any necessary on-the-job training, to discuss periodically his appraisal of them and of their career prospects, to listen to their suggestions and proposals, and to facilitate their interaction with one another. And if any of them in turn is a manager with subordinates, he must be able to monitor their managerial activities, plan establishment, assess potential in promotion in individuals, hear appeals. In short, the situation must enable him to act as an effective manager.

There are two main factors which determine how many subordinates a manager may have before it begins to be a strain upon his ability to act as their manager: first, the amount of time the manager must spend on his own activities away from his subordinates; and second, the complexity of the technology involved. The two factors interact to some extent.

The main features can be illustrated by first taking the simplest case; namely, the one in which the manager has nothing to do but to be with his subordinates and to supervise them, and the technology is simple in the sense that the manager does not have to develop it. Such situations occur, for example, in a ditch-digging task using pick-and-shovel technology; or in a highly standardized and computerized retailing activity where, for example, the store managers are provided with their goods at predetermined stock levels, stock replenishment is centrally controlled, advertising is standardized and carried out by a central department.

It is in these circumstances that it would appear that some managers may be capable of managing as many as fifty to sixty direct subordinates and more. The only limitation here is the psychological limitation of how many people it is really possible for a manager to know in the managerial sense. There are some managers who could cope with perhaps as many as a hundred[21] direct subordinates, but by and large more than fifty is very heavy even under the simplest of conditions.

If the technology is nearly standardized but not quite, and if the manager must take part in various types of meeting which take him away from the immediate workplace, he may still be able to have up to fifty or more subordinates, so long as he is given one or more supervisory assistants. (The role of supervisor is discussed in Chapter 17)..

As the technology becomes less standardized, demanding more collateral contact between the manager and his colleagues, or frequent encounters between the manager and production method specialists, or production controllers, or research and development people, or customers, or higher management; or as the manager himself must devote his own personal time to planning, or design, or social work, or therapy, or research, or selling; or as complexities in work require him to spend large amounts of time with each of his subordinates working out operational problems; so the number of subordinates a manager can manage will decrease.

In short, there is no golden rule for determining the optimum number of immediate subordinates that a manager can manage and for whose work he can be accountable. There is a minimum of one – and a maximum of about fifty or sixty or possibly more in exceptional circumstances. Where between those limits a manager's immediate command will fall will depend upon conditions such as those described – and the number may require to be changed as those conditions change.

This description of the number of subordinates there might be in an immediate command group is an empirical one. There is an absence of systematic research on the problem. Thus, for example, the research on small groups and small-group dynamics is not relevant, for a manager's command is not a small group, it is a collection of individually accountable persons in separate detached roles. The research results which set a maximum of ten to twelve for an effective face-to-face group simply do not apply to managerial commands. What is needed is experimental work which simulates the conditions of manager-subordinate *accountability* in manager-subordinate pairs, with varying degrees of colleague interaction among the subordinates under the control of the manager.

The objective of such research would not be the study of communications patterns as for example in Bavelas' work,[22] nor of personal interactions as for example in Bales'[23] studies. The research would follow from the fact that managerial systems are primarily accountability

---

[21] This number is exceptional; but I have met such situations in which it did seem that the extant situation was that the manager was really in charge and did know each of his subordinates on first-name terms and was able to maintain a sound appraisal of the competence of each one in detail.

[22] A. Bavelas (1942), 'Morale and the Training of Leaders'.

[23] R. F. Bales (1950), *Interaction Process Analysis*.

systems in a social exchange setting, and only secondarily systems of communications and personal interaction. Its object would thus be an exploration of accountability with authority.

The Collegium

The foregoing description has been concerned with the bureaucratic hierarchy. This type of structure provides a framework for utilizing large numbers of people of different levels of ability. The nature of the work may, however, call for a governing body to appoint a number of people all with more or less the same level of ability to work together in a common endeavour perhaps in relation to a bureaucratic system and sharing the same resources.

Such a situation occurs, for example, in the case of consultants appointed by a governing board to a hospital. The level of work thrown up for consultants in medicine or in surgery is no different from that thrown up for consultants in obstetrics or in dermatology. Although individual consultants will certainly vary in capacity, the role requirements are satisfied by the same capacity in each case. Appointment of colleagues under such circumstances creates a collegium.[24]

Since the members of a collegium have no common managerial superior other than the governing body itself, they must sort out among themselves the day-to-day problems arising out of interaction of their work, including especially priorities on allocation of resources. When they cannot agree on these issues, they must find means of making policy proposals to the governing body that will enable that body to resolve the differences by policy decisions.

The means by which the members of a collegium can collaborate are twofold. They can meet all together to discuss common problems. If, however, the group is larger than face-to-face size – that is, greater than eight to ten in number – they will require to elect representatives to act as an executive group on their behalf. This elected executive group is accountable to the members of the collegium. It must express the consensus of those members. It must assist those members to arrive at a consensus.

A collegium cannot extend much beyond one hundred members. Its satisfactory functioning requires mutual recognition among the members. Without mutual recognition the meeting together of all members of the collegium becomes an impersonal mass meeting. Effective interaction can-

---

[24] It is not my intention in this book to consider the collegium at any great length. My concern is with the bureaucratic hierarchy. The significance of the collegium and its interaction with the bureaucratic hierarchy, for those who wish to pursue the matter further, is described in detail in connection with the organization of consultants in hospitals, in *Hospital Organization*, by R. W. Rowbottom *et al.* (1973).

not occur. Universities, for example, lose their collegiality when they grow beyond this number of academic staff – and can get it back only by dividing into relatively autonomous colleges or departments.

Members of a collegium may themselves be managerial heads of departmental hierarchies within the institution. The extent of this process of departmentalization is limited by the intensity and frequency of contact required between the departments.

It is possible for one institution to encompass both bureaucratic systems and a collegium or collegia. Such a mixture requires an interface institution in which the head of the bureaucratic system meets the elected representatives of members of the collegium or collegia, as in the organization of hospitals and of academic staff in universities.

Retrospect

In summary, a manager-subordinate role relationship is one in which one person is held accountable for the performance of another person. In order to be accountable it is necessary for the manager to have the minimal authority needed for him to have subordinates who are not unacceptable to him: he must have the right of veto of appointment; he must be able to decide just which of his own activities he will delegate to his subordinate; he must be able to decide the assessment of his subordinate's competence in that role; and he must be able to de-select or initiate transfer of an unsatisfactory subordinate.

If the manager does not have this minimal authority described, and yet is held accountable, then his subordinates will be able to dismiss him. In such circumstances the manager-subordinate relationship becomes paranoiagenic, at least as far as the manager is concerned.

The relationship is potentially just as paranoiagenic from the subordinate's point of view if he does not have reasonable safeguards. He must have the right of appeal (to be discussed in Chapter 15). He must also have the right to be fairly warned about any shortcomings and to have his manager devote training attention to him to help him to make the grade. Without such steps he will feel more like a chattel than a human being. He must finally have the right to know what is being reported about him, and not to have other people reporting about him behind his back to his manager. Secret reporting spreads anxiety and suspicion and is death to confidence in social relationships and in social institutions.

5

Bureaucracy and Associations Contrasted

This chapter briefly describes some of the properties of the functioning of associations which are particularly relevant to an understanding of bureaucracies. The functioning of associations is contrasted with similar situations in bureaucratic systems as a means of highlighting some of the properties of the latter.

An understanding of associations is essential to the understanding of bureaucracy in several respects. It is associations (including nations and local communities) which establish the vast majority of bureaucratic systems. Associations set the direction for the activities of their dependent bureaucratic systems. They thereby set the functions to be carried out. Satisfactory organization design depends upon an understanding of these functions. An organization structure can be no better than its relevance to the work to be done.

An understanding of associations is also needed for any analysis of the important issue of employee participation. For employees can and do form associations – trade unions, staff associations, and other types of representative body. Once such an association has been formed, there is a complex power relationship to be worked out – that between the employing association on the one hand and the employee association(s) on the other. The successful constitutionalization of this power relationship between employing and employee associations is necessary for the legitimation of the objects and authority of employing associations and of the authority they delegate to their bureaucratic systems.

Non-bureaucratic Ways of Getting Work Done

In order to examine more closely the relationship between associations and bureaucratic systems, it may be useful to consider first of all the other ways by which men can get work done. These other ways in industrial societies are three-fold: men can simply work as self-employed individuals; they can work as families without employees; or they can join together and work as partners. Let me briefly examine each of these methods in turn.

First, a man may work on his own, by himself, for himself. He is self-employed – a genuine *entrepreneur*. He risks his livelihood against his own capacities. He earns no wage or salary: he is not responsible to anyone who could pay him one. He gets his income from the services he renders. Many professional men – solicitors, physicians, actors, writers, artists – and business men – from large and small traders, investors and landholders, to sales agents, window-cleaners and taxi owner-drivers – may choose to be in this position. It provides maximum individual freedom in work; it incurs maximum personal risk; and it demands self-reliance.

Recognition of the difference between self-employed people and employees is important. There is often confusion between the two. For example, the 'pay' of authors, film stars and professional sporting heroes is sometimes compared with the general level of wages and salaries in industry and commerce: there is a failure to recognize that such persons are self-employed entrepreneurs whose income waxes and wanes with their popularity at any particular moment. They are not employees with a continuous wage or salary.

Second, men may organize for work on a family basis. The family may be the immediate family, possibly with grandparents, and with father, mother and children, or it may extend to brothers and uncles and to others genealogically more remote who are absorbed into the family circle.[1] The family so constituted lives, as does the self-employed individual, upon the income it gains from its endeavours. How this income is distributed among the members of the family varies from family to family and with changes in family circumstances such as sons and daughters growing up, marrying and having families of their own. Farming, fishing and small trading businesses are readily established on a family basis. The success of the arrangement depends upon the quality of the family relationships. If intra-familial stresses develop, tension may run high because family ties cannot be disbanded.

Third, men with or without family ties may enter into partnership with each other, sharing the risks and the earnings of their work. These partnerships may be short-term for a special purpose, such as a group of men joined together to finance and build themselves houses. Or they may be enduring, formally established and registered partnerships, such as firms of solicitors, or consultants, or financiers, or insurance brokers or estate agents. How the proceeds of the partnership are to be divided is determined by the particular agreement setting up the partnership. Greater or lesser degrees of independence may be built into the arrangement – partners sharing completely or dividing the proceeds in proportion to their individual earnings. Partnerships demand close personal working relationships; they therefore require procedures whereby individual

[1] Or it may extend outside the immediate family to hired hands, retainers, servants, counter assistants or clerks, who live with the family or in the shop or office and are covered legally by the law of master and servant. This arrangement was exceedingly common in the nineteenth century and is still a common type of organization in non-industrial societies.

partners may leave or be bought out, or the partnership dissolved, should interpersonal stresses develop.

There are severe limitations to the possible size not only of family enterprises but also of partnerships. Thus the law in various countries usually sets an upper limit of between 20 and 50 partners – a reflection of the fact that partners must be able to work closely together; in groups of 50 or more it becomes no longer possible for every partner to be able to know and to work with all the others.

Types of Employing Institution

None of the foregoing arrangements for work can cope when larger-scale enterprise is required. Even with extended families or partnerships there may be at the very most a working group of 25 to 50 people who can work together without forming a hierarchical system of managers and subordinates. Where it is necessary to get together a larger work force than, say, 50 persons for a particular endeavour, some kind of additional arrangement is needed. There are two alternatives which have so far emerged: the first is to have an agglomeration of families, as in the practice of war on a tribal basis in primitive societies; the second is to set up bureaucratic systems and employ people to do the work (even slavery on a large scale required the employment of a bureaucratic managing system for its functioning and control).

In order for people to be employed, there must be an employing institution. The main types of institution which set up bureaucratic employment systems may be categorized as follows:

1. individuals – either professionals or private entrepreneurs;
2. families;
3. partnerships – entrepreneurial and professional;
4. permanent associations, including:
   (a) co-operative associations, such as religious associations, trade unions, co-operative communities (e.g. kibbutzim);
   (b) profit-distributing associations (companies);
5. central and local governments on behalf of nations and local communities, which are in effect national and civic non-voluntary associations.

I shall be limiting myself to a consideration mainly of associations and governments in the setting up of bureaucracies. I do so for two reasons: they are the largest employers, both in the sense of employing the largest bureaucratic systems and in the sense of employing the majority of the employed population; and they are the source of much of the trouble in the bureaucratic sector.

While there are some individuals, families and partnerships who set up large-scale bureaucracies, they are mostly employers of small groups of staff from tens to a few hundred. They run the small enterprises whose employees share many of the feelings of entrepreneurs.[2] They are also notoriously difficult to legislate for in terms of policies governing such matters as industrial relations or incomes. But in general terms my analysis of the functioning of bureaucracies set up by governments and by associations applies to the smaller-scale bureaucracies as well, as I shall indicate.

Membership of Associations

The association is a political or quasi-political institution based upon individual power; a few members are elected into representative offices constituting the governing body. By contrast bureaucratic systems are totally made up of offices – they are individual accountability systems based upon authority in office. The members of associations join as individuals, and the impact of each one upon the functioning of the association is determined by his individual power. This power is expressed in the number of votes he can control. Votes may be garnered by combining with other members, by gaining the support of other members, or – in shareholding associations – by these means plus the gaining of control of shares.

While members of associations may seek to influence one another and to combine in voting, no individual member has the authority to instruct any other member to do anything, nor can he be held individually accountable for the activities of any other member. That is to say, power has not been legitimated and transformed into individual accountability and authority attached to manager-subordinate role relationships, as is the case in the bureaucratic system.

Membership of permanent associations is obtained by diverse means, depending upon the nature of the association. Thus, membership of associations such as co-operative societies and trade unions is obtained by application and acceptance if and when the conditions of the association have been complied with, in contrast to the membership of a company which is achieved simply by buying shares in it.

Once a person has become a member of an association it is usually not at all difficult to remain a member. It is necessary only to obey the rules, and the rules are generally simple and straightforward. Usually no positive performance is required, not even, for example, that of being an active

[2] Indeed, D. R. Miller and G. E. Swanson refer to these small-scale concerns as entrepreneurial rather than bureaucratic because the outlook and attitudes of their employees coincide in many ways with the attitudes of true entrepreneurs: (1958) *The Changing American Parent.*

member or of standing for election to one of the offices in the governing body. So long as you do not break the rules you may remain. Members of associations are not held individually accountable as members for using their own initiative in achieving things for the association, and hence the vexed questions of transfer, de-selection, or dismissal do not arise as they do in bureaucratic systems. Nor do associations declare redundancy: they do not need to garner income, either by grant or by earning, in order to remain in being.

Representative Systems of Associations

Bureaucracies function through the exercise of managerial authority in appointed roles, associations function through elected representatives of the membership as a whole. The consequential effects of this functional difference are manifested in many ways: in the profound differences between managerial and representative leadership; in corporate versus individual accountability and authority; in the interaction between the chief executives of bureaucracies and the elected representatives of the trade union and staff associations formed by those employed in the bureaucracy; in the nature of the activity of the institutions themselves.

The institutionalization of the power of an association *qua* association takes place by means of the establishment of elected representative roles (offices) whose incumbents, the officials, are authorized to act on behalf of the association. Those officials may be directly elected by the membership or they may be elected by a representative assembly elected by the membership. Either way, an association operates through its responsible governing body elected by the members to act on behalf of the members. These governing bodies, be they a board of directors of a company, or central committee of a co-operative society or trade union (or a central government), usually carry corporate liability for their activities. Governing bodies are true groups in the sense that they make group decisions. The employees in bureaucratic hierarchies are individually accountable and cannot be combined into accountable working groups.[3]

It is through its governing body and its elected officials that an associa-

[3] This distinction between group decision-making in associations and individual accountability in bureaucracies is of considerable theoretical and practical importance. As I shall show in Chapter 12, failure to make the distinction (in line with the current fad to make everything into group situations) has led, for example, to an inappropriate application to industrial employment of the group decision-making studies of Lewin, Lippitt, White and others, as in the so-called functionally autonomous work groups which have been formed, or in the use of group decisions by a manager's immediate subordinates as a means of participation. And for many years group bonus payment schemes have been used in bureaucratic systems with inevitable adverse effects, since in reality it is individuals and not groups who do the work and are accountable.

tion may make an impact upon its individual members. It may do so, however, only to ensure that its members conform to the rules and regulations of the association. It cannot instruct its members individually to undertake any particular activities other than to obey the rules. (Nations and their governments are, of course, different in this respect from all other associations.) Associations are thus essentially institutions composed of equals, founded upon power, in which representative authority is vested in a governing body. The association, unlike its bureaucracy, is not a hierarchy of members; it is a hierarchy only in the very limited sense that the members as a corporate body stand above their elected officials. These officials most certainly are not in a manager-subordinate relationship with the members.

Relationships between members of an elected governing body are colleague relationships. No one member is the manager of any other member, nor is he accountable for the work of any other member. The chairman may speak on behalf of the governing body between its meetings. Complications in relationships within a governing body may arise if it contains members who also occupy positions as employees of the association. This situation arises in many companies whose boards are composed of a mixture of so-called executive and non-executive members, the executive members being senior employees and usually including the chief executive and some or all of his employed immediate subordinates. These executive members occupy two roles: as shareholders they are members of the association and are thus eligible for election to the board: as employees they are members of the bureaucratic system, with an accountable manager in a position of superordination over them.

The employee members in their executive roles will be in superior-subordinate relation with the members of the governing body as a whole, while within that body they are colleagues. It is essential that they should be consciously aware of this feature of their double role carrying (especially the chief executive and his subordinates) if they are to be able to behave in appropriately different ways in each situation. Many countries preclude such an arrangement by using a two-tier board structure – a top non-executive board and a subordinate executive board.

It is often said that members of associations do not have much control over their governing bodies; for example, that shareholders in companies or in co-operative societies, or the members of trade unions, have little control over their boards of directors or central committees. This view is oversimplified and misleading. It fails to take into account the significance of being able to set the contextual limits or boundaries within which people are free to behave. Elected governing bodies must be sensitive to the views of the members of the association, as these views either implicitly or explicitly set limits on the decisions which the governing body may make.

If a governing body pursues policies outside the limits acceptable to the members of its association, then the members may decide not to re-elect it; or in the case of a company, they may sell their shares and the board may find it increasingly difficult to obtain financial support. Thus, whereas members of associations may not involve themselves in a continual review of the activities of the governing body they elect, they do inevitably set the context within which that body shall work. Continual failure of a governing body to conform to those limits will lead sooner or later to a day of reckoning when the association may act to remove it. The membership most often gives sanction by omission rather than by active consent: but elected committees are always aware that they have to judge carefully just how far they can go in order not to antagonize the membership.

At the same time, it is also true that the context within which many elected representatives act may in some respects be a very wide one. Boards of companies and central or branch committees of trade unions, for example, are usually not much bothered by the members they represent so long as they make profit or continue to gain improved working conditions. They may then take part, for instance, in many kinds of political activity, nominally on behalf of the company or the union but with their members in reality not at all involved. In such activities, they will find themselves working in a context so broad as to leave them unhampered unless they overstep the very boundaries of national political propriety or indeed the limits of the law. To this extent associations are vulnerable to political manipulation (see Chapter 13).

Public Objects and Private Motives

It is essential for the design of requisite organization of bureaucracy that the objects of employing associations should be made as explicit as possible. For it is these objects which establish what the bureaucratic organization is for, and from which, therefore, the pattern of that organization must follow. These objects are not commonly stated as explicitly or in as much detail as is requisite. One of the reasons is that the objects of associations tend to get mixed up with the wide range of personal motives of their members. Let us consider therefore the question of private motives of individuals and public objects of social institutions.

The coming together of people to form an association cannot happen fortuitously. There must be an object or objects around which a group of like-minded people can come together: to seek some service, or improved conditions, or a dividend payment, or an opportunity to forward a cause. If this condition is not fulfilled the co-operation necessary for association cannot occur. When common objects are lost associations disintegrate.

But to say that the members of an association require to unite around a common object or objects does not mean that all members of the association must have identical motives or purposes in pursuing that object. Each one may have his own personal reasons for joining the association, and those personal reasons may vary widely. The satisfactions obtained by one person will not necessarily be the same as those obtained by others: one may seek a quick financial profit; another may seek to fulfil a political aspiration; another may seek personal power; another may seek the status that he believes to be conferred by being made a member; another may seek to do something for the social welfare of others; another may believe in co-operative action; another may feel forced by social pressures to join; others may do so for a combination of any or all such purposes, and many other purposes; and all will have strong unconscious motives besides.

We may distinguish, therefore, between: the private and personal motives of individuals – their own purposes – with respect to which they may differ; and the object or objects which they will share with respect to their association and which must be explicit and publicly formulated so that all can be agreed. Individual purposes are psychological things and must requisitely be allowed to be private; association objects are social things and must requisitely be public. Even a secret society must be able to make known its objects to its members.

The right of individual members of an association to the privacy of their personal motives may be accepted without argument in a democratic society. By and large this principle is accepted without query. To deny the principle is to establish the scrutiny of personal motives in addition to acceptance of the objects of an association as a criterion for acceptance for membership. It can be predicted that any such criteria will be experienced by individuals as an invasion of the self. Certain types of managerial training which have become widespread do in fact invade the psychological privacy of the individual, and predictably induce anxiety, suspicion, and mistrust.

The objects of associations determine the operational activities of the bureaucratic systems they employ. The structural aspect of bureaucratic organization therefore lends itself readily to analysis in structural-functional terms. The organizational structure of the bureaucratic work system must requisitely follow directly from function as defined by the association's objects. The starting point for the design of organization for a bureaucracy must always be the detailed analysis and explicit formulation of the functions which the bureaucracy is employed to undertake to achieve the objects of the association.[4]

---

[4] In pointing out this functional implication of the analysis I do not intend to establish the whole argument as within the so-called functionalist theory of the nature of society, in con-

Service to the Community

Most associations are engaged in exchange with other institutions or with individual consumers in a market. The objects of associations are thus of concern not only to their members but also to others in the social surround. It is impossible for some members of a society to band together to pursue a common object without others wanting to know whether or not they are going to be affected. Society is continuous. No one sector can be carved out without affecting its neighbouring areas. Associations and their employed bureaucracies must therefore be open systems if they are to survive.

This fact of the continuity of a society provides the basis for establishing one important characteristic of the objects of associations if those objects are to be requisite. The characteristic is that since the objects of each particular association concern transactions with the surrounding community, they must not be centred upon gain for the association's members at the expense of the community, or upon the maintenance of careers for its employees. Personal gain should derive from service; employment and career security should derive from the economy as a whole and not from particular enterprises (see Chapter 11).

If the governing body and its chief executive orient an enterprise towards the dominant interests of its members or its employees only, the community or market will become aware of this fact, if not from the public statements of the enterprise then certainly from the behaviour of its members and its employees. Rogers[5] has shown how unconscious motivation in the directors of a business primarily towards understanding and serving the needs of others can lead to sound growth, whereas unconscious motivation primarily to use the market to satisfy personal aggrandisement can have deleterious effects. Society may go on tolerating this situation if circumstances, especially those of monopoly, force it to. But in these circumstances social tension builds up. A situation of increasing disequilibrium is likely to develop. It may, however, endure for many years. The same type of social disequilibrium is observable in governmental institutions whose elected officials and employees forget that they are rendering a service and begin to behave in a manner to suit their own convenience rather than that of the public they are supposed to serve.

---

trast to systems theory or conflict theory. My point is that in analysing bureaucracy it is essential to clarify and help to make explicit the objects of the employing association as *one* of the critical factors determining the pattern of requisite organization. Establishing in this way the 'functions' of the bureaucratic system as sought by the employing association, is entirely consistent with an analytical treatment of bureaucracy in terms of systems theory. And it certainly does not preclude the consideration of conflict between employers and employees and between different employee power groups as well.

[5] K. Rogers (1963), *Managers: Personality and Performance*.

To be requisite, therefore, the objects of associations must have as one of their outcomes the provision of some kind of service to the community or at least to its members. What then of the purposes of the members of an association? To the extent that the motives of members are dominantly in the service-giving direction, then their motives and the objects of the association can be consistently requisite. It is possible, and not uncommon, however, for the motives of members to be inconsistent with the objects of the association. Conflict and an undermining of the pursuit of requisite objects will result, contributing to the weakening of an enterprise or the debasement of a government and of governmental process.

The first and essential step in all organization analysis is to establish the nature, policies and structure of the association. From these policies and structure flow the functions and requisite structure of the bureaucratic systems which may be employed. If this rule of defining the association first were followed, it would overcome many difficulties in analysing and clarifying the structure and functioning of many institutions such as universities, churches, trade unions and co-operative communities.

PART THREE

AN EXPLANATION OF
BUREAUCRATIC SYSTEMS

6

Work and the Measurement of Level of Work

In Part Two we have outlined the defining features of bureaucracies and of the associations which establish them. The manager-subordinate role relationships which constitute the social structure of bureaucratic systems have been described. It is these networks of role relationships which give to bureaucratic systems their familiar pyramid-shaped hierarchical structure. Against the background of these definitions a number of major propositions about bureaucracy and the nature of human capacity may now be put forward.

These propositions are concerned with explaining how it is that a recognizable class of social institutions which we are calling bureaucratic systems can exist at all; why they have their hierarchical structure; how they manage to provide a setting for the deployment of human talent in working inter-relationships between people; how they manage to retain a recognizable structure while they contract or grow and while the people who occupy roles in them develop and change, transfer from one role to another, leave and are replaced; how, in short, they manage to give scope for the individuality of each person, his development and change, while yet functioning as integrated social systems.

In order to consider these issues it will be necessary first to confront the question of what constitutes work. For these systems are work systems: they are the means by which associations get work done. Our understanding of bureaucracy will therefore depend upon our understanding of the processes of human work.

Work (in the sense of human work and not the $W = FS$ formula of physics) is defined as that plane of human activity in which the individual exercises discretion, makes decisions, and acts, in seeking to transform the external physical or social world in accord with a predetermined goal. Bureaucratic systems are social systems which call upon individuals to work in a setting in which the goals of the activity are set by the employing institution through its managers in the form of assigned tasks, rather than by the individual himself.

Bureaucracies are hierarchical systems. They contain a range of different levels, reflected in different levels of work. An operational definition of level of work is given in the form of a measuring instrument based upon the maximum time-spans during which people are required to exercise discretion.

These definitions of work and level of work are used to begin the task of constructing our theoretical propositions. The first proposition is that there exists a universally distributed depth-structure of levels of bureaucratic organization. It is this depth-structure to which stratified hierarchies of bureaucracies tend to conform and which gives a feeling of there being something similar about the pattern of stratification of all bureaucratic systems. Evidence is presented which suggests that there are natural lines of stratification at the 3-month time-span level, 12-month, 2-year, 5-year, 10-year, and at higher levels as well, and that managerial strata can and should requisitely be built around these boundaries.

The second proposition is that the existence of the stratified depth-structure of bureaucratic hierarchies is the reflection in social organization of the existence of discontinuity and stratification in the nature of human capacity. The capacity is referred to as work-capacity, which is further analysed in terms of a person's level of abstraction. A multi-modal distribution of capacity is postulated, each person falling into one particular mode or level of abstraction. This proposition represents a radical departure from the assumption so commonly made in the social sciences that human characteristics are distributed in accord with a uni-modal Gaussian curve.

The third proposition is that the rate of growth of the work-capacity of individuals follows regular and predictable paths. Maturational shifts in the quality of function of an individual's capacity occur as he moves across the boundary from one level of abstraction to another.

These propositions can be applied not only to the design of organizational structure for bureaucracies but also to coping with changes in these systems induced by the developing capacities of their employees, particularly their senior employees. If the propositions are valid and reliable, they will show that the relationship between bureaucracy and individuality is not an unresolvable conflict to be softened by uncomfortable compromise, but rather a dilemma which can be dealt with by creative interaction between social institution and individual.

The Process of Working

Bureaucratic systems are social institutions established to enable associations to employ people to do work for them. They are rational institutions, as Weber has described, especially in the sense that the work of each person in the system is linked to the work of every other person in the system in such a manner that the whole institution functions to provide an integrated and unified output. That is what the division of labour is about. Seen from one point of view, each person is a mere cog in the machine. The social institution is seen as determining what each person does. The sociologist who adopts this view perceives bureaucracies as a fine example of how social structure and role relationships can be the sole and sufficient causal agent in explaining individual behaviour. The employer who adopts this view perceives his employees as instruments of economic action.

That real life is not and cannot be so simple is demonstrable if we examine the process of work itself. Work as an activity in the bureaucratic situation can give the clearest possible picture of the person-in-action, with his own particular being and nature, functioning in a social setting which provides a unifying context within which he expresses himself. If that context is sufficiently differentiated to provide roles which allow freedom of individual expression with respect both to interest and to level of ability, then social system and individual personality can be mutually reinforcing. If this matching of role and personality does not occur, then each person will simply not behave in accord with the demands of the social system: his individuality will express itself eventually in an attack upon the social context itself.

Let me first describe the main components of the process of work in general, and then turn to work more specifically within the constraints of the bureaucratic system. The term work refers to activity, to behaviour, to that human activity in which people exercise discretion, make decisions, and act so as to transform the external physical and social world in accord with some predetermined goal in order to fulfil some need. The aspect to be changed may be a physical object to be modified or created, a person or persons to be influenced, a social institution to be changed, or the person himself to be changed relative to the surrounding field. When the work has been done, something has been manifestly transformed – there is an objective output to be observed.

Work is thus a goal-directed activity. It begins with a feeling of something lacking, something desired. That something arises as a feeling but comes through into consciousness as an idea of something to be created, something to be brought into being. The lack may be experienced as something missing in the environment or as something missing in the self. In either case the lack will be experienced as a missing or incomplete object.

The idea of something missing begins to formulate itself in terms of what Schutz has called the *project*:[1] a subjective idea of a situation which would satisfy the felt need, a model in fantasy of something to be sought after in the objective world and a means of seeking it.

The project serves to focus *attention* on the field in the search for objects which could be transformed so as to match the project. As Merleau-Ponty has put it in another context: 'Empiricism cannot see that we need to know

[1] A. Schutz (1967), *Collected Papers I.*

what we are looking for, otherwise we would not be looking for it, and intellectualism fails to see that we need to be ignorant of what we are looking for, or equally again we should not be searching. They are in agreement in that neither attaches due importance to that circumscribed ignorance, that still "empty" but already determinate intention which *is* attention itself."[2]

The objects attended to may be physical objects: physical materials to be transformed into tools or goods; or indeed, a lump of stone within which a sculptor can perceive his work of art. Or they may be human objects: people who are to be persuaded, or instructed, or asked, to do things. Or they may be cultural objects: ideas to be revised or developed, things to be written, laws to be created.

The transformation of the object may not require any change in the object itself, but merely a change in the relationship between the object and the self. Thus, for example, an object which could entirely satisfy a person's need – such as food or clothing – might exist but might be unavailable because it was physically or economically out of reach. The transformation required here is a positional one: it is to overcome the difficulties by getting the object located differently. The acquisition of learning would have this same quality.

The initiation of work then requires a field situation composed of an individual with a subjective idea or project related to an external object which, by some modification in its nature, could be transformed into an object sufficiently like the projected model to satisfy the individual's need. The transformation of the object to approximate to the project is the goal. It defines the *direction* of the person's work.

There is one other aspect to the goal, without which it cannot exist in the world of reality. The achievement of the goal must have a time limit, a *target completion time*. The problem in work is never simply to achieve an object never mind when; it is to achieve an object in a limited period of time. If no time target is set, then in fact there is no felt need. Real needs require to be fulfilled within real time limits.

The construction of the goal is an unconscious intuitive process. It is done by touch-and-feel, by intuition, by hunch, by guess, by flashes of insight. It is done by the person-in-action using discretion and judgment. The result of this process is a conscious subjective outcome: a conscious awareness of need, the construction of a project, the seeking out and selection of a suitable object to be transformed, and the fixing of a target completion time.[3]

[2] M. Merleau-Ponty (1974), *Phenomenology, Language and Sociology* (ed. John O'Neill), p. xxiv.

[3] The process is of course never quite as tidy as this in practice. Needs are never completely explicit: they always have unconscious undertones, complexities, ties to other needs

The goal having been set, the person is faced with the problem of constructing a plan for achieving it. He must figure out how to manage the transformation of the object. Not only must he establish a plan, he must determine how the plan is to be carried out. In doing so, he will use whatever knowledge he has about similar situations, about the resources available, or indeed about anything which for whatever reason seems relevant to the situation. His sense of relevance will be intuitively determined. Ideas will occur to him. Alternative plans will suggest themselves. He may play these ideas over in his mind, savour them, choose the one which he thinks most likely to succeed. It is this process of deliberation which John Dewey has described as 'a dramatic rehearsal (in imagination) of various competing possible lines of action . . . an experiment in finding out what the various lines of possible action are really like.'[4]

In order for a plan to be satisfactory it must fulfil two criteria: first, it must promise the creation of a satisfactory end-product or output, and second, it must have a reasonable chance of getting to completion within the time that has been targeted. To produce a plan to achieve a transformation in an object or a field situation is one thing; to produce a plan that will achieve this end in a given time is quite another. *Balancing pace of work against quality of output is at the heart of the process of work.*

Having decided his plan, the individual will begin to act. As he acts he will meet unexpected obstacles. He will modify his plan to overcome these obstacles. He will observe how his plan is unrolling, testing it as he goes, changing a bit here or there, elaborating and detailing as he encounters each successive stage. As he works he will note the accumulating result as the object becomes transformed, judging just how quickly he can go, just how much needs to be done, just how satisfactory is the process, and finally judging when a sufficient transformation has occurred and a satisfactory output has been achieved.

This process of behaviour and on-going adjustment of behaviour towards a goal is readily interpretable in terms of a cybernetic feed-back model. The individual homes in on a target, taking correcting action in the light of his observation of his progress towards the goal; and, indeed, modifying the goal itself if necessary.

Working in a Bureaucratic System

In employment work in bureaucratic systems many of the features of the situation are determined by a person's manager (or someone higher up)

---

and desired gratifications, denials and secondary gains, some of which may be connected with individual psychopathology. I have described many of the features of such pathology connected with work in (1970) 'Disturbances in the Capactiy to Work'.

[4] J. Dewey (1922), *Human Nature and Conduct*, p. 190.

rather than by the person himself. This assignment of duties is in sharp contrast to entrepreneurial work whose outstanding quality is that the individual himself decides what work he will undertake.

In bureaucracies the goals of the working activity are always managerially assigned or sanctioned (implicitly or explicitly). These goals are set in terms of tasks or assignments. By *task* I refer to the activities to be undertaken by a subordinate on behalf of his manager within prescribed limits in order to produce a particular output required by the manager. *Activity* refers to the observable behaviour of the individual. *Output* refers to the end-product of the activity − a physical object, a service or a formulated idea; it can be seen, or read, or listened to, or used. Tasks are assigned in terms of a description of the output, the quantity to be produced, the standards of quality, and the target completion time for carrying out the activity and finishing the total output. The institutional boundaries are set in the form of *prescribed limits* which are the real rules, in the form of policies (both written and unwritten), procedures, physical controls, signals, and other types of control which are objectively set and which must be obeyed.

Some examples of tasks would be: produce 1,000 units of these goods, to this quality, within two weeks, with these prescribed methods and tools; carry out this research investigation within two months, within these resources and testing these three hypotheses; type 20 invoices a day, accurately and neatly and using the standard forms and layout appropriate to each one; prepare a written recommendation on this subject by the end of next month, ensuring that it is consistent with these particular governmental policies which are relevant; give these specified services to clients who request them, but do not undertake any which are likely to extend for more than a year without checking first.

It can thus be seen that a task always has the character of an instruction about carrying out a particular activity so that 'that' may be realized − where 'that' is an idea in the present of something which it is desired should exist in the future. The completion of the task is manifested in 'that' having been brought into existence in the present as an output.

In bureaucratic systems tasks are activities carried out by subordinates for managers. The tasks may be initiated in any of three ways: they may be directly assigned by the manager; they may be a response by the subordinate to requests or initiatives from elsewhere in the organization or from customers or suppliers outside it; or they may arise from the subordinate's own initiative. But however they arise, the tasks will all have been either explicitly or implicitly sanctioned by the person's manager, or lie within an area of general responsibilities which the manager has instructed the subordinate to discharge.

Tasks in bureaucratic hierarchies are always carried out within prescribed limits: it is these limits which provide the institutional zone of the channel or area of relevance within which the activities of the person-in-action are to flow. An employee can never be given *carte blanche* to do whatever he likes in order to carry out the task set. Any such open terms of reference would leave his manager and the employing organization with no control over expense, and with no opportunity for the use of standardized methods and procedures. They would also leave the employee free to carry out the task in his own time.

The essence of employment in bureaucratic systems is to carry out tasks and achieve outputs within target completion times, within expense and quality limits, and conforming to such prescribed methods and procedures as have been fixed as a matter of policy. In general terms activities within bureaucracies are always within the policy of the institution. It is these policies which give to the bureaucratic system the quality of rationality described by Weber. They do so by ensuring that all the tasks which are carried out are organized towards a common final output and within a common time-scale of planning.

The prescribed limits of tasks can be learned. Response can therefore become automatic. Because the prescribed limits are objectively definable, there is no uncertainty as to whether the subordinate has obeyed or not. Failure to obey the prescribed limits constitutes negligence or insubordination. The subordinate can know with certainty if he has been negligent.

The work, however, in carrying out a task consists not in conforming to the prescribed limits but in deciding how within those limits to carry out the task – deciding what has to be done in the moving present in order to bring the future idea into being. The work is what is left to the person to use his own discretion to do. If there is no discretion or judgment to be used in carrying out a task, then the task can be done by an automatic machine tool.[5]

[5] The prescribed limits as I have defined them link closely to Durkheim's concept of moral duty in his *Moral Education* (1961). His description of the interaction between 'prescribed behaviour' and 'individual initiative' demonstrates that the concepts of prescribed limits and discretionary content may be very general concepts indeed, applied in Durkheim's case to the analysis of morality rather than of work. He writes: 'In the first place, there is an aspect common to all behaviour that we ordinarily call moral. All such behaviour conforms to pre-established rules. To conduct one's self morally is a matter of abiding by a norm, determining what conduct should obtain in a given instance even before one is required to act. This domain of morality is the domain of duty; duty is prescribed behaviour. It is not that the moral conscience is free of uncertainties. We know, indeed, that it is often perplexed, hesitating between alternatives. But then the problem is what is the particular rule that applies to the given situation, and how should it be applied? Since each rule is a general prescription, it cannot be applied exactly and mechanically in identical ways in each particular circumstance. It is up to the person to see how it applies in a given situation. There is always considerable, if limited, leeway left for his initiative. The essentials of conduct are determined by the rule. . . . Thus, we can say that morality consists of a system of rules of action that predetermine conduct. They state how one must act in given situations; and to behave properly is to obey conscientiously.' (p. 241)

Let me give a few examples of what is meant by the exercise of discretion in work. Work lies in the judgment that a machine operator uses in setting a machine tool, in deciding whether the finish is good, in using hand tools, in discovering *ad hoc* means for using an ill-made tool or jig; or in the judgment used by a sales representative on how and when to approach a client; or in the judgment used by a typist in laying out her work; or by a research worker in organizing a programme of research projects, or in taking notice of unusual results; or in the judgment used by a manager in assessing the adequacy of a subordinate; or by a managing director in deciding budget allocations; or by an accountant in interpreting expense trends; or by a personnel manager negotiating a pay structure; or by a time-study engineer assessing a task carried out by an operator; or by a planning engineer doing a layout; or by a production controller organizing a schedule; or by a patents officer preparing a patent; and so on.[6]

Size of Problem, Time-span, and Level of Employment Work

In short then, in working in a bureaucracy a person has his goals and direction of activity set by his assigned tasks. The channels within which he acts have a boundary zone set by his manager which dictates a range of prescribed limits within which he has to work and the maximum time during which he is allowed to finish the task and produce the required output. In order to carry out the task he must construct his own subjective project, comprising his picture of the goal and output and a plan of how to achieve it, and must go into action using his best discretion in order to move towards the goal within the prescribed limits set. That part of the boundary zone composed of the maximum target completion time within which he has to organize his activities in carrying out tasks turns out to have an interesting and unexpected significance. It is concerned with the objective measurement of the level of work, or to put it another way, the level of responsibility which a person carries in his work.

We have seen that the direction, boundaries and goal both in output and completion time have been set for the subordinate by his manager on behalf of the employing institution. But it is equally important to remember that it is the subordinate himself as the person-in-action who does the work: it is he who uses his judgment in producing his own plan within

---

Weber also made this distinction between prescribed limits and discretionary flow of activity in his analysis of the technical rules or norms regulating conduct in offices, and of the authority to act within those regulations.

[6] All individuals occupying roles in bureaucratic systems must bear accountability for the exercise of discretion and the making of decisions. In this limited sense I would be in accord with Simon's description of employment systems as decision-making systems (H. Simon (1957), *Administrative Behaviour*).

whatever broader plans might have been set, and in overcoming obstacles in traversing the path towards the goal. He does it all in his own personal way, which will differ from the way anyone else would do it. He must be interested. He must have the knowledge and the experience, the touch-and-feel, to place himself in context; he must feel comfortable in the time context, and he must have the ability to cope with the size and difficulty of the task. What can we say, then, about this question of size of task?

One way of investigating the question of size or difficulty of task in bureaucracies is to take note of the way they break problems down into sub-problems – into a series of steps on the way to the future. The solving of those sub-problems is then organized in accord with a sequence and timing which allows the solution of each sub-problem to contribute to a larger part, until all the larger parts are solved and come together in an output from the institution to society.[7] But the moment we speak about problems and sub-problems it may be obvious that we are speaking about larger and smaller problems, larger and smaller steps, about parts and wholes. In what way, then, can one problem be said to be larger than another? Certainly if problems a_1 and a_2 are parts of problem A, then A is bigger than a_1 or a_2. But how much bigger? And is a_1 bigger than a_2, or vice versa? And is problem A bigger or smaller than another problem, B, where neither includes the other? If we could answer these questions we might be able to understand more clearly the structure of bureaucratic hierarchies. For example, is there any systematic order in the size of problem to be assigned to any particular level in the hierarchy? Do roles at different levels carry problems of different size and therefore require individuals of different size in capacity?

To consider these questions let me summarize my findings which have been reported previously but which are relevant here.[8] First there is the following simple and obvious fact: when a problem A is broken down into sub-problems a_1 and a_2, then the target completion time for the sub-problems is inevitably shorter than that for the total problem. Could it be, then, that the time-span within which people work is somehow associated with the felt magnitude of the tasks they are carrying out? If so, it might be possible directly to measure the level of work in terms of the time context of the work.

Research has demonstrated this view to be correct, but not directly in terms of each discrete task. What has emerged is that the maximum time-span within which a person is required to act with respect to all of his tasks

[7] This description of work coincides with Critical Path Analysis. The goal G is the objective event OE, the sub-goals are events on the critical path. A critical path diagram is simply a diagram of the organization of a problem-solving process.

[8] See especially my (1956) *Measurement of Responsibility*, (1961) *Equitable Payment*, and (1964) *Time-Span Handbook*.

in a bureaucratic role does appear to give a measure of the level of his work. The sense of responsible effort in work seems to be directly connected with the sensation of having to exercise continuous judgment in problem solving and to tolerate the accompanying sense of uncertainty. The sense of size of effort in working, or the sense of size of the responsibility in role occupied, seems to vary directly with the length of time within which a person has to organize his problem-solving activity. The longer forward in time is the overall goal of his work, the heavier his responsibility feels to him.[9] It would appear that the further distant the future that has to be realized, and the longer the moving present that has to be organized and traversed, the weightier the feel of the task.[10]

I had the opportunity in the Glacier Project to follow up this notion that level of work is related to the time for which an individual is expected to exercise discretion on his own account. The resulting findings suggest that the burden of work as man experiences it is related to time directly and exclusively. Considerations such as size of command, resources to be deployed, skill, danger, public utility, and so on, are irrelevant to the measurement, notwithstanding their popular appeal as factors which 'should' determine the importance of various types of work. Let me summarize some of the data which have led to this conclusion.

The Time-span Instrument

An instrument was constructed for objectively measuring the maximum periods of time during which individuals in roles in bureaucratic

[9] This finding is consonant with the interesting view recently put forward by the biologist D. Stenhouse about the importance of what he terms the postponement or P factor. The P factor refers to the individual's ability to delay or withhold the instinctive responses as 'an essential precondition for the emergence of adaptive variability from within the rigidity of instinct systems'. Stenhouse postulates a strong connection between P and intelligence. (1974) *The Evolution of Intelligence*, p. 80.

[10] Relating this finding to Lewin's concept of life-space would suggest that the *size* of a person's life-space can be measured in terms of its organized extensiveness in time: that is to say, how far forward the person is really working in the present, and how much of his past he can bring into organized and usable focus in doing so. This suggestion would be consistent with Lewin's view that as the life-space of unemployed persons contracted so did their forward planning shorten.

Lewin, in fact, was quite aware of the importance of the time dimension for measuring the size of life-space but he never developed the idea. Thus, for example, we find this allusion to the relationship between life-space and temporal duration: 'During development the scope of the psychological time dimension of the life-space increases from hours to days, months and years. In other words, the young child lives in the immediate present; with increasing age an increasingly more distant psychological past and future affect present behaviour' (K. Lewin (1952), 'Regression, Retrogression and Development', pp. 103–4).

Basil Bernstein makes the same point: 'Necessarily, the child lives in the here-and-now experience of this world, in which the time-span of anticipation or expectancy is very brief.' (B. Bernstein (1971), *Class, Codes and Control*, p. 55.)

hierarchies were required by their managers to exercise discretion or judgment in pursuit of a goal in the form of delegated tasks or programmes of tasks. This instrument was named the time-span of discretion. Its existence as an objective measuring instrument is made possible by the fact that time targets for the completion of tasks are objectively discoverable facts in bureaucratic systems. It is only by virtue of the fact that there are objectively planned time targets that bureaucratic systems can function as coherent systems with outputs.[11]

The definition of *time-span of discretion* is the longest period which can elapse in a role before the manager can be sure that his subordinate has not been exercising marginally sub-standard discretion continuously in balancing the pace and quality of his work. This period in effect gives the maximum time during which the manager must rely upon the discretion of his subordinate and the subordinate works on his own.[12]

Measurement of level of work in time-span terms reveals two major categories of role in executive hierarchies: those in which subordinates undertake only one task at a time in the sense that each task can be completed before the next is commenced – single-task roles; and those in which the subordinates undertake many tasks at the same time in the sense that it is not possible to finish each task in turn because some or all of them are discontinuous and cannot be finished at one go – multiple-task roles.

The time-span of discretion in single-task roles is determined by measuring the task sequences with the longest target completion time to the point of review of quality. If the subordinate is working too slowly, that fact will become evident at the end of each task. Quality may often not, however, be reviewable until well after one task is completed and the subordinate has moved on to successive tasks, and this leads to a longer time-span of uncertainty of outcome.

The time-span of discretion in multiple-task roles is determined by measuring the task with the longest target completion time in the role. Poor quality will become evident at the end of the shorter tasks. Poor pace, however, can persist undetected for longer because work on the longer tasks can be put off, borrowed against, temporarily.

Time-structure of Activity and Subjective Sense of Level of Work

The special significance of the measurement of time-span of discretion emerged in the first place through the accidental discovery of its unique

[11] By 'objectively discoverable' I do not mean that these time targets are always immediately obvious or explicit. As often as not they are implicit. But I do mean that they exist in the sense that they can always be found by discussion with the manager and the subordinate. The time targets are there and acted upon even though not explicit. If they were not there in actuality, the work system would rapidly degenerate into chaos.

[12] The method of measurement is described in my *Time-Span Handbook* (1964).

correlation with an employee's sense of fair pay for his work. Strikingly, employees at the same time-span level – in effect, working to the same point in the future – state very closely the same payment levels when asked privately what they think would be fair for the work they are given to do – regardless of their occupation and regardless of their actual pay. There is growing evidence that this relationship between time-span and felt-fair pay holds from the lowest wage-earning groups to top salaried executives (see the more detailed data presented in Chapter 14).

This relationship supports the idea that time-span measurement can give an objective indication of the subjective experience of the level of work demanded by the tasks in a role.[13]

There is further evidence for the relationship between time-span and level of work in the following findings. If the tasks in a role are modified so that the measured time-span is decreased – the future to be planned for in the project and pursued by the person-in-action is brought closer – the incumbent feels that his level of work is dropping; and *vice versa* for an increase in measured time-span. Conversely, if the incumbent complains that his level of work feels as though it is dropping, it will consistently be found that the measured time-span is decreasing; and *vice versa* for a felt increase in the level of work. The farther away the future to be worked to, the greater the feeling of weight of responsibility in the work and of the value of the achievement.

This view of the importance of time is reinforced by the following apparent paradox. It might be argued that if a manager has a subordinate who he feels is not quite good enough to carry out the programme of tasks in a role, then surely he would give that subordinate longer in which to do it; that is to say, the worse the subordinate the longer the time-span he is given and thus the higher the level of work. But in fact that is not how managers behave. They do not increase the time-span of the programme of tasks, they do not increase the distances into the future towards which the subordinate must work, give him more time: that would be fatal. What they do is to break the programme down into a sequence of parts, the subordinate being given each successive part to do as he finishes the one he is working on – the subordinate is given a series of less distant futures to work towards.

The measured time-span thus reflects the manner in which a manager allocates tasks. As the subordinate improves he may eventually be given the whole programme intact, in which case he will have received a consequent increase in time-span. This kind of case which at first seemed to falsify the conjectured relationship between time-span and level of work,

<hr>

[13] The argument for this conclusion is presented in E. Jaques (1956), *Measurement of Responsibility* and (1961) *Equitable Payment*.

on further examination turns out not to do so. It is but one example of the testing that has been carried out through the search for instances which might falsify the hypothesis. There have been many other examples, such as the apparently short time-span that goes with high responsibility in the airline pilot or the diamond cutter, or the apparently long time-span that goes with the routine work of being engaged continuously in painting very large bridges. But so far the actual analysis of very many such instances[14] has turned out to support the hypothesis rather than to falsify it, the actual time-span turning out in fact longer or shorter than first impressions might suggest, and to be consistent in each case with felt-fair pay.

This finding that measured time-span – or measured distance of goals into the future – corresponds to subjective feelings of level of work, is like the finding that the measured length of a column of mercury in a thermometer corresponds to subjective feelings of warmth. Time-span measurement has all the characteristics of equal-ratio scale measurement in the natural sciences. It is possibly the first such measurement in the social sciences. I have been encouraged by the fruits of its use so far to believe that the discovery of further measuring instruments of the equal-ratio type will have the same revolutionary consequences for the social sciences as the discovery and use of the new measuring instruments during the eighteenth and nineteenth centuries have had for the natural sciences.[15]

From such evidence it may be concluded that time-span is significantly related to level of work. As will be seen, this hypothesis is an important element in the general theory to be elaborated about the nature of levels in bureaucratic hierarchies. The very strongest evidence that time-span by itself can measure the level of work in each role in bureaucratic systems will be presented in Chapter 8. This evidence comes from the finding that there is a general pattern of hierarchical levels which seems to underly all bureaucratic systems, each successive level in this underlying structure precipitating out at the same successive increase in the time-span level. Before turning to this evidence, however, it is necessary to tease out some of the theoretical implications of this analysis of work in connection with the nature of human capacity involved in doing work.

---

[14] See E. Jaques (1964), *Time-Span Handbook*, Chapter 8.
[15] See E. Jaques, (1970), 'Time and the Measurement of Human Attributes'.

7

On the Nature of the Capacity to Work

In this chapter the nature of work is examined in greater depth as it appears from within the person, in order to understand the way bureaucracies are formed and shaped in relation to the work process in human beings. Bureaucratic systems are systems for controlling, channelling, and directing the work behaviour of many individuals to combine towards the creation of planned outputs. These processes of channelling and direction of behaviour cannot be clarified unless the nature of the behaviour itself is clarified.

Work is considered in terms of the whole person-in-action, engaged in goal-directed behaviour. This special behaviour requires a consideration of some of the more general characteristics of behaviour: the unconscious, on-going, unstoppable flow of intuitive mental activity and behaviour occurring in the ever-moving present (or durée); the modes of setting goals in a conceptually stoppable clock-time future; the creation of boundaries within which the flow of behaviour may be contained and regulated; the processes of discretion and decision; and finally the concepts of knowledge and of uncertainty.

Against this background I shall outline some current developments in our thinking about the nature of the capacity in the person which is necessary to do work: the levels of abstraction; the modes of ordering and patterning of data; the categorizations in depth and at the surface. A relation will then be suggested between work-capacity and the distance, measured in clock time, to the planned goal which a person is capable of encompassing in action.

Work and the Person-in-action

Work is an activity of the whole person. It is not some special aspect of a larger field of activity. It is that behaviour which constitutes the primary plane of reality in which the individual relates his subjective world to the external world, transforming each in the process of creating some socially manifest output. It is a realization in the external world of a subjective project. It is the behaviour through which the individual experiences the reality of his core identity.

It is because work is a goal-directed activity, the goal being an output in the external world, that work, in contrast for example to a fantasy or a dream, is the primary plane of reality. It is in Popper's terms[1] an activity in the psychological or second world (subjective world) which produces an output in either of or both the objective worlds – the first world of material objects or the third world of cultural objects. The first and third worlds are objective in Popper's sense because they are socially shareable – people can co-operate in relation to their contents, and it is in the sense of this social sharing that the products of the work process can be said to be externally objective outputs.

Work may therefore be defined in the philosophical sense in the following manner: the person-in-action can be said to be working when his behavioural flow is aimed towards the transformation of a specific part of the objective world so as to bring it into a state consonant with a state which he has in mind; or to put it in other words, to produce an objective output which is the realization of a subjective project.[2]

Work is thus to be distinguished from all types of activity which lack the specific *intents* and *acts* necessary to change the objective world. Sleeping, dreaming, fantasying, musing, are levels of reality different from the primary plane of reality which is work. Schutz, for example, makes an important distinction between work and performance. By performance he refers to the subjective processes which precede work, and which become a part of the process of work only if they are acted upon. Performance comprises the subjective preoccupation with desires, with thoughts of things which might satisfy, with the elaboration of trial projects, with thoughts of how things might be achieved, even with plans for achieving them; but – and here rests the essential point – without taking any action with the intent to change the objective external world.

Performance remains part of the internal mental processes of the individual. It flows into the process of work only at the point in time when the person-in-action commits himself to decisions expressed in real acts upon real physical or social things in the objective world of which other persons can become aware. Such acts transform external things and are therefore objectively irreversible.[3]

Work, in short, is the central theme of the philosophy of the act, of the plane of action – of the primary plane of reality. It enables the person-in-action to know himself and his existence through his shared perception of

[1] K. R. Popper (1972), 'On the Theory of the Objective Mind'.

[2] In the sense defined by Schutz. This definition is also related to the description by Wilfred Bion of normal psychic processes (α processes as he calls them) in which a concept seeks its realization in external reality. In his formulation, the infant's first experience of the breast is that of a primal 'concept' (a primal project) which seeks external realization and finds it in the real feeding breast which it transforms and internalizes both physically and psychically. W. R. Bion (1962), *Learning from Experience*.

[3] A. Schutz (1967), *Collected Papers I*, pp. 211–12.

his effects upon other things in accord with his intent.

From this philosophical definition of work three themes require further consideration. Each is essential for my theory of how the behaviour of individuals can be patterned and ordered and made into a coherent functioning bureaucracy. These themes are: first, the person-in-action, the behavioural flow or flux, and durée or the moving present; second, conscious subjective processes, performance, and the construction of the project, in the physical or clock-time world which contains the past and future; and third, the direction and control of action (of the behavioural flux) by boundaries, by the establishment of external goal zones, and by feed-back control.

The Behavioural Flux and the Moving Present (Durée)

Kurt Lewin has defined behaviour in field terms as a function of the person and the environment (B = fPE). That definition conceives of a dynamic unbroken field in which behaviour is a continuous process in a context or setting. Behaviour never stops: it flows on and on, endlessly, changing direction, changing pace, changing in mode, apparently pausing but only in eddies, always in flux. The person-in-action is like the amoeba, putting out and retracting its pseudopodia, withdrawing, moving on, ingesting and excreting, in continuous transaction with its environment. This continuous amoebic process, this stream of action, is but one expression of the active organism as an open system in a complex and shifting relationship with its environment. It is by its work that the organism maintains itself as an open system.

There is one outstanding feature of the behavioural flux: it can never be consciously appreciated as it occurs. In a literal sense behaviour occurs, and goes on occurring, as a process of which the person can become conscious only in retrospect by observing what has occurred. And even then, only aspects of the process can be articulated and described, only some of the consequences or end-products, but never the whole process, because it has already gone by.[4]

To say that the behavioural flux occurs unconsciously is not necessarily to use the concept of the unconscious in the sense employed in psychoanalytic theory – namely, a part of the mind containing the products of repression and the source of conflict and psychopathology. It is used in the sense employed by some experimental psychologists, such as, for example, D. O. Hebb, who use it, if at all, to refer to all on-going mental mechanisms. Describing how all mental acts, from great discoveries and creations to the

---

[4] As Bergson puts it, 'Practically we perceive only the past': (1911) *Matter and Memory*, p. 194.

most simple and mundane mental acts such as simple arithmetic, are un-observable by introspection (as shown by Külpe as early as 1910), Hebb writes, '*All* mental acts are in this class, a fact that may help the student to see why objective psychology considers that all mental processes are "un-conscious" in the sense that they are not reportable or known directly by the subject but must be studied theoretically....'[5] The behavioural flux just is; it is not open to direct introspection and cannot be made so. It occurs as a process in a relentlessly moving present; its effects can be consciously perceived only in retrospect, in the past. It cannot therefore be subject to direct conscious control, but only to indirect control.[6]

It is just as true for an observer as for the person-in-action, that the behavioural flux is not immediately consciously articulable but can be articulated only in retrospect, in the immediate past. All conscious processes are about past events. As Freud[7] described the matter, con-sciousness is a long-circuiting of on-going mentation; it is a piece of mental activity temporarily removed from the on-going stream of mentation for reflection, consideration, analysis, use. It is as though mentation has been temporarily stopped; but of course that is not so. Conscious ideas are like eddies or backwaters, apparently still but in fact part of the flow and moving along with it.[8]

The temporal quality of the unconscious behavioural flux is that of Henri Bergson's concept of durée (duration) rather than that of William James' concept of the stream of thought or stream of consciousness. James' conception, brilliant as it was at the time, is too limited, too tied to the conscious thought processes and too little connected to what is after all the important matter, namely the on-going flow of full behaviour, of action, and not just of the reflection of action in conscious thought.

---

[5] D. O. Hebb (1972), *Textbook of Psychology*, pp. 249–50.

[6] Our language makes it exceedingly difficult to describe these processes. We split con-scious and unconscious, thought and feeling, ideas and action, body and mind, and cannot get them back together again. It is interesting to note that the sense of Eastern thinking for the emotive, feeling, acting content of thought underlying the more conscious processes may possibly be expressed in the Chinese character for thought. This character contains the idea of unconscious emotion in its primary radical which represents the heart as the seat of thought and passion, and the idea of conscious image in the secondary phonetic above it which represents the eye perceiving wood.

[7] S. Freud (1923), *The Ego and the Id.*

[8] It is the ability of observers to become aware consciously of the external manifestations of the behavioural flux as soon as or even sooner than the person-in-action that is, I believe, an important component of a person's sense of external reality. It provides for an experience, in an inter-subjective relationship, of another who is aware of one's behaviour, and who by interpreting non-verbal communication can often formulate and point out one's feelings and intent before one can do so oneself. This being known by the other gives strong evidence of the reality of the existence of the external other, and is the antithesis of the view that only the individual himself can know his own subjective world because only he can be aware of his own sensations.

Bergson himself tended to define durée in terms of a past-future relationship, but the foregoing description in terms of the moving present is an accurate paraphrase of his view. As he put it, for example, '. . . durée (duration) is the continuous progress of the past which gnaws into the future and which swells as it advances'.[9] The emphasis is upon the notion of *continuous* progress, for it is in these terms that he differentiates durée from the clock time of physics in which particular events are abstracted, located at particular points in clock time, and then said, for example, to be in a cause and effect relationship with one another.[10]

Consciousness, Performance, and the Project

If the person-in-action behaves unconsciously in a continuous present in an unbroken space-time continuum, where then does consciousness enter in relation to work, and what are its time characteristics? Consciousness has to do with abstraction, discontinuity, categorization, or − in the phenomenological terms of Husserl and Schutz − with typifications. Consciously formulated perceptions, therefore, are always of events which have already occurred: they are in the past. Conscious ideas equally are collections of data from the past. They are typifications which pull together given characteristics to give the idea of categories of things like dogs, or memoranda, or letters, or cars, or customers.

In general it may first be noted that conscious perceptions and ideas are related to clock time rather than to durée. Events or things, to be considered consciously, have to be treated as slices taken out of the stream of behaviour (including mentation). In this sense they can be said to have occurred at such-and-such o'clock, or to have taken so many hours. Moreover —and here is a point of great importance − they can be thought of as to be planned to take place at some time in the future. Consciousness has a clock-time past and future but no true present.

Such conscious events and ideas are of course mental abstractions only. Mentation and the behavioural flux have not in fact in any way stopped. And indeed the conscious ideas themselves, carried along upon the behavioural flux, are in continuous process of change and modification as they are played over in the mind, however constant they might appear. The behavioural flux has no more stopped than, for example, has the flow of music in the pauses between notes in syncopation.[11]

[9] H. Bergson (1911), *Creative Evolution*, p. 6.

[10] This difference between durée and clock time is lucidly described by Victor Zuckerkandl. He shows that clock time − the time used in physics − is really spatial time: it is static; it has no flow. He then argues that it is in music that real time is most readily observed and the data for the existence of durée are to be found − rhythm, melody, form, all have to do with accumulated experience in the moving present. (1956) *Sound and Symbol*.

[11] V. Zuckerkandl, op. cit.

Because of its quality of pausing and externalization, it is in consciousness that work plans can be formulated. A goal may be established, to be completed at a given time in the future. Plans can be thought out as to how the goal may be achieved, goal and plan composing the project. Boundaries may be thought of and mentally established. Various ways of testing the plan may be carried out in imagination, and potential results assessed by means of conscious mental performance.

This process of performance and project maturation is the person-in-action: it occurs in durée. But the conscious mental content of the action is an abstraction, and is stated in physical time, so that plans and projects may be dated, time-sequenced and time-targeted. All behaviour is thus a combination of continuous intuitive mental activity and action, within a framework set by conscious perceptions and ideas.

Boundaries, Goals, and Feed-back Control: The Actual Work Process Illustrated

Since the behavioural flux cannot be directly introspected as it occurs, by the same token it cannot be subjected to direct conscious control. It can be consciously controlled only by pointing it in a particular direction — towards a goal, by channelling it within boundaries, and by using feed-back controls to change the boundaries so as to keep moving in the direction of the goal. The following example illustrates these processes of control, as well as the interaction between unconscious flow in durée and conscious abstractions in clock time.

Let us say a toolmaker has been given a particular fixture to make, and he is instructed to complete it within two weeks. The goal, the fixture, is described in the form of a drawing. This drawing is a typification, a model of the intended output. It can be studied, and taken into the conscious thoughts of the toolmaker in the form of the subjective picture he creates of what the finished product should look like. The particular picture he constructs arrives out of his intuitive unconscious flow of behaviour interacting with the consciously perceived drawing. When he is satisfied with his picture he stops, and holds it in an apparent state of suspended animation.

The toolmaker must then think out how to make the fixture. He knows first of all that there are certain institutional boundaries to which he must conform; for example, only certain metals are to be used, certain tolerances are to be maintained, the fixture must be able to be fitted in a special way with screws and fittings of a certain size, and so on. Within these boundaries he may think up a number of different ways by which he might make the fixture, test these in his mind's eye, mentally experience the likely difficulties and obstacles on the way, and choose what he thinks is the best path. His picture of the finished product plus his plan of action including the materials he intends to use, constitute the project.

All through this performance, the toolmaker has of course been behaving. He has been relying upon his intuitive judgment to throw up ideas which, when they become conscious, he seizes upon and tests. He has also used his conscious aim to keep his behaviour within the area of relevance of the task in hand. But he has not yet irrevocably committed himself. Now he does so. He goes into action in the external world. The performance phase is over and he now gets to work. What happens?

The first thing is that he directs his behavioural flow by orienting himself in general terms towards his pictured goal, and more specifically directs himself towards his most immediately planned sub-goals on the way. He also bounds his behaviour within certain constraints: the cultural and legal constraints, the institutional constraints including those set by his immediate manager; the inter-subjective constraint in which he takes account of the particular personality characteristics of his manager and of his interaction with his manager; plus his own subjective boundary set by his work sub-identity and his ideas about the use of particular tools and procedures. Having set the direction for his behaviour, and having added his own subjective boundaries to those fixed from outside himself, all he can do is to let himself loose – to behave and then continually to observe what happens.

As he begins to work at his tasks he keeps under continual review the results of his actions upon the materials he is shaping, comparing the emerging external object with his subjective picture (the project) of the final planned result. In the light of this continuous feed-back, he both unconsciously adjusts his behavioural flow and consciously adjusts the direction and pathway bounding that behaviour so that he will act more closely in accord with the planned goal. He behaves in continuous flow, using intuitive touch-and-feel adjustments framed within a consciously controlled channel, moving step by step towards his goal, namely the emergence within the stipulated clock time of the fixture required.

In effect – and this point is of the highest importance – the toolmaker exercising discretion and judgment in carrying out his tasks is always and continuously exercising discretion about the pace at which he is working. He is using as good judgment as he can in the time available. He must not only carry out the task well enough in quality; he must do that, certainly, but he must do it within the target completion time. If he had more time he could do better. But he does not have more time. He must do well enough. In short, he must use each moment of the present sufficiently to be able to move consistently towards the realization of the goal whose target completion time is moving steadily nearer. Work has to do with bringing an idea of the future into present reality – or of continuously shaping the present to realize that idea. It is a Bergsonian becoming. As Ortega y Gasset has expressed it, 'Whether we like it or not human life is a constant preoccupation with the future. In this actual moment we are concerned with the one that follows. Hence living is always, ceaselessly, restlessly, a *doing* . . . all *doing* implies bringing something future into effect.'[12]

Work is thus concerned with doing what you do not know for sure. The sensation of work lies in the experience of uncertainty about the future when exercising discretion or judgment in the present. The quality of the discretion used cannot be known until the final outcome, at which time it will be seen whether the task has been carried out in a manner and at a pace which the manager judges to be satisfactory.[13]

The behaviour of the toolmaker thus flows continuously. But it is channelled and directed. It is constantly aimed towards the final output. It is channelled within particular methods and techniques. It is framed within two clock-time markers, the beginning and the end points. Both these markers are conceptual abstractions – the start being in the past as soon as it is consciously perceived to have occurred, and the target completion time being an abstract idea of the future contained within the person-in-action.

This behaviour also illustrates the continuous interaction between unconscious flow of behaviour and conscious knowledge and ideas. The adjustments to behaviour through the use of discretion, judgment, *nous*, skill, touch-and-feel, insight, trial and error, are all part of the normal unconscious flow drawing upon organized past experience. In effect, work, judgment, decisions, are all carried out unconsciously. But this constructive unconscious process is controlled by being constrained within very complex conscious processes: channelled within socially institutionalized boundaries refined by a subjective boundary zone; consciously directed towards a goal expressed in a conscious project; and using consciously learned knowledge and methods, such as tools, arithmetic, drawings, etc.

Social institutions and conscious individual knowledge are thus frameworks or boundaries. They can channel and direct the work process, but themselves can do no work. The work behaviour of the person-in-action is unconscious and intuitive. That is why *all* work is creative. Moreover, work behaviour occurs in durée: it is continuous and non-stop, although it changes in direction, in pace, in content. The consciously formulated channels and goals, however, occur in the physical clock-time

---

[12] J. Ortega y Gasset (1932), *The Revolt of the Masses.*

[13] Many authors have pointed to the importance of uncertainty in work. Bavelas, for example, described leadership as the absorption of uncertainty; von Neumann differentiated between work and games on the basis of the openness and uncertainty of outcomes in work. I have analyzed the significance of uncertainty in some detail in Chapter 7 of my (1956) *Measurement of Responsibility.*

world, including the conceptual abstractions called the beginning and the target-completion times for a task.

One last point abut the function of explicit boundaries must be pointed out. Whereas the focusing of attention by means of facts and explicit formulations can facilitate decision-making, it also reduces the possibility of original solutions being discovered in the areas excluded by the narrowing of focus and the channelling of thought. Knowledge is always both helpful and limiting. The best example of this is a good theory: it helps to solve a wide range of problems; but it distracts — draws attention from other problems and solutions. Newton's theory of mechanics was an enormously powerful problem-solver; it was also an enormously large set of blinkers, which Einstein finally managed to see round.

In bureaucracies it is therefore essential that policies, administrative procedures, rules and regulations be kept adequately under review. On the positive side they are the regulating framework which binds the bureaucratic system into a rational whole, framing the intuitive work processes of each employee. On the negative side they can be the blinkers which inhibit employees from using their judgment to the full. This dual feature constitutes one of the prime dilemmas of bureaucracy. Its resolution lies in sound policies subject to scrutiny and modification, set in such a manner as to provide blinkers or constraints large enough to provide an adequate channel, but not so large as to interfere with the abilities of individuals. It requires that everyone should have the opportunity to be employed at a level of work consistent with his capacity.

Analysis of Subjective Work Process

To define work as problem-solving activity is simply to say that all goal-directed behaviour is work and all work is goal-directed behaviour, regardless of the nature of the goal and regardless of whether a person earns his living from work. The subjective state of the person may be illustrated by a simple Lewinian type of diagram. The person must get from x to y within time t, overcoming obstacles a, b, c, d . . . etc., many of which are unknown, while staying within limits L. At the beginning the picture is simply as shown in Figure 7.1 (a) opposite.

The next stage (Figure 7.1(b) is for P to plan how to arrive at the Goal G. This plan calls for a differentiation of G into sub-goals, $g_1, g_2, g_3, \ldots g$ to be reached on the way, the totality of the sub-goals being able to be assembled into the final product.

Then as each sub-stage is completed, P moves to the next phase of his plan. He may, of course, have to modify his plan as he goes, altering his sub-goals and his routes to them. At t_4, the situation might be represented as in Figure 7.1(c):

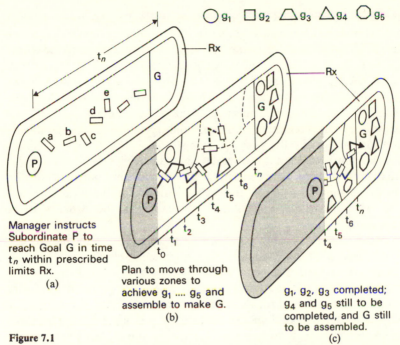

$\bigcirc g_1 \quad \square g_2 \quad \triangle g_3 \quad \triangle g_4 \quad \bigcirc g_5$

Manager instructs
Subordinate P to
reach Goal G in time
t_n within prescribed
limits Rx.

(a)

Plan to move through
various zones to
achieve $g_1 \ldots g_5$ and
assemble to make G.

(b)

g_1, g_2, g_3 completed;
g_4 and g_5 still to be
completed, and G still
to be assembled.

(c)

Figure 7.1

At the final stage, the goal zone G is entered, with the sub-goals completed, and the assembling of G (the bringing together of the parts) is carried out. P is able to return his completed output to his manager.

It will be noted that each diagram deals only with the present. But it is a present which contains G (g_1, g_2, g_3 . . .) as conceptions in the present of a future extending to t_n with various stages t_1, t_2, t_3 . . . on the way to t_n. As the present flows, t_1, t_2, t_3 . . . – and sub-goals g_1, g_2, g_3 . . . – become realizations in actuality, leaving the goal residues to be completed by t_n which steadily moves in closer in psychological space-time.

The Psychological Future and Measurement of Work-capactity

Work has been described as a stochastic process, as goal-directed behaviour, and therefore as activity directed to a goal in the future. Does this imply, then, a mystical teleological conception of human activity? On the contrary, this definition of work implies a definition of the future as a particular psychological state in the present.

The experience of the future is an experience in the present of a lack, of something missing, of something to come or desired;[14] but especially of

[14] As Bergson says: 'In a general way, human work consists in creating utility; and as long as the work is not done, there is "nothing" . . . nothing that we want.' (1911) *Creative Evolution*, p. 314.

something to be worked for. It is a conception in the present of something not yet realized but which might be realized by activity involving the exercise of judgment and discretion; that is, activity involving psychic effort.

The sense of the future may vary between two extremes. At one extreme is the vaguely sensed future concerned with vague wishes or hopes in the present that somehow things can and will be better, or with idealized fantasies of a world that can never be realized. At the other extreme is the organized future connected with work: the experience of the aspiration or goal, and a plan of activity for achieving the goal. The idea of the future is thus nothing more than the experience in the moving present of a sense of frustration and need, the conceptual construction of a potential satisfier, the formulation of a plan for the realization of that satisfier, and the conceptual construction in thought of the stochastic process to be negotiated.[15]

In the light of this definition of the future as a region in the moving present life-space of the individual, we can begin to establish some of the main features of the kind of capacity necessary for the person to do work. It is a great human quality, one which enables the person to organize the moving present so as to work through into the future, and to make what begins as an idea gradually take shape, and eventually to bring about its realization as an output. There is no name for this quality. It is certainly more than is expressed by the words intelligence, skill, ability, capacity, competence, initiative, motivation. It has to do with the psychological state and size of the whole person. It is the quality which Piaget has tried to define in his concept of functional intelligence,[16] McLelland in his concept of operant ability,[17] and Stenhouse in his concept of the Postponement factor (P).[18]

I considered the possibility on this occasion of starting afresh with an entirely new term without associations – such as parvenance (achieving) or stochacity (moving towards a goal). But it seemed a simpler and more practical solution to adopt the phrase *work-capacity*, and thus link it directly with the concept of work which we have established, as contrasted with capacity to dream, capacity for fantasy, physical capacity, or any of a score of other types of human capacity.

[15] Saint Augustine had a clear sense of this view of the future as psychological expectation. In his scintillating analysis of time, he wrote: 'From what we have said it is abundantly clear that neither the future nor the past exist, and therefore it is not strictly correct to say that there are three times, past, present, and future. It might be correct to say that there are three times, a present of past things, a present of present things, and a present of future things. Some such different times do exist in the mind, but nowhere else that I can see. The present of past things is the memory; the present of present things is direct perception; and the present of future things is expectation. If we may speak in these terms, I can see three times and I admit that they do exist.' (1961 ed.) *Confessions*, p. 269.

[16] J. Piaget (1953), *Origin of Intelligence in the Child*.

[17] D. McLelland (1973), 'Testing for Competence rather than "Intelligence".'

[18] D. Stenhouse (1974), *The Evolution of Intelligence*.

What then is the nature of this work-capacity in the individual? A fuller treatment of this question will be given in Chapter 10, after we have added further information about certain discontinuities in level of abstraction in this capacity. But two preliminary sets of observations may be relevant at this stage. The first has to do with a summary of some of the main features of work-capacity. The second has to do with the nature of the amount or, more precisely, the level of work-capacity.

Among the main features of work-capacity which we may summarize are the following. There is an overall ability to pattern and order experience in both space and time – or in space-time as a continuum.[19] This patterning and ordering shows in the construction of the project – the subjective picture of the goal and plan for reaching it – the pulling together and ordering of external information about the required task, and its organization into a patterned sense of the finished output accomplished in a particular block of time.

In connection with this patterning and ordering of the project there must be an unconscious mobilization of relevant past experience, intuitively brought into play. It is this intuitively available material, learned from experience, which comes into the discretion, *nous*, touch-and-feel, insight, skill, employed by the person-in-action in constructing the project and carrying out the task.

In the making of a decision, a person can approach a problem with more or less information and a more or less explicit set of propositions for its solution. The data and propositions serve to focus attention upon particular solutions, eliminating all other possibilities from consideration. The more facts available, the more sharply focused and constrained is the attention, the more narrowly delimited is the field of play for the unconscious mental processes and behavioural flux. But finally, it will be from within these unconscious mental processes that the decision will emerge, and along with it the sense of the degree of probability that the decision taken is likely to resolve the problem satisfactorily. The end reasons for any judgment or decision can never be conscious; they emerge as the outcome of learning from experience.[20]

In the light of the unconscious intuitive nature of the experience which comes into the task, the person-in-action must be able to tolerate uncertainty. He cannot be sure of success until the final output has been produced and tested. Only at that point is he in a position to know whether his efforts have been successful in creating either a physical or social thing and in the time allowed.[21]

---

[19] As formulated in G. Stamp (1974), 'Mental Function and Human Capacity.'
[20] W. R. Bion (1962), *Learning from Experience*.
[21] E. Jaques (1954), *Measurement of Responsibility*, Chapter 7.

The control of discretion and uncertainty requires that the person-in-action should have a sound sense of direction in the behavioural sense. Along with this sense of direction he must have the necessary knowledge, to ensure on the one hand that his behavioural flow is staying within externally prescribed channels, and to be able on the other hand to construct the immediate personally created context necessary for the fine tuning of his behaviour in the required direction. To control the direction of his behaviour, he must be able to maintain an effective feed-back loop, allowing him to readjust the context of his behavioural flux by adjusting its channels or direction or both.

Work-capacity is concerned with the actively behaving person, the person engaged in problem-solving, the person engaged in goal-directed behaviour, the person doing things, working, creating. Work-capacity so defined includes both the afferent and the efferent neural processes, in contrast to intelligence which is concerned mainly with the afferent processes.

This summary description does not, of course, tell us much about the nature of these processes of patterning and ordering, of project and context construction, of knowledge and intuition, of feed-back and readjustment. Nor does it take us any further towards an understanding of how the unconscious intuitively coloured behavioural flux interacts with the objective knowledge and conscious processes out of which explicated directions are set and goals and channels constructed.[22] The question of this interaction between unconscious process and conscious framework or context is a matter of enormous importance, but quite beyond the scope of this book. What may be noted, however, is the way in which our present analysis of work behaviour highlights the conscious-unconscious interaction; it illustrates the fundamental constructiveness of unconscious processes; and, most important, it gives a preliminary formulation of the nature of the interaction in terms of unconscious process bound in a conscious contextual

[22] There is one passing observation which might be worth making. We are dealing here with the interaction between verbally formulated and therefore conscious facts, data, propositions, rules, laws, and other explicit analytical tools, on the one hand, and intuitive non-verbal patterning activities on the other. This interaction fits closely the formulation of R. W. Sperry (1966, 'Brain Bisection and Mechanisms of Conscious Experience') and S. Dimond (1972, *The Double Brain*), who have demonstrated the difference in functions between the right and the left hemisphere of the brain. The left hemisphere controls speech and analytical functions. The right hemisphere controls non-verbal patterning and integrative functions. R. Ornstein (1973, *The Nature of Human Consciousness*) links these two different types of functions to the Western analytical-scientific-verbal outlook and the Eastern thought-in-feeling outlook respectively – the 'Word' as against 'Om'. It is not unreasonable to postulate an interaction in which the left hemisphere is more involved in the conscious attention-limit setting and focusing functions, setting direction and channels within which the right hemisphere acts in unconscious forwarding of the on-going constitution-based behavioural flux which must be fundamentally an expression of the 'touch and feel' of the lower centres of the brain and of the peripheral nervous system. (See also V. B. Mountcastle (ed.) (1962), *Interhemispheric Relations and Cerebral Dominance*.)

channel and direction, unconscious durée punctuated by conscious clock time, and unconscious intuitive sense guided by conscious knowledge.[23]

Level of Work-capacity

We can, however, be more precise in our analysis when we turn to the question of level of work-capacity. Here we may start with the evidence given in the previous chapter that felt level of work itself is experienced as bearing a direct relationship with the time-span of discretion in a role. Transposing this finding to our analysis of the work process in the individual, we may note that the longer the time-span in a role the greater is the psychic distance between the person (P) and the goals (G) within the person's life-space.

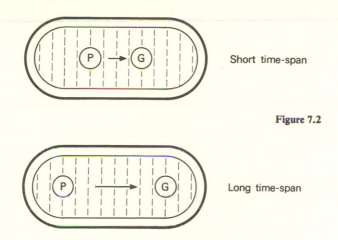

Short time-span

Figure 7.2

Long time-span

The psychic distance is greater because as the time-span gets longer the path to be traversed gets longer and more complex, and there is an increase in the number of intervening regions to be crossed, in the number of obstacles to be encountered, and in the number of detailed bits of information to be garnered, patterned and ordered. Moreover, the longer the time-span within which the person-in-action works, the wider the range of data and detail he has to take into account from the very beginning in order to construct an adequate project. There is more to be organized and dealt with.

It is suggested therefore that level of work-capacity can be expressed in

[23] From the psycho-analytic point of view, the concept of making the unconscious conscious would imply the explicit formulation of some of the consequences of the behavioural flux. These conscious formulations then become useful for directing and channelling the unconscious behavioural flux.

terms of the longest time-spans with which an individual can cope. Putting this proposition another way, it may be argued that the size of the life-space of an individual can be expressed in terms of the longest time-spans of goals within that life-space with which the person is able to deal. In effect, the size of the psychic life of an individual may be measured by the distance into the clock-time future up to which he is capable of organizing projects and acting upon them so as to produce an output. We shall now apply this proposition about the nature of capacity and see whether, and how, it may help to forward our understanding of the fundamental nature of bureaucracy.

8

The Stratified Depth-structure
of Bureaucracy

We have now considered the associations which establish bureaucratic hierarchies, the manager-subordinate molecules out of which they are made, and the nature of the work which they are established to get done. That gives enough material to make it possible to approach one of the central questions about the bureaucratic hierarchy, the question upon which our theory will hinge; namely, why is it that this structure is the only type of human organization so far discovered for bringing large numbers of people to work together in one united enterprise?

For bureaucratic systems are divided into a hierarchy of horizontal strata and tend to be pyramid-shaped. These hierarchical strata do not at first sight appear to be established in any uniform way, there being variations in the number of manifest strata in different organizations and in different parts of the same organization. Work with time-span measurement, however, has revealed that underlying this conglomeration of manifest strata there is a consistent and definable depth-structure[1] from which neither the manifest nor the extant structure can depart too far without collapsing. This underlying system of organizational strata appears to be universal and constitutes one of the fundamental properties of bureaucratic hierarchies.

Once the fixed pattern of these strata is grasped, a general view of bureaucratic organizational structure can be obtained which is like looking into the symmetrical and regular structure of a crystal. The time-span structure of these strata is a fundamental quantitative characteristic of bureaucracy.

Consequences of 'Too Many' Levels of Organization

It is an almost universal disease of bureaucratic systems that they have too many levels of organization. This disease manifests itself in a number of commonly known symptoms. Among these familiar symptoms are: the occurrence of much by-passing because of excessively long lines of command; uncertainty as to whether a person's manager is really the next one up on the organization chart, or the one above him, or even the one above

[1] In the sense defined in Chapter 2, pp. 42–3.

him; uncertainty as to whether a manager's subordinates are really just the ones immediately below him on the organization chart, or perhaps the ones below them as well; too much passing of paper up and down too many levels – the red tape phenomenon; a feeling on the part of subordinates of being too close to their managers as shown on the chart; a feeling of organizational clutter, of managers 'breathing down their subordinates' necks' of too many levels involved in any problem, of too many cooks, of too much interference, of not being allowed to get on with the work in hand.

Consideration of these symptoms raises the question of just how many levels there ought to be in a bureaucratic hierarchy. Another way of asking the same question is to consider what ought to be the length of the vertical line joining two roles in manager-subordinate relationship. Scrutiny of the literature makes it apparent that no general rules have been formulated. Controversy has been framed in terms of the advantage of 'flat' organiza- tion as against 'steep' organization, but in none of these arguments has the question even been asked, much less resolved, of how many levels there ought to be.

Three or four levels may be realistic, or even five or six or seven. But most people would consider a hundred levels or even fifty, or perhaps even twenty, to be surely too many. Why? What is it that determines how many levels there ought to be in any given hierarchy? In considering this question of number of levels it is essential to state what kinds of level or stratum. The usual meaning is that of so-called grades. Grades are strata used for ascribing status to individuals, for stating payment brackets, and for ad- vancing individuals in pay and status. These grading systems commonly become used also for describing the organization of work and manage- ment. This second use occurs uncritically and by default. It is a source of enormous confusion. In discussing bureaucratic levels, therefore, we shall confine our attention to work-strata – the strata concerned with work organization and managerial levels. Grading will be dealt with in Chapter 18, where it will be shown that about three times as many grading levels are needed as the more fundamental work-strata.

True Managers, Quasi-managers, and Bureaucratic Levels

This problem of how many working levels there ought to be can be illus- trated by reference to a number of different types of bureaucratic hierarchy. Here, for example, are descriptions of four lines of command (examination will show them to be based upon gradings) as set out in the manifest organization charts in a factory, in a civil service department, in a hospital nursing organization, and in the infantry. Let us examine each in turn in terms of one factor: namely, who is experienced as manager of whom.

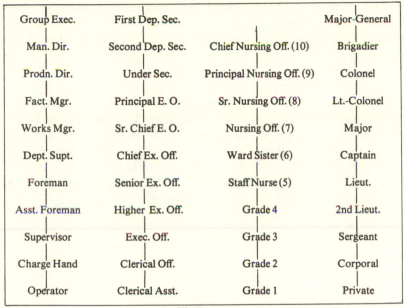

Group Exec.	First Dep. Sec.		Major-General
Man. Dir.	Second Dep. Sec.	Chief Nursing Off. (10)	Brigadier
Prodn. Dir.	Under Sec.	Principal Nursing Off. (9)	Colonel
Fact. Mgr.	Principal E. O.	Sr. Nursing Off. (8)	Lt.-Colonel
Works Mgr.	Sr. Chief E. O.	Nursing Off. (7)	Major
Dept. Supt.	Chief Ex. Off.	Ward Sister (6)	Captain
Foreman	Senior Ex. Off.	Staff Nurse (5)	Lieut.
Asst. Foreman	Higher Ex. Off.	Grade 4	2nd Lieut.
Supervisor	Exec. Off.	Grade 3	Sergeant
Charge Hand	Clerical Off.	Grade 2	Corporal
Operator	Clerical Asst.	Grade 1	Private

Figure 8.1

In the factory, if you ask the operator who is manager, he will probably ask if what you mean by his manager is his 'boss'. He will then want to know whether you mean his 'boss' or his 'real boss'. The distinction here is between what the operator would call 'my real boss' – the one from whom he feels he stands a chance of getting a decision about himself – and the 'middlemen' or 'straw bosses' who are pushed in between him and his real boss, and through whom he must go if he wants to see his boss. The operator would then probably pick the assistant foreman or foreman as his real boss, with the charge hand and supervisor (and possibly the assistant foreman) as middlemen or straw bosses.

The same phenomenon occurs higher up as well. For example, the invoice department manager might well refer to the accounts office manager as his manager for 'administrative purposes', but the chief accountant as his direct manager where 'real accounts work' is concerned. Or the vice-presidents of a corporation might work with the deputy president as being their 'co-ordinative' manager, the president being the real immediate manager who meets directly with them all in the planning and control of corporate activities. Nowhere in the line of command is it possible to predict whether or not a subordinate will experience the next up on the organization chart (the manifest situation) as his real manager (the extant situation).

From the manager's point of view a mirror image is obtained. He may wish to appear well organized, and emphasize that his immediate subordinates are those shown immediately below him on the chart. But he too will admit that it does not necessarily always work quite that way, and that he must often make direct contact with subordinates two and three levels down 'in order to get work done'. This by-passing is seen as necessary even though it might not make good management theory!

In a department in the Civil Service the same answers can be obtained, perhaps couched in slightly different terms. A Senior Executive Officer (SEO) says, 'The CEO is my manager, and I am the manager of the HEOs. But what you probably cannot understand is that in the Civil Service we work in teams. It's not like in industry. The CEO, the HEOs and myself all pitch in together and work as a team.' The meaning of this statement becomes clear when further analysis reveals that the extant situation is that the SEO is really a staff assistant to the CEO and helps him to control and co-ordinate his (the CEO's) HEO subordinates;

that is to say, what is manifestly

Figure 8.2

is extantly

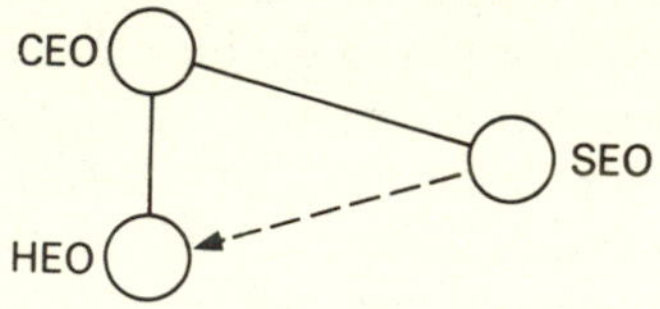

Figure 8.3

Again, as in the industrial example, the same kind of unclarity can be found at any or all levels in the system.

In a nursing organization, a Chief Nursing Officer (CNO) of a hospital group describes her relationship with her manifestly subordinate Principal Nursing Officers (PNOs) as one in which 'I am really the co-ordinator of a group of colleagues and not really their manager. You can't work in nursing with these strong managerial relationships. You all have to work together in the interests of the patients.' The extant situation is that of the CNO's being a co-ordinative colleague, in contrast to the manifest manager-subordinate relationship.

And again, in a military organization – in this case the infantry – it is easy to draw the organization chart as shown.

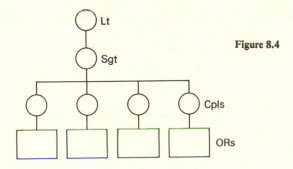

Figure 8.4

But what does it mean? A corporal — whatever the manifest organization — is not extantly accountable for the performance of the soldiers in his section; he is really an assistant, like a leading hand or a charge hand — someone who helps the real commander to control the platoon. Similarly, the platoon sergeant is not the platoon commander, however the organization chart is drawn. He is an assistant to the platoon commander. It is the platoon commander who is directly accountable for the performance of everyone in his platoon, including the sergeant and the corporals. This accountability is indicated in the distinction between being a commissioned officer as against a non-commissioned officer. The manifest situation might be drawn as above, but the extant situation is more nearly —

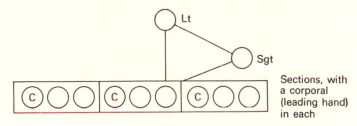

Sections, with a corporal (leading hand) in each

Figure 8.5

Equally, higher in the line of command it will never be found that a Lieutenant-Colonel battalion commander has majors as direct fighting subordinates, who in turn have captains, who in turn have lieutenants, who in turn have second lieutenants, and so on down into the NCO levels. They would all be killed while trying to sort out who was giving orders to whom. It is only in managerial text books (and, unfortunately, increasingly in military training now that it is incorporating managerial theory) that military organization takes on this manifest form.

The conclusion from these and other experiences of bureaucratic organization in some twenty different countries including Eastern Europe, is that it is never possible to tell from an organization chart just who is manager of whom: in effect, it is a wise manager (or subordinate) who knows his own subordinate (or manager).

Just how confusing it can all become can readily be seen the moment the concepts of deputy and assistant are introduced. Is a deputy president, or deputy secretary, or deputy works manager, or deputy catering officer, or deputy engineer, or deputy accountant, and so on ('assistant' for 'deputy' can be substituted in each case) a genuine managerial level,

A

Dep. A   Figure 8.6

B

or is he a managerial assistant,

A

Dep. A   Figure 8.7

B

or is he merely someone who acts for the manager when he is away?

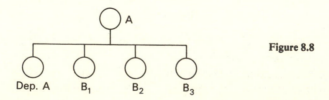

A

Figure 8.8

Dep. A   B₁   B₂   B₃

It is usually difficult to know just what is the extant situation – the occupants of the roles being confused. Organizational confusion of this kind is tailor-made for buck-passing, everyone willing to be manager in accord with the manifest organization chart when everything is going well, but retreating to the extant situation when things are going badly.

Time-span Boundaries and Managerial Strata

The manifest picture of bureaucratic organization is a confusing one. There appears to be no rhyme or reason for the structures that are developed, in number of levels, in titling, or even in the meaning to be at-

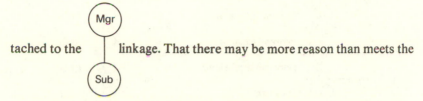

tached to the   linkage. That there may be more reason than meets the

eye, however, in the underlying or depth-structure of bureaucratic hierarchies became apparent from an accidental series of observations, hit upon quite separately and independently in Holland and in England during 1957 and 1958.[2] The findings were accidental in the sense that they were discovered in the course of studies being carried out for other purposes. The same findings have since been obtained in many other countries and in all types of bureaucratic system including civil service, industry and commerce, local government, social services, and education.

The findings may perhaps best be described as follows. Figure 8.9 on p. 134 shows a series of lines of command in which time-spans have been measured for each role. The diagram is schematized to show the time-span bands within which each role falls. It will be noted that as one moves higher up the hierarchy there is a fanning out of the time-spans, a phenomenon which occurs universally. The arrows from each role denote the occupant's feeling of where his real manager is situated as against his manifest manager.

What might at first sight appear to be a rather messy diagram reveals on closer examination the following interesting regularities: everyone in a role below 3-month time-span feels the occupant of the first role above 3-month time-span to be his real manager; between 3-month and 1-year time-span the occupant of the first role above 1-year time-span is felt to be the real manager; between 1- and 2-year time-span, the occupant of the first role above the 2-year time-span is felt to be the real manager; between 2- and 5-year time-span, the occupant of the first role above the 5-year time-span is felt to be the real manager; between 5- and 10-year time-span, the occupant of the first role above the 10-year time-span is felt to be the real manager. Sufficient data have not been obtained to show where the cut-off points are above 10-year time-span, but preliminary findings suggest a boundary at the 20-year level.

---

[2] In Holland by F. C. Hazekamp and his co-workers at the Dutch General Employers Confederation, and in England at the Glacier Metal Company.

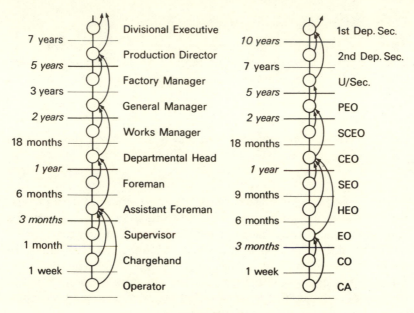

7 years	Divisional Executive		10 years	1st Dep. Sec.
5 years	Production Director		7 years	2nd Dep. Sec.
3 years	Factory Manager		5 years	U/Sec.
2 years	General Manager		2 years	PEO
18 months	Works Manager		18 months	SCEO
1 year	Departmental Head		1 year	CEO
6 months	Foreman		9 months	SEO
3 months	Assistant Foreman		6 months	HEO
1 month	Supervisor		3 months	EO
1 week	Chargehand		1 week	CO
	Operator			CA

Figure 8.9

This regularity – and it has so far appeared constantly in over 100 studies – points to the existence of a structure underlying bureaucratic organization, a sub-structure or a structure in depth, composed of managerial strata with consistent boundaries measured in time-span as illustrated. The data extend to over 15-year time-span, and there has been the suggestion of a boundary at 20-year time-span in some very large employment systems, although this finding has not been confirmed by measurement.

Time-span	*Stratum*
	Str-7
(?) 20 yrs	
	Str-6
10 yrs	
	Str-5
5 yrs	
	Str-4
2 yrs	
	Str-3
1 yr	
	Str-2
3 mths	
	Str-1

Figure 8.10

The data suggest that this apparently general depth-structure of bureaucratic stratification is universally applicable, and that it gives a formula for the design of bureaucratic organization. The formula is easily applied. Measure the level of work in time-span of any role, managerial or not, and that time-span will give the stratum in which that role should be placed. For example, if the time-span is 18 months, that makes it a Str-3 role; or 9 months, a Str-2 role.

If the role is a managerial role, not only can the stratum of the role be ascertained, but also how many strata of organization there should requisitely be, including shop- or office-floor Str-1 roles if any. Measure the level of work in time-span of the top role of the bureaucratic hierarchy – say, chief executive of the hierarchy, or departmental head of a department within the hierarchy – and that time-span will give the stratum in which that role will fall, and therefore the number of organizational strata required below that role. For example, if the role time-spans at 3 years, it makes the bureaucracy a Str-4 institution, and calls for four levels of work organization including the top role and the shop- or office-floor if the work roles go down to that level. If the bottom work role, however, is above the 3-month time-span – say, for example, 6 months, as may be the case in some types of professional institution – then the institution will require only three levels of work organization, namely, Str-4, an intermediate Str-3, and the bottom professional Str-2.[3]

One-stratum Distance and Optimum Manager-subordinate Relationships

The occurrence of too many levels in bureaucratic systems creates difficulties, both for the staff members personally and for the effectiveness of the institution. These difficulties can be illustrated by reference to the self-explanatory conception of roles being within the same stratum, or at

---

[3] The progression of the time-span boundaries of strata has an interesting geometric-logarithmic quality; above 3-month time-span they occur at 1 year, 2 years, 5 years, 10 years, 20 years; that is at approximately equal logarithmic intervals. This progression suggests the operation of a fundamental psychological process in line with the Weber-Fechner law (to produce the psychological experience of arithmetically equal increase in sensation the stimulus must increase geometrically).

If we treat each executive stratum as one arithmetic unit of responsibility, the equitable work-payment scale can then be plotted against those units (*see* Figure 8.11 on p. 136). A possible interpretation of the straight-line geometric progression from 3-month time-span is that logarithmic increases in responsibility input as represented by the logarithmically increasing felt-fair pay are necessary to produce the experience of arithmetic increases in responsibility as represented by each work-stratum. If this interpretation could be validated it would help to explain the shape of the equitable work-payment scale and would strengthen the notion that all work-strata are arithmetic unitary equivalents from the psychological point of view.

one-stratum distance (in contiguous strata), or at more-than-one-stratum distance.

Optimum manager-subordinate relationships require that the time-spans of the two roles be such as to place them in contiguous strata – the *one-stratum distance hypothesis*. When the actual differences in level of work between manager and subordinate posts deviate from this pattern of one-stratum distance, certain effects can be observed. Thus, for example, if B is set up as the manager in charge of C, and they both fall within the same stratum rather than within contiguous strata (there is less than one-stratum distance between them), then a full-scale manager-subordinate relationship will not occur. The subordinate will be found to have a great deal of contact with his manager-once-removed. Regular by-passing of the manifest immediate manager occurs. At salary review time it is the manager-once-removed rather than the immediate manager who reviews the subordinate's performance and decides the assessment, taking recommendations from the manifest manager. Similarly, when it is a matter of appointing somebody to the subordinate role, the manager-once-removed tends to involve himself not only in setting policy for the selection but also in the selection itself.

In such circumstances the manifest manager is in the difficult 'middleman' or 'straw boss' situation. He may try to make up for his muddied authority by throwing his weight around in order to gain a semblance of authority, or else he may just retire into doing the minimum necessary and staying out of trouble. The manager-once-removed (who is the extant manager) is also in trouble in that he cannot have the untrammelled contact he requires with

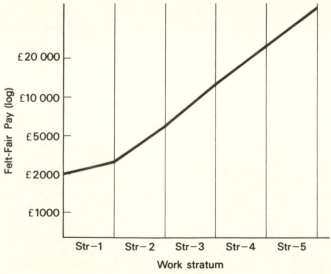

Figure 8.11

his extant subordinates. He does have a natural scapegoat in the apparent manager, should anything go wrong. As for the subordinate, his manifest immediate manager is not his real manager. He will be in an uncomfortable relationship with that manager if he attempts to by-pass him, and tied up with red tape if he does not. He will not be able to have much confidence in his manifest manager's assessment of his performance.

Some of the worst features not only of red tape in bureaucracy but of autocratic dominance and rigidity, or of laissez-faire withdrawal, are created by the widespread occurrence of this less-than one-stratum distance situation. If this analysis is correct, then many of the social psychological studies of managerial or supervisory behaviour and styles[4] may need to be looked at again in terms of whether the managers and supervisors were extantly in a manager-subordinate relationship with their so-called subordinates, or only manifestly so. The latter is the most likely, unless proved otherwise.

In short, something less than a full-scale manager-subordinate relationship will be found extantly to exist between the apparent manager and subordinate. But because the manifest situation calls for the apparent manager to act as though he were manager, it can only encourage non-responsible management. Fortunately most people are sufficiently constructive in orientation to work to get on in spite of these organization-stimulated difficulties.

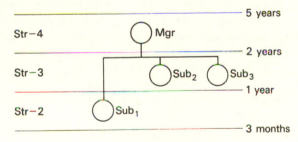

Figure 8.12

If, on the other hand, as in the diagram, the manager and his subordinate Sub_1 are in non-contiguous strata (and therefore, more than one-stratum distance), Sub_1 is not experienced as being in the same category as the manager's other subordinates, Sub_2 and Sub_3, who are in the contiguous stratum. Typical of the situation of more-than-one-stratum distance

[4] There are countless such studies; for example, to mention only a few: J. R. P. French, Jr., and R. Snyder (1959), 'Leadership and Interpersonal Power'; R. Lippitt *et al.* (1952), 'The Dynamics of Power'; P. Lawrence (1958), *The Changing of Organizational Behaviour Patterns*; R. L. Kahn and D. Katz (1953), 'Leadership Practices in Relation to Productivity and Morale'.

between manager and subordinate roles is the relationship between a manager and his secretary or his personal assistant, the level of work in whose role may be two or more strata lower than that of the manager and one or more strata lower than that of the team of immediate subordinates. Secretaries and personal assistants are not conceived of as part of the immediate command. They are not considered to be full-scale colleagues of the manager's other subordinates. They are assistants to that manager in helping him to do detailed parts of his own tasks such as typing, gathering information, conveying his instructions, etc. – which he would have to spend a lot of time doing himself if he did not have such assistance.

But it can happen that a manager's extant operational subordinates are at more than one-stratum distance. If they are, they will feel too far away from him; he will have to get down to too much detail in order to manage them; he will wish that he had an interposed manager between himself and them – and that is in fact the requisite solution to the problem. On the subordinate's side, the manager appears too distant also; he seems impatient, and expects too much and too quick understanding; the subordinate feels it difficult to cope.

In summary, then, what is postulated is the existence of a universal bureaucratic depth-structure, composed of organizational strata with boundaries at levels of work represented by time-spans of 3 months, 1 year, 2 years, 5 years, 10 years, and possibly 20 years and higher. These strata are real strata in the geological sense, with observable boundaries and discontinuity. They are not mere shadings and gradations. Requisite organization of bureaucracy must be designed in such a way that manager-subordinate role relationships will be established at one-stratum distance (except for personal assistants of various kinds).

The question, then, is why this postulated depth-structure should occur. Where does it come from? What is it caused by? What can be the source of these boundaries and the discontinuous stratification which they create? These questions are taken up in the next chapter.

9

Levels of Abstraction and the Stratification of Mental Activity

It is generally assumed in the social sciences that human characteristics when measured would prove to be distributed in populations in accord with a uni-modal Gaussian distribution curve. The assumption underlying this view is that these characteristics are parameters with single attributes, which appear in single rather than multiple states. It is worth noting that the opposite assumption informs most other sciences; namely, that the parameters in nature are most likely to be multi-attribute, and that changes in quantity in any given parameter will lead at certain critical points to changes in state.

This chapter will present the evidence so far accumulated to support a multi-attribute theory of the nature of work-capacity; that is to say, that work-capacity is subject to discontinuity and to change in state with change in quantity, and that it is multi-modally distributed in the population. This idea could serve to explain the systematic discontinuities which occur in bureaucratic systems and which create the depth-struture of the work-strata which have been described. The levels in the depth-structure of bureaucratic hierarchies follow from the existence of sub-populations each with its own particular state of work-capactiy.

How any two people perceive the same problem or activity will be different according to the differences in their level of abstraction. This postulate will be of considerable importance when we consider the consequences of consistency or inconsistency between a person's work-capacity and the available level of work in his bureaucratic employment.

Further evidence in support of the theory will, however, be presented in subsequent chapters where the high predictive power of the hypothesis will be demonstrated.

Single-attribute Versus Multi-attribute Parameters

If it is the case that there is a universal and uniform depth-structure in the form of regular layers and boundaries towards which bureaucratic systems tend — a system of regular stratification — then the question arises as to why this phenomenon should occur. There would appear to be two main possibilities: the first would postulate the existence of various lines of stratification in the external social or physical world, the world outside man; the second would postulate facts about the nature of man himself: such qualitative differences in men's capacities or other aspects of their make-up connected with problem solving and with personal interaction, as to divide them into stratified sub-groups with natural lines of cleavage between. Consideration of these two sets of possibilities has led me to choose the second as the most likely explanation. If this explanation is correct, the consequences would be far-reaching.[1]

The reason I have discarded the first postulate is that I have been able to find no evidence to support it. If there were external causes, they must be either in some inherent quality of social systems or in the properties of tasks. Yet there is no constant class or caste system, or other system of social stratification, whose existence could explain the apparently universal and timeless character of the stratification of the structure in depth of bureaucratic systems.[2]

The almost universal commonsense view is that bureaucratic stratification and hierarchy exist because they are necessary for large-scale work organization. This view is reflected in the functionalist outlook in sociological theory, succinctly expressed, for example, by Kingsley Davis in connection with social stratification generally: 'We said that it came from the fact that every society has to pay some attention to functional importance and to scarcity of personnel (in terms of talent and training) in filling its positions. In order to satisfy these requirements, differential rewards must be given for different positions – and these differential rewards are precisely what we call stratification.'[3]

Davis does take account of human abilities in his reference to talent, but in terms of scarcity rather than in terms of a hierarchy and stratification of talent. He then uses differential reward synonymously with social stratification. In both these respects his usage expresses the mainstream of sociological thought. We shall find it useful, by contrast, to differentiate between the continuity of inequality in economic differentials and the discontinuity implied by stratification. And we shall take human ability as the key. For the functionalist type of argument that bureaucratic systems are

---

[1] Melvin Tumin suggests such a possibility in the structure of human motivation as the explanatory principle for the occurrence of social stratification. Finding no evidence, however, for this particular hypothesis, he writes: 'If we cannot rest the case for the inevitability of stratification on inescapable facts about human mc‘:vation, we cannot rest it upon anything at all ... We are dealing with something optional in human affairs' (M. M. Tumin (1967), *Social Stratification*). I believe that Tumin's intuition was right in trying to connect social stratification with psychological factors. But he picked the wrong human characteristic for his explanatory conjecture and was then led to a wrong general conclusion.

[2] The Imperial Roman Army, with its centurions and cohorts, manifests the same character of stratification as Str-2 and Str-3 in modern armies and businesses.

[3] K. Davis (1949), *Human Society*, p. 388.

economically efficient and that these systems were established in order to get the necessary work done, is at best incomplete. Social systems cannot endure in the way the bureaucratic system has endured if they are not closely attuned to man's nature. If, for example, all men were equal in work-capacity, the bureaucratic hierarchy would be an impossible social system. It would never have been discovered. Men would have worked together in leaderless groups or in partnerships, or in other types of small face-to-face size associations, but a bureaucratic hierarchy, never!

Nor can the nature of tasks readily explain the phenomenon. For tasks are man-made things. They are products of human desire and aspiration, created by human imagination of the objects to be produced as the output of the task. Any evidence that there might be not only of a hierarchy of tasks but of an inherent discontinuous stratification of tasks, would therefore point to a stratification of populations with respect to the mental functioning of their members.

Discontinuity and Multi-modality in Mental Functioning

The regularities in stratification of bureaucratic hierarchies must surely reflect an equivalent stratification in human populations, otherwise why would bureaucratic hierarchies ever have occurred at all? The postulate to be considered is that with respect to work-capacity people are divided into distinct and separable categories which are hierarchically stratified; that is to say, as work-capacity increases in amount it undergoes changes in state. A parallel case would be if in the case of intelligence as measured in IQ, there were critical points at which a further increase in IQ produced not only a further increment in intelligence, but a change to a different quality, the emergence of a new quality; as though the 110 to 130 IQ group not only had higher IQs than the 90 to 110 group and the 70 to 90 group, but also had a different kind of intelligence, different in some significant quality as steam differs from water. And there would be another significant difference between the 90 to 110 group and the 70 to 90 group as water differs from ice.

If intelligence as measured by IQ in fact had such characteristics, the discontinuities would show up in a multi-modal distribution, in contrast to the uni-modal distribution which is found. Human qualities with discontinuity of this kind would divide populations into discrete groupings. If the quality related directly to competence to carry given levels of work, the discontinuities would show in divisions of the population into hierarchically placed strata.

This kind of postulate is not common in the social sciences. We are deeply committed to the idea of single parameters represented in uni-modal normal distribution curves. The notion of multi-attribute parameters with accompanying multi-modal distributions is rarely used. And yet discontinuity of just this kind is normally expected in the natural sciences. The experience of changes in state at critical points with changes in quantity is a familiar phenomenon; as, for example, in the ice-water-steam-superheated steam series of discontinuity and change of state, or in the Böhr discontinuity model of the atom. It is also an integral part of developmental biology, where changes of state and discontinuity are part of ordinary thinking; the idea of emergent evolution phylogenetically or of development stages in orthogenesis. This latter type of thinking is also very much a part of developmental psychology.

It is interesting to note, however, that discontinuity theory to some extent has been a part of psychological thinking in connection with levels of abstraction and conceptualization. Ever since Goldstein and Scheerer published their distinction between concrete and abstract modes of thought[4] a qualitative shift between at least these two levels of mental functioning tends to have been assumed. Harvey, Hunt and Schroder,[2] however, illustrate some of the discomfort about making such an assumption, when they take William James' argument for the existence of a continuous stream of consciousness in the individual as a possible argument against the conception of discontinuity between different categories or populations of individuals. 'We shall leave unsolved,' they write, 'the issue of whether concreteness-abstractness is more appropriately viewed as a qualitatively continuous or discontinuous dimension.'[5]

More specifically our postulate is that there are discontinuities in the nature of work-capacity at the 3-month level, the 12-month level, the 2-year level, the 5-year level and so on. These changes in state are such as to divide any population into a series of separate modalities with respect to work-capacity, the group up to 3-month capacity forming one normally distributed modality, the group from 3-months capacity to one-year capacity another normally distributed modality, and so on. It is these different modalities in any population which are at the root of the discontinuities in the depth-structure of bureaucratic organization. To put the conjecture another way, any human population is stratified with respect to the work-capacity of its individual members as measured in time-span, and the depth-structure of bureaucratic systems is stratified in accord with these changes in state in work-capacity.

If the conjecture about qualitative jumps in the nature of human competence in work, and in all goal-directed behaviour, is valid, then there ought to be qualitative differences which can be observed in the way people

[4] K. Goldstein and G. Scheerer (1939), *The Organism*; and K. Goldstein (1948), *Language and Language Disturbances*.
[5] O. J. Harvey, D. E. Hunt and H. M. Schroder (1961), *Conceptual Systems and Personality Organisation*, p. 28.

at different work-strata actually work: differences in their perception of tasks, differences in the planning and organization of their work, differences in how they carry their relationship with the external task in which they are engaged, and, indeed, in the fullest sense, qualitative differences in the way they picture the world in which they are working.

There are such qualitative differences, such discontinuities, and they manifest themselves in many different ways. Two such types of phenomena will be described, and at a number of different levels: the first type is concerned with the relationship between the individual and the physical resources he uses in carrying out his tasks[6]; the second type is concerned with his relationships with people and social systems. This latter theme has been formulated and developed by my colleagues David Billis and Ralph Rowbottom.[7]

The emphasis throughout the description will continue to be upon behaviour, upon action, or as Piaget has described it,[8] 'upon the sensory-motor ability to organize the outer world'. The field of description is thus the individual, in a bureaucratic role system, at a given organization level, interacting with the outside world in connection with a task or tasks which he is employed to carry out.

Each of the discrete levels to be described will be termed level of abstraction. Each shift across a boundary represents a shift in the capacity of individuals to deal with problems in an increasingly abstract way. The observations may contribute to the development of the concept of level of abstraction itself.[9]

A series of examples will be given to illustrate each point. These examples are real. In describing them we must refer to the title of the particular role (for example, typist, supervisor, research investigator, etc.) and to the time-span of each. In doing so, it is *not implied that all other roles with these same titles have the same time-spans*. It is common practice for the same title to be used for roles of very different levels of work.

[6] B. Bernstein uses a similar criterion: 'The predisposition to form relationships with objects in a particular way is an important perceptual factor.' (1971), *Class, Codes and Control*, p. 44.

[7] R. W. Rowbottom and D. Billis, 'The Stratification of Work and Organizational Design' — to be published in *Human Relations*.

[8] J. Piaget (1953), *The Origin of Intelligence in the Child.*

[9] Level of abstraction is often loosely used to refer to the level of generalization at which a person functions. Its more systematic use as a rigorously defined concept has been markedly limited. Goldstein and Scheerer distinguished between two levels only, the concrete and the abstract, an analysis which is much too restricted: see K. Goldstein and G. Scheerer (1939), op cit.; O. J. Harvey, D. E. Hunt and H. M. Schroder (1961), op. cit., in their review of the literature were unable to produce a formulation which went much beyond the distinction between concrete and abstract. They do support the present argument in stating the view that there probably exist many discrete levels, but they do not give any indication of what these levels might be.

First Level of Abstraction: Perceptual-motor Concrete

It is a general feature of roles with time-spans below 3 months that the tasks are assigned in concrete terms and are carried out in direct physical contact with the output. The project can be pictured and constructed by means of direct perception of examples of the output to be produced. For example; a copy-typist is given a typed memorandum to copy, and works physically with her machine in doing so; a manual operator is given a drawing from which to carry out a particular operation on a piece of metal either by hand or by a machine; a laboratory assistant is given a particular test to carry out; a clerical officer is given a set of administrative data to search through and check; a supervisor is given a particular group of operators to watch over; a sales assistant is required to give customers the articles they ask for, wrap them and take payment.

If there is no immediate perceptual contact with the output, no work is done at this level. The whole of the task is at hand in a concrete sense. Either the output itself, or the controls of the machine or equipment affecting the output, can be reached out to, touched, manipulated. Words and other abstract data may be used in the instructions for the task, but these abstractions have an immediate reference which can be concretely pointed to – the piece of material to be worked upon, the drawing or sample to be worked from.

The working relationships with people are also concrete in mode in the sense of being prescribed in content. Rowbotton and Billis describe this as 'working towards objectives which can be completely specified (as far as is significant) beforehand, according to defined circumstances which may present themselves; but not expected to make any significant judgments on what output to aim for or under what circumstances to aim for it.'[10]

This view of relationships with clients can also explain why no managerial roles can be found below the 3-month time-span level. Manager-subordinate relationships require that the manager should be able to do much more than react in a prescribed and delimited way to the needs and demands of their subordinates.

The quality of capacity at this level is thus one of concreteness in the sense of needing to be in immediate perceptual contact with the physical output – visual, tactile, kinaesthetic, auditory – and to be able to manipulate it motorically as work progresses and the task is carried out. This concreteness goes along with mechanistically prescribed relations with others as necessary in the work.

The concreteness of work activity at this level connects with the use of very concrete modes of expressive movement, such as hitting or pushing

---

[10] R. W. Rowbottom and D. Billis, op. cit.

or tapping the other person, as described for example by Miller and Swanson[11] and by Basil Bernstein[12] with reference to working-class communication.

This first level of abstraction may be termed the perceptual-motor concrete, and the population which works in this mode Work-Capacity Group I.

Second Level of Abstraction: Imaginal Concrete

At the 3-month time-span level and up to the 12-month time-span, tasks are characterized by new qualities not found below 3-month time-span. The goal can no longer be completely specified; imagination must be exercised in the construction of the project, although the task is still concrete in the sense that output can be imagined in concrete terms. For example: a ward sister in charge of a ward in hospital had to be able to interpret the doctor's prescriptions and assess the needs of patients where the doctor had not specifically prescribed, she also had to set terms of reference for each of her subordinate nurses in the light of her assessment of the needs and competencies of each one, all within the general planning of activities and priorities which she carried out; a social worker had to interpret the needs of clients with whom she was doing casework, and not just accept at face value what they said was wrong or needed; a civil service executive officer had to decide how to plan a six-month investigation of how to improve the implementation of a piece of departmental policy; a research investigator had to plan and carry through a six-month research programme to examine certain new methods of bonding metals; a foreman had not only to plan the work of his section from week to week, but also to plan and carry out a retraining and development scheme for his operators in preparation for new methods of production which were to be operating efficiently in nine months' time.

In none of these tasks are there terms of reference which can be specified completely or pointed to physically, nor can the tasks be carried out solely by perceptual-motor manipulation of the object. They all require the ability to imagine, but to imagine in concrete terms, what requires to be done, to picture it in the mind's eye, and in imagination also to work out and prepare plans and methods for overcoming problems.

[11] D. R. Miller and G. E. Swanson (1958), *The Changing American Parent.*
[12] B. Bernstein links his qualitative distinction between the behaviour of his so-called working-class and middle-class children to time-span as well: 'The school is an institution, where every item in the present is finely linked to a distant future, consequently there is not a serious clash of expectations between the school and the middle class at all. The child's developed time-span of anticipation allows the present activity to be related to a future, and this is meaningful.' (1971) *Class, Codes and Control*, p. 29.

Rowbottom and Billis[13] have pointed to the interpretative content of the work of professionals such as social workers in dealing with clients; they have to use their imaginations in getting a picture of underlying needs, and cannot simply deal with things as presented to them in concrete terms. They describe the work as requiring a 'situational response – carrying out work where the precise objectives to be pursued have to be judged according to the needs of each specific concrete situation which presents itself; but not expected to make any decisions, i.e. commitments on how future possible situations are to be dealt with.'

The location of the output is also no longer given in immediate concrete perceptual-motor terms. It is not available for touching and motor manipulation, although it may be possible physically to oversee the whole of the area of responsibility.

The quality of the capacity involved is that of being able to hold the concrete problem firmly in imagination and to work with it mentally, without the support of being able continuously to test judgment and imagination by tactile manipulation of a physical thing. A physical detachment from the field of work is required, but without losing the subjective sense of the output in concrete terms.

This second level of abstraction may be termed the imaginal concrete, and the population which works in this mode Work-Capacity Group II.

Third Level of Abstraction: Imaginal Scanning

At time-span levels of 1 year to 2 years the emergent characteristic of tasks is that it has become impossible physically to oversee or to imagine all at once the whole of a person's area of responsibility. The scope of activity has become too wide for this, although it is still possible to do so by mentally scanning the whole, one bit at a time. For example: the owner of a small business employing 150 people was not able to look at all that was going on all at once, but he could run over all the activities in his mind and was up to date in his knowledge of existing sales and stock levels, forward order book, profit position, and other aspects of his business; a sales manager with eight level-two sales subordinates could not picture all at once all the customers for whom he and his subordinates were accountable, but he could run over them one by one in his mind and reconstruct the total sales position; a battalion commander could not picture the whole of the terrain in which his troops were fighting, but he could cover it by riding physically over the whole, and could build up the total picture as he went.

The instructions received at this level tend to be in conceptual terms of load data and programmes, expense variables, indices, ratios, vectors.

---

[13] R. W. Rowbottom and D. Billis, op. cit.

These conceptually formulated tasks must be translated into an imaginal picture of the tasks controlled. The totality of the duties must be scanned continually so that progress can be tied up with new instructions.

The effect of scale at this level is that the project can never be constructed as a coherent mental picture. The project itself can be pictured only by scanning: it has become more elusive, it cannot be pictured all at once, but only in a series of time slices. The interplay between project and output, therefore, has become qualitatively more complex. Feed-back is in terms of comparing what is happening in various parts of the output region with equivalent parts of the subjective project. The whole has to be bound together in feel rather than by direct perception, feel supported by conceptual data about the whole. The relationship between project and object is still in terms of concrete comparisons, but perceptual part to part rather than perceptual whole to whole as at level two. The process of scanning is thus one in which a person must be able to sense the interplay of the various parts without the support of being able physically to perceive at one time the various parts making up the whole.

Rowbottom and Billis have conceptualized work at this level in terms of their observation that it always includes system development – 'systematic service provision – making systematic provision of services of some given kinds shaped to the needs of a continuous sequence of concrete situations which present themselves; but not expected to make any decisions on the re-allocation of resources to meet as yet unmanifested needs (for the given kinds of services) within some given territorial or organizational society.'[14]

The third level of abstraction may be termed the imaginal-scanning level, and the population which works in this mode Work-Capacity Group III.

Fourth Level of Abstraction: Conceptual Modelling

At the 2-year time-span capacity level there emerges a profound change in the quality of abstraction used in carrying out tasks: it is a change from the concrete to the abstract mode of thought and work.

When a designer is asked to get out a design (or indeed when anyone is asked to get out any kind of proposal for a new method or procedure or policy), the higher the level of capacity of the designer the more generalized the form of his design will be in the special sense that the less it will be like things that already exist. What is noteworthy is the fact that in the time-span band from 2 years to 5 years, designs (or method, procedure or policy) will frequently require the designer to start from existing designs

[14] R. W. Rowbottom and D. Billis, op. cit.

but to depart from them to produce new ones which are not recognizably like those which existed originally.

In one such case a designer was instructed to design a new large-scale piece of machinery to do the work of an existing machine but to be based upon different principles so that it would be more versatile and less expensive. He had to analyse the existing mechanism and express it completely in abstract terms of force fields, vectors, power, stresses, direction of movement, degrees of freedom. He then had to detach himself from his picture of the existing machine and immerse himself in the manipulation of his abstractions with a temporary suspension of reference to existing machines – while he continued to retain a firm grip somewhere in the back of his mind on the realizable goal of his work, which was to produce a design which could be translated into something concrete which could be constructed.

Other examples: a civil service assistant secretary and his department were given the task of producing proposals for a new type of service to the community, including an analysis of the organizational changes which would be required, costs, and a practical programme for implementation if agreed; the general manager of a factory employing 1200 people was instructed to work out and implement a programme of change in the factory such that in $3\frac{1}{2}$ years' time over half the factory would be working on entirely different products for new markets and the other half would be using new methods and equipment which would be introduced during the period and brought up to full productivity; a purchasing manager had four years in which to develop an entirely new supply network to enable the enterprise to stop producing certain components and to have regular supplies on contract to do so instead.

The common feature in all these examples is that the task requires the individual to retain mental contact with what exists, but then at the same time to achieve a detachment from this experience and to work with ideas of things which are different from what exists – which look different, function differently, do different things. The new thing is not a modification or extension of the old; it is a departure from it.

Rowbottom and Billis have referred to this level in the following way: 'making comprehensive provision of services of some given kinds according to the total and continuing needs for them throughout some given territorial or organizational society; but not expected to make any decisions on the re-allocation of resources to meet needs for services of different or new kinds'.[15]

Another feature of this same level of work is that the possibility of direct command is lost. Unless the department is very small (say under 50

[15] R. W. Rowbottom and D. Billis, op. cit.

people), it is unlikely that staff working at this level and above will recognize all the other members of the department. The junior members at the first level will be found to be organizationally very distant. In larger departments there may be up to 1500 or 2000 people. The geographical environment is no longer conceivable *in toto* in concrete terms. It is too extended, contains too many departments, too far-flung customers, too many competitors known and unknown. The transition is often referred to managerially as 'becoming chairborne'. In military organization the abstract quality is reflected in the emergence of red tabs, oak leaves, and patches at regimental and brigade levels. Such symbols substitute for the direct quality of command based upon individuals' mutual knowledge of each other at lower levels of organization.[16]

The qualitative jump from level three to level four is that at level four neither the output nor the project can be foreseen in concrete terms, even by imaginal scanning. The project cannot be completely constructed. It remains a combination of a conscious subjective picture, incomplete in itself, whose specific total form and content are unconsciously intuitively sensed but cannot quite be consciously grasped. The cross-comparison between project and emerging output is thus a process with much intuitive feel in the early stages as to whether the work is proceeding satisfactorily; as the work proceeds, the project becomes more and more explicitly filled in through perception of the emerging output, until in the finishing stages the final output can be completely projected and completed. In short, at level four the construction of the explicit project can be completed only during the process of work itself.

This level is the one at which what is usually referred to as innovation can begin, innovation in the sense of taking existing things or services as a starting point but being able to detach mentally from a picture of these things and to work in this detachment, returning to concrete representation with new ideas different from existing ideas precisely because of the detachment. In the first three levels of abstraction continual reference to the concrete case either perceptually or imaginally is needed and available in order to be able to work. By contrast, from level four and higher the ability to work in phases of interrupted perceptual or imaginal contact with real things is the essence of work.

The notion of an abstract mode of work does not simply mean thinking in the abstract in the sense of being a 'back-room boy' or an 'academic' thinker; that is to say, it does not refer to 'abstract' as against practical and down to earth. Nor does it imply merely using abstractions whether words,

[16]It is significant that the title 'General' emerges at the 2-year time-span level in military services. In commerce and industry, the same title tends to come into play, although this fact is less recognized because it is used in the adjectival form of General Manager, or of General Sales Manager rather than as a noun as in the case of Major-General, etc.

ideas, conceptions, beliefs or even high-level and abstruse mathematics. The central quality is that of detachment; of abstraction in the sense of being able to work at specific and concrete problems without dependence upon mental contact with existing things, and with the ability to contact things without becoming mentally fixed on them.

In short, the transition in capacity from the third to the fourth level of abstraction (the transition to work capacities above 2 years) is a transition from concrete to genuinely abstract work. This fourth level of abstraction may be termed conceptual modelling, and the population which works in this mode Work-Capacity Group IV.

Fifth Level of Abstraction: Intuitive Theory

It will be apparent that these descriptions of levels of abstraction are descriptions derived from work-in-progress. At the fifth level of abstraction at 5-year time-span and up to 10-year time-span our experience is limited. The roles analysed include a number of chief executives in industry and in the public services, a number of under-secretary roles in the Civil Service and a number of specialist and professional roles in various services.

The central finding from the point of view of qualities in the task which are not to be found at lower level can be illustrated in the following example. A manager operating at 7-year time-span, on being pressed by his subordinates to come to see the latest prototype of a newly developed product, replied that he had already examined the prototype at an earlier stage of its development. He did not have to take another look but would be content with a verbal description of the new development. His subordinates continued to press him to see for himself, but he insisted that he would prefer to get down to examining the figures of performance, available markets, etc., so that necessary decisions could be made. He did not require physical contact with additional examples. In the discussion two different frames of reference – different levels of abstraction – are interacting, the higher level sifting out a decision from the application of intuitively held generalizations requiring only passing contact with the concrete; that is to say, generalizations having the characteristic of an intuitively constructed theory.

At this level of work we are dealing with chief executives, heads of service, managers of enterprises, departments, army divisions, which may be employing five to ten thousand people. There is no possibility whatever of having other than a very limited contact with the concrete reality of the total field of responsibility – contact with a specific detail or datum here or there, but for the most part activities go on without the head knowing anything about what is happening. He must be occupied in fashioning the longer-term future and leave the present to take care of itself in the hands of his subordinates with the policies and plans he had already laid down.

Rowbottom and Billis refer to this level as that of comprehensive field coverage and describe it in the following terms: 'making comprehensive provision of services within some general field of need throughout some given territorial or organizational society; but not expected to make decisions on the re-allocation of resources to provide services outside the given field of need.[17]

The level of abstraction concerned can be described in terms of the relationship between these periodic contacts with some very few details of implementation and the general policies, strategies, plans, and statistically co-ordinated bodies of information which are the everyday content of these roles. The relationship is similar to that between a general theory and a specific and detailed point of application of that theory. A good theory applies over a wide range of concrete cases in such a manner that, given the theory and one detailed example of its application, it becomes possible to understand what will happen in other cases similar to the example and covered by the theory.

In similar vein, the fifth level of abstraction is based on the mental possession of intuitive theories built up from experience. Such intuitively constructed theories then allow the person to function with what might be called one-time contact with the concrete. Each specific case or specific problem or specific example is generalized and absorbed for use as part of a general formulation.

It can be conjectured that the construction of the project has now become a matter of unconscious intuition, with a complex of apparently disconnected facts and figures. These facts and figures are intuitively sorted over. Those intuitively felt most relevant are elevated and elaborated in subjective consciousness, and the intuitively felt irrelevancies are put to one side. New data are sought and sorted over for connections, for pattern, so that an ordered pattern of relevant facts is gradually constructed, and decisions can be taken. Feed-back control continues in relation to a largely intuitive and unconscious project, as for level four, except that to the extent that it becomes conscious it does so in terms of a general policy the concrete details of which are to be filled in by subordinates, rather than in terms of a project in itself eventually specifiable in concrete terms.

This fifth level of abstraction may be termed the level of intuitive theory, and the population which works in this mode Work-Capacity Group V.

[17] R. W. Rowbottom and D. Billis, op. cit.

Sixth and Seventh Levels of Abstraction

Because of the evidence from bureaucratic organizations that there exist at least two further levels – a level beginning at the 10-year time-span and a level beginning at the 20-year time-span, and perhaps higher levels as well – it may be postulated that new emergents in the qualitative characteristics of time-span capacity would be found to occur towards the 10- and 20-year levels. In very broad terms it can be noted that if the technology allows, there is a shift towards managing in terms of policy setting and away from directing and co-ordinating the activities of subordinates with collateral relations. That is to say, if the technology is light- or medium-scale manufacturing or services (rather than heavy large-scale technology such as in steel or in oil refining where production cannot be broken into small-scale units) then there is a tendency for the enterprise to differentiate into a series of independent trading subsidiaries each managed by a profit-and-loss account chief executive.

This process is consistent with another notable tendency at levels 6 and 7, and that is that the management of institutions turns into the creation and establishment of new institutions. These institutions are among the most prolific creators of new bureaucracies. Insufficient observational work has as yet been done at these levels, however, even to attempt to distinguish the qualitative changes in mode of work being assumed. What can be said is that these institutions can employ tens and hundreds of thousands of people, and commonly have working relationships with central governments or are national departments or services employed by central governments.

The table on p. 153 summarizes the scheme of levels of abstraction described.

An Experimental Study of Discontinuity and Multi-modality

The foregoing descriptive material is far from satisfactory from the point of view of testing the discontinuity and multi-modality hypotheses in relation to the stratification of bureaucracy. Descriptive cases readily lend themselves to biased interpretation, and in consequence are never useful for refuting hypotheses. But a much more powerful set of tests has been carried out in a research programme that has gone on for ten years now and is still continuing. So far this work has not refuted the hypotheses, and certain predictions based upon the discontinuity hypothesis have been strongly sustained.

The work has been carried out by D. J. Isaac, joined more recently by B. M. O'Connor. Isaac postulated both a system of discontinuity in the make-up of mental activity and an equivalent developmental discontinuity. In

Summary of Strata and Levels of Abstraction

		Stra-tum	Time-span	Level of Abstraction	Equitable Payment (1975)	Maximum No. of Employees (labour intensive)	Types of Unit			Normal Location of Work Facilities	Nature of Group
							Industry & Commerce	Military	Civil Service		
ABSTRACT Indirect or General Command		VII		?			Corporation	Army	Perm. Sec.	World-wide	?
			20 yrs		£70 000	150 000					
		VI		Institution creating			Group	Corps	Deputy Sec.	In several nations	?
			10 yrs		£35 000	20 000					
		V		Intuitive Theory			Full DMS	Division	Under Sec.	Spread over one nation	?
			5 yrs		£18 000	2500					
		IV		Conceptual Modelling			Medium-sized Business	Brigade	Asst. Sec.	Regional	?
			2 yrs		£9000	350					
CONCRETE Direct Command		III		Imaginal Scanning			One-man Business or Unit	Battalion*	Princ'l	50 000 sq. ft.	Mutual recognition
			1 yr		£4800	50					
		II		Imaginal Concrete			Section	Company Platoon	Asst. Princ'l	5000 sq. ft.	Mutual knowledge
			3 mths		£3000	1					
		I		Perceptual-Motor Concrete			Supervisors & Shop-& Office-floor	NCOs* & ORs	Clerical & Office Supervisors	Supervising up to 500 sq. ft.; Shop & Office Floor up to 150 sq. ft.	Face-to-face

* This same type of structure applies to the cohort and centurion in the Imperial Roman Army, and to the military organization in China in 1000 B.C.

short, his working assumption was that as each individual developed, there would emerge a succession of new modes of working, each new mode appearing in conjunction with a maturational step. This assumption was, of course, consistent with the developmental discontinuities postulated by Piaget and the subject of so much of his experimental work.

A very practical problem, however, was to construct situations which accurately modelled the work situation, and which could be used for research purposes. I had the good fortune to work with Isaac from the early stages. One thing soon became clear: it was no use setting up intelligence-test types of problem – for intelligence tests differ from work in real life in at least two important respects. The first is that the nature of the problem is always explained; the second, that the problem sits still while the subject works upon it. In real-life work, by contrast, the first problem is to decide on the nature of each problem. Then especially on longer-term tasks, the problem rarely remains static; rather it changes as circumstances change and as unexpected difficulties arise. Isaac therefore set about designing problem-solving situations which would be active in the sense that the test situation would change as the test went on, because the presenting information would keep changing, and in which the subject's first task would be to discover what the problem was about through limited and controlled feed-back.[18]

One of these tests, for example, is a card-sorting test in which the 'subjects were given a pack of 96 cards — 3 of each of 32 patterns — to sort into 3 piles, two of which were marked with a display card. ... The patterns on the cards in the pack could differ from each other in one or more of five ways: colour — yellow and red; shape — round and square; size — large and small; number — one and two; content — filled and unfilled. ... The problem was simply to continue to sort cards from this pack into the three piles until they were all being placed "correctly", i.e., sorted according to a particular principle selected by the experimenter prior to the test. Each time a card was placed, the subject was told "right" or "wrong", which provided a guide to recognizing the principle. The criterion of success was 20 successive cards placed without error. ... When, after solving the problem, subjects were asked to verbalize the principle by which they had been sorting, not all of them could do so, even when expressing it in more concrete statements than those given above.'

The hypothesis to be tested was that to the extent that these problems approximated to the conditions of real work as a problem-solving process, a multi-modal distribution of scores would be found, instead of the uni-modal distribution usually expected and found with performance tests including intelligence tests. The research workers postulated not only that the number of modes would increase with the age of the population tested, but that additional modes would appear at certain critical ages, just as pubertal maturation occurs at a critical age. For reasons which cannot be elaborated here, the critical ages were thought to be at about 5 to 6 years, 10 to 11 years, around 17 years, and perhaps other critical points later still (these older critical ages being the subject of further work).

Figure 9.1 on p. 155 shows the results from one of the experimental runs.[19] The emergence of new modes can be clearly seen as occurring at the critical ages predicted. When the same tests were carried out under conditions similar to intelligence tests — for example when practice runs were given — the more familiar uni-modal distributions of scores were obtained. Thus, the hypotheses about multi-modality and about developmental discontinuity were not refuted by these carefully controlled experiments.[20]

---

[18] Some of these tests and the first set of experiments are described in D. J. Isaac and B. M. O'Connor (1969), 'Experimental Treatment of a Discontinuity Theory of Psychological Development'.

[19] For these and other similar results, see the Isaac and O'Connor, op. cit.

[20] It is of interest to note that the types of problem used by Isaac and O'Connor are what Thorndike would have called the co-ordinative type of task in his research on comparing

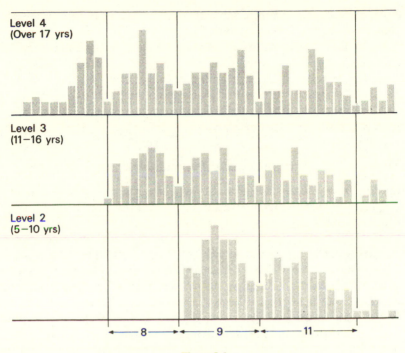

Figure 9.1

Of equal interest is some of the current Isaac and O'Connor work in
which they hit upon the idea of using information overload for determining
the level at which performance breakdown would occur.[21] Here again they
predicted discontinuity around their critical age points. They postulated,
for example, that an age range of 11 to 23 years would contain separate
groups of members in each of two different stages or levels (in their terms,
modes three and four). They argued that 'if some measurement could be
made of the maximum rate of information/input tolerable in a particular
situation without breakdown in performance, the distribution of scores

the performance of groups and individuals in problem-solving. On such tasks individuals
did better than groups (R. L. Thorndike (1939), 'On What Type of Task will a Group do
Well?'). But it is precisely such tasks that characterize the employment work situation.
Employment work is individual – it is not, and cannot be, done by groups. It is to be
expected, however, that in the experimental situation – as well as in real life – groups would
prove more effective in deciding policies than in carrying them out; that is to say, in determining policy limits and frameworks (as committees do) than in solving the types of
problem encountered in the implementation of policy (as individuals do). The clearest
examples of groups doing work are boards and other corporate governing bodies: the very
fact that they are corporate bodies means that they are true groups – and the work they do
is to consider and agree policies for others to implement.
[21] One of their starting points was in the work of James Miller. See, for example, his 'Input Overload and Psychopathology' (1960).

provided by a large number of subjects within an age range presumed to include two stages would be bimodal.'[22]

The well-controlled experimental work produced the predicted bi-modal distribution and thus strengthened the hypothesis. This result is of considerable importance, since it strengthens the idea of a possible link between the capacity to plan and proceed into the future (work-capacity) and the capacity to process and categorize given amounts of information without breakdown in the present.

Time-span, Work-capacity, and Information Processing

In Chapter 7 we began an analysis of the nature of work-capacity. It is now proposed to develop that analysis in the light of the discontinuity theory which has been put forward. In that chapter it was suggested that the higher the level of abstraction a person can manage, the longer the tasks or projects which he will be able to plan and further in full-time employment. It is this relationship which is necessary if time-span in fact measures level of work. It is also the reason why individuals demand time-spans which are consistent with their capacity seen in terms of level of abstraction. For no matter how interesting the tasks, if their general framework is not sufficiently extended in time the individual feels constricted, hemmed in, in the present.

How then may the relationship between time-span and the work-capacity of the individual be explained? It has to do with the organizing capacity of the mind, its capacity to pattern and order, to categorize, to generalize, or in the language of information theory, the capacity to chunk information bits.[23] For it may be apparent that the longer forward the object of the task to be achieved, the greater is the amount of information or detail to be organized, from the very beginning. The longer the task, the more complex it can be, the greater the number of circumstances to be anticipated.

That the longer the task the greater will be the complexity to begin with, can be shown, for example, by the fact that the greater number of sub-events in a critical path diagram the farther forward the objective event or goal. The 'future', the goal, shows up as a complex field in the present, as I postulated in Chapter 7: longer time-spans are reflected in a larger initial field, with a greater information input-load, with more sub-activities to be undertaken, requiring more complex categorization, with the ability to encompass detailed bits of information into sub-categories, sub-categories into categories, categories into larger categories, and so on. In effect, the in-

[22] See D. J. Isaac and B. M. O'Connor (1973), 'Use of Loss of Skill under Stress to Test a Theory of Psychological Development'.
[23] C. Cherry (1957), *On Human Communication*.

dividual has to be able to take a higher or wider perspective at the start in order to traverse a longer time-span path to a goal.[24]

It is this assumption about categorization or chunking of information bits, which may explain the discontinuity phenomena described. For categorization is a discontinuous process. Take for example the process of definition: four sticks do not define a chair; nor do four sticks and a board; but four legs, a back and a seat do: there is a sudden linking of information bits (themselves each composed of information bits) which pulls the various bits together into a category which can be dealt with as a single chunk containing the several bits. And once the category has been constructed, additional bits of information can be added and thus taken into account in describing many different types of chair, for example, but all still within the same single category. The category chair can then become one bit of information within a wider category; for example, if put together with the categories of table, bed, etc., to constitute the inclusive category, furniture.

It may be noted that a jump or discontinuity occurs each time in moving from each separate item to the new encompassing category. There is, of course, an infinite regress in this process of boundary definition. In one direction, increasingly inclusive categories are discovered – by processes of scientific generalization and theory building, or of artistic creativity; and in the other direction, by increasingly refined and microscopic analysis, and the revealing of the sub-structure of already defined and known things.

It may thus be seen that discontinuity is the essence of definitory categorization and indeed is contained within the meaning of the term definition itself: de-finire, to set boundaries around. The relationships are relationships of inclusion, with boundary-defined discontinuities.

The principle involved can be stated in the following general terms. The capacity to manage activity through time is the counterpart of, and depends upon, the capacity to analyse and detail situations, to pattern and order the detail. The capacity to analyse, pattern and order detail depends upon the organizing and conceptualizing capacity of the mind. The wider the span of the hierarchy of concepts a person is capable of manipulating, the greater is the range of detail he is capable of organizing and therefore the greater his work-capacity. Since categorization is a discontinuous process, so too will work-capacity in populations be found to be discontinuous.[25]

---

[24] This view has an interesting counterpart in the work of Van Lennep and Muller for Shell International. They describe what they call the 'helicopter principle' in assessing individual capacity. They use this phrase to refer to the height from which the individual is able to survey the work situation while still metaphorically keeping his feet upon the ground. The higher the helicopter view a person can take, the greater his capacity.

[25] The same phenomenon occurs in physics. Thus, for example, to move the temperature

There is one further type of support for our theory; namely, its explanatory power. The opportunity will arise in many of the succeeding chapters to demonstrate that this theory is able to identify and to explain most of the important phenomena associated with the structure and functioning of bureaucratic systems better than existing assumptions.

Activity Versus Level of Work

Meanwhile, one last assumption may be added about the expression of a person's level of abstraction; it is not possible for a person to perceive the world in any and all its aspects other than through glasses coloured by the particular level of abstraction which he possesses. That is to say, there are no problems and activities which are exclusively level one, level two, etc., but there are individuals in the first, second, third etc., levels of abstraction. Some problems may require analysis into so many details as to be beyond the ordering and patterning potentialities of persons of lower levels of capacity; but that does not place the problem at any particular level higher up. Under such circumstances the person feels overwhelmed by the problem, becomes disorganized, and inevitably fails.

But the more interesting case is that of a number of people of different levels of abstraction, say capacity group I, II, III, and IV, tackling 'the same problem', say one which is within the competence of the group I person; let us say, the task of doing some copy-typing and let us say each is able to type equally well. Each will be able successfully to complete the task in the sense of producing a satisfactory copy. But each will also have been doing a different task in a very significant sense. The person in capacity group I will have perceived the task in the concrete terms of the production of a fair copy. The group II person will have wondered whether it was this particular task which would best fulfil the needs of the person for whom it was being done, and would seek an opportunity to discuss what was really needed. The group III person would take the experience as one example of tasks which could be assigned to Stratum 1, and would get ideas from the experience which could be used as part of the building up of work systems designed to cope with such tasks. The group IV person would react to the experience by wondering why copy-typing had to be done in the manner assigned; he would be able to put the experience together with other observations, and to use it as material for the develop-

---

of water across the steam boundary requires a sudden increase in the amount of energy absorbed; that is to say, a jump in the amount of heat is required to move the temperature the one degree from 99 °C to 100 °C as compared with the heat required to raise the temperature from 97 °C to 98 °C or from 98 °C to 99 °C. These jumps are characteristic of change-of-state discontinuities.

ment of new systems to be invested in, which could eliminate copy-typing altogether.

In effect, it was quite impossible for Newton to perceive falling apples in the way that a group I apple picker would perceive falling apples. Similarly, it was impossible for Sir Alexander Fleming to perceive spoiled bacteriological plates in the same way that they were perceived by his laboratory assistant as he threw them out. Different pictures of the world, based on different levels of abstraction, lead to different accumulations of experience, different patterning and ordering of detail, and different final outcomes.

This particular conclusion, simple enough in all conscience, will become a cornerstone of our argument that industrial societies must as an absolute condition of democracy and human freedom provide a range and distribution of levels of work that correspond to the range and distribution of work-capacity in the population – regardless of the so-called demands of technological advance. To require a person of, say, group III capacity, to work in a Stratum-1 role, and to confine his output to the level-one concrete output is to cage him; its effect would be like that of employing Newton to pick apples, and Fleming to clean up the laboratory, and to force them to keep their ideas about gravity and about bacteriocides to themselves because that was not what they were being employed for.

There is an implicit distinction here which must be made clear and explicit: it is the distinction between the content of an activity and the level of work of the task to which that activity is directed. By activity is meant what a person is actually doing, without reference to his goal in doing it; for example, writing with a pen; using a slide rule or a micrometer; operating a machine tool, or a business calculating machine, or a typewriter; speaking on a telephone; sitting at a desk talking to someone; drawing some designs; walking about; driving a car.

Unfortunately, such activities are often taken to denote the nature of a role, and to indicate its level of work. Examples from the foregoing list of activities would be: machine tool operator; typist; accounting machine operator; telephonist; interviewer; commercial artist. In fact, these denotations of activity can no more give an indication of level of work than describing a judge as a desk-sitter or a chief accountant as a fountain pen operator. Nor can any chain of activities denote the level of work; as, for example, in denoting a managing director as telephonist-pen user-interviewer-letter dictator.

The level of work in a role results not from the activity but (as we have demonstrated) from the time-span of the *goal* of the activity. Level of work, responsibility, derive from the purposes of human activity, from the nature of the output to be achieved. Thus, it cannot be assumed that any two typists, or drivers, or machine operators, or telephonists, are necessarily carrying the same level of work. We have argued this point in Chapter 7.

But it might be thought that there is a contradiction in our argument. If a person inevitably carries out an activity at the level consonant with his level of work-capacity and demanded by it, how is it possible for anyone ever to be under-employed? This apparent contradiction is readily resolved. To be under-employed is not a feature of the activity, it is a feature of the goal of the activity and its time-span. Thus, in our example above, a person with the capacity to work at Str-2 would be under-employed and feel frustrated if given typing to do whose object was simply to make good copies day by day. He would not be under-employed, however, if the object of the typing was to produce copies of long and complex manuscripts, checking for errors, making suggestions for improving the formulations, preparing the bibliography and index, and getting copy ready for the printer – a three – to six-month task in all.

The frustrating effect of under-employment comes from requiring the person-in-action to confine his attention and his activities to shorter-term and less responsible goals than his work-capacity would cope with. As he carries out these lesser tasks, his higher level of capacity inevitably expresses itself, and he experiences the longer-term possibilities, the higher levels of task and output of which he is capable: the possible new methods; the easier ways of doing things; possibly better decisions; the advantages of doing some other investigation in place of the one he is doing; and so on. But he is not allowed to express these ideas. His manager is not interested in these other ideas, but only in getting the assigned tasks done and on time. At best there might be a suggestions scheme to be used, but that calls for work at home and does not get over the soul-destroying eight hours of frustration at work every day.

In short, under-employment is frustrating because it requires an individual to swallow the inexorable expression of his level of work-capacity, to conceal it, to keep it to himself, to throw it away. The measure of that frustration is the discrepancy between the time-span of the person's work-capacity and the time-span of the objectives of his activity. This discrepancy can be shown in its most dramatic form when capacity is constrained by physical imprisonment of the individual, as Farber has shown in the constriction of time perspective in the life-space of men serving long prison sentences.[26] Forced under-employment through lack of availability of adequate levels of work in the bureaucratic sector of industrial societies has effects akin to imprisonment.

[26] M. L. Farber (1944), 'Suffering and Time Perspective of the Prisoner'.

10

Growth of Individual Capacity and the Dynamics of Bureaucratic Systems

The foregoing two chapters have outlined the evidence for the existence of a bureaucratic depth-structure composed of a universal and uniform pattern of organizational strata, and have postulated the existence of this uniformity – indeed the existence of the bureaucratic hierarchy itself – as being a consequence of the hierarchical stratification of work-capacity. Further evidence will be adduced for this discontinuity theory by linking it to the concept of developmental stages in human growth. In doing so it will be possible to consider the important question of change and growth in bureaucratic systems.

People become capable of undertaking higher levels of work as they grow older. As might be assumed from the work of Piaget and others, this maturational process occurs in stages, with discontinuity. At stages before the full maturation of work-capacity the non-matured potential in people will reveal itself in the quality of working.

The maturation of work-capacity continues to a later age than is ordinarily assumed for the maturation of intelligence: at least to 40 years of age or later, and in higher-capacity people the maturation may continue throughout life.

Bureaucratic systems are markedly influenced by the rate and amount of maturation in work-capacity of their members. Each time one member traverses the boundaries of a work-stratum a serious disequilibrium is created. If this event occurs at the top of a bureaucratic system or at the top of a department within it, then that system or the department will be under enormous pressure to grow. The dynamics of bureaucracy will be examined in the light of these assumptions and findings.

Changes within Bureaucratic Systems

The question of change is concerned both with people and with institutions undergoing development; for example: what are the conditions under which bureaucracies change and what does the process of change look like? How do individuals grow in work-capacity – does it mature, is there a continuous or discontinuous development, does it increase throughout life or does it begin to fall off at some point? Is there a discernible pattern of growth? Do people differ constitutionally in work-capacity or is it infinitely extendable by education? What is the impact of technological change upon bureaucratic organization? Up to this point we have been dealing with the statics of bureaucracy. We shall now introduce the dynamics.

One approach would be to start from the fact that bureaucracies are open systems and subject to change through interaction with forces in the environment. Many systems theorists have adopted this course.[1] Although it is true that bureaucracies are open systems, our present interest is slightly different and perhaps more limited. The question with which we are concerned is what are the important factors within any one bureaucratic system which will determine whether or not it responds to external forces or to internal forces, and how it may adapt and change – that is to say, what type of theory may be developed to explain the special features and the dynamics of change within particular bureaucracies.

The dynamics of each individual bureaucracy must be seen in the relation between the distribution of work-capacity of its members and the distribution of levels of work in roles in the system. Growth or stability will tend to occur depending upon the extent to which there is a match or mismatch between the work-capacity of the chief executive and senior members of the system and the level of work in their roles, and upon the extent to which changes are taking place in the distribution of those capacities as the work-capacity of those individuals develops through time. Equally, the dynamics of change in parts of the system will be connected with similar changes in the senior officers in those sections. The relationships to be understood are those to do with the degree of fit between the level of work and organizational structure on the one hand, and the distribution and changing distribution of work-capacity of employees on the other.

It is, of course, true that the governing body on behalf of the employing association can decide to introduce major changes into their employed bureaucratic systems. In certain circumstances governing bodies may impose such changes, but these have to do not with the dynamics of bureaucracy but with the dynamics of employing associations. As far as the analysis of bureaucracy is concerned, imposed changes are best analysed in terms of response to a coercive force.

Regular Pattern of Growth of Individual Capacity: the Capacity Progression Array

The following are the data which suggest that work-capacity has a regular and predictable pattern of growth in each individual. They have already

[1] For example, A. K. Rice (1963), *The Enterprise and its Environment;* R. L. Ackoff and F. E. Emery (1972), *On Purposeful Systems*; D. Katz and R. L. Kahn (1966), *The Social*

been published[2] and are here summarized.

The prime data were obtained by plotting the progression in annual total earnings of a large population of individuals.[3] These earnings were adjusted to a common level of the annual earnings index; that is to say, a curve for each individual's earnings progression was obtained which represented changes in real earnings as compared with other people's with the effects of inflation taken out.

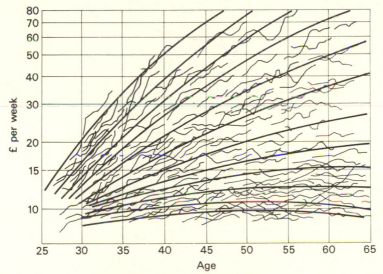

Figure 10.1   Earnings progression data

When curves are plotted in this way, an array of individual progression curves is obtained as illustrated. These curves manifest a regular tendency, as though directed into line by some underlying force, as a magnetic force field causes iron filings to line up on a sheet of paper. It is postulated that this underlying regularity is a reflection of a regularity in growth of in-dividual work-capacity. As each person develops, he strives for a level of work consistent with his capacity, and a level of pay consistent with the level of work, and this striving shows in the pattern of the curves.

My best current hypothesis about an underlying and uniform pattern of growth of work-capacity in individuals is expressed in the 1963 revision of the capacity progression array as illustrated. The hypothesis expressed in this array of curves is that the growth of a person's work-capacity will

---

Psychology of Organisations; and F. E. Emery and E. L. Trist (1965), 'The Causal Texture of Organisational Environment'.

[2] E. Jaques (1961), *Equitable Payment* and (1968), *Progression Handbook*.

[3] Such data have now been obtained for over 250 000 individuals in over 20 different countries.

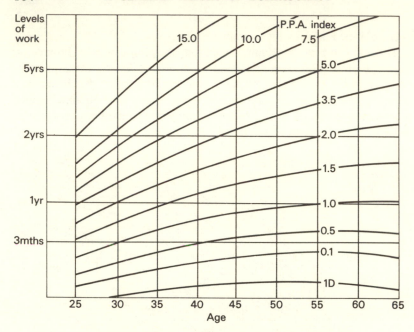

EARNING PROGRESSION DATA SHEET (AMENDED 1970)

Figure 10.2   Capacity progression array

follow the capacity growth curve which intersects his work-capacity represented in time-span at any particular age.[4]

Individuals' Predictions of their Development

The careers of over one hundred individuals have been followed, with their co-operation, for periods of five to eighteen years. Once the high mark at any given point in a person's career is established (that is to say, a time-span of work at which he felt he was working at absolutely full stretch), that high mark appears to have good predictive value for high marks in his subsequent career. If the time-span of discretion in his role falls more than 10 per cent below that value called for by his particular capacity progression curve he feels under-employed, and at 20 per cent below the work feels monotonous. If the time-span of discretion goes 10 per cent above this value, he feels over-stretched and begins to show the signs of disorganization described in Chapter 11 and at 20 per cent above this value will show signs of breakdown in capacity to work.

The predictive power of the array of curves was studied under controlled conditions by Dr Edna Homa.[5] She showed that the anticipated gain in

---

[4] For example, if his work-capacity is equivalent to a time-span of two years at age 35, it could be predicted that he would have grown to 5½ years' time-span by the age of 55.

[5] E. Homa (1967), 'The Inter-Relationship Among Work, Payment, and Capacity'.

earnings that an individual thought of as fair for his anticipated growth in capacity could be predicted from his current age and sense of current fair pay. She asked each subject two main questions: first, his current sense of fair pay for a level of work that would be just right for him; and, second, his sense of fair pay under assumed constant economic conditions for a level of work that he thought would be just right in five years' time. The upward slope for subjects of different ages and felt-fair pay was consistent with the slope of the appropriate curve in the capacity progression array, if felt-fair pay translated back into time-span was taken as an indication of the individual's sense of a just reasonable level of work.

Dr Homa's explanation for her findings was that each person seemed to have a strong sense of how his work-capacity would grow – individuals of the same age and felt-fair pay apparently looking up along the same capacity progression curve. The prediction based upon the capacity progression array hypothesis were thus not refuted, and the hypothesis was strengthened.

Developmental Stages in Maturation of Capacity

If the work-capacity of individuals grows and develops in accord with this capacity progression array, what then of the hypothesis of the discontinuity with discrete levels of abstraction? This hypothesis would lead to the assumption that work-capacity would mature in developmental stages; as a person's work-capacity progressed across the boundaries of work-strata and levels of abstraction, a qualitative reorganization would take place over a period of time, with the emergence of the new qualities associated with the next higher level of abstraction.

Take, for example, a person, A, with a potential work-capacity of 6 years – that is, the potential to reach and to work in Str-5. As he progresses, say into Str-3 he will work successfully for some 10 years in that stratum. There will then come a critical period as he approaches 35 to 37 years of age when he will begin to be recognized as changing, as becoming ready for promotion. He appears to be maturing in outlook. This developmental change shows most clearly in the fact that he now seems ready to take over the management of his erstwhile colleagues in Str-3. A maturational step has been traversed.

If he is promoted at this stage there is an adjustment period while he takes over his Str-3 command and relinquishes his former subordinates in Str-2 to another manager, possibly one of his own new Str-3 subordinates. During this adjustment period he may need training for his new role. The period of adjustment may take from a few months to a year or more. It happens faster if the individual is young and has very high potential. It takes longer the higher the stratum involved.

But what can be said about the nature of the potential Str-5 capacity when the person is still working at, say, Str-3? The potential is there. But the full capacity has not yet completely emerged. If his performance is compared with that of another manager, B, much older but at the same current level of work, the following will be noted: the older man will produce a more rounded and reliable performance and will be more experienced in coping with a wide range of eventualities; the younger man will be less to be relied upon in various emergencies and will require more frequent direct supervision – but he will also be inclined to think up new ideas, to be innovative, to push for new developments and to welcome new methods, although some of his ideas may still be a bit wild and his proposals lacking in control.

In other words the as yet incompletely matured high potential capacity applied to lower levels of work expresses itself in imaginativeness and creativity. The higher level of abstraction is there and can be observed, but it cannot yet be used in a full or reliable way; the judgment is still faulty. Thus, the potential Str-5 individual at 25 years of age can be seen to be able to detach himself from the concrete; that is how he achieves his initiative and his imaginativeness. The great industrial innovators were never bound down to a perceptual relationship with the concrete, even when employed as youths in starting positions as manual workers or clerks.

In short, a person's potential ability shows in the form of evidence of his level of abstraction applied at all stages in his working life. The maturation of his ability to use his level of abstraction consistently and reliably over a full range of activities takes place gradually with periodic developmental shifts forward across critical boundaries. With maturation and experience, the individual's work-capacity opens out and fills with usable information – eventually filling out to its fullest limits. The higher the capacity the longer into adulthood this filling-out process takes. In individuals of 10-year work-capacity and above, it is unlikely that the filling-out process is ever completed: maturation of work-capacity is still progressing until over-taken by senility or death.

Changes in Bureaucracy Induced by Internal Forces

The nature of the on-going dynamics of bureaucracy may be revealed if we put together: the capacity progression array; the postulate of discontinuity and development stages in work-capacity with critical boundaries at 3 months, 1 year, 2 years, 5 years, etc.; and the postulated stratification of bureaucratic hierarchies with boundaries at these same time-spans. This internal dynamic is a critical factor in determining the response of bureaucratic systems to external forces, and to the capacity of the system to adapt and change.

The capacity progression data sheets can be used as an instrument for amalgamating these postulates; for example, by plotting on them the age and current level of work of any particular groups or departments, or indeed, of the total population of a bureaucracy. Let us take as a first example a group of four relatively simple cases, especially selected because they are the most important types of situation in considering bureaucratic dynamics.

On the diagram are plotted the current ages and levels of work of the chief executives and their immediate groups of subordinates of four different bureaucratic systems. These examples are all taken from actual cases, but have been schematized for purposes of illustration. Many actual examples of a wide range of different situations are to be found in my *Progression Handbook*. How these plottings are made is also described in detail in that book.

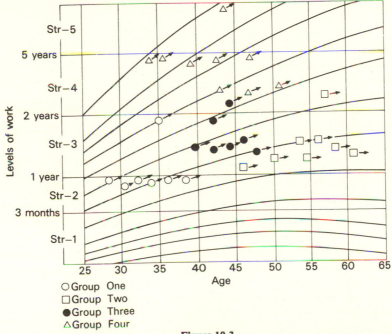

Figure 10.3

Group one shows a chief executive about to cross the boundary from Str-3 to Str-4, and his subordinate group all about to cross the Str-2/3 boundary. This pattern is predictably associated with growth by vertical extension. It is the so-called 'young and dynamic group' which will seek ways of extending the activities of the association, and will be growth-minded. Their philosophy will be that growth is good, that growth is essential for survival, that an enterprise either grows or it decays. What they will be unaware of is how much their rough and ready economic theory of the enterprise is but a reflection of their own growing capacities and a seeking to express that growth.

If the group succeeds in getting the necessary resources for growth – and unless it does it can be predicted that it will break up – the bureaucratic system it is managing will have to add another work-stratum. This process of vertical extension is a significant change: it requires what will be experienced as a reorganization. It involves much more than mere growth by lateral extension, in which more employees are added by increasing the size of existing managerial commands, or even by adding whole new departments. Consider what must happen.

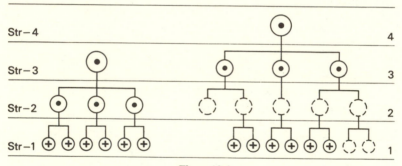

Figure 10.4

As the chief executive and his subordinate group each moves up one stratum (to Str-4 and Str-3), a managerial gap is left in Str-2. This gap must be filled, either by finding new managers from outside or by finding enough Str-1 members who are promotable. In either case, the remaining Str-1 members will find themselves with new managers interposed between themselves and their erstwhile managers. Moreover, the chief executive and his immediate subordinates must all learn how to operate at a new and higher level of abstraction.

This shift in which a Str-3 system moves up to become a Str-4 system is one which also lays the foundation for a very considerable expansion; an expansion which could encompass an increase of something of the order of ten times the activity and ten times the number of employees (say, from 200 up to 2000 if the activities of the system are labour intensive). The change is not just one more increase, it is a jump into a new and different scale of magnitude.

Group two shows a chief executive well established in the middle of Str-4 with subordinates well established in the middle of Str-3; each has reached his full potential level of abstraction and no further upward movement is likely. The philosophy of this group is most likely to be that economic stability is a good thing, and that consolidation and slow and regular adaptation make sound sense. Its outlook would be dubbed conservative. Under good conditions, such an enterprise – or indeed such a division within an enterprise – can continue successfully for years. It is simply not true that growth is always an essential ingredient of survival.

Group three shows a manager well established in the middle of Str-4 with subordinates in Str-3, one of whom is capable of moving across the Str-3/4 boundary but without there being a place for him to do so. This group would react in a manner similar to group two, except that the progressing subordinate would be attempting to stimulate change – or at some later stage (if he stayed) challenging the leadership of the manager. But the likelihood, given moderately full employment, would be that he would seek and find higher employment either in another department or division or in another enterprise.

Group four shows a chief executive about to cross the Str-5/6 boundary; half his subordinates are ready to cross the Str-4/5 boundary, the other half being older and well established in the middle of Str-4. Situations of this type are not uncommon. They lead to changes of the type described for group one, but with the complication that only half the subordinate group has the competence to move up. Requisitely, the top management group should be reconstituted by interposing a new group of subordinates between the chief executive and those of his subordinates who are unlikely to progress further. The trouble is that these circumstances are ordinarily not faced up to. There is a widespread taboo against talking openly about the fact that some members of a group of colleagues may outgrow the others. What usually happens is that the team is maintained, and those who are not up to the new situation become disorganized and suffer breakdown. They are then replaced in their roles. More requisite methods of dealing with such problems are described in Chapter 23.

Changes in Groups Inside Large Bureaucracies

These schematized cases used for illustration have concentrated on the top executive group, because the situation there impinges most heavily upon the bureaucratic system as a whole. But the same types of example may also be used to consider what happens in sections and departments within larger bureaucratic systems. The same phenomena may be observed, but affecting only that portion of the bureaucracy without necessarily making a strong impact upon the whole system (although the effects may resonate elsewhere).

When the internal situation is considered, there is, however, one additional feature worthy of note, and that is that different types of function will have different dynamic characteristics. In the diagram, for example, are illustrated the young university graduate members of a research department, a group of first-line managers in manufacturing and accounts and a group of works police and their manager.

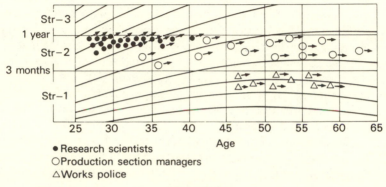

• Research scientists
○ Production section managers
△ Works police

Figure 10.5

The research group is rapidly moving towards and across the Str-2/3 boundary. The section managers are mainly moving within Str-2. And the works police are an older population who are moving through Str-1 and their manager through Str-2. The dynamics of these three situations are very different. The research group needs an active policy of rapid progression, followed either by promotion or by planned leaving. The section managers need steady progression, and some few need watching for promotion. But the work requires people of experience likely to remain in post for many years because it is necessary to have stability in managerial leadership over long periods of time in order to maintain production and accounting consistency. The works police also require a stable and trustworthy population of older men. The requisite, therefore, is to appoint top-level Str-1 staff at about the age of 40 whose capacity progression has flattened off, and thus to provide for staff in post till retirement after 25 years.

These few examples are meant only to set up a picture of bureaucratic systems as internally live and changing, as the occupants of the systems join, develop, change and leave. There is a continual ebb and flow, with stable periods, critical change periods, and then stability again for a period. At the same time different parts of the system change at different rates, as do the individual members of these parts of the system. These variations inevitably produce varying degrees of stress and conflict, not as a matter of pathology but simply as a reflection of the fact that human beings are alive.

Responses to External Forces

These few examples may illustrate how bureaucratic systems are constantly in greater or lesser flux from within through the developing capacities of
their members. These developments can never be absolutely in phase,
though some of the schematized examples may have given the impression
that they can be. In real life different members of a bureaucratic system are
developing at different rates, hitting boundaries at different times and with
different force. These differences produce stress as well as change in the
systems – the net effect being that bureaucratic systems are always to
greater or lesser degree under stress from within.[6]

How bureaucratic systems respond to external forces will also be very
much influenced by the internal situation I have described. The second
group in our example for instance, will attempt to take external changes in
its stride, accommodating and adjusting as it can and incorporating such
changes in service or goods provided, in technology, and in methods
generally, as can be absorbed without fundamentally restructuring the
system.

The first group, by contrast, will be looking for opportunities in the
external world, and will believe that in growing and reorganizing it is merely responding to the requirements of the environment. Even in the depression years there were great advances in scale of bureaucratic systems
through mergers and takeovers, although it could hardly be said that there
were economic pressures for growth.

Bureaucratic systems can also be changed by the employing authority.
Civil service departments, for example, are bureaucracies which *par
excellence* can be subject to massive changes as a result of changes in
governmental policies which make certain departments obsolete and call
for other new types of department to be established. The dynamics of this
kind of change, however, are tied up with the dynamics of governmental
processes and not with the dynamics of bureaucracy.

It may also be noted in passing that government departments and other
types of grant-income bureaucracy may at times continue for long periods
on an unchanging course with the same scale and content of activity. It is
often thought that in these circumstances such systems will inevitably
become 'bureaucratized' in the pejorative red-tape sense. Such an outcome
is not necessarily inevitable. Whether or not it does occur is likely to depend upon the internal dynamics of the system. Two factors in particular

[6] It ought to be possible, theoretically, to calculate these internal stresses at any point in
time. The calculation would consist of an analysis of the match or mismatch of work-
capacity and level of work of all the employees. Each point where employees were crossing
or had crossed boundaries would be known. Areas of the bureaucracy which were more or
less in balance could be distinguished from those areas of imbalance where a significant
number of employees were over- or under-employed.

may lead to trouble: the first is a tendency in stable departments to save expense by filling roles at salaries and at levels lower than are required for the work to be done; the second is the tendency to sub-divide levels of organization, giving longer and longer lines of command. Given a combination of these two factors, rigidification, red tape, impersonality and other monolithic features do then become practically inevitable.

Size of Population and Available Capacity Levels

There is a very general statistical implication of this hypothesis of stratification into a series of normally distributed sub-populations which warrants examination. If one is dealing with the same phenomenon but in populations of different size, the larger populations may be expected to throw up a longer tail on the distribution curve, whereas the smaller population throws up statistical sports – occasional outstanding individuals with no telling whether they will be replaced or at what level.

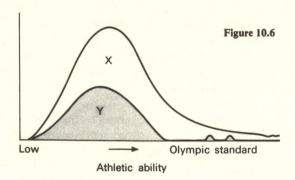

Figure 10.6

This phenomenon is illustrated in the diagram, which depicts, say, the athletic ability of two nations – X with, say, 250 million people, and Y with 5 million people. Country X will throw up a population of potential Olympic medal winners in many fields. Country Y may throw up occasional Olympic winners in one or other field, but it will never be possible to predict when or in which field. In other words, country X has a population large enough to provide succession at these higher levels, whereas country Y has not. In this same way, small nations occasionally throw up world leaders of world stature but large nations do so regularly.

This statistical finding can be applied to our analysis of bureaucratic systems. The diagram shows a series of sub-populations of decreasing size to represent the populations capable of working at successive work-strata. Three distributions are conjectured, for countries P, Q, and R with populations of 10 million, 50 million, and 250 million respectively.

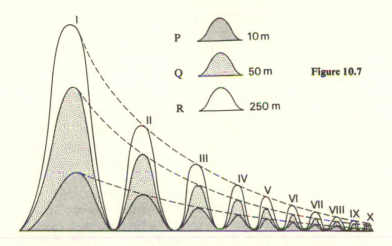

Figure 10.7

P   10 m
Q   50 m
R   250 m

For purposes of illustration, population P provides succession up to Str-6, Q up to Str-7, and R up to Str-8. With such an assumption it would be expected that if all three countries were fully industrialized, then P might be able to sustain several enterprises employing Str-6 bureaucracies with leadership from among its own nationals, Q would be able to sustain a number of Str-7 bureaucracies, while R would be able to sustain a number of Str-8 bureaucracies. None of the countries would be able to sustain enterprises with bureaucracies at higher levels, because none or them can provide succession at those higher levels – only occasional sports.

These examples have in fact not been chosen entirely at random. They represent Holland, the United Kingdom, and the United States. Superficial analysis of these three countries serves to show that Holland can sustain a fair number of Str-6 bureaucracies, but when it comes to Str-7 bureaucracies they must go into joint ventures and establish joint boards with Str-6 companies in other countries (for example, Unilever and Shell). The United Kingdom sustains a fair number of Str-7 bureaucracies, and, in order to take part in Str-8 bureaucracies, must co-operate, by means of mergers, with Str-7 organizations in other countries.

The United States, by contrast, is able to sustain a number of super-corporations on a national basis with Str-8 bureaucracies – most of which have become multi-national. Indeed, it is one of the main stated aims of the Common Market to provide – as a result of having a population of over 250 million – a base for the development of corporations of a magnitude to compete world-wide with American (and, increasingly, Russian) super-corporations. The foundation for such corporations lies not only in size of domestic market (the explicit EEC argument) but also in size of population needed to sustain managerial leadership of these very high, Str-8, levels of bureaucracy.

These conjectures can and will in due course be tested. The analysis is not too difficult. And indeed, other predictions also may follow; for example, that nations like China and India, if they become fully industrialized and if they retain the character of single nations, will throw up and sustain super-super enterprises, with Str-9 bureaucracies of a kind represented by the merger of two or three of the current largest multi-nationals. The Str-9 leadership necessary to sustain the bureaucratic systems of such enterprises would be of very long time-spans of work-capacity, longer than the life-time of the individual. But that would mean only that the managerial leadership would never themselves carry through the longest of their development operations. They might start them but others would have to finish. This fact need occasion no surprise, for individuals with such long time-spans have probably always existed as statistical sports. By and large, they tend to be called geniuses[7] – a concept which may be defined as a person with a time-span capacity longer than his life span, and who therefore is always growing and developing a lifetime's work but must bear the constant frustration of being aware that he may never see the completion of what he has started.[8]

Innate and Environmental Factors in Work-Capacity

Finally, there are two questions with sensitive political overtones which must be faced in connection with the postulate of a natural process of growth and development of the work-capacity of individuals. The first has to do with whether a person's work-capacity is a biological given, something fixed at birth and immutable, or whether, on the contrary, it is a flexible quality influenced by social background and opportunities which can be developed and increased by education. Associated with this first question is an ancillary question of whether a person's work-capacity can be measured. These questions are sensitive because they raise the issue of whether an implicit and unwarranted elitism is being imported into our analysis of bureaucracy – an elitism deriving from the postulated connection between stratification of human capacity and stratification in work systems, and therefore with inevitable socio-economic inequality deriving from the differential economic rewards to be obtained from work at different bureaucratic levels.

[7] I have elaborated this notion in (1970) 'Time and the Measurement of Human Attributes'.
[8] There may, of course, occasionally occur an abnormally high concentration of geniuses in nations with small populations. Under these conditions, as Alfred Kroeber wrote, '. . . the highest aesthetic and intellectual achievements in history occur(red) in temporary bursts of growth, as indicated by the clusterings of geniuses in space and time.' A. L. Kroeber (1944), *Configurations of Culture Growth*. The point about these bursts of growth is the existence of a statistically improbable number of geniuses at the same time, but without succession because of the size of the population from which they come.

The nature versus nurture question is one on which I have no occasion to have a very strong view in either direction but on which the data suggest a particular slant. The data are derived from adults in employment in industrial societies. They suggest that certainly by the age of 20 or 25 the level and pattern of development of a person's work-capacity have been fixed.[9] From there on, it is postulated, the course of development can be predicted from the curves in the capacity progression array.

It may be, however, that the discontinuity hypothesis provides a sounder framework within which the nature/nurture argument may be considered. This hypothesis, with its associated conception of stratification into levels of abstraction, makes it possible to separate out two critical questions. The first question is whether the level of abstraction – the stratum within which a person functions – is constitutionally set; the second question is whether position within the level of abstraction is constitutionally set.

In order to establish a likely postulate about the answer to these questions, let us consider some of the issues. It ought to be possible to assess work-capacity in very young children, indeed perhaps in infants. What would be required would be observations on the ability of the child to handle frustration or delayed gratification for given periods of time. The earlier the age and the longer the periods that delayed gratification can be tolerated, the higher the work-capacity.[10] It would not be inordinately daring to postulate observable wide differences in young children in this respect; preliminary studies in nursery school children have given strong support to this hypothesis.[11]

That work-capacity in very early childhood would be a good predictor of work-capacity in adult life – regardless of family setting, schooling or

[9] I must here emphasize one point, for I find I have often been misunderstood: I do not mean that every individual always achieves the level of work and earnings he deserves – that is to say, a level consistent with his work-capacity. Nor, similarly, do I mean that it is possible to assess a person's work-capacity from the employment role he occupies and the salary he earns. The work-capacity of the individual, the time-span of discretion in the role he occupies, and the salary he earns, are independent variables. Each must be analysed in its own right. My analysis is concerned to show the conditions under which these three variables may be experienced as in satisfactory balance, to show the symptoms which accompany various degrees of imbalance, and, most important, to show how social arrangements may be created which give the maximum chance of providing satisfaction and opportunity for the individual and benefit to society.

[10] D. Stenhouse (1974), *The Evolution of Intelligence*.

[11] Lewin, and his colleagues Barker and Dembo, have described this phenomenon in young children (R. Barker, T. Dembo and K. Lewin (1945), 'Frustration and Regression'). As Lewin states: 'The infant lives essentially in the present. His goals are immediate goals; when he is distracted, he "forgets" quickly. As he grows older, more and more of his past and future affect his mood and action.' (K. Lewin (1942), 'Time Perspective and Morale'.) The hypothesis is currently being tested as part of a more general research at Brunel University into work-capacity and its development.

work – would be a slightly more controversial postulate, however, but one which it would nevertheless be useful to make and to test. Such an exercise would require a long-term study. Reconstructions back from adulthood would be extremely difficult if not impossible.

The reason why work-capacity is likely to pursue a regular course of development regardless of circumstances is that we are dealing here not merely with the ability to learn in school or to handle materials used in schools, as is the case with intelligence testing. We are dealing with the person-in-action and his ability to handle his primary plane of reality. Real life provides every day opportunity for this encounter in work of some kind. It is to expected, therefore, that if it becomes possible to measure work-capacity,[12] everyone will be seen to have received a good deal of op- portunity to exercise his own level of capacity – whether in an industrial society, an agricultural society, or a primitive tribal society.

One opportunity for testing this hypothesis would be in studies of the populations of the so-called developing nations. There is evidence that, when sudden opportunities have arisen for local populations to take over control of their own government, civil service and enterprises, there have been individuals ready to take over high time-span positions. Their work- capacity had already developed through dealing with their work situations in their occupations and in their families. Some training might have been needed. But such training assists a person to use his capacity in relation to particular technologies; it does not increase innate capacity.

In the light of the foregoing considerations, it would also be reasonable to postulate that a person's eventual level of abstraction is innately deter- mined. Ordinary life experience should provide plenty of opportunity for this innate level of abstraction to mature, and the particular type of oppor- tunity is unlikely to make much difference.[13]

A person's eventual level of work-capacity *within* a given level of abstraction, however, might well be influenced by experience and oppor- tunity. Early childhood experience and education might enable him to reach a higher point in a given level of abstraction than he might have done without that experience and education. If this postulate could be verified, it would provide considerable scope for education and for individual development and would not in effect be forcing everyone into his 'proper place'.

In short, work-capacity may prove to be innate as far as level of abstrac- tion is concerned, but influenced by environmental factors within the limits

---

[12] Any such tests will of course have to be problem-solving performance tests and not verbal tests or tests based primarily upon the use of verbal skill.

[13] Unless of course a child were subject to severe and crippling mental disturbance, in which case I would expect inhibition of the development of the child's capacities, although there would still be signs of the talent potential which was disturbed or destroyed by illness.

for a given level. Does this assumption, however, not limit each person to a future in which he is slotted into a particular station in life? Is it not really a reactionary feudal type of outlook?

This type of question confuses two issues — the nature of the individual and the nature of social institutions. Feudalism, used in a pejorative sense, and reactionary social systems, are reactionary not because they seem to assume innate qualities in individuals by an elitist assigning of each one to his proper station in life. They are reactionary because they use mechanistic criteria such as family, race, or religion, to assign these statuses within the society or indeed to outlaw groups from the society. And they use these mechanistic criteria, falsely, as evidence of personal characteristics in the individual.

To say that individuals are born with different constitutions, different endowments, different capacities, is a far cry from saying that all members of a particular social class, or race, or religion, possess certain superior or inferior characteristics. It is to aver only that there are constitutionally determined individual characteristics, and that environmental factors can have some effect upon an individual's development, but not an unlimited effect.

Indeed the burden of the argument is to emphasize the great importance of social institutions for the individual. For if it is true that, as a result of everyday experience, most individuals will mature to that level of abstraction with which they have been innately endowed, it becomes an even more critical issue to provide abundant employment in industrial societies. The likelihood is that there are still large numbers of people with innate capacities higher than their level of work but who are working as, say, Str-1 manual or clerical workers because of their working-class backgrounds and lack of education and opportunity. Their capacity will have matured despite their work careers. They will be understandably bitter and disillusioned because they are intuitively aware that they are leading a life of under-employment and lack of fulfilment. Advancement to higher levels of work with special training or job enlargement opportunities ought to be readily available to such individuals.[14]

Indeed, the postulates would have implications for the design and interpretation of many of the studies of effects of social background upon individual development. Some of these studies might also be useful for testing the foregoing hypotheses. If, for example, the postulate about the innateness of level of abstraction were true, evidence for this ought to come to light in studies such as those carried out by Basil Bernstein and his colleagues on language development in children from working-class and

---

[14] I have described in (1961) *Equitable Payment* cases of men of 45 years of age and older able to cope with rapid advancement and promotion after years of languishing in levels of work below their capacity, when chance opportunities have arisen for them to move into roles at higher levels.

middle-class families.[15] There ought to be evidence, for example, that it is the children in capacity group I who — regardless of whether they are from working-class or middle-class families — absorb the concrete linguistic modes characteristic of working-class communication patterns. Equally, children from either working-class or middle-class backgrounds who are in capacity Group II or higher ought to manifest the ability to use the more abstract linguistic modes which are described as characterizing middle-class communication patterns. Unless work-capacity can be measured, studies such as Bernstein's have an uncontrolled and floating variable which may be of critical importance. Measurement of IQ is not an adequate substitute, for reasons described in the previous chapter.[16]

We have argued from the structure of bureaucratic hierarchies to the existence of a stratified structure of the work-capacity needed to do work. It is precisely by recognizing differences in individuals, and being able to identify them, that a society can accomplish two important social ends: first, it can arrange social procedures to make it possible for everyone to gain a level of work and career consistent with his work capacity; and second, it can bring political power and legislative control to bear to ensure that bureaucracy is managed in a manner consistent with the political outlook of the society, including determination by political means of the distribution of the socio-economic rewards of bureaucratic work. Thus, whether or not bureaucratic organization would lead to economic elitism would be a political decision, and certainly not an inevitable consequence of the present analysis.

Social understanding, like any other kind of understanding, does not produce any particular outcome. Outcomes have to do with how understanding is used and applied, and that must always remain a matter of human judgment. That judgment will be expressed in the final analysis in social policy determined by political means, and is not a matter to be determined by technocracy or scientific robotism. The scientific problem is to ensure that our understanding is valid and reliable, so as to inform political judgment and not to mislead it.

[15] B. Bernstein (1971), *Class, Codes and Control.*
[16] The measurement of work-capacity may soon become possible as a result of the work of Isaac, O'Connor and Stamp to which I have referred earlier. The break-through has, I believe, come with the assumption of discontinuity, multi-modality and stratification, as against the more usual assumption of continuity and uni-modality. Experimental work is being pursued to develop methods for determining not absolute work-capacity scores but rather the level of abstraction at which an individual is potentially capable of functioning.

PART FOUR

SOCIAL JUSTICE AND
BUREAUCRATIC EMPLOYMENT

11

The Right to Abundant Employment and Individual Opportunity

In view of the emotionally charged nature of work, and in view of the fact that in industrial societies almost the sole opportunity for work is in bureaucratic systems, it is essential that the basic rights and duties of employees in bureaucracies should be specified and agreed. The issue is that of the rights of the individual in a situation which without satisfactory protection of rights contributes to anomie and to alienation.

Rights must be balanced by duties, and *vice versa*. The duties of employees have generally been clear enough. Employees are bound by the employment contract to carry out the agreed work within the agreed conditions of service. The conditions of service have, however, been much too narrowly drawn from the point of view of the essential rights of employees. These conditions are a hangover from nineteenth-century employment contracts between master and servant, and are in certain major respects irrelevant to bureaucratic employment with its complex managerial structures and large-scale labour market.

There are four basic rights of employees that must requisitely be taken for granted in every employment system if bureaucracy is to be humane and creative. The efficiency of the organization, the satisfaction of the individual, and societal equilibrium depend upon them.[1] The proper application of these rights will be seen to depend upon the existence of a structure of manager-subordinate relationships such that every employee has a full-scale manager at one-stratum distance and every manager has full-scale subordinates.

These four basic rights of employees in an industrialized democracy are:

1. the right to abundant employment and individual opportunity;
2. the right to participation in the control of changes in policy in the employing organization;
3. the right to equitable reward;
4. the right to individual appeal against decisions which are felt to be unfair or unjust.

These rights might be argued in a moral, political, philosophical or

[1] Preliminary statements of these basic rights will be found in my paper (1970) 'The Human Consequences of Industrialization'; and in W. Brown (1973), *The Earnings Conflict*.

religious sense. They will be presented here, however, as one part of our analysis of requisite organization. Failure to provide these conditions gives rise to social pathology, the symptoms of which are predictable. Some of these symptoms are considered along with the procedures necessary for establishing the four basic rights and making them real.

The Meaning of Abundant Employment

The question of the rights of employees arises because work is a positive and necessary human activity. It is not a negative process, something unpleasant as opposed to leisure which is pleasant, or something a person is forced to do as opposed to something he likes to do, as is so commonly assumed. Indeed, a person's use of his time in his occupation and in his leisure activities are both work – they are both creative aspects of living and of being. The more a person's occupation accords with his interests and his capacity, the less it feels like 'work' in the pejorative sense. It is when in their occupation there is dissatisfaction and frustration that people try to shorten the working week to as near zero as possible, and to increase leisure time in which they have more opportunity to function at whatever level they choose.

The first right to be satisfied, therefore, is the right of abundant employment; that is to say, the right of every individual who takes up employment work to be able to find work reasonably in line with his interests and experience and at a level consistent with his capacity. This right must be fulfiled by the provision of a buoyant employment situation in the nation. It cannot be fulfilled by any one enterprise.

No individual can expect the enterprise in which he is employed to provide him with just the right post for him at each stage in his career. He may sometimes have to move from one enterprise to another to find the employment he desires; or in the case of very large enterprises, from one division to another. Genuine freedom to move does not exist, however, unless there is a buoyant employment situation sufficient to allow everyone who seeks employment to be employed at full stretch.

A nice balance must be maintained. There must be sufficient employment available for everyone to be able to seek and find his own level. But there must not be such abundance of employment that no enterprise can settle down to get its work done without having to bribe its employees to stay, or somehow hold on to them by other illicit and anti-social means.

Since no single enterprise can guarantee fully to employ the growing capacities of all its employees, then society must do so. Abundant employment is a requisite condition of any industrial society precisely because the livelihood of over three-quarters of the people in industrial societies depends upon earnings gained in employment in bureaucratic hierarchies.

A society whose work is organized in bureaucratic hierarchies is in for trouble if it cannot guarantee appropriate work in them for everyone.

In an industrial society the right of abundant employment is nothing less than the right to be a human being in contact with reality. Any society which does not provide it is not entitled to call itself civilized. It is socially utterly destructive to argue that modern technology and mass production methods may preclude appropriate work for everyone in the interest of the provision of goods in plenitude. The technological problem of an enlightened society is to create a production technology which is not only economic but which provides a balance of work roles suited to the spread of talent and ability of the population at any given time.

Under-employment and Boredom

The consequences of the under-employment of the capacities of individuals wishing for the chance to work at full capacity are readily observable. So too are the consequences of over-employment — that is to say, employment at a level of work above the work-capacity of the individual. Let us consider each in turn.

The first and outstanding feature of under-employment is boredom. There is no work at any level which is inherently boring. Boredom is the response of a person whose level of work-capacity is too high for the work he is employed to do. Too often when one person looks at another's work and finds it boring, all he means is that he would himself find it boring because it is below his own level of work-capacity. Thus, boredom and monotony occur at any and all levels of work. The most senior employees of organizations, right up to and including the chief executive, will become bored with their work if it is below their level of work-capacity.

With boredom and monotony come restlessness, resentment and despair — feelings which can be alleviated only by giving the individual opportunity to move to another position in which he is more likely to make use of his work-capacity. Denied such opportunity, a person will frequently seek outlets in other activities either inside or outside the organization. Some of the most competent and effective shop stewards, for example, are individuals of higher work-capacity than their employment demands, but through identification with the working class or because of barriers to higher employment, they remain in lower-level work posts and use their full work-capacity in their representative activities. This statement must not be taken to mean that everyone who takes part in activities outside his work is under-employed. Far from it. It is only to say that under-employed individuals may seek to compensate in other activities for their boredom at work. People seek a more or less varied range of activity. The shop steward or staff representative example is the prototype in the sense that, through being a shop steward or representative, a person under-employed in his employment role can find not only a compensating activity but an activity at a satisfactorily high level which often allows him to be away from his work role for hours at a time on trade union and representative activities.

Long periods of under-employment – or indeed a career of under-employment – can lead to a chronic semi-depressed resignation in people and a lack of conscious awareness of their true capacity.[2] Somewhere inside something tells the individual that he is capable of greater things, but he hardly believes it. It is not till some shaking event occurs which forces him out of his groove that he allows himself to realize his capabilities. The shake-up of a war, or massive reorganization, or long-term absence of one's manager, are the kinds of event which throw up such opportunities.[3] Without this kind of opportunity the individual may continue in his chronic state of torpor. Whole communities can be forced into such a state by chronic under-employment or unemployment. Initiative is lost. It eventually becomes exceedingly difficult to regain it.

There is one circumstance in which an individual may choose under-employment; that is under piecework or other individual bonus schemes. For one of the features of a person's being employed at a level below his capacity is that he can do the work more rapidly than a person of the right capacity can. He works more rapidly not by increased pace but by applying his ability for higher level of abstraction to organize his work better and to overcome flaps and crises. He can thus often defeat the bonus scheme and earn an artificially inflated income, higher than the income he could have earned even at a level of work consistent with his work-capacity. Very high piecework earners tend to come into this category.

But this type of bonus earning is soul-destroying. The *Modern Times* caricature of the industrial worker-cum-automaton is a representation of the high-capacity low-level-of-work human production machine turning out as much as he can so that he can get as much money as possible while the going is good.

Goldthorpe and Lockwood (1968) in *The Affluent Worker* describe the effects upon automobile workers in England of employment below their work-capacity. Work becomes instrumental – a tolerable means of earning enough money to buy the good things of modern life – but basically unsatisfying in itself. However, just because some manual workers express such an instrumental interest in work, it does not necessarily follow as a generalization that manual work can be nothing more than instrumental,

---

[2] As Kurt Lewin has observed: 'Studies in unemployment show how a long-drawn-out idleness affects all parts of a person's life. Thrown out of a job, the individual tries to keep hoping. When he finally gives up, he frequently restricts his action much more than he has to.' K. Lewin (1942), 'Time Perspective and Morale', p. 103.

[3] See, for example, E. Jaques (1961), *Equitable Payment*, Chapter 11.

that it can have no inherent interest, that it is inevitably boring, that it can only be an activity undertaken under sufferance in order to live.

The *Affluent Worker* is a good example of social research workers' taking their own pejorative attitude to manual work and attributing that attitude to manual workers. In fact there is not necessarily a low level of work in manual tasks. It depends on how the tasks are organized, as the Volvo Company in Sweden are demonstrating with their job enlargement programmes in which operators have the opportunity to organize how they do their work. Contrariwise, the automotive industry in the United States and Great Britain is a good example of how an industry can come to dominate whole communities by carrying mass production techniques excessively far and setting a distribution of work roles at too low a level for the population.

This problem is not of course limited to the automotive industry. The process of standardization has gone too far in other types of industry and, equally important, in many types of office work. Accounting and invoicing procedures, documentation and filing and related types of clerical work, routine types of test (laboratory, mathematical and others) all contribute to the production of more roles with time-spans of less than a day than there are people with ability limited to that level.

Given the same rewards, a person will gravitate to a role that gives him satisfaction in the sense of being a challenge to his abilities rather than merely providing him with the same reward for a level of work which is below his abilities. And if society provides abundant employment, and an individual still prefers to remain in a role with boring work below his abilities, then society can at least claim to have discharged its obligations to the individual as far as work is concerned.

Over-employment and Anxiety

To emphasize the fact that an imbalance between a person's capacity and his level of work produces symptoms of anxiety or disquiet, and to sharpen the picture of the consequences of under-employment, we may also look at what happens to individuals when they are employed at a level of work beyond their capacity – that is to say, when the time-span of the tasks in the role is longer than the individual can cope with.

The effect on the individual can be disastrous. He becomes overwhelmed by the mass of detail which he is unable to organize because he is unable to deal with it conceptually in categories. He is not able to construct the project or the context that will enable him to group and thus control the details. It is a source of distress to the individual to experience this situation, and if he is a manager, even more distressing to those whom he manages and those with whom he works, to watch his difficulties. He tries to control the work by clutching at details. He finds it exceptionally difficult to delegate tasks to his subordinates since he cannot set an appropriately broad framework within which they can work.

He therefore seems continually to be doing everything himself. He is involved in too much detail, leaving for his subordinates a host of tasks that are in turn much below their capacity. He is a chronic bottleneck, keeping to himself many activities which his subordinates could readily deal with on his behalf but which he cannot delegate because he is unable to construct an adequate controlling framework of prescribed limits. If his subordinates have the capacity to carry their own established roles they will find themselves under-employed. For the manager will be breaking tasks into too small pieces for delegation. Intense frustration results.

The department subordinate to the manager suffers from constriction. The forward planning necessary to keep the section at its existing level or to enable it to grow simply does not occur. Everything is on too short a time-scale. The organization shrinks and withers. Subordinates may be blamed and used as scapegoats. Lack of work or support may be blamed. The over-employed individual tends to blame everyone and everything but himself – to recognize and admit publicly his own shortage of capacity for his role is too grave a threat to public identity and self-esteem.

Is Widespread Under-employment Inevitable?

These situations may be sufficiently familiar to need no further elaboration. They may serve to indicate how serious can be the effects of a mismatch between work-capacity and level of work. But how serious then is it for governments to employ economic policies which produce or increase unemployment: or even to use unemployment itself as one of the techniques for attempting to control cost-push inflation – in the jargon, to help to cool the economy?

Even so-called marginal unemployment weakens the total employment situation by acting as a force in the direction of spreading under-employment among those who are at work; thus, for example, 5 per cent unemployment ends up as 5 per cent under-employment for those who do have jobs. With significant levels of unemployment the spread and degree of under-employment becomes correspondingly serious. For with unemployment it becomes more difficult for an individual to find a position at the appropriate level, or to change to a position at a higher level if he is already under-employed. The greater the unemployment the greater the difficulty.

Nevertheless, much pessimism surrounds the possibility in modern industrial societies of ensuring the abundant employment that is necessary to guarantee individual opportunity. Mass-production methods are said to require such intense specialization and de-skilling of work that the many will simply have to suffer more or less boredom and monotony at work in order that all may receive the compensatory benefits of the accompanying economic security and affluence. Alan Fox gives thoughtful expression to this view of the consequences of the division of labour. He argues that modern industrial organization requires a plethora of low-discretion roles on grounds of economic efficiency and that these low-discretion roles tend to be low-trust inducing. Economic exchange relations are seen as submerging the high-trust inducing social and moral exchange relations. 'Here and there particular groups may ... be led by technological or organizational change to adopt a marginally more diffuse perspective towards their work, supervision and higher management. But the probabilities of the temper and tenor of the whole society being fundamentally changed by tactics such as these seem small indeed.'[4] 'In sum, then a wholesale transformation of industrial society, structurally geared as it is to a complex set of interdependent institutions, expectations, and values shaped predominantly by the principles of low-trust economic exchange, would involve adjustments and adaptations totally beyond our power to cope with even given the (in practice inconceivable) condition of a mass political will. For good or ill, according to the point of view, there can be no reversion to the small-scale operations, handicrafts, and local markets which would constitute the most fruitful structural context for high-trust roles and relations.'[5]

In these passages Fox expresses succinctly two important and widely held views, both of which I believe to be wrong: one, that low-discretion roles are inherently anti-requisite; and two, that handicrafts and other small-scale operations must inevitably provide better opportunities for people than mass production work could possibly do. It is precisely these two propositions which must be questioned, for if they are valid, then industrial society is certainly in for chronic trouble.

There is no such thing as an inherently too high- or too low-discretion role. The question is whether the level of discretion which obtains in a role matches the level of ability of the incumbent. If it does, then it is neither high nor low but in balance; and the individual will experience the corresponding sense of equilibrium, of satisfaction, in the core region of his self-identity. It therefore becomes a central task of any democratic society to guarantee a distribution of level of work in its bureaucratic systems which matches the distribution of capacity in the population: the availability of such a distribution of level of work is the sign of abundant employment.

[4] A. Fox (1974), *Beyond Contract*, p. 353.
[5] A. Fox, op. cit., p. 355.

Given the existence of abundant employment, there is no need to go hankering after the yesteryears of the guild craftsman and the small-scale operations, handicrafts and local markets. On the contrary, bureaucratic systems can provide outlets for the full expression of individual skill and ability. The social problem is to ensure that every individual has the opportunity to do so: that is why an abundant-employment economy is crucial.

There is no economic reason why abundant-employment economies cannot be created and sustained. Abundance of employment occurs, indeed, in any successful economy.[6] The accompanying problem, of course, is to contain the wage-and-salary-push inflationary force which occurs in such circumstances. That problem could be overcome by the construction of institutions to ensure an equitable differential distribution of income, as will be shown later in Chapter 25.

The Impact of Automation and Rationalization

It may of course still be argued that even with abundant employment the process of rationalization and automation will go on under the pressure of technological advance and so continue to throw up an excess of roles at levels below the level of competence of the population. Widespread under-employment would thus be maintained at the manual-worker end of the spectrum. I have given careful attention to this view, held as it is by so many distinguished authors,[7] but can find no evidence to support the idea of the inevitability of this process.

Indeed, the evidence tends to refute the argument that specialization must inevitably proceed to the point where work becomes dehumanizing and ego-constricting. This argument overlooks the fact that a practical production technology must be designed or rationalized in relation to the available work force. In an abundant employment situation employees will, if they so wish, be able to move to roles at levels consistent with their work-capacity and away from under-employment. The designers of production technology will be forced to adapt, in such circumstances, in two ways: first, they can absorb the very lowest levels of discretion into the machine by automated technology, leaving the higher levels of discretion or entirely new types of discretion to the operator;[8] second, they can design the discretionary content of technology to match and attract the necessary labour force.

[6] Recent and current experiences in West Germany, Sweden and Switzerland demonstrate this fact.

[7] R. Blauner (1964), *Alienation and Freedom*; R. K. Merton (1957), 'Bureaucratic Structure and Personality'; and W. E. Moore (1963), *Social Change*.

[8] Blauner has described how operators in the chemical industry talk of the newly automated plant in terms of 'I control the machine.' (R. Blauner (1964), *Alienation and Freedom*.)

The first of these adaptive mechanisms – elimination of very low levels of work by automation – is familiar. The second has been less recognized but is equally common. The design of production technology and of office technology to allow for higher or lower levels of work, is much more flexible than seems ordinarily to be realized. Recent developments in so-called job enlargement or job enrichment have made this possible flexibility more apparent. The local availability of abundant employment opportunities can be a strong stimulus to designers of production methods. It can concentrate their attention wonderfully upon the task of providing efficient production systems containing roles which will attract the necessary employees because they provide levels of work attractive to those employees.

If as one of the effects of rationalization the number of employment roles is reduced in a given locality, then conditions must be provided to adjust for the loss. If an industrial society is to continue to gain economic security and affluence by the use of bureaucratic employment systems, then it is essential that that society makes work available in bureaucracies at local level for all who want such work – whether by governmental provision of advantages to attract employers or by direct investment in government-financed work. In such a manner bureaucratic opportunity may serve to reinforce and secure the personal identity of individuals and the existence of a sound local community, rather than to weaken personal identity and the fabric of community relations by causing unexpected and undesired local unemployment and economic distress. It is simply no use hoping community ties will somehow strengthen if human dignity and self-esteem are destroyed because the essential economic underpinning of community life is constantly at risk and socio-economic continuity cannot be reasonably assured.

Certainly unemployment is non-requisite and unacceptable for what it does to people, for the economic insecurity it brings, for the wastage of human capacity. It also forces upon society the less noticed under-employment phenomenon. This under-employment undermines a society and saps its strength. Requisite procedures and the avoidance of societal imbalance call for a continually buoyant economy and full employment. Socialist planning makes this possible – but the cost is the loss of opportunity for individual entrepreneurial initiatives and risk. Capitalist societies gain the freedom for more or less individual enterprise, but manipulate the employment situation. The requisite solution requires getting the best of both these worlds. I shall reserve for the final chapters a fuller analysis of how requisitely organized bureaucracy might help towards this end.

12
The Right to Participate in the Control of Change

One of the great issues in the management of bureaucratic systems has to do with the rights of employees to participate in the control of these systems. Participation has been given many different meanings, but one common thread runs through all of them: the power exercised in these systems must be authorized and legitimated by resting on consensus if it is to be effective. The general theme is that of the legitimation of power and its transformation into authority.

Employee participation will be defined as the right of employees collectively to take part in the control of any changes whatever which they feel might adversely affect their future employment opportunities as a group. In the long run no industrial society will be able to survive in democratic form if its bureaucratic sector is not firmly planted in employee consensus.

Four main types of participative arrangement will be critically examined. First, the common type of advisory joint consultation. Second, so-called participative management and functionally autonomous work groups. Third, the currently popular but abortive conception of workers' directors. Fourth, the syndicalist type of arrangement associated with workers' councils in Yugoslavia and the small industrial units of the Israeli kibbutzim.

Each of these arrangements is unsatisfactory because of a failure to differentiate adequately between the employing association, the bureaucratic hierarchy and the associations formed by employees. In so doing, all these arrangements fail to give attention to the realities of the power relationships and social conflict between the employing and employee associations as interacting power groups.

In the next chapter the Glacier Project experience will be used to establish the main conditions essential to allow for adequate employee participation. These conditions will be described in terms of constitutional arrangements to be created to mediate the relationship between employing association and the associations formed by employees.

The Significance of Employee Participation

The meaning of participation was best summed up by John Locke when he wrote in *Two Treatises of Government* that 'participation in the making of laws is essential for consciously willed adherence to those laws.' To exclude people from taking part in policy-making, to impose policies or policy changes upon them, is a sure way to court rejection of those policies or changes. Participation is thus intimately associated with belongingness and alienation. For a person to have a sense of belongingness requires the opportunity to belong. The opportunity to belong calls for the right to have a say in what goes on which will affect him. Without that right he will feel alienated.

Participation has to do with the right to take part in the control of change by taking part in formulating and agreeing new policies or modifications to existing ones. It is this control of the setting – the rules and limits – within which social relationships will be carried on (within which the social structure will function) that is so very important. It is important not so much for any immediate effect upon output or productivity: there is little evidence to support the notion that the introduction of opportunities to participate will act as a form of incentive scheme. Opportunity for participation is an essential element for the survival of democratic industrial society itself.

The lack of the right to participate in the control of the policies which affect groups – whether or not this right would be exercised if it did exist – is intensely paranoiagenic. Without the right, one group can be subject to coercion by another. A society which provides for such coercion to occur is a society which thereby makes the acts of one group potentially unacceptable to other groups. All acts in such circumstances are therefore suspect until proven otherwise. Role relationships become clogged with suspicion and mistrust, regardless of the personal motives and integrity of the individuals involved. The quality of social exchange is undermined.

It is necessary only to consider a continuation of industrial society without such opportunities for employees to participate in the control of change, to become aware of the gravity of the issue. Anywhere from 70 to 90 per cent of the working population would continue to spend some 40 hours per week in bureaucratic systems *all their working lives* without a proper say in what their lives were to be like in those systems! Trouble would gradually build up as a result of unacceptable imposed policies experienced as unwarranted coercion.

Folkways, Policies, and Social Change

In considering this issue of participation it should be recognized that not all policies need to be made explicit. In any effectively functioning society the operation of the bureaucratic sector will rest upon the normal folkways of that society. Most of the content of policies and of role relationships in bureaucratic systems can thus be taken for granted: the normally expected modes of speech and of address; ordinary courtesies; allowances in work for personal or family difficulties; degree of trust and confidence; tolerance of security measures; expectations of continuation of work in the absence of direct supervision; style of exercise of authority; acceptable minor perquisites. All these are learned as part of the established processes of socialization.

Most social change takes place in terms of a gradual and unrecognized moulding and remoulding of this on-going flow of folkways. These changes do not need identification and formulation. Indeed, to formulate them disturbs the unexpressed underlay of social relationships. It rigidifies what should be a malleable and flexible social process spontaneously carried through at the level of unconscious mentation in the individuals involved.

There are at least two conditions, however, in which folkways by themselves can no longer be relied upon, and in which explicit policies become necessary. The process is the same as that described by Sumner with respect to the formulation and transformation of various aspects of folkways into explicit law.[1] The first condition is where changes in environmental circumstances or in attitudes and outlook call for adaptation and changes in behaviour which have not been established as part of the ordinary process of socialization. The second is where the changes are of an order which creates new conditions which are controversial and would arouse conflict.

Under such conditions, where intuitive adaptation of folkways will not suffice to cope with change, explication of policy is necessary. Relevant parts must be picked out from the flow of relationships, abstracted and made concrete by means of verbal formulation, and held constant like small visible peaks of a huge iceberg. Once the proposed changes have been made explicit, participation in the sense of negotiation and debate becomes possible.

The gradual adaptation of folkways depends upon there being no developing conditions which are unacceptable to any significant power groups which may be affected. There may be imperfections and short-comings, but that will not matter so long as they are consensually acceptable. If these power groups do not have the constitutionally established right to take part in debating the unacceptable changes and in negotiating modifications until the changes are no longer unacceptable, all changes will tend to feel coercive. Suspicion and mistrust will increase. The effect will be that the folkways themselves will be poisoned by suspicion, and social relationships will have to become governed by explicit rules and regulations to an increasingly harassing degree. Spontaneity in

[1] W. G. Sumner (1959), *Folkways*.

relationships will be choked off. It is the situation commonly described as becoming entangled in red tape.

Unresolved conflicts do not disappear. They may remain walled off for a time because one or other group does not feel sufficiently powerful to do anything about them. But they fester, they coalesce; they build up into greater potential conflict; and they are magnified greatly by the endemic suspicion which exists in the absence of previously agreed constitutional means of resolving conflict should it arise.

Constitutional mechanisms are required, therefore, which can detect and pick out for consideration those issues which are likely to give rise to continuing social conflict unless agreement is arrived at between the conflicting groups. It is not a question of preventing or eliminating social conflict. It is a matter of recognizing that social conflict is always present to some extent, and that it will inevitably pile up from time to time. It is at these times that conflict must be somehow resolved and reduced unless a situation of dissensual conflict is to develop.

Unlimited Nature of Employee Participation

What then should be the rights of the employees when it comes to the running of bureaucratic systems? Are there no limits? Can everything be subject to debate? For after all, are bureaucratic organizations not 'owned by' the employing association – whether shareholders, trade union members, government on behalf of the people, or other types of association? Is there no such thing as 'management prerogative': that is to say, are there no areas of decision in which the governing body must have the right to decide regardless of the views of the employees?

The foregoing questions are among the most vexed questions besetting industrial societies today. They have to do with the rules within which bureaucratic employment is carried on; rules which delimit the exercise of power, and which thereby may legitimate power, transforming it into authority. These rules, or policies, matter enormously to people. Policy-making does not mean some vague esoteric general statements beyond the ken of the ordinary employee. It refers to matters of great concern to all employees; such things, for example, as: the emotive question of differentials in pay and in other conditions; the authority possessed by their managers in judging the employees, rewarding or disciplining them; their conditions of work and progress; changes in methods of work; office or plant closure, modification, or extension; sickness benefits; transfer from one role to another; size of dividend declared by public companies; and any of the hundreds of issues which may arise and become the subject of negotiated agreement. Each of these policies when agreed becomes part of the prescribed limits within which managers and subordinates must work.

Yet, despite the undoubtedly critical importance of these issues to employees, the notion that employees should be entitled as a matter of constitutional right to a voice in the policy-making decisions for the enterprise through institutions explicitly established for that purpose has been highly unacceptable if not downright repugnant to most governing bodies. Boards of directors of public companies commonly argue that the shareholders own the company and that it must be their prerogative in the final analysis to determine policy. Governments, whether central or local, do not often feel that they can allow themselves to be 'dictated to' by their public service employees – whether civil servants, teachers, employees of nationalized industrial or other public or social services – since after all they 'act democratically for all the people' and cannot allow employees to determine public policy.

These short-sighted attitudes lead to inadequate institutions being established when the issue of participation arises. There is a tendency to set up either largely ineffectual advisory meetings, or meetings limited to negotiation between employer and employee representatives on limited matters of 'rightful and reasonable' concern to the employees – a definition usually limited to wages and salaries and other negotiated conditions of work – issues which are certainly of great import but are far from covering the whole field of concern. And even this right to negotiation – to collective bargaining – has had to be won through the intense and familiar struggle of the trade unions in the nineteenth and twentieth centuries for recognition and a legitimate role. Employers have not often taken the initiative in encouraging employees to form associations, to elect representatives, and to take part in policy-making.[2] Legislation of recent years in West Germany and France with respect to works councils and workers' directors had gone some way to redressing the balance, but these particular changes do not get to the root of the problem of participation.

Association, Consumer, and Employee Power Groups

None of the arguments about the rights of shareholders, as owners, or the rights of government, as democratic representatives of the people, to have the 'final' say about the policies of the enterprise except for negotiated conditions of work, can in fact be upheld. When an association, whether private, or charitable, or national, decides to employ people, it certainly does not own them. But more than this, it can no longer make any decision whatever, large or small, which does not to some extent affect those

---

[2] There have, of course, been notable exceptions such as, in the UK, the Scott Bader Organization, Richard Baxendale and Sons, Limited, some Airport Authorities, the Glacier Metal Company, Stirling Industries.

employees. There is no way out. And it is those employees who contribute to the development of the enterprise. Their contribution within a social exchange relationship is something more than is merely paid for in wage or salary: it includes the employees' trustworthiness, loyalty, initiative and concern, and the employing body's interest in the individual's development, progress and well-being. If this social exchange relationship is accepted, then the rights of employees to a say with respect to any change in the enterprise cannot be denied.

But in a much more serious vein, the reluctance to allow fully for employee participation overlooks the realities of the power situation. Rights and prerogatives are nothing more than the legitimated transformation of power. This legitimation process, if it is not to result in dissensual conflict, must include the sanctioning of power by those towards whom it is to be exercised: in this case, the employees. If they decide to take collective action and not turn up for work, the enterprise cannot function. And what needs to be emphasized is that in democratic nations there are no restrictions, nor can there be any – legal or otherwise – upon the reasons which might move an employee collective to go out on strike or to sit in. They may do so in connection with any change whatever which disturbs them to such an extent as to be strongly unacceptable.

In general terms, the analysis of the power field within which enterprises operate requires that note be taken of three dominant power groups. The policies and activities of any bureaucratic system are of immediate concern not only to the members of the association which employs the bureaucracy: they are of concern also to the consumers of the goods or services produced by the system; and inevitably to the employees who work in it. All three groups are necessary for the functioning of the system.

The members of the association are concerned because they wish to ensure that their objects are being pursued and that their resources are being properly used. The consumers are concerned because they want to ensure a supply of satisfactory goods and services. The employees are concerned because they want assurance of continued work of the right kind under acceptable conditions. As Wilfred Brown[3] has described, each of the three groups constitutes an interested power group with a very important type of power – the power not only to contribute to the functioning of the system, but *unilaterally* to put it out of action.

It is the social fact of the existence of these three power groups in connection with any enterprise, each with the power to impede the functioning of the enterprise, which gives the basic meaning to participation in the control of the enterprise. The initial and inescapable social fact is that each power group does inevitably participate in control to a significant extent

[3] W. Brown (1960), *Exploration in Management*, and (1971) *Organization*.

simply by continuing to make it possible for the enterprise to function. Each time consumers accept a service without complaint, each time the employees turn up for work, they are in actuality giving a minimal sanction to the policies and activities being pursued. They may not be saying that the activities leave nothing to be desired; but they are in a real sense voting with their custom or their feet to the effect that the activities are at least not totally and utterly unacceptable.

Power and conflict of interest are neither good nor bad in themselves. They are human facts. They are indications that people are alive. Only dead human beings exercise no power and are involved in no conflict. The issue is how power is to be expressed and mediated in human relationships, how it can be used for the common good rather than for human destruction. As Pascal wisely wrote: 'Justice without power is unavailing; power without justice is tyrannical. Justice without power is gainsaid because the wicked always exist; power without justice is condemned. We must therefore combine justice with power, making what is just strong, and what is strong just.'[4] The linking of power and justice is in essence what participation is about.

Employees and consumers inevitably participate by omission if not by commission in sanctioning, with respect to the effects upon themselves, the policies pursued by each and every enterprise – in industry and commerce, in the civil service, in social services, in local government. The question is whether more explicit institutionalization of participation is necessary. The existing situation is uneven. There are always explicit constitutional means by which association members influence policy (it is usually referred to incorrectly as 'determining' policy, for they determine policy only up to a point): these constitutions always include at least an elected governing body which can act corporately for the association and arrive at its policy viewpoint.

The consumers are not necessarily so well catered for. In commerce and industry, just as the relationship with shareholders is mediated through the institution of the Board, so there is an institution for mediating the relationship with customers – namely the sales organization. Such institutionalization of the consumer relationship is not so true, however, of grant-income institutions as it is of earned-income institutions which after all depend for their existence upon the support they receive from their customers. Earned-income institutions are directly aware of consumer power, except of course under monopoly conditions. And even there, consumers set up countervailing institutions, as Galbraith, for example, has described.[5]

Grant-income institutions tend by and large to be less sensitive to con-

[4] B. Pascal (1941 ed.), *Pensées and Provincial Letters*, p. 298.
[5] J. K. Galbraith (1957), *American Capitalism: The Concept of Countervailing Power*.

sumer reactions, and are slow to set up institutions for mediating relations with consumers. Government departments, governmental social and health services, public education, trades unions, charitable bodies, do not often have such institutions. There is a tendency, however, in the opposite direction. Some countries, like Sweden with its socially oriented governmental services, have gone some distance towards seeking the views of the public about governmental services. In the UK and other countries as well there are gradually increasing numbers of official consumer advisory groups, and market research firms are being used in special cases.

When it comes to the power of the employee associations, however, the institutions for mediating that power are very wanting indeed. Trade unions and staff associations will act to mediate parts of the power field, in particular those parts concerned with the negotiation of wage and salary levels and other associated employment conditions. But they are not commonly involved in the negotiation of other equally significant activities and policies. And they are rarely if ever involved in the negotiation of differential conditions as between the groups concerned: the almost universal practice is for each power group to insist upon its 'democratic right' to negotiate its own conditions separately with the employer. It is equally universally overlooked that this assumed independence of action is a fiction; the extant situation is that the employer is not free to negotiate any conditions with one group which might be unacceptable to others.

In the final analysis all significant power groups must be minimally in accord with any given agreement. They do not like to admit this fact because it appears to diminish their freedom by tying their conditions to other groups. But the fact is that conditions of work are always questions of relativities, even if it is decided that on certain matters (for example, holidays) there should be no differential. There must be unanimous acceptance by all significant power groups of any differentials in conditions between them. Even when a strike occurs, it cannot be brought to a conclusion unless the representatives of any significant power groups who have remained at work also accept the conditions for a resumption of work. For if they do not agree, as sometimes happens, they in their turn go out on strike. When a number of power groups are involved, unanimous agreement among them is required, as I shall show later.

What are 'Significant' Policy Changes?

When a governing body on behalf of an association brings a bureaucratic hierarchy into being, it brings into being another potential association – or a complex of associations – for it creates a gathering of the people it employs. These people are provided with a most active common interest – their conditions of work and the consequences for them of the developing policies and plans of the enterprise. All the conditions exist ready-made for the formation of an association. And that is precisely what happens. Employees do form associations: they form trade unions; they form staff associations; they may form into single associations in one enterprise, or they may form into a multiplicity of associations – into different trade union or staff groups combining higher or lower status groups, or different technologies, or even different religious or ethnic groups.

These associations form attitudes towards the policies and activities of the enterprise. The policies and actions may be judged to be satisfactory, with the wish that they should be continued; or unsatisfactory, with the wish that they should be changed; or in so far as the policies are experienced as affecting the employees in a new or unexpected manner – that is to say, in so far as they are experienced as changing the situation of the employees in some significant way, or as being likely to produce such a change – then the wish will be to be able to discuss and negotiate the nature of these changes and the effects upon their lives.

What then is a 'significant' change? In practice it is nothing less than any change whatever which the people concerned judge to be significant to them. Which changes are likely to be felt to be significant and which not, is always difficult to predict, either by those who wish to introduce the change or by the representatives of those affected, or, indeed, even by those likely to be affected. The change has actually to be proposed and the proposal pursued and actual reactions tested before the full reaction can be known. It depends on the current mood, anxiety or security, the particular people, the degree of confidence at the moment in the governing body, and many other factors besides. That is a familiar fact in all political activity. Why this should be so is quite another matter. It raises the deeper issue of opinion formation and its sources, and that is a question beyond our present scope.

Any issue may therefore be felt by employees to affect them significantly: projected new production methods; a planned expansion in another district or even in another country; a change in management methods; a company-level reorganization; changes in products or services or in markets – any or all such matters, or others, may sometimes be felt as a threat to employment or to employment conditions and therefore arouse anxiety, and at other times will give rise to no concern and be accepted without discussion. There can be no issues which do not affect the lives of employees and the social exchange relationship to some extent, and many issues affect their lives immensely.

The Need for Constitutional Procedures

Neither the community through government nor private employers can requisitely have the right to employ people without those people in turn having the constitutional right to influence the policy of the enterprise in which they are employed. By constitutional right I mean a right made explicit and manifest in a constitutionally established institution with known and agreed procedures.

Failure to provide this right through proper constitutional mechanisms has two important effects. First, it leaves employees with concerns and anxieties without legitimated routes for their expression – a recipe for the damming up of potentially and eventually explosive power, over months, years, or decades, with an inhibition of any full or enthusiastic expression of their abilities in work – an effect greater in some individuals, less in others, but of significance in sum total.

Second, it leaves governing bodies and chief executives unclear about the limits within which they are working, and leads to less active, imaginative or adventurous policies and actions than might otherwise be undertaken. The absence of constitutional rights for employees to participate in determining change most certainly does not leave top managements free and unhampered in their decisions. On the contrary, it leaves them in the dark with respect to the likely reactions of their employees to any given decision. It increases uncertainty. It is conducive to pussy-footing on the grounds that care will have to be taken because a given policy might be too disturbing. And it is all too often just those decisions which are avoided and set aside for this reason, which would have been quite acceptable; and those decisions over which no trouble is anticipated which suddenly cause a blow-up. The reactions to given policy proposals are unpredictable.

It may be concluded, therefore, that firm, strong and effective management of bureaucratic systems demands equally strong and effective employee participation in the control of change. Such participation gives that essential sanction to managerial authority which it requires to make it workable. By means of this sanction, employee power is invested in the management process, and enhances the power of employer and employee, manager and subordinate, alike. And the strongest reason of all, perhaps, for providing opportunity for participation lies in the political fact that the citizens of a democratic nation have the right to be taken account of in matters which effect their livelihood, their careers, their self-esteem, and their socio-economic status in society.

The question, then, is what type of institution and constitution? In order to answer this question, let me first consider four common types of solution which I believe are wrong in principle; they offend in varying degrees against the properties of bureaucratic systems, but they can point the way to better solutions.

Advisory Joint Consultation and Group Decisions

The first type of solution is that of advisory consultation often referred to as a joint consultation committee, where the committee discusses all matters except negotiation of pay and conditions, which is left to other machinery in parallel to the committee. Such committees are inevitably lame duck institutions. They do not deal with the fundamental issues of pay and conditions. Nor can they do anything with the issues which they do consider except discuss them on an advisory basis. They are well-intentioned talking-shops. It may be predicted that they will attract as elected representatives those who are content to spend their time in unimportant talk. It may further be predicted that their existence will not arouse any very great excitement in the enterprise, since they cannot take any decisions which are binding upon anyone. The evidence is of difficulty in finding representatives to stand for election, and of patronizing boredom on the part of managers who must attend.[6]

Participation in Group Decisions and Autonomous Work Groups

A second type of institution and procedure is that described by Rensis Likert.[7] It has to do with consultation between a manager and his immediate subordinates in order to arrive at a group decision before taking action. Its background is Lewinian group-decision theory[8] and the Lippitt and White[9] work on democratic, autocratic and laissez-faire leadership. The original notion was that it would be more democratic if a manager were able to arrive at an agreed group decision with his subordinates on what should be done, rather than having to order them to do it; resistance to change would be overcome, and effective implementation assured.[10]

This approach overlooks the important fact, however, that group decisions cannot extantly be taken in manager-subordinate terms in bureaucratic hierarchies, whatever the manifest position. A manager is accountable for his decisions. He cannot transfer any of his managerial accountability to his subordinates. Therefore, even if he consults them he cannot transfer his authority to make the decision. It is therefore not a group decision but the manager's decision taken after consultation with his subordinates. In effect, the group is free to take any decision it wishes – so long as the manager is in agreement!

The work of Likert and his colleagues illustrates the dangers of transferring results between dissimilar institutions. It also demonstrates

---

[6] The literature on advisory joint consultation committees is vast. See for example, P. Blumberg (1968), *Industrial Democracy: The Sociology of Participation.*

[7] R. Likert (1961), *New Patterns of Management.*

[8] K. Lewin (1952), 'Frontiers in Group Dynamics'.

[9] R. Lippitt and R. K. White (1947), 'Experimental Study of Leadership and Group Life'.

[10] See. L. Coch and J. P. R. French (1948), 'Overcoming Resistance to Change'; and D. Katz, N. Macobby and N. C. Morse (1950), *Productivity, Supervision and Morale in an Office Situation.*

the importance of distinguishing between associations and bureaucracies. For the Lippitt and White research was carried out in a boys' club. A boys' club is an association. It is not a bureaucratic hierarchy. The club leader is *not* the manager of the boys: he may be either a voluntary association member or an employed officer of the association. But whichever he is the boys are not his subordinates. They are either members of the association or consumers of its service, but are most certainly not in any way whatsoever its employees. Therefor it is not just 'best' for him to help the boys to arrive at their *own* decisions by majority voting (the 'democratic' leadership style), it is requisite for him, incumbent upon him, to do so. Moreover, it can be shown to be non-requisite in such a situation for the club leader (even though he be an officer) to tell the boys what to do (the 'autocratic' leadership style): for if the boys are members of the association they are the superiors of the club leader, or if they are consumers of its service then they are his equals.

We may thus note that the types of leadership behaviour which Lippitt and White have called democratic as against autocratic styles are in fact not generalizable to any and all institutions. Voting on decisions is requisite in associations – the issuing of instructions is not. In bureaucratic hierarchies, however, for a manager to get his subordinates to vote on managerial decisions is not democratic. It is rather more what Lippitt and White would have called laissez-faire. What is requisite is for the manager to make decisions and to issue his instructions – so long as those decisions are within agreed policies. While such behaviour would be autocratic in an association, it would not necessarily be so in a bureaucracy.

The fallacy is to label as autocratic any and all behaviour in which A orders B to do something. It is a serious fallacy in that it has led to much sociological romanticizing in which democracy is incorrectly interpreted in attempts to impose group voting on situations, such as the bureaucratic hierarchy, where it is not only irrelevant but destructive of morale and sound human relationships. The prevention of autocracy in management lies not in the elimination of managerial authority but in processes for sanctioning and controlling the limits of that authority by elected representatives of all employees. What is called for as a role requirement is not autocratic (or 'authoritarian') behaviour but authoritative behaviour – and there is a world of difference between them.

These same criticisms of group decision in bureaucratic hierarchy apply to the related notion of autonomous work groups.[11] There can extantly be no autonomous work groups employed in bureaucratic hierarchies, regardless of the manifest description. There must extantly be an employed

[11] F. E. Emery and E. Thorsrud (1969), *Form and Content in Industrial Democracy*; E. Thorsrud and F. E. Emery (1970), *Industrial Relations in Norway*.

manager accountable for the work of the members of the group, and he must extantly assess each member's performance.[12] A general principle may be stated; namely, that work is done by individuals and not by groups, and in bureaucratic systems each individual is accountable for his own work. Autonomous work groups in bureaucracies are an organizational fantasy, giving the shadow of democracy without its substance.

A further point overlooked by the Likert type of formulation is that consultation between a manager and his immediate subordinates is in any case requisitely an ordinary and everyday aspect of normal managerial work. Bureaucratic hierarchies are not 'formally' one-way downward communications systems and only 'informally' two-way systems. Such a formulation is to confuse the hierarchical structure of managerial accountability and authority in bureaucracies with their much more complex structure of communications – a structure which certainly includes a manager's seeking advice from his subordinates and the subordinates' offering advice and criticisms to the manager and making demands upon him. It is a serious mistake to conceptualize this process as a group decision, or to make something special of it and call it participation. It can be accurately conceptualized as part of the two-way manager-subordinate communication in bureaucracy – leaving the concepts of group decision and participation to do their own work in other settings.

Workers' Directors

The third and fourth types of non-requisite solution which I wish to consider are related. They have to do with the presence of employees in the employing association or its governing body.

The third type is the provision for workers' directors which has become widespread in West Germany and France. The idea of having workers' directors looks good on the surface. But at best it is a mere palliative; it will not help to satisfy the democratic aspiration towards greater participation, but will, on the contrary, be more likely to increase despair about the democratic process.

The creation of workers' directors simply does not fulfil the requirements of participation with power. Do such directors give up their positions as elected trade union representatives – in which case the workers have lost good representatives? Or do they retain their trade union roles and accountability – in which case there is a conflict of loyalties which would make it impossible for them, for example, to be present at board meetings when preparations were being made for negotiations on

---

[12] Apparent but not true exceptions are special contract groups, such as an independently employed plate-laying gang in shipbuilding with a ganger in charge, who are really self-employed entrepreneurs on sub-contract work.

wages and salaries and other conditions of work.

Moreover, what are the powers of workers' directors? Can they hold up change? If they cannot, does it mean that they are acquiescing in board decisions? If they can, then it is not a proper board made up of individual members: it is in fact a negotiating meeting between two groups – the 'real' board members and the workers' representatives – thus pre-empting eventual negotiations.

One proposal for overcoming such difficulties is to have workers' directors make up 50 per cent of the board. But it confuses matters to call such a body a board. It would in fact be a statutory negotiating council – a two-sided body in which both sides have the power to veto proposals for change. It would be better to recognize it for what it is: for then a properly constituted council could be set up. Let the appointed directors continue to be the board, for they will need to meet together anyhow; let representatives for a council be elected from all employee groups; and let the negotiations proceed in the council (see next chapter).

The major point here is that the employing association is one body – it may be the nation, a local community, a group of shareholders, trade unionists, co-operators, an Israeli kibbutz. It is an institution in its own right with its own properties, its own mode of granting membership, its own particular interest. None of the members of the employing association receives a salary as member of the association (though they may receive pay if they are *also* employees) – it is for them to ensure that wages and salaries are available for the employees. But the employees too can form an association. It also has its own properties, one of which is that to gain entry a person must be an employee of the enterprise.

There are thus two different associations, and the problem of constitution building is to create a working relationship between them. Simply to take employee representatives and put them on the governing body of the employing association is unsatisfactory, because it distorts the nature of the governing body and leaves the employee representatives without a viable role.

Employee Ownership

The fourth type of participatory arrangement magnifies the problems of workers' directors. It is the type of institution used, for example, in Yugoslavia and in some Israeli kibbutzim: it is a syndicalist type of organization, an employee co-operative, in which the immediate employees are the owners; they make up the employing association. What is required in such a set-up is to recognize that everyone has two roles – that of member of the employing association and that of employee. Their relationships with one another in the two roles are different – everyone is in a colleague relationship in the association, but differentiated out into manager-subordinate relationships in the employment situation.

What is required is to have two different types of institution – the one elected by the employing association and the other in the shops and offices. But if precisely the same people are involved it is fruitless to pretend that there are in reality two separate associations in negotiation with each other. People cannot negotiate with themselves. The situation arises, therefore, in which the same people are expected to be able to reconcile the conflicting viewpoints of a community-oriented employing association and of a self-interested employee association.

The inherent conflict of interest will lead either to the adoption of too narrow a local employee outlook at the expense of service to the community (the Yugoslav government has frequently complained about such narrowness[13]), or an unrealistic bending over backwards to place the interest of service to the community before the interest of the employee group, with an imbalance at the expense of the employee group. The necessary constructive tension and conflict between the two requisite associations are lost. Strikes can occur (and are now officially allowed in Yugoslavia), but have the extraordinary quality of sub-groups striking against their colleagues and themselves.

Employment in a syndicalist group is via membership of the employing association. All members of the association must be employed in the bureaucratic system. A frozen employee group tends to result, without the normal social respiration provided by labour turnover.[14] The enterprise will become involuted, its policies too strongly dominated by the need to provide just the right employment for the members of the association, reinforcing the tendency towards excessive concern for the employee group. It is the nation which must provide an abundant employment economy, for no individual enterprise can guarantee continuously to maintain just the right pattern of work for its employees. When the individual enterprise attempts to do so it tends to become rigid and unadaptive.

Experience in both Yugoslavia and some Israeli kibbitzim[15] suggests that difficulties may also arise because the senior managerial group begins to behave like a political caucus and tends to arrogate special power to itself, or is seen to be in a position to do so and hence is suspect.[16] In Israel the attempt is made to overcome this problem by requiring senior

---

[13] W. A. Westley (1971), *The Emerging Worker*, and (1972) 'An Evaluation Model for Worker Participation in Management'; and W. A. Westley and J. Kolaga (1965), *Workers' Councils – The Yugoslav Experiment*.

[14] See J. M. M. H. Hill (1951), 'A Consideration of Labour Turnover as a Resultant of a Quasi-Stationary Process'.

[15] D. Billis (1971), 'Process of Planning in the Kibbutz'.

[16] Indeed in many cases they are there by virtue of election rather than appointment and have to behave like part politicians in order to survive.

managers to rotate every three years and to return for further experience on the shop-floor.[17] But rotation of this kind can succeed only in deposing the best people from appropriate roles and under-employing them. Artificial solutions have inevitable debilitating side-effects.

In short, employee co-operative ownership does not eliminate the bureaucratic hierarchy. It requires that the employee owners somehow dispose themselves within a bureaucratic system of their own making: they find themselves in two roles – owner and employee – in which their interests differ. The general tendency of such enterprises is to become closed social systems; systems which few people leave or enter, and in which the work to be done in the bureaucratic system and the work-capacity of the employee-owners become increasingly mismatched.

[17] The same rotating arrangement is currently used in Communist China (C. Howe (1973), 'Labour Organization and Incentives in Industry, Before and After the Cultural Revolution'). There is further evidence that the same problems of anti-requisite bureaucracy are being met there as everywhere else. The cultural revolution attempted to sweep aside monolithic bureaucracy, with its attack upon Chou En Lai and the '10 000 rules of bureaucracy' for which he was held to be accountable. The committee structure which replaced the normal managerial structure failed pitifully within two years, being supplanted by a more rational and less red-tape entangled managerial system.

13

Requisite Conditions for Employee Participation

What type of institution, then, is requisite for employee participation in the control of change in the enterprise? This chapter will set out a number of conditions necessary for such institutions. The analysis is based upon generalization of the Glacier Project experience of seeking to establish conditions for the achievement of employee consensus.[1]

First, a distinction is made between policies and executive decisions within policies. Policies can be negotiated between employing associations and representatives of employees. Executive decisions are not negotiable in the same way but must be subject to employee participation: managers must be individually accountable for them, but must be open to challenge by elected employee representatives as to whether those decisions are consistent with optimizing the future employment opportunities of their constituents.

Second, all significant employee power groups are recognized as having the right to participate through elected representatives: a significant power group is any organized group which through collective action can exercise effective coercive power to cause the enterprise to stop. Third, the matters in which participation is to be allowed are defined as any matters whatever which are of concern to any significant power group: no so-called management prerogatives can be allowed. Fourth, the members of power groups must accept as binding upon them the agreements arrived at on their behalf by their elected representatives. Fifth, employees and their representatives must be kept informed about changes which the governing body or chief executive are contemplating, so that they can determine whether those anticipated changes need explicit consensual acceptance or not.

The sixth and final condition is the establishment of a constitutional body or council on which the elected representatives of all significant employee power groups can meet with one another and with the chief executive acting for the governing body. Voting on such a council must be unanimous, to express the fundamental principle that no power group can impose changes on any others, nor can it have unacceptable changes im-

---

[1] The Glacier Project experiences in participation are described in E. Jaques (1951), *The Changing Culture of a Factory* (Chapter 5 describes how the development occurred), and in W. Brown (1971), *Organization* (Chapters 16 and 19).

posed upon it. This unanimous acceptance of good enough arrangements is in turn based upon majority consensus within each of the power groups. This combination of majority and unanimity voting arrangements reflects the realities of power in bureaucratic systems. It provides the necessary constitutional means for identifying social conflicts as they arise, and for holding off change until consensus has been achieved on the proposal or some modified form of it.

The chapter will close with a brief section on consumer participation.

Policy, Executive Actions, and Future Employment Opportunity

The difference between policies and executive actions may be derived from our analysis of work in Chapters 6 and 7. Policies are frameworks or contexts within which executive decisions are taken and actions carried out. They have no target completion times because they are criteria for action and not actions. Policies can be explicitly formulated in words. They set context in the sense of both direction and channel. Thus there are operational policies to the effect that certain directions of development will have higher priority than others. Or there are boundary-setting policies, for example, that payment levels for certain occupations will be kept within certain limits. The policy statements indicate the direction or the limits within which action shall be taken *if* the need for action should arise.

By contrast executive decisions *are* actions and do have target completion times. Employees, including managers, must be able to take executive actions on their own authority or they cannot be held individually accountable for the work. But requisitely those executive actions should be carried out within policies which are consensually acceptable to any employees who might be affected.

Policies, being explicitly formulable frameworks, can readily be the subject of negotiation between a manager on behalf of the employing association and elected representatives on behalf of employees. Once they are constitutionally agreed, they form part of the institutional context and the managers can then work within them. Executive actions, by contrast, cannot be the subject of negotiation and agreement between a manager and his subordinates without removing his individual accountability, substituting an anti-requisite group accountability, and undermining completely the exercise of individual work-capacity.

The fact that policies can be negotiated and agreed but executive actions cannot be, poses a difficult problem for employee participation. For many executive actions are of as much concern to employees as are the more general policies. Thus, for example, decisions to close a factory or to open another elsewhere, or to introduce certain new rationalized production methods, or to declare a redundancy, or to change to a new product line, or to increase the dividend, or to invest in an overseas country, may not be policies but they are certainly emotion-stirring executive actions which cause strong desires among employees to be able to 'participate'.[2] They wish to be involved.

Examination of this problem reveals, however, that although employee representatives certainly wish to be consulted in such decisions, they cannot be held accountable for the outcomes. Even shareholders or employee-owners expect their chief executive and senior management to make such decisions and to accept their accountability for what they do. To participate but not be accountable, that is the dilemma. This dilemma is resolvable once the following facts are recognized.

The first fact is that the central concern of employees about executive actions has to do with the effect of these actions upon the future employment opportunities of those employees.[3] As elected representatives would argue, only the people whose working role requires them to make particular decisions can be held accountable for those decisions. But the representatives want assurances, on behalf of their constituents, that the manager concerned is paying serious attention to the future employment opportunities of the employees. Even if an action seems in the short term to worsen employment prospects, can the manager show that in taking the decision he genuinely considered that it would enhance these prospects in the longer term and that everyone would thus be better off in that regard?

In short, consideration of executive actions leads to a fundamental underlying policy of all bureaucratic systems; namely, that managers will behave in such a way as to attempt to optimize the future employment opportunities of employees in the enterprise as an integral element in their executive decisions.

Given the recognition and acceptance of such a policy, discussion between a manager and elected representatives about particular executive decisions has the following character. It is not a matter of negotiation or agreement about the particular decisions. It is a matter of the manager's having to show why he believes that the decisions will optimize future employment opportunity. His integrity and competence are under scrutiny. If the representatives do not oppose the decision they are in effect simply affirming a belief in the integrity and competence of the manager concerned in carrying out the policy of optimizing future employment opportunity. If they strongly oppose the decision they are in effect proclaiming their loss of confidence in his integrity or his competence, or both: a serious situation will have arisen, the outcome to be decided by the relative power of the contenders and the degree of loss of confidence.

---

[2] Large-scale decisions of this kind are often referred to as policies. In fact they are not policies but simply high-level far-reaching decisions and actions.

[3] J. G. Collyear has formulated this idea in (1975) *Management Precepts.*

We will refer to the process of discussion between a manager and elected representatives (or direct subordinates) about executive actions, as *consultation*. Negotiation between a manager and representatives with respect to arriving at agreement on policies will be referred to as *legislation*. The process of employee participation comprises both legislation of policies, and consultation to establish and monitor managerial integrity in implementing these policies.

Let now turn to the conditions necessary for making effective participation possible.

No Limit to Issues Subject to Participation

There can be no limits whatever with respect to the issues on which employee participation shall be allowed. Thus, for example, it is not possible nor is it necessary for all matters of policy to be negotiated. Most policies are in any case implicit – contained in the prevailing folkways of the institution and its surrounding society. But there must be opportunity explicitly to legislate any policy issue whatever which is of concern to the members of any significant power group and which they wish their representatives to consider and negotiate before the policy is adopted.[4]

The same openness must also apply to executive decisions. Most of a manager's decisions will be straightforwardly within well-established practice and policies. There needs to be sufficient opportunity, however, for periodic review of actions and for prior notice to be given of any decision which the manager considers might arouse anxiety or concern. For successive executive actions cumulatively modify the context of action by adding new precedents, small or large, which become part of the operating folkways. Policies and actions thus interact to form one field of activity. That is why no policies or actions can in principle be excluded from opportunity for employee participation: any exclusion is to rupture the total field.

So long as this principle of non-exclusion is constitutionally accepted, all power groups can approach proposed changes in a relaxed frame of mind. They know that nothing can be slipped over on them or go by default. If they are worried about a proposed change they need only raise it as a matter for negotiation or consultation, whereupon the proposed change must be deferred until it is finally adopted, rejected, or accepted in a modified form. Under such conditions it becomes easier for people to listen to one another in debate and to consider alternatives. By contrast, in a coercive power situation, everyone is too consumed by suspicion and mis-

---

[4] The Glacier Policy Document defines policy as 'any statement adopted by a council or laid down by a manager, or any established practice or custom, which specifies behaviour required of members in given situations'.

trust to listen constructively to anyone else – the art is to exercise cunning in order to outwit the others[5] – and cunning behaviour is highly paranoiagenic.

Freedom of Association on Independent Sites

All employees must have not only the opportunity but the facilities to form associations by means of which they can elect representatives to express their point of view. In enterprises which are geographically split up between two or more different localities, there must be opportunity for association and representation on each site as well as centrally. Employees who find themselves on a common site experience common problems – of pay and conditions related to local conditions, of work and work allocation and investment policy related to the site, of common local traditions and culture – and these common problems and outlook combine to create the particular and local reactions to policy proposals. Employees on different sites may well react very differently to the same policy proposals.

Site representation is an essential component of the potential contribution of bureaucracy to the strengthening of *gemeinschaft* in community life. When local conditions are negotiated locally, the local community interest can be expressed and taken into account. When all negotiations are centralized, due regard cannot be given to local differences, and the general feeling is increased of everyone's being ensconced in a large, impersonal and geographically and emotionally distant monolith.

Local policy cannot of course be created without regard for the total needs of the employing institution as a whole. But participation in policies affecting all sites will have to do mainly with issues which have a differential effect upon local employment opportunities; for example, transfer of resources from one site to another; closing down or decreasing the size of one site and enhancing other sites or opening new ones; investing in new resources in such a way as to favour employment in some sites relative to others. Issues of this type can be extremely emotion-provoking, and at the same time difficult for employee representatives to handle. In Glacier it has been found necessary to arrange periodic company-wide conferences of elected representatives from all sites and the members of the Board. These conferences are exploratory, any decisions requiring subsequent endorsement by all the site negotiating bodies.[6]

Another important feature of site negotiation is that the representatives

---

[5] Melanie Klein vividly described the role of cunning as an outstanding feature of personality functioning in the paranoid-schizoid position: (1946) 'Notes on Some Schizoid Mechanisms'.

[6] Further development work is currently being carried out to improve the institutionalization of this process.

and their constituents are all local employees. These employee representatives may be assisted in the case of trade unions by outside paid officials, but it is up to the union to empower the local elected representatives to act on its behalf. By this means the common split between shop stewards and union officials is overcome. The shop stewards are the official representatives in all respects. The union officials must ensure that they act within official union policy.[7]

Keeping the Representatives Informed

It is useful if employing associations and their top management realize that they would be privileged if their employees were willing to elect representatives to negotiate with them on policy issues, and are prepared to cooperate in this. It is for the most senior manager on site to act as management member of the site council and to meet with the representatives and seek to arrive at agreements with them on all policies governing the whole site. It is for this management member to keep the representatives regularly informed about the anticipated decisions and actions of top management – in advance of change – so that those plans can be considered and the integrity of the managers put under scrutiny with respect to the policy of optimizing future employment opportunity. It is this senior manager who speaks on behalf of the chief executive and the governing body and thereby on behalf of the employing association.

The regular information provided to representatives by the management member of each council is a crucial element in the procedure. By keeping the elected representatives informed about anticipated or projected changes as far in advance as possible, the opportunity is provided for the representatives to decide whether any of the proposed changes are likely to be matters of serious concern to their constituents. If they are concerned they can raise these matters as requiring debate in the light of their possible effects upon future employment prospects. If they are not concerned, they need not challenge the report, and the effect will be that they have sanctioned the proposal.[8]

[7] In the Glacier situation all representatives are elected by scrutineered secret ballot within works hours, ensuring a 100 per cent vote. The trades unions grant shop stewards' cards to representatives elected in constituencies where more than 75 per cent of the employees are members of that union. Except for Str-3 staff, employees who are not union members are disfranchised for election purposes but are represented by the shop steward who is elected. All council agendas and minutes are sent to the District Trade Union Offices so that any potential problems may be picked up. Any manager getting in touch with a shop steward who represents his subordinates is officially in touch with the union – it is up to the shop steward to decide when he wants to call the union official in.

[8] In the Glacier Works Councils the management member gives a management report at every meeting, in which he gives an up-to-date picture of on-going management plans, using *in camera* meetings if any confidential matters have to be reported. It is furthermore an

Individual Anonymous Consensus and Committal

The employees must on their part be willing to elect representatives to meet the senior site manager. These representatives must be empowered to commit the constituents who elect them to any decisions arrived at. If employees are to take part in policy-making they must be prepared to sanction their representatives to act for them, and to abide by the decisions taken. It should be a matter of employment contract.[9]

The separation of the representative system from the managerial system overcomes another problem of manager-subordinate relationships in consensus formation. The manager relates with his subordinates individually with respect to their views *within* the manager-subordinate work situation; that is to say, with respect to how the policies affect them in their employment work. In the representative system these same employees can argue out among themselves and the subordinates of other managers their personal views about those policies; that is to say, how they are affected by them in general life terms – including effects upon their home and family life and the community. The outcome of this discussion is then presented to the managers as a group consensus, without need to reveal the views of any individual member of the group. Nor indeed are the representatives' personal views revealed, since they are speaking for the group and not for themselves.[10]

The representative process is thus an individually anonymous process as far as managers are concerned. Each employee has the opportunity to influence the consensus of view in his colleague group without having to be concerned with how he might be influencing his manager's attitude towards him. It also avoids toadying to the manager, a situational role which there always seem to be some individuals ready to take up, particularly if the manager is present in a non-managerial relationship.

agreed policy that it is a manager's duty to communicate his views to his subordinates, and not to use elected representatives for this purpose. Their London Factories agreement states: 'During negotiations, the structure of communication on the matter under negotiation between the determining manager and the subordinates represented in the negotiations is changed from the normal two-way pattern to the following: the elucidation of the official executive point of view remains a direct executive relationship between managers and their subordinates; communication for purposes of negotiating is between the determining manager and the representatives; communication of the group consensus is from the members as constituents to their representatives, and from the representatives to the determining manager.'

[9] The decisions of the legislative bodies are binding on all employees.

[10] The Glacier Policy Document says: 'A manager shall recognize that the views put forward by a representative are views he is expressing for his constituents, and may or may not be the same as those that the representative would express in his executive role. He shall recognize that the individual views expressed by a member to his representative are confidential to that member in his constituent role and to his representative, and shall not use his executive authority to try to discover those individual views or to influence other members with regard to their representative activities.'

Constitutional Council

Finally, it is essential to have some form of constitutional meeting – let us call it a council – between the senior site manager and the elected representatives in which agreement requires a unanimous vote without abstention. Here we come to a major point of principle. Since both the top management and the employees have the power unilaterally to close down the site, this power must be reflected in the council. How? By an arrangement in which the power to close down can be constitutionally represented in the voting – that is to say by unanimous voting without abstention, whereby each member of the council has an effective veto. By this means no changes can take place which are not accepted by every member of the council: the manager accepting on behalf of the governing body of the employing association, and each of the elected representatives accepting on behalf of his constituent group.

Such a council, it may be noted, is a meeting between the employing association whose policies must be taken into account and represented by the management member of the council, and the association or associations of employees acting through elected representatives. We have then three interacting sub-systems: the managerial system of the bureaucracy; the system of elected representatives of employees – the representative system; and the meeting place between these systems in councils made up of a senior manager and elected representatives – a legislative system.

Unanimity as the Expression of Consensus Among Power Groups

It is this last condition – the unanimous voting council – which raises some of the deepest questions. For surely, it might be argued, it could never be possible to gain unanimous agreement between employing association and the employees. Such doubts go straight to the heart of the issue of the transformation of power into authority within bureaucratic hierarchies, through the legitimation of power by consensus.

How, it may be asked, can sufficient consensus be arrived at within an enterprise – be it public service or social services, industrial or commercial – to enable the enterprise to function satisfactorily? The answer is that unless sufficient consensus exists, the enterprise will not function; so long as it is functioning, then by definition there must implicitly be consensus, and the problem becomes one of getting it explicitly formulated.

Such an answer is not to deny power and conflict, or to seek to push them to one side. It is to recognize that associations and bureaucratic systems are power systems, just like all other human institutions. There is and always will be conflict within them. Power and conflict are among the essential constituents of all social life. The object of requisite institutional design is not to eliminate power and conflict. It is to have built-in procedures whereby conflict can find constitutional channels into which to flow, to be worked over and to be sufficiently resolved for social life to continue.

The prime channel through which power flows, or is designed to flow, in the bureaucratic system is the hierarchical manager-subordinate network, for it is in the roles in this network that power is transmuted into the authority needed for accountability to be discharged. But the transformation of power into authority is never a perfect transaction, since sanctioning processes can never be perfect. The discrepancy is reflected in conflict or potential conflict.

What we are here considering, therefore, is how sufficient consensus can be gained and recognized so as to legitimate power into sanctioned managerial authority and to tackle conflict as and when it arises. By consensus I mean that sanctioning and acceptance of policies which allows the members of an institution to agree to remain together and to support its constitution, even though at any given time some may be opposed to the policies then current and actively engaged in trying to change them by *constitutional means*.[11]

Consensual processes cannot in and of themselves eliminate all possibility of dissensus and social disintegration. Constitutional provisions for consensual agreement can, however, help to avoid unnecessary dissensus; that is to say, the development of dissensus under conditions where the social atmosphere favours consensus but there are no adequate institutions to provide an outlet for the consensual aspiration.

In any one association, consensus is usually defined in terms of the majority view, expressed if necessary in voting, a definition deriving from the democratic tradition. What must be noted, of course, is that a majority view is by itself not sufficient for consensus to exist. There must also be a willingness on the part of the minority to accept the majority view. Consensus concerns the attitude of the total population – it is a social centripetal force, binding an association together. Dissensus is precisely the opposite – a social centrifugal force, causing an association to fly apart. An opposi-

[11] The Glacier Policy Document explicitly recognizes this issue, stating: 'Realism forces the recognition that power [coercion] may be resorted to from time to time, and the constitution broken. Such use of power does not necessarily, however, destroy the constitution. Part of the value of having a constitution is to be able to recognize clearly when it is being broken, so that due care may be exercised to avoid destroying it by such frequent breaks as would bring it into disrepute. . . . In the final analysis, even when power [coercion] is used, agreement must eventually be arrived at between the contending groups. The Works Council procedure provides a setting where agreement can be sought before recourse to power, under conditions where those concerned are faced with the fact that if they cannot find a solution, then there is nothing else to be done.'

tion minority is thus also taking part in consensus formation if it chooses to keep the association intact.

The problem of consensus in a bureaucratic system is that the employees may form more than one association, all of which must relate to one another as well as to the employing association. There are thus several associations involved, each a separate power group: the employing association plus one or more employee associations. What is to be done? Two steps are required. First, each of the associations must maintain its own consensual process by majority. Second, on policy all the associations must come to an agreement unanimously – for the overall inter-association consensus must be able to encompass the consensual view within each of the associations. Failure to get acceptance by each of the associations leaves a situation where one group (not an individual) has had its consensus rejected by the others. That becomes socially intolerable.[12]

The question of whether it is right for the employees to form more than one association can have no final answer. It will be decided by the degree and nature of the commonality of interest at any given time. It is the same question, with the same answer, as how many political parties there ought to be. The question, however, of which associations of employees should be entitled to representation on a unanimous voting council does have a general answer: those associations whose members have the power unilaterally to close the enterprise – that is to say have the power to act coercively. It is by the acceptance of this principle that such councils can be bodies which reflect in an accurate and living manner the play of significant power and conflict within the enterprise. By the same token, a unanimously accepted decision is no more than the practical expression of the discovery of a reciprocal arrangement which reduces conflict sufficiently to enable the endeavour in the enterprise to continue *pro tem* and with more or less enthusiasm, in the common interest.

Constitutional Channelling of Power

The procedure described is designed to enable such consensus as exists to be discovered. It gives a constitutional basis for consensus in the complex of associations which constitute the enterprises of which bureaucracies are a part. It provides for majority voting within associations; and for unanimity voting when the representatives of associations meet together to agree on changes in policy. This unanimity voting prevents any one association from dominating any other. Giving to the association or associations of employees the right to hold back changes which are against

---

[12] Wilfred Brown has analysed these differences in terms of stable and unstable committees: see (1973) *The Earnings Conflict.*

the consensus of view of those employees, gives employee power a constitutional form within which to express itself. The alternative is that in the final analysis change will be held up by the mechanism of the strike, or by eventual dissensus of sufficient strength to destroy the enterprise.

The question of course arises as to what happens if an emergency situation requires a decision and action before the legislative system is able or prepared to be consulted or to arrive at a decision? This issue was faced early on in Glacier, and it was agreed that the chief executive could take such a decision, but only on the condition that no precedents were thereby established and that the matter remained under active consideration in council until an agreed policy was hammered out which would avoid the problem recurring.[13] It has rarely been found necessary to use this mechanism in the past twenty-five years.

Giving employee power a constitutional form creates the channel by which managerial power can be transformed into explicitly sanctioned authority. The Glacier experience has confirmed that explicitly sanctioned authority can be much stronger than authority which has been only implicitly sanctioned.[14] Once the accountability and authority of all managers have been publicly debated and defined in a legislative system, then each and every manager knows where he stands. He is expected both to exercise that authority and to accept his managerial accountability. The employees as a body have the safeguard of participation in the legislative system. And each individual employee has the additional safeguard of the right of appeal (as discussed in Chapter 15).

With these participatory and appeal safeguards, it becomes quite possible to reach explicit unanimous agreements in legislative councils.[15] Such an outcome should not really be surprising. For unless the members of one or other of the associations contained within an enterprise are genuinely determined to destroy that enterprise, the overriding consensus can be found. If there is a dissensus situation and destruction is the real goal, then

[13] The actual policy states: 'Legislative bodies shall accept, pending a unanimous decision, either: (a) the continuation of existing policy, or (b) such immediate decisions as the management member thinks fit, where the matter under consideration is not covered by existing policy or where there is disagreement on the interpretation of existing policy, and where the interests of the Company demand that action shall be taken. The manager concerned shall, where possible, make every endeavour to give representatives prior information on the steps he intends to take, to enable them, if they so wish, to inform him of their views. Acceptance of the decisions shall be without prejudice to the final decision of the appropriate council or councils, which shall make every effort to reach a unanimous decision without delay.'

[14] The definition of managerial authority worked through and agreed in the legislative system is that described and discussed in Chapter 4.

[15] Hundreds of such agreements have been arrived at in Glacier including: all wage and salary differentials; all other employment conditions for all groups of employees at all levels; conditions governing transfer of work between sites; procedures for dealing with redundancy; policy on managerial authority.

institutions to provide for participation are in any case irrelevant. Participatory institutions can help, to prevent dissensus arising by default. The opportunity for all concerned to take part by constitutional right in agreeing policy change can itself become a powerful consensual force within the enterprise.

In this process of participation, the chief executive at the peak of the bureaucratic hierarchy is in a situation worth noting. He is at the focal point of interaction of the three important power systems – employing association (and governing body), employees, and consumers. The interplay of power can be intense, and one of the main characteristics required in a chief executive is the ability to mediate these power relationships. It is a position of personal isolation and may at times feel intensely lonely. A chief executive must have the competence to exercise judgment from within himself to ensure satisfaction for the members of the three power groups upon whom he is dependent for the successful exercise of his role.

The total arrangement of executive system, representative and legislative systems, and employing association and consumers, is illustrated in the following diagram.

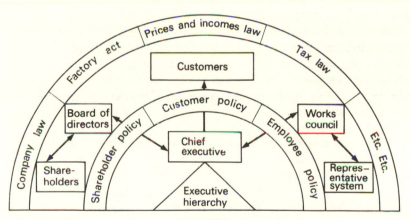

Figure 13.1

Participation Where Government is the Employer

In developed industrial nations, the government becomes one of the largest employers of staff, and in socialist economies it becomes the sole or practically sole employer: in administrative departments (civil service), in military services, in social service agencies, in education systems, in production systems and in nationalized industries. The problem of employee participation where government policies are concerned becomes a particularly sensitive political and constitutional issue. It calls for special mention.

A government acting as employer is acting as the employing agent for the nation as a whole, The people are the employing association, in short are the employers. When the members of a government bureaucracy of any kind become dissatisfied, and perhaps go on strike, they are acting against their co-citizens. They are in effect saying that the rest of the nation is not giving them an adequate position in the national scheme of things. It is anti-requisite for the rest of the nation to respond by saying it is wrong to strike against the government, that it is an unconstitutional political act.

If the people of a nation want government services they must accept the role of employer. It is not socially just to argue that because a government has been democratically elected, then the employees of that government must somehow accept whatever conditions it lays down. There is no guarantee whatever that the nation as employing association will ensure fair and just conditions *differentially* for those it employs. On the contrary, the nation is every bit as capable – to take one important example – of arguing inability to meet the cost of the pay and conditions demanded by certain of its employees as against the claims of others, as is any private employing association. It does so usually by being unwilling to meet the higher taxes or charges which would ensue.[16]

The difficulty is that when the nation feels threatened by any group of its employees, it may feel inclined to exercise its special emergency powers in the so-called national interest, bringing in troops to get work done, or conscripting employed staff. It is in this possible recourse to powers over the citizen which only the government on behalf of the nation possesses, that the great difference between the nation and all other employing associations may be seen.

It should also be noted that nationalization of an industry does not put that industry under the control of its employees.[17] What it does is to give its employees the same share in control as any ordinary citizen has.

Governments act through various agents for the management and control of their bureaucracies. They commonly use government ministers in a second role broadly equivalent to that of a company chairman. The

---

[16] Every nation has had its experience of public servants striking or threatening to strike, and the national complaints which are aroused. Recent examples in the UK are the miners, the electrical power workers, the railway workers, and the health service nurses and ancillary workers; and in Sweden, the Army officers.

[17] Many miners made this mistake in the UK when the mines were nationalized in 1947. They thought they were taking over the mines, but discovered that they were exchanging private associations for the nation at large as their employers. Their managers were quite unchanged, for they were employees also. The situation felt little different, and the subsequent paralysing national strikes have been every bit as bitter as those under private ownership, with large sections of the nation complaining that the strikes were political.

departments they control are thereby bureaucracies which have chairmen who change periodically in accord with a political time-table. Or they may appoint separate boards or political authorities with varying degrees of independence of the government itself, to manage the department or service. These differences in organization may be of great significance politically. They make little or no difference from the point of view of the bureaucratic systems employed. To the employees there are no significant differences between a minister of state, the chairman of a political authority, or the appointed head of a nationalized service of industry, as agent of the nation as employing association. They are 'the employer,' and require to win the sanction to manage by consensus in the same way as any other employer.

Consumer Participation

Finally, I wish to mention briefly the question of the participation of consumers in policy formation for enterprises. Here we must return to the distinction between earned-income and grant-income enterprises. For earned-income enterprises have a built-in mechanism for consumer participation – unless they are in a monopolistic position. The consumers affect policy by their decisions to purchase or forego the goods or services of the enterprise. That is what competition is about.

The institution mediating the relationship between consumer and enterprise is the marketing organization of the enterprise's bureaucratic system. It is via its chief executive and marketing organization that the enterprise carries out its negotiations with the consumer. It is they who must seek to understand consumer needs and wishes and to so formulate them that the enterprise may develop and produce what the consumer seeks. In modern marketing it has come to be known as market-orientation in business as against product-orientation.

This problem of consumer participation arises especially in connection with such institutions as schools, hospitals and health services, social services. The question is what ought to be the rights of those directly in receipt of service – the parents and pupils, the patients, the recipients of social services – to influence the policies which determine the type and availability of service. In particular, what special rights, if any, ought the immediate consumers to have, as compared with the views of the tax-paying community as a whole?

The starting point is of course that the services are provided by governing bodies on behalf of the whole community. But only parts of the community benefit directly at any given time. The direct consumers thus constitute a special sub-group *within* the employing association. This sub-group cannot be allowed to override or push to one side the normal democratic representative process in the community. What, then, can it do without interfering with due community process? Three things are needed: it must be entitled to be consulted by the employed bureaucracy – by the principal, or head, or director; it must be enabled to inspect what is happening and to report to the political authority; and individual consumers must have the right of complaint to an independent body.

The first point, that of consultation, can be illustrated in schools. The immediately involved parents must have the right to be consulted by heads and teachers, to state their needs and to advise.[18] If dissatisfied they must be able to report higher to political authority, so that difficulties may be taken up by normal political processes. Such a procedure does not interfere with political mechanisms. It reinforces them.

The second point, that of inspection, can be illustrated in local citizens' committees connected with public hospitals.[19] There must be opportunities for the local public to come into those hospitals and to know at first hand what is going on. They must be able also to be informed about the policies and policy developments for the institution. And they must finally be able to report not only to the hospital authorities but to the political authority acting as the employing authority, so as directly to influence the formulation of policy as well as the assessment by the authority of its employed bureaucracy.

The third point is concerned with the individual who receives services: what is he to do if he is not satisfied with the service he receives and wishes to complain? Is he to be made to feel small and helpless against a great and faceless bureaucratic giant? Even if he withdraws his custom it will have no effect. As with appeals systems in law and within bureaucratic hierarchies, there must also be an appeals mechanism for the enforced consumers of public and social services.

A model for such appeals is the Scandinavian Ombudsman and the UK Parliamentary Commissioner for Administration with whom individual complaints may be lodged against unacceptable treatment by civil servants, or by employees of other public or social services. Without such a mechanism, the grant-income type of bureaucratic hierarchy tends to become involuted and impersonal, and takes on the characteristics of anti-individual 'bureaucracy' in the pejorative sense. Bureaucracies are open systems, and need to be kept open to influence by their consumers if they are to avoid becoming blocked up.

---

[18] M. Kogan and G. F. Packwood (1974), *Advisory Councils and Committees in Education.*

[19] See, for example, the Community Health Council provision in National Health Service in the United Kingdom.

14

The Right to Equitable Differential Reward

We now turn to one of the fundamental rights of employees which is one of the most potent sources of industrial strife – the right to fair and just payment differentials. It is commonly overlooked that payment problems are problems of differentials, of who gets how much relative to others. At stake is the relative socio-economic status of every employee and his dependents, and the more general issue of the degree of equality or inequality in a society.

These differential pay questions are currently settled by collective bargaining procedures. These procedures, rationalized by unsound economic theories of labour supply and demand, are in fact coercive and anachronistic. They lead eventually to dissensual conflict in society.

A resolution of this problem is to be found in the relationship between time-span measurement and felt-fair pay mentioned in Chapter 6. This finding suggests that it ought to be possible to establish an equitable distribution of differential wages and salaries throughout the bureaucratic sector, since the norms for such a distribution can be demonstrated to exist. The need for an institution whereby employee representatives can adopt or modify these norms of equity is discussed. The prime issue is the introduction of constitutional methods for achieving social justice in the payment sphere, in place of social coercion and injustice.

The Question of Differentials in Payment

A point that is too rarely noted in explicit terms is that something of the order of four-fifths of the wealth created in industrial societies is distributed through the wages and salaries paid to employees.[1] The differential wage and salary structure of the intermediate zone in an industrial society is thus the main factor determining not just the economic status of its citizens but their economic status relative to one another, the general pattern and scale of economic inequality among them. Wage and salary levels cannot therefore be regarded as merely a matter of a bargain between an employer

---

[1] The distribution of income in fully industrialized nations tends to be around 80 per cent in wages and salaries, 15 per cent in entrepreneurial earnings and dividends, and 5 per cent in rents.

and employees to get some work done. The issue is more complex that that. For in addition to each wage or salary providing each individual or family with a livelihood, the total pattern of payments determines one of the absolutely fundamental social characteristics of any society – the differential range of standard of living from the poor to the rich. Indeed, it serves to designate what each society means by poor and rich, and in so doing it establishes the degree of inequality.

There are of course other factors which affect economic status and inequality, such as fees, dividends, rents, inherited wealth, success in speculation, windfalls. Such factors are often spectacular and may be of great importance, but they occur in only a small proportion of cases. The fact remains that it is through wage and salary income that the vast majority of the population of industrial societies find their socio-economic positions. By the same token, they change their economic status as a result of changes in their wage or salary income.

The question then is what should decide relative economic status? Or should there be any differences in status in the first place? There seems to be a generally accepted consensus in favour of differential reward: somehow, the feeling runs, those who carry higher responsibility should have a higher economic status. But why should that be so? Why should some individuals have a higher economic status and standard of living than others? These questions of inequalities and differentials in income and economic status have plagued all societies.

At core will be found that great issue of the meaning of justice and equality in contemporary society. Should it mean an egalitarian distribution of all wealth? – that result is more difficult to achieve than may at first sight be apparent, even in small co-operative communities in which wealth is commonly owned and shared.[2] Or should it mean 'from each according to his abilities; to each according to his needs?' – socialist societies have not been able to find how Marx's idealist maxim can in fact be applied in social reality. Or should it be limited to equality of opportunity – educational, social, political, occupational – as has tended to be the aim in most democratic nations? – that interpretation begs two practical questions: how to provide equality of opportunity; and how, even if equal opportunity is achieved, should the fruits of everyone's using such opportunity be distributed.

One mode of explanation has been in terms of distributive justice and status congruence, a notion which as Homans points out goes back at least

---

[2] I have put forward a possible explanation of this phenomenon in terms of differences in capacity for discriminating expenditure which coincide with differences in capacity in work. I would still keep to this explanation as my strongest hunch (E. Jaques (1961), *Equitable Payment*, pp. 157 ff.).

as far as Aristotle:[3] it is the idea that each of the various aspects of a man's status and activities should be congruent in the sense of carrying the same rank-order, so that his general social status and esteem are clear and un-ambiguous.[4] These ideas find one psychological explanation in Festinger's cognitive dissonance theory, which has been applied by Adams and by Vroom in their researches on equity.[5]

There is, however, an important vacuum in this idea of distributive justice and status congruence. Congruence by itself at no matter what level is unlikely to prove satisfactory. It must be congruence at some particular level, a level whose rank-order in the general order of statuses is acceptable to the individual. The question then is what should that level be for any given individual; what is it that causes a person to opt into a particular status level in the first place?

The congruence or equilibrium in question revolves around three critical factors: first and foremost, a person's level of work-capacity (C); and second and third, the level of work (W) he is given to do and his level of payment (P), which must be experienced as in equilibrium with each other and with his work-capacity: what I have termed a C-W-P equilibrium.[6] That is to say, a person gets satisfaction from having a level of work con-sistent with his current work-capacity, and a level of pay which is equitable for that level of work. For equilibrium between capacity and work (C-W) to be assured requires the abundant employment condition described in Chapter 11. The question which remains is what is equitable reward, and how it can be assessed and related to payment so that the nature of work-payment (W-P) equilibrium can be formulated.

One of the difficulties in attaining precision in these propositions has been that the size of responsibility or level of work carried for a particular level of reward has not been assessable. Thus it has been impossible to link wages and salaries in any systematic and known way to responsibility. All kinds of seeming anomalies arise leading to chronic and gross disaffection and disruption. Whether or not distributive justice is at work cannot, therefore, be readily ascertained.

No analysis of bureaucracy can reasonably evade these issues. It is not proposed to do so. But it is unlikely that there is any final social or philosophical or political answer to the vexed question of whether or not

---

[3] G. Homans (1961), *Social Behaviour*, p. 245.

[4] See also E. Shils (1968), 'Deference'; and H. H. Hyman (1942), 'The Psychology of Status'.

[5] L. Festinger (1954), 'A Theory of Social Comparison Processes'; J. S. Adams (1963a), 'Wage Inequities, Productivity, and Work Equality'; (1963b), 'Toward an Understanding of Inequity', and (1965) 'Inequity in Social Exchange'; and V. H. Vroom (1964), *Work and Motivation*.

[6] I have described this equilibrium, and the consequences of various types of dis-equilibrium, in *Equitable Payment*, pp. 213–25.

there should be socio-economic status differentials. Every industrial society must create the means for adopting an explicit policy with respect to the
pattern of distribution of wages and salaries, whatever that pattern might
be at any given time – differential or not. It is possible in practice to determine this distribution in a systematic, controllable and equitable manner.
To demonstrate how to do so, we will use certain findings which appear
strongly to relate the sense of fair and equitable differential pay to level of
work as measured in time-span.

The Shortcomings of Collective Bargaining

The universal method of determining payment differentials so far has been
by leaving it to the play of forces on the open market – the so-called labour
market. A man earns what he can get – whatever the going rate is. We are
not here referring to a free market, or indeed to any particular kind of
market. For labour markets have rarely if ever been entirely free.[7] They are
subject to many controls – royal or presidential dictatorial decrees,
governmental regulation, or collective arrangements among employers
and employees.

The outstanding feature of the play of the labour market is that labour is
regarded as a commodity, the same as any other goods or service. Its value
is seen as deriving fundamentally from demand and supply, just as for any
other commodity. As supply or demand changes, so goes the theory,[8] the
differential value of different types of labour changes, and the socio-
economic status of different types of labour changes in consequence. In
short, different types of human labour are not regarded as having any inherent differential value. The very same work may be properly and fairly
treated as warranting a higher or lower position in the general scale of earnings in accord solely with whether there happen to be more or fewer
people available in a given locality to do that work as compared with the
number of vacancies available. A person's status may thus change without
any change having taken place in himself.

Bargaining depends upon a combination of guile and power. Collective
bargaining depends upon the strength and power of the collective and the
guile of its representatives. With collective bargaining, therefore, – or indeed with individual bargaining – the pattern of differentials is strongly influenced by *ad hoc* forces and power. Collective bargaining, established in
the nineteenth century to overcome and to prevent gross abuses of
employees by employers, can also become a dominant source of dis-

[7] J. Robinson (1933), *The Economics of Imperfect Competition*; and M. Friedman
(1962), *Capitalism and Freedom*.
[8] Every standard text in economics or labour economics, such as for example, P. A.
Samuelson (1964), *Economics*, sets forth the theory.

equilibrium once a society has become wholly industrialized. To the powerful go the rewards. Anyone employed in the intermediate zone comes readily to appreciate the situation. Most groups accordingly attempt to use coercive power to enhance their differential position. Those who do not do so get left behind in the economic struggle. The outcome is that the general level of wages and salaries keeps being pushed up by power bargaining. A chronic inflationary leap-frogging is kept in motion without anyone's necessarily being sure of gaining in the end.

These phenomena are painfully familiar. The inadequacy of conceptualization of work and of reward for work, and the anti-requisite nature of the bargaining procedures for determining rewards, have brought about the most obvious and manifest symptoms of social unrest. The institutions mediating payment demand the expression of the most negative qualities of greed, devil-take-the-hindmost, envy, rivalry and dissembling. A constructive concern for the welfare of others or of the nation cannot be expressed without utterly undermining the power of a bargaining position. Collective organization has become a banding together of employees against other groups of employees, although ostensibly against employers.

This last point is of vital importance. In the final analysis, what constitutes a fair pattern of differential payment is not what employers think is fair but rather what employees think is fair. The most general conclusion from this postulate is that the structure of differential wages and salaries is a matter to be determined by the representatives of employees: the representatives of employers and government have no reasonable role in this process.[9] This conclusion refers solely to the *differential* distribution of wages and salaries and not to the absolute levels of earnings. Most of the emotion and stress arise from feelings about differentials.

Whether or not this last postulate is accepted, it is a fact that there is a strong tendency among trade unions and staff and other types of employee association to deny that they are competing differentially with one another. Each likes to believe that it is 'bargaining with management' and that this bargaining has nothing to do with anyone else. Each trade union, for example, likes to profess its independence in bargaining.

Yet what actually happens is that every individual compares his pay with other individuals and is satisfied or dissatisfied in relation to whether he considers the comparison favourable or unfavourable. In the same way every small group, every trade union, every staff association, not only compares the earnings of its members with those of other groups, but also uses this comparison as its main base of negotiations. The language used is that of relativities, or of position on the pay ladder, or of position in the pecking order or 'league table'.

[9] A postulate first stated by W. Brown in (1973) *The Earnings Conflict*.

Reaction to Felt Inequity in Differentials

Anyone who thinks that negotiations are about anything other than differentials would be well advised to consider the matter again. Bargaining and negotiation by themselves can do nothing more than change a group's relative earning position at the expense of others. They do not and cannot increase the amount of wealth available, nor does an increase even necessarily improve a particular group's standard of living. As Keynes pointed out, the absolute levels of earnings are determined by economic forces other than negotiations,[10] and so too is the standard of living.

It is because wages and salaries are concerned with standard of life that they arouse such understandably passionate feelings. But it is the further fact that pay is concerned with relative status, with relative standard of living, that causes negotiations to be so dramatic. Everyone has his eye on his neighbour, his friend, his workmate, his colleague. It is a struggle by each one for his proper position, and for a proper position for his reference group. All the intensity of reference group values and behaviour are to be expected.[11]

These feelings are revealed every day – when teachers complain that they earn less than semi-skilled workers; when coal-miners claim that they are losing out to others; when office staff feel they get unreasonably less than shop-floor workers; when foremen resent the fact that the operators whom they manage take home a bigger pay packet than they do because of piecework and overtime and other premium payments; when the shop-floor and office staff feel it is unfair for higher-level management to enjoy longer holidays, or better pension or sick pay arrangements; when skilled men strike because the differential between them and the so-called semi-skilled is being narrowed.

Every single benefit gained by another group is experienced as an actual loss by others – even if one group is given a daily ration of milk for industrial health reasons, then other groups will argue for milk – or for safety clothing, or for clean overalls. Those who are not included in some new provision somehow feel deprived, left out, worse off, impoverished, badly treated, unloved, envious. If one group goes up, others do not feel as though they have simply stood still: they feel that they have gone down, lost out. And so, differentially, they have.

[10] He wrote: '. . . the struggle about money-wages primarily affects the *distribution* of the aggregate real wage between different labour groups. . . . The effect of combination on the part of a group of workers is to protect their *relative* real wage. The *general* level of real wages depends on the other forces of the economic system.' J. M. Keynes (1936), *The General Theory of Employment, Interest and Money*, p. 14. The italics are his.

[11] H. H. Hyman and E. Singer (1968), *Readings in Reference Group Theory and Research*; and E. E. Maccoby, T. M. Newcomb and E. L. Hartley (1958), *Readings in Social Psychology*.

This point can be illustrated by the following example. Take three groups, A, B, and C, each of which gets an increase. A is earning say £50 per week (say $300) and is given a rise of £5 ($30) to £55 ($330); B is earning £40 per week (say $240), and is given a rise of £5 ($30) to £45 ($270); C is earning £45 per week (say $270) and is given a rise of £3 ($20) to £48 ($290). The feeling of group C will be that they have had a decrease instead of an increase, for they will be concerned that they have lost out relatively to A and B. Their actual feelings are best expressed in percentage differential terms. Taking A as 100 per cent, C will feel they have actually lost out by dropping from 90% to 88% of A, whereas B has gained by moving from 80% to 82% of A. An increase in actual pay can thus constitute a decrease in relative pay, and will be experienced as a loss in relative status.

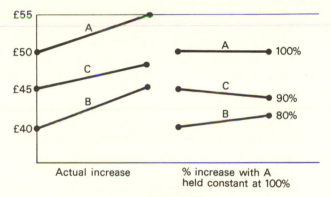

Figure 14.1

It is these feelings about relativities which count. They are the prime source of the sense of getting ahead, staying even or losing out. If everyone gets exactly the same percentage increase, then everyone may be a bit better off, or not so badly off, but no-one feels that he has made any advance. It is when one group feels that another is differentially too high or is moving differentially ahead without justification, that the real trouble starts. The deepest and most hostile bitterness will be stirred. This bitterness cannot be over-emphasized. It is virulent; stirs violent primal envy;[12] sets friend against friend and work group against work group; is the main cause of intractable strikes; and is resolvable in any real sense only by correction of the differential dislocation. It is, after all, gross differential inequity between top and bottom in a society which is one of the powerful sources of revolutionary ferment.

Once differential inequity favours any given group for an appreciable

[12] In the sense used by Melanie Klein: see (1957) *Envy and Gratitude*.

period of time, that group will try to hold on to its advantage.[13] I have elaborated this point in *Equitable Payment*.[14] The attitude is readily understandable so long as the exercise of power is the major factor regulating differentials and there is no constitutional means of ensuring fairness and equity all round. In such circumstances it is not only the weak who fall behind: those who are altruistic, who are concerned about others as well as themselves, also fare badly. Power unregulated by adequate constitutional mechanisms favours those who can be strong, hard and self-centred, saps the will to social cohesion, and is in the end socially corruptive.

The Time-span/Felt-fair Pay Relationship

If the problem of differential payment is as critical an issue as experience would suggest, what then is to be done? A possible lead has been provided by the curious finding which first suggested that level of work might be measurable in terms of time-span of discretion; namely, that for each time-span level there is a corresponding level of pay felt by employed persons to be fair. This finding was referred to in Chapter 6; here are the detailed findings.

In work over a period of some twenty years in The Glacier Metal Company a correlation of about .90 has been found between time-span and felt-fair pay, for all types of work – manual, technical, managerial, research, sales, finance, etc.[15] In a study at the headquarters of the Honeywell Corporation in Minneapolis, U.S.A., Richardson found a correlation of .86 for managerial and staff personnel in manufacturing, sales and research. He further found by means of regression analysis that time-span explained some 75 per cent of the variation in felt-fair pay, as compared with actual pay (10 per cent), and 28 other variables, none of which accounted for more than 1.5 per cent of the variation.[16] There is further support for the validity and reliability of these studies in work in Holland[17] and in Canada,[18] and in less systematic and unpublished testing in a number of other countries besides.

There have been other studies in which the results have been less conclusive, but none of these so far reported has been based upon satisfactory

---

[13] The typographers in Great Britain are often cited as an example of a group heavily engaged in restrictive practices to retain a favoured differential position.

[14] See especially pp. 133–6.

[15] E. Jaques (1969), 'Fair Pay: How to Achieve It'.

[16] R. Richardson (1971), *Fair Pay and Work*.

[17] F. C. Hazekamp (1966), 'Werk, Capaciteit en Belonging in het "Glacier-Project" '.

[18] D. R. Hansen (1973), 'Some Results of a Test at Canadian Forces Base Uplands of a Measure of Work and Responsibility'; (1974) 'Results of a Test at a Land Base of a Measure of Work and Responsibility'; and (1975) 'Tests of a Measure of Work and Responsibility in Some Naval Units of the Canadian Forces'.

use of the time-span measurement procedure. Goodman, for example, merely assumed what the time-spans were, without any measurement at all.[19] In another research which might have provided a serious test with manual workers of the relationship between time-span and felt-fair pay, it was unfortunate that time-span measurements were taken from data obtained from the managers only without being checked with the subordinates actually doing the work.[20] Such a procedure is unsatisfactory where the research worker has had no previous knowledge of the work the time-span of which is being measured. When time-span measurement is first carried out in an organization, careful checking back and forth is required between manager and subordinate, to ensure that sufficiently accurate data are obtained about the tasks assigned. When the work is more familiar to the person doing the measurement, less of this checking is necessary.

Very recently, however, even stronger support has emerged from the analysis, reported by G. E. Krimpas, of a study he carried out in collaboration with J. S. Evans and R. L. Miller of twelve different firms in the United Kingdom. Krimpas concludes that

> The quantitative work presented here is a severe test of Jaques' hypothesis in that it covers a broader range of observations than his own, particularly at the bottom end, over a rather extreme variety of firms, locations and types of job. Such testing is necessary to get away from the possible peculiarities of the special case. The method of public in contrast to confidential analysis also brings the technique nearer to the hands of its natural users, the firms' management. This study therefore confirms that time-spans exist in the simple sense that they can be measured with objectivity and rigour. The three versions of Jaques' hypothesis are all confirmed with some amendment for the stricter one among them.

We can summarize the quantitative basis of Jaques' proposition as follows:

(a) The total of 11 firms, giving 195 observations, fit a cubic relationship with $r^2 = 0.89$.

(b) Jaques' original data (Glacier) fit a cubic relation with $r^2 = 0.94$ for 70 observations.

(c) The new sample (10 firms) fit a cubic relation with $r^2 = 0.84$ for 125 observations.

(d) Individual firms vary, in terms of closeness of fit, between $r^2 = 0.25$ and $r^2 = 0.98$, according to range of observations and position within the overall scatter.

[19] P. S. Goodman (1966), 'An Empirical Examination of Elliott Jaques' Time-Span'.
[20] Department of Employment (1976), *Felt Fair Pay*.

(e) The relation can be presumed to fall into two natural parts, divided by the kink in the middle of the (logarithmic) range. The association between time-span and felt-fair pay appears generally weaker to the left of the kink, but it is not possible to attribute the cause as between the value of time-span as such and/or characteristics of specific firms, as it is a single firm which dominates the lower range with 46 observations.

(f) Jaques' 'Equitable Payment Scale' falls mostly within the 95% confidence limit of the best overall cubic relation but has slightly different slope from it.

(g) Both halves of the relationship are statistically significant for all firms and all levels of work.

(h) Hence the time-span of discretion is a good predictor of felt-fair pay even if all other factors which may be considered to affect felt-fair pay are ignored.[21]

In short, there is a steadily growing amount of evidence of a close relationship between measures of time-span of the tasks in a role and the attendant feelings of fair pay of the people carrying out those tasks. I have taken this relationship as support for the idea that time-span measurement

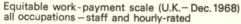

Equitable work-payment scale (U.K.– Dec.1968)
all occupations – staff and hourly-rated

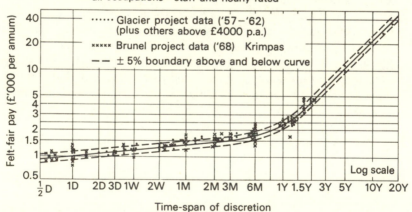

Time-span of discretion

D = days W = weeks M = months Y = years

Figure 14.2

[21] G. E. Krimpas (1975), *Labour Imput and the Theory of The Labour Market*, pp. 66–7.

Krimpas goes on to propose a highly imaginative and important new economic theory of the nature of the labour market, using the kink in the curve to which he refers, to discriminate a dual market, each with different economic properties, one concerned with the 95 per cent of employees who are the shop- and office-floor workers, and the other with the 5 per cent who are managerial, technological and directorial personnel. He shows how these two different markets respond differently to price and to supply.

can give an objective indication of the subjective experience of the level of work demanded by the tasks in a role.[22]

When the individual data on felt-fair pay and time-span measurement are plotted, the curve in Figure 14.2 is obtained. I have called this curve the equitable work-payment curve, the hypothesis being that it represents that distribution of wages and salaries in relation to level of work, which would generally be experienced as fair and just. Whether, and how, this curve might change with time and with circumstances is not known. Nor have sufficient data been obtained in countries other than the United Kingdom to determine whether the shape of the curve is universal.[23]

Payment at equitable level for the time-span of work involved appears to induce a feeling that in principle the wage or salary is reasonable. A person might want more, wish the country were richer and that everyone had more, or resent the fact that some groups appeared to be paid at above equity rates. He might, moreover, feel he was entitled to more because he was capable of a higher level of work but there were no opportunities for him to get a job at his warranted level. But he would still be of the view that his pay level was equitable for the work he was being given to do, even though he himself was worth more.

Other findings first reported in *Measurement of Responsibility* and *Equitable Payment* also continue to be confirmed; namely that those who are paid below the rate called for by the equitable work-payment scale feel underpaid, while those paid above this scale have the feeling of being overpaid even though they may not always admit publicly to that feeling. When actual pay falls below equity there is disaffection; when it rises above equity there is a sense of uneasy gratification. The intensity of these feelings varies directly with the extent of the deviation of actual pay from the equitable scale.

An Interpretation of the Equitable Work-payment Scale

This discovery of a relationship between time-span of discretion and felt-fair pay is an instructive demonstration of the value of precision in the definition of social facts. For with the boundary definition of work in terms

[22] The argument for this conclusion is presented in my (1956) *Measurement of Responsibility* and (1961) *Equitable Payment*.

[23] Available data suggest at least a similar shape. Thus for example, felt-fair pay data for equivalent time-spans in England and the United States show a factor of about $7 to £1 to have been operating for at least the past ten years, and not just the rate of exchange $1.90 to £1. This factor indicates the relative levels of the incomes ladder in the two countries: a person moved by his employer from London to New York in a role of the same kind and the same time-span would have to be paid at $7 for each £1 of his London salary to find himself among his economic peer group in New York. This factor of $7 to £1 sterling seems to apply about equally at all income levels, suggesting that the equitable work-payment scale has the same shape in the two counties.

of discretion, and the operational definition of level of work in terms of measured time-span, there came into view new findings about payment that are simply unobservable without time-span measurement. These findings provide a basis for the objective study of differentials and of people's actual feelings about payment. They also make it possible to compare wages and salaries for like time-spans right across the whole of the intermediate zone: in industry, government, social services, and so on.

Most striking, these findings give strong support to the view that whatever the selfish and envious impulses in people, they are equally moved by an essential fairness and reasonableness, and have a capacity for concern about others.[24] It would appear that deep inside people seek what they think to be a proper place for themselves in the economic scheme of things. They will not be out to do each other down so long as each can be assured that equity will be served all round. The tragedy is that the norms of fair economic reward on which all are apparently intuitively agreed are prevented from effective expression and influence by the power bargaining procedures which are current and which leave no place for fairness.

Moreover, it may be noted that these findings suggest that supply and demand theory and the marginal utility of labour do not explain wage and salary levels. What they serve to explain is deviations of actual pay from equitable pay. There is an intrinsic differential value of labour connected with level of work. Labour shortage allows individuals to seek above-equity rates. And conversely, labour surplus makes it more difficult for anyone in the over-supply group to gain equity in pay.

A realistic hypothesis would be that the equitable pay curve represents what the actual distribution of wages and salaries would be in a full employment economy. Such an economy would give a labour supply and demand situation that was in balance: the right people would be available to fill posts at every level, and every person would stand a chance of finding the post he wanted at the right level at the right time. The effect of imperfections in the balance of labour supply and demand, caused by unemployment and other factors, is to induce deviations between equitable earning levels and actual levels – and that is where the trouble starts.

An Equitable Differential Wage and Salary Distribution

The demonstration of the existence of equitable payment norms suggests that the wage and salary structure of the intermediate zone ought requisitely to follow this pattern if unnecessary social unrest is to be avoided, and that the rights and liberty of the individual would be best served by this

[24] This conclusion is supported by the work of the equity theorists such as Stacey Adams. See footnote, p. 223.

procedure. The rights of individuals cannot be served simply by the right to get what they can, either collectively in bargaining or individuallly through any one of dozens of payment-by-results systems.[25] Neither of these processes of unrestricted self-seeking can bring peace and freedom to the intermediate zone of society.

Resolution of conflict by coercive power is the fate of a society which knows of no principle by which to resolve the conflict. It can never be a principle of freedom in a democratic society. The principle of equitable payment offers that freedom which derives from the recognition of a social reality. It offers the opportunity of extending a scientific understanding of society into one more area where, in the absence of principle, resolution of conflict has inevitably been by coercion.

It is not necessary to argue for the application of the particular scale of felt-fair pay differentials which has been described. The actual payment differentials must be politically debated and agreed. The basic issue is that of introducing into the intermediate zone of society not only a principle of economic justice for all individuals in the reward they gain for their work, but an objective mode of implementing the principle. The outcome would be a transformation of the intermediate zone of society from an area of economic inequity, of social disturbance, where individuals learn to suspect and hate their society, into an area of manifest equity from which society as a whole could learn about economic justice.

Establishment of a system of equitable payment would be a major step towards eradicating the possibility of economic exploitation of individuals by employing organizations. By contrast with bargaining and similar techniques which reinforce the conception of people as greedy and self-seeking and require them to behave as such if they are to look after their own interests, the objective formulation of equitable payment differentials would allow for the expression of people's constructive concern for each other and would touch their deepest feelings of fairness.

Universal application of time-span measurement would thus require a political mechanism for agreeing what pay levels to attach to what levels of work. Various types of solution are possible. Wilfred Brown's proposal for a National Council for Regulating Differentials is likely to be the most realistic.[26] Brown suggests a two-part procedure as required for an adequate institution. The first, is the governmental part. It is for government to determine by its financial policies broadly how much of the national income should go into wages and salaries, how much into social services and pensions, how much into dividends, how much into providing

---

[25] Much has been written about the apparent gains for employer and employee under such schemes. Less has been written about the disruptive consequences for everyone. Wilfred Brown has covered the field well in (1962) *Piecework Abandoned*.

[26] See his book (1973) *The Earnings Conflict*.

employment opportunities in under-employment districts, and so on. Any rational system of income distribution must be based upon central decisions as to how much – if anything – a nation can afford by way of increases in real wages and salaries. Central government is the only body in a realistic position to make such decisions and capable of making them democratically.

The second part is the mode by which the differential distribution of the total amount available for wages and salaries is to be established. This issue is for the wage and salary earners to determine. Brown suggests a pragmatic way in which these decisions could be made. He calls for the establishment of a National Council for the Regulation of Differentials (NCRD), to be composed of some 300 members representative of all major trade unions, professional associations and other employee negotiating bodies. This NCRD would decide annually, by near-unanimity voting procedure, whether any changes in differentials should occur and which groups should move higher or lower in the economic scheme of things. In this manner the system of economic ranking within the bureaucratic sector would be achieved as a matter of agreement among employee groups, with the results binding not only upon all employees, but upon employers and government as well.

The main point, however, is not whether Wilfred Brown's proposal is the best method of coping with the problem of equitable payment. There is work to do, and much to learn, before the best method or methods can be determined. What is essential is that there should be universal recognition of the existence of the problem and of its nature.

The discovery of time-span measurement and of its relationship to felt-fair pay demonstrates that the equitable pay problem is resolvable. It demonstrates further that classical economic theories of the marginal utility of labour are themselves marginal. The central factor of an adequate theory must be the assumption of an inherent differential utility of a man's labour related to the level of work involved rather than to the condition of the labour market. Such a theory can settle also the question of differential economic status in theories of distributive justice and status congruence.

If society could become more aware of the nature of the problem, power bargaining and spurious methods of productivity payment could be relinquished in favour of equity, fairness and justness. Social cohesion would be enhanced. The rights of the individual employee to equitable economic treatment would be assured. This issue will be returned to in Chapter 24.

15

The Right to Individual Appeal

There is plenty of scope for conflict between individuals in bureaucratic systems. When these conflicts occur between individuals in laterally related roles, the conflict will be resolved in the final analysis by reference to the common crossover-point manager. When, however, conflict occurs between individuals in vertically connected roles – that is to say, between manager and subordinate – the resolution of the conflict is more difficult; there is no common crossover-point manager.

Manager-subordinate conflict can be particularly virulent because the subordinate's status and progress can be so much affected by his manager's judgment of him. What is required is for the subordinate to have a channel of appeal whereby his conflict with his manager can be reviewed higher up the executive line, and if necessary at the top of the hierarchy. Arrangements for such an appeal system are discussed in this chapter, and their implications for social justice for the individual are considered.

Subjectivity of Managerial Decisions About Subordinates

Even with a requisitely accountable manager, abundant employment, participation in control of policy change, and assurance of equitable differential reward, there is yet one other personal safeguard required for the individual: it is the individual's right of appeal over decisions of his manager which he feels affect him unfairly. A manager makes many decisions that relate directly to his subordinates that are of great personal import to them. He decides what work they shall do. He decides what resources they shall have. He judges their performance. He trains them. He criticizes them. He compliments and praises them. He decides whether they shall receive merit increases or whether they shall receive accelerated progression. And in the final analysis he decides whether each of them is above or below the minimum level of competence required, and decides whether or not to continue with each of them as subordinate.

Even though all these decisions are made within the constraints of policy, there is nevertheless plenty of scope for a manager's decisions to affect his subordinate. All the delicate intricacies of their inter-subjective relationship come into play, with varying degrees of fit between the sub-identities involved in the subjective interaction of the particular individuals in each particular manager-subordinate pair.

There is plenty of scope for personality clashes to occur, and for the manager's judgment of his subordinate's work and performance to be influenced by his feelings about his subordinate personally. Indeed, the manager's judgment must inevitably be influenced by his personal feelings: the only question is how much his judgment might be distorted by such feelings.

The situation is further complicated by the manager's having to depend upon his subordinate. Every manager will know the private feeling of irritation and resentment that grips him when a subordinate makes a mistake and he is left with the resulting complications to sort out, perhaps at a time when he is heavily occupied with problems of his own. Then there is the annoyance and impatience the manager may feel when a subordinate keeps pressing new ideas for consideration which might be good ideas but are nevertheless unrealistic because there is no time to attend to new methods at that moment. Or the simple dislike the manager may have for a subordinate for quite irrational reasons, the source of which is not consciously accessible.

The relationship between manager and subordinate is an intensely human one, in which liking and disliking, admiration and envy, jealousy and contempt, favouritism and animosity, patience and anger, sympathy and exasperation – the full range of feelings and emotions may all play a part. And there is also the full flow of a 40-hour-week (or thereabouts) encounter in the Goffman sense between managers and their subordinates taking place within the established constraints of the bureaucratic role relationships. The full panoply of situational roles of the cultural role repertoire may be seen – in the interplay between the manager and each subordinate and in the group composed of the manager and all his subordinates; for example, the role of scapegoat, of yes-man, of domineering bully, of father figure, of denigrator of authority, of oracle, and so on. All these interpersonal relations and situational role relationships are factors influencing managerial judgment in the manager-subordinate role relation.

How then are managerial judgments to be objective? They cannot be. Precisely because they are judgments they are inevitably subjective. They are influenced by the play of feelings and emotions; and in the final analysis based upon an unconscious, intuitively felt Gestalt. Subordinates may therefore be subject to feelings of unfairness and injustice, to feelings that others are getting better treatment, to feelings of being victimized.

There is nothing inherently wrong in such judgments having to be made. The issue is to ensure that justice can be done. If judgments were not necessary then a bureaucratic system would not be required. Work would be controlled in a mechanical way and people would not be needed. In actuality people are needed, and, therefore, so are bureaucratic systems. The greatest point about these systems lies precisely in the fact that they can put to practical use some of the finest of human capabilities – the capability to feel concern and to be accountable for getting things done, and, in proper conditions, to make sound judgments about the competency of others in helping to get those things done, in spite of the play of distorting personal and situational forces.

Such human judgments are, however, never perfect. 'Could any one person,' asked Junius Brutus, 'be relied upon to safeguard another's life and welfare? Any one man was too mutable, too unruly and weak against his passions, to be so trusted.' In practice the intensity of play of feelings is such that any manager is unlikely ever to be entirely free from a situation in which at least one of his subordinates has some feeling of being badly treated or even personally victimized. Such feelings are endemic in bureaucratic hierarchies. It is practically inevitable even under the most nearly requisite of organizational patterns that personality clashes will occur and a sense of victimization will arise. That fact is true of all institutions, and of living society itself.

The solution to this problem lies not in trying to root out the personality difficulties. Of course, the better the emotional balance in individuals the less likely it is that unnecessary stresses in relationships will occur. But even well-adjusted personalities can grate and jar upon one another in subjective interaction. And in any case it is no business of a bureaucratic organization to undertake to change the personalities of its employees.

The solution is to be found in the provision of safeguards for individuals so as not only to make victimization impossible but to make it apparent that victimization can be seen and dealt with. In order to do this, it must first be recognized that although a subordinate works at any given time for a particular manager, his employment contract is with the governing body of the association. Therefore, the requisite safeguard is to provide the opportunity for the subordinate to appeal higher up the managerial hierarchy against those decisions of his manager which affect him in a way which he thinks unfair or unjust. He must have the right to cause his manager's decision to be reviewed by higher authority: in the first instance by his manager-once-removed, and subsequently, if he is not satisfied with the decision at that level, by the next higher manager, and so on up to the top.

An appeals procedure is the necessary guarantee to the individual that authority to make important decisions about him will not rest finally and without review in the hands of one person, his own immediate manager. Paradoxically, an appeals procedure is also the necessary safeguard of the manager's authority to make decisions about his subordinates. For so long as the appeal review procedure exists, the assignment of clear and appropriate authority to managers becomes tolerable and acceptable. Without such procedures it is managerial authority itself that must be continually called into question and repeatedly attacked and undermined.

Effective managerial power, in the sense of sanctioned and authorized power, must be power within requisite limits. Power that cannot be appealed against is *prima facie* unjust power. It is autocratic and coercive. It is one of the strongest conceivable stimuli to suspicion and mistrust. Contrariwise, power that is not only authorized but can be subject to appeal at any time is potentially just and fair power, for it is constructively limited by the appeal action which the subordinate can himself take in his own interest.

Appeals as Review of Reasonableness of Managerial Behaviour

The procedures whereby appeals can be heard may vary in different types of bureaucratic hierarchy. The procedure in military organization, for example, is established strictly in accord with legislated rules, since military organizations are vested with their own internal legal system – the final step often being questions raised at government level. In the vast majority of bureaucratic hierarchies, however, what is required is simply a regularized procedure whereby a subordinate can go to his manager and tell him that he is not satisfied with his decision about him and that he wishes to see his manager-once-removed about it. The manager-once-removed will see the immediate manager and the subordinate together, otherwise he is allowing the subordinate to talk to him about the manager without the latter's having the opportunity to know what is being said and to reply – a situation which would be tantamount to tale-bearing. Brown [1] has described many of the necessary features of appeals procedures.

The manager hearing an appeal is faced with judging, among other things, whether his managerial subordinate has been unduly influenced by feelings extraneous to the work situation in making judgments about the subordinate who is appealing. It is an exceedingly difficult decision to make. For the immediate manager is much better placed to judge his subordinate's performance than is the manager hearing the appeal. What is required in the course of the discussion is to discover whether the manager is in fact behaving too harshly, or restrictively, or unreasonably towards his subordinate; or whether he, as a manager, has particular weaknesses or blind spots. Or alternatively, the question may be whether the subordinate has an unnecessary chip on his shoulder; or whether he is trying to say that he ought to be transferred or promoted or receive some other special action or recognition. Or it may be a matter of deciding whether the manager and the subordinate are both satisfactory, each in his own way, but perhaps just not capable of working together.

[1] W. Brown (1960), *Exploration in Management*, and (1971), *Organization*.

The circumstances and content of appeals are legion. They are as varied as the lives and circumstances of human beings. Was the subordinate's time-keeping really so bad if his statement about his difficult home circumstances is taken into account? Did he start the fight, or was he goaded into it? Did he carelessly cause the scrapping of the work, or was he contending with bad tooling and materials? Has he been chronically 'swinging the lead', or has he been given all the bad jobs to do? Has he been passed over for too long for a merit increase, or does he have an inflated evaluation of himself? Is he marginally impatient with customers, or merely firm and realistic? Was he impudent and abusive, or justifiably annoyed? Was suspension for three days too severe in the circumstances? And so on. There is no telling what issue will arise next. The manager hearing the appeal must use his best judgment in coping with these human situations.

The central issue for the higher manager is that he should ensure that his subordinate managers and his subordinates-once-removed are behaving in a fair and resonable manner. He is curbing autocratic tendencies in his subordinate managers, and making it clear that subordinates do not simply have to bow down in silence to unfair and unjust treatment. He is at the same time supporting and reinforcing firm but fair treatment of subordinates by his managers against inroads that might be made by subordinates who would act out personal problems and grievances at work.

In his decisions in appeals the higher manager is demonstrating in a practical way how he wishes his section of the organization to be run. An appeal procedure is thus an important opportunity for on-the-job training for managers and subordinates. It is also an important mechanism for helping to fix the style of management in an organization. This fact underlines the necessity of there being sufficient difference in capacity between manager and subordinate. For if an appeal is heard by a manager who is in the same work-capacity group as the manager appealed against, nothing is happening as far as the subordinate is concerned. The appeal is a mere formality: a mere climbing of an unnecessary and excess rung in the executive ladder. What is required is not only a fresh look at the situation but a fresh consideration at a significantly higher level of abstraction and of authority.

Final Resolution of Appeal Within Bureaucratic Systems

If a manager is so dominated by personal qualities or by involvement in situational-role relationships as to be pushed outside the limits of the behaviour required in the manager-subordinate relationship, for example behaving in an autocratic manner, then without adequate appeals mechanisms an explosive situation may develop. There may be continuous arguments. Labour turnover may go up. Chronic unco-operativeness may be established. Complaints may go by roundabout means to higher authority, a reflection of inadeqate organization often included under the rubric of informal organization.

The absence of an appeals system is a good example of the type of situation that gives rise to so-called informal organization. That concept not only overlooks the issue of requisite organization but stands as an intellectual block against striving for requisite organization. Where mechanisms are missing, people in executive organization will seek to fill the gap by mechanisms outside those explicitly ('formally') provided. Many therefore have concluded that this type of informal organization is not only needed but to be encouraged. The approach here is different. These informal mechanisms are seen as signs of social pathology — as pieces of extant organization pointing to shortcomings needing to be rectified by the development of more nearly requisite organization.

Given an appeals procedure, it becomes possible for the subordinates to draw the attention of higher authority to any situation of felt injustice. A spate of appeals against decisions of the same manager is a cause for a more general consideration of that manager's behaviour. Is he managing adequately? Are his subordinates trying to get at him? What are the reasons for the repeated appeals?

But what of the appeal or appeals that go to the very top of the bureaucratic hierarchy, to the chief executive himself? Suppose his decision is still not satisfactory to the appellant? The general trend today is to have a tribunal of people completely outside the enterprise to judge the merits of the case independently. Such a procedure is unlikely to be requisite. The decision is about standards, and an outside body could impose upon the enterprise a precedent for standards which may in fact be acceptable to no-one inside it — and without being accountable for the consequences as the chief executive is.

One example of the type of procedure which is likely to be more requisite is for the aggrieved individual, if dissatisfied with the chief executive's decision, to be able to take his grievance for consideration by the representatives of his peers. This procedure requires a representative system as described in Chapter 13. If these elected representatives decide that the individual has a case they will approach the chief executive on his behalf, bringing their power and influence to bear to get the chief executive to revise his judgment. By this means representatives can consider with the chief executive, in the setting of specific examples, the style and modes of behaviour to be accepted as appropriate in the organization.[2]

---

[2] Social analysis of this issue in the Glacier Project proved enormously instructive. The initial policy adopted by the Works Council was for an outside Tribunal to be used as the final stage of appeal. This Tribunal was to be composed of an outside arbitrator to be appointed by the Law Society or other independent body, plus one member appointed by the

This procedure points up the fact that in hearing an appeal the chief executive is setting standards of managerial and subordinate behaviour for the total organization. Such decisions ought requisitely to be a matter of concern to elected representatives within the enterprise. It is decidedly not a matter for outside interference, so long as the organization and its chief executive are working within the law of the community.

Individual Appeals and Policy Implementation

The distinction between regulated policies and subjects for individual appeal must be strongly noted. It is a conceptual distinction that must be made if appeals – which have to do with justice with respect to specific and particular judgments about particular individuals – are not to be confused with policy formation and implementation – which has to do with providing a framework of explicitly stated rules or established precedents applying in general and to everyone.

If an individual considers that his manager has acted fairly and within policy, but that nevertheless the decision is unsatisfactory in his particular case, then he should not have recourse to appeal, but should challenge the policy itself through the representative system. The requisite procedure is to take the issue up with the manager. If he cannot rectify the matter, then the subordinate with his representative should take the matter directly to the determining manager – that is to say to the manager at the level where the particular policy is determined. If the determining manager cannot, or will not give satisfaction by modifying the interpretation of policy, the member can then seek to have his representative take it up via the representative machinery. For that to happen would of course require a consensus among the other members that they too considered the policy unsatisfactory.

The question of individual appeals arouses very deep feelings of personal victimization and anxiety. Interpretations of policy do not: they tend rather to arouse anger on behalf of the group. Policy is external to the individual. It is a limit applying equally to all. The substance of an appeal, however, is concerned with the subjective interaction between manager

---

appealing member's representative committee. When after some years the procedure was called upon for the first time, it proved exceedingly difficult to find an independent outside member who could understand the Company's policies and mode of operation. The appellant on this occasion left the Company without bothering to complete his appeal. This unsatisfactory experience led the Works Council to call for further analysis. It was the shop stewards who then began to question the wisdom of having tribunal members from outside, on the grounds that their decisions would be final and would likely to be binding in perpetuity. It was far too inflexible a procedure, and inhibited the working through of problems to an acceptable solution. It was at this point that the procedure described in the foregoing text was worked out and became part of Company policy.

and subordinate, and with the kind of person the manager is and the kind of person the subordinate is. There must therefore be adequate procedures for appeals to be dealt with and to be handled with despatch. It is in the appeals procedure that the bureaucratic hierarchy touches most directly upon the general political and legal question of the freedom of the individual.

FUNCTIONING OF BUREAUCRATIC SYSTEMS

16

Operational Spine and Delegation
of Tasks

The chapters which make up Part Five of the book probe more deeply into how bureaucracies actually function: they deal with the elaboration of a range of different role relationships, with varying degrees of accountability and authority, concerned with the carrying out of operational tasks and supporting activities; the separation of grading systems and career progression from the organization of managerial levels; and an analysis of different types of leadership. Much of the data comes from the Glacier Project, added to and sometimes modified by other project work. The goal is to analyse this material afresh to seek out in detail those working arrangements within bureaucracy which will strengthen *gemeinschaft* and community; and to identify those which stimulate exploitation, suspicion and mistrust, so that they can be eradicated.

First, in Chapter 16, we shall establish the general nature of the operational spine of a bureaucracy, that part of the system which directly produces outputs which the system was set up to produce. This operational organization comprises the development of the goods or services, their production, and their presentation to clients or a market for sale or delivery.

In considering the nature of the organization for these operational transactions, three different modes of organization will be separated out: that used, for example, in manufacturing, where the direct output activity is all delegated to the shop- or office-floor and managers spend all their time managing; that used, for example, in design and research, where direct output is provided higher up with assistance as necessary from subordinates; and that used, for example, in some selling; where a manager and a subordinate may share responsibility for direct output, in this case sharing responsibility for work with different areas of a customer organization. Failure to make this distinction leads to all areas of bureaucratic systems being analysed as though they were manufacturing systems, an approach which unnecessarily stultifies and gives a mechanistic quality to the design of organization for other types of work.

How Objects Define Operational Tasks

Governing bodies assign operational activities to their bureaucratic systems in pursuit of the objects of the association. It is these operational activities which can be broken down into specific tasks which a manager assigns to a subordinate to achieve. The task can be assigned in terms of a describable output to be achieved, and when the task is completed the output can be observed.

The tasks that will be available to be assigned within the bureaucratic hierarchy will be determined by the objects of the association and the operational activities which the governing body has decided shall be carried out in pursuit of the objects of the association. It is essential therefore that the objects of the association be clearly formulated and made manifest.

One of the difficulties in attaining clarity about the objects of an association is that there tends to be confusion between its objects and the motives or purposes of its members. This confusion usually results in a failure to define objects. Failure to define objects tends towards non-requisite organization. The reason is that there is a resulting failure to set out clearly the operational tasks to be carried out by the employed bureaucratic hierarchy, and therefore executive organization will tend away from the requisite.

For example, the purposes of those governing a hospital may be a humanitarian concern to ensure that sick people receive treatment. That is also the reason why a mother takes care of her sick child. But the fact that the mother is moved by the same type of purpose as hospital staff does not make her home a hospital. It is not the motives of the individuals concerned that determine the nature of an institution. It is the objects they set as a result of those motives that matter. The objects of the authority governing a hospital must be more precisely detailed if we are to see the difference between it and a home in which a sick child is being treated. These objects involve among other things the provision of medical diagnosis, prescription and treatment; nursing care and treatment; hospital rooms and hotel facilities; medical rooms and equipment; teaching and research facilities; facilities for discovering new needs and for modifying the services provided. It is when these objects are stated that the operational tasks can be discovered, and requisite organization for the activities of the hospital can be realistically considered. The form of organization sets the framework within which the efforts of employee staff can be deployed so as to achieve the objects of the association.

A second example: the purposes of the individual members of a group of entrepreneurs in setting up a business may include the desire to make a profit, the desire to be occupied in running a business, the desire to provide a service to consumers, and other motives as well. The executive hierarchy of the business cannot be organized, however, in terms of these statements of motives or reasons. It must be organized in terms of those activities which the governing body decides shall be pursued in providing the particular services they shall offer to the market. These objects will need to include the continuing assessment of market needs and the development and production of the specific goods and services calculated to fulfil those market needs and to satisfy customers.

Failure to avoid the confusion between personal purposes and organizational objects can lead to endless debate and recrimination on the question of who is to be held accountable for what. In business enterprises everyone may argue that he and his department are 'responsible for profits', whereas in fact each one contributes to those profits by pursuing his own particular operational tasks deriving from the objects. Many accounting techniques make this error by getting out profit and loss accounts for factories; in fact, since the factory manager controls only the operational activity of production, and usually has no control over prices or selling activities, or research and development, it is anti-requisite to hold him accountable for anything other than his manufacturing activities. In hospitals the argument may take the form of who is responsible 'for curing patients'; the fact is that no one section of the hospital is accountable for such an object, whatever might be their personal motives and desires. Nursing, medical and administrative staff are accountable for their own specific parts of the range of objects which it has been decided that the hospital shall try to achieve, all of which contribute to the treatment of the patient.

Operational and Support Tasks

The translation of the objects of an enterprise into actual work requires the assigning of the specific tasks to be carried out by employees of the enterprise. Tasks that are directly concerned with the objects and operational activities of the enterprise are here termed *operational tasks*. They can be distinguished from all other types of task concerned with supporting and facilitating the discharge of the operational tasks, which will be referred to as *support tasks*.

The distinction between operational and support tasks is an important one for organizational purposes. It lays the basis for precision in assigning accountability and in fixing the authority relationship between different positions in the hierarchy. In the actual process of constructing an organization, it is essential to outline first the organizational pattern for the operational activities – to construct what I would term the *operational spine* – and to build the organization of support activities around this operational spine.[1]

---

[1] This distinction between operational spine and support organization may seem to be the old familiar distinction between line and staff dressed up in a new language. It is not the same. The reason it cannot be the same is that line and staff have never been given any boundary definition or systematic meaning at all. I would emphasize that by operational

The concepts of operational and support task can be illustrated if we take the example of a secretarial agency which has as one of its objects the provision of secretarial services for customers. The task of doing secretarial work for a customer who pays for it is an operational task; the task of doing secretarial work for the manager of the agency to assist him to do his tasks, is a support task.

In more general terms, the operational tasks of bureaucratic systems can be formulated in terms of social exchange theory.[2] Bureaucratic systems are social exchange systems. They are the means by which associations transact business with one another or with consumers. Operational tasks are the tasks which constitute the content of the business transactions. The term business is used here in the widest sense of any and all provision of goods or services – industrial and commercial, public services, social or educational services.

Human transactions in social exchange would appear always to differentiate into three main dimensions: development and modification of the content of the transaction according to the perception by one person or group of the needs and interests of another; production of the goods or service involved in the transaction; and assessment of the needs and interests of the other, and maintenance of contact in order to effect the transaction.

From these three dimensions of human transactions may be derived the three major operational activities of any bureaucratic system: the development of goods and services (D); provision of these goods or services (M);[3] and their selling (S). When a governing body sets up a bureaucratic employment system the chief executive of that system is always accountable for the co-ordination of the D, M, and S operational tasks of the organization. If in turn, that chief executive is authorized to establish subsidiary bureaucracies, then the appointed chief executives of those subsidiaries would also be accountable for their delegated D, M, and S activities. In short, the definition of a chief executive role is one that carries accountability for D, M, and S. All three are necessary to constitute a full operational transaction, and it is only the chief executive who can be accountable for all three together.

The role of chief executive of a bureaucracy always includes D, M, and S duties. It is within the chief executive role that these three functions come

---

tasks I mean precisely those tasks which a bureaucratic system is established to carry out. The definition of support organization is a much more complex matter and will be analysed in the next chapter.

[2] G. C. Homans (1951), *The Human Group*; and P. M. Blau (1964), *Exchange and Power in Social Life*.

[3] Production of goods and provision of services have designated by the symbol M because this analysis was first carried out in the Glacier Project in manufacturing industry where the production part of the transaction was concerned with the manufacture (M) of goods. See W. Brown (1960), *Exploration in Management*.

together and are seen in relation to one another in the formulation of operating strategies and tactics – marketing, in a commercial or industrial enterprise. It is for the chief executive to ensure that there is an adequate balance of activity: enough investment in design and development of new goods or services to secure the future, but not so much as to sink the enterprise in the present; the right amount of production capacity and development of production methods to be able to cope with fluctuating and changing market or client demand; and enough contact with the market and with clients to maintain effective negotiations for current service provision and to assess likely future needs.

This description of the chief executive role does not refer particularly to industry, or to government departments or to social services, or to any other special kind of bureaucracy. It refers to all types. Thus, within *goods and services* are incuded provisions of all kinds – industrial and consumer goods; commercial services; central and local government services; education, hospital and other social services. Making and provision (M) of the goods or services are manifestly necessary in all. Design and development (D) of goods and services are also required in all types, although this fact is often overlooked in the public and social services and sometimes overlooked in all. So too in the case of sales or client relationships – it is often overlooked in public and social service organizations that the maintaining of good public relations and a continuing understanding of community needs are absolutely essential if a good service is to be provided.

The particular D-M-S activities established by the chief executive are determined by the object set and controlled by the governing body. That is to say, the kinds of service he provides, the outline of the market or clients he will serve, and the general direction of service design and development must be governed either by explicit general policies fixed by the governing body or by the accumulation of decisions on capital provisions and on budgets. The chief executive must then organize his bureaucratic system to achieve these objects by carrying out operational tasks. Once the association and its objects have been identified, the establishment of the operational spine is the first act in systematic organization of bureaucratic hierarchies.

Organization of D, M, and S Systems

The D, M, and S activities are the sub-systems of bureaucratic systems which manifest the open system characteristics of the whole. D exchanges energy in the form of new knowledge and ideas; M exchanges energy in the form of raw materials bought in and goods and services delivered; S exchanges energy in the form of active negotiation with the client and market environment. It is essential that these systems should be organized in terms of those operational transactions. This proposition may seem self-evident. That it is far from self-evident can be shown, for example, by the very common tendency to organize these systems in terms of the career structure, or professional outlook, or other interest of employees.

Thus, for example, Development (D) is commonly organized in groupings based upon academic research disciplines such as physics or engineering or chemistry; or in product or customer or market groupings. In fact, the operational tasks in D are projects concerned with exploration, research and design directed towards modification of the existing products or services or the development of new ones. They should thus requisitely be organized into departments or sections based upon categories or projects concerned with the development of the same or related products or services. It is this principle of organization which maintains the open system character.

Each of these project groupings, of course, might require to bring together several academic disciplines. But to organize in terms of academic disciplines *per se* produces a fragmentation of the operational activity of the modification and development of products or services. It also tends to turn the D function into a closed system, turned in upon the staff rather than turned outwards towards the needs of clients.[4]

The operational tasks in M are concerned with the manufacture of goods or the provision of services, and are organized requisitely in product or service groupings. They are not uncommonly organized in terms of customer or market groupings, with consequent loss of production specialization. If the scale of production for a particular market is such as to allow for a separate and continuous facility, then the establishment of a D-M-S subsidiary, large or small, is probably called for. There is more opportunity for setting up small entrepreneurial subsidiaries of this type than is often recognized.

The operational tasks in S are concerned with the assessment of market and consumer needs and negotiation with those consumers, including information and publicity. These tasks are requisitely organized in connected consumer groupings or markets. In multiple organizations where the services of two separate subsidiaries are produced for the same consumer, it may often be useful for the S organization of one to have complete consumer responsibility, the other subsidiary retaining responsibility for the provision of its own products or services to those consumers while at the same time getting an S service from the other organization.

None of the foregoing implies that contact with consumers is the sole right and responsibility of S. D and M also require direct contact with con-

---

[4] Professional identity must also be reflected in organizational structure. How this result can be achieved alongside operational task organization is discussed in the next chapter.

sumers – to experience the difficulties and shortcomings which arise in existing products or services, and to sense potentially useful new developments; and to experience directly the quality and delivery standards demanded for the goods or services being provided. It is by this means that the three operational sub-systems may function best as open systems, and thus as human systems. The greater the extent to which all operational sectors of a bureaucracy have direct consumer contact and function as open systems, the more the bureaucracy may be humanized.

It is of course often argued that 'research types' cannot be allowed contact with customers. It is said to be too risky because they are after all 'boffins' or 'back-room boys' and in the back room they should be kept. Our argument here is precisely the opposite. D is most decidedly a front-room activity, concerned not with research for its own sake but with the use of research methods to try better to satisfy human needs – the needs of consumers. It is by bringing D into the front room that one of the most important steps can be taken to bring bureaucracy alive in the sense of bringing product and service development work directly into contact with the community to be served. Here is a social link and social interaction of more than passing significance in industrial societies, with particular relevance to avoidance of the centralization of taste.

This analysis ought to be familiar enough to those in industrial and commercial organizations, in central and local government departments providing direct services to the public, and in social service organizations and agencies. In all these organizations the goods or services to be provided can be clearly enough described and so can the requisite need for their modification and development. So also can the consumer be identified – whether as an explicit customer in a describable market, or as a member of a group of potential consumers of a service, known as the public.

The notion of a consumer contact function, S, in relation to public service grant-income institutions may be less familiar, since it smacks too much of earned-income institutions attempting to persuade consumers to buy their goods or services. This is far too narrow a view of consumer contact and selling, however. This concept in the broader sense adopted here relates to the idea of understanding the needs of the consumers of goods or services; of providing the best and most satisfying goods or services within the limits set; and of maintaining good personal and public relations with those consumers. Such an outlook is as essential to grant-income as to earned-income institutions. Both ought requisitely to be the servants and not the masters of those for whom they are providing. Such an outlook would requisitely be reflected not only in a client- or a marketing-orientation, but in more widespread provision of the D function in public services. It is noticeable that when grant-income institutions are 'hived off' and become earned-income institutions, they very soon set up both S and

D organizations.

Many government services have grown up within a regulatory quasi-policing orientation, such as income tax regulation, or within an orientation of providing help to the needy and destitute 'who cannot help themselves', or within an orientation of being a monopoly utility for a public that cannot do much about the service it gets because there is no alternative. Against this background, the notion of government services having to orient themselves towards consumer interests makes only slow headway. It must rapidly become more common if the nature of public services is to help to reinforce the idea that government is for the people and not the other way around. This orientation of bureaucracies towards public service is one critical element in the metamorphosis of bureaucracy to *gemeinschaft* within the framework of *gesellschaft*.

Three Modes of Managerial Work: DDO, ADO, DOS

There is a marked tendency in the literature on organization of D-M-S activities to use a single model – that based upon the organization of mass production manufacturing. This model does not in fact serve well for all activities. More than one model may be needed. One of the consequences of over-stretching a single model when several different models are required, is a preoccupation with concepts such as variations in managerial style, or special arrangements for professional staff, to make up for the short-comings of the single model used. Thus, for example, it is often argued that management in factory production work requires a very different climate or style from the management of research or professional work. The former is said to allow for a more autocratic or mechanistic climate or style, whereas the latter two are supposed to call for a more organic, or open, or collaborative, or participant climate or style.[5]

One of the studies on the Glacier Project began as a study of the possible need for different managerial styles. The outcome of the analysis, however, was not a need for a different climate or style, but a need to recognize that there were at least three different managerial situations, each one requiring to be the subject of its own model. In order to describe the three different models, it is first necessary to establish the concept of *direct output* (DO). By direct output is meant the actual production of an end-product or service or of a constituent part of an end-product or service. Thus, for example, a direct output (DO) would be: machining a piece of metal; typing a letter; carrying out a research investigation; doing a design on the drawing board; getting out an estimate; seeing a customer with a view to a sale;

[5] See, for example, such writings as: R. Tagiuri and G. H. Litwin (1968), *Organizational Climate*; and L. R. James and A. P. Jones (1974), 'Organizational Climate: A Review of Theory and Research'.

dealing with a client; conducting an interview. That is to say, a direct output (DO) is any activity directly concerned with the output of a particular department, as against managing the production of the direct outputs of others.

In the production model of managerial organization in bureaucratic systems direct output is wholly and exclusively at Str-1 level – mass production by hourly-rated operators of machine tools. The managerial line above the operators is wholly and exclusively engaged in managerial activities. The production managers do not themselves operate machine tools and produce direct outputs. We shall call this model *delegated direct output* – the **DDO** model – because managerial activity is concerned only with the delegation and control of direct output tasks.

Very different models of managerial activity are needed, however, with respect to activities which require direct output work above Str-1 level. One of these models is concerned with direct outputs which may require to be done anywhere from Str-2 and above, but where the employee doing them may need assistance; for example, most research work; most design work; some personnel selection; drafting replies to questions in Parliament; social work or district nursing; physiotherapy; etc. In such situations what is often required is for the person carrying out the direct output to be assigned one or more subordinates as assistants or aides; in other words, the direct output is at Str-X with parts or bits and pieces done by a subordinate or subordinates at Str-(X-1) and possibly at Str-(X-2) as well.

In these circumstances the person engaged in direct output is primarily so engaged, but he must secondarily be the manager of whatever subordinates he may have to aid him in his direct output. We shall refer to this model as *aided direct output* – the **ADO** model. It is an essential model for the organization of all professional work in bureaucracies.

The third model, which applies mainly to some sales situations, is one in which the direct output is mainly delegated, but from time to time the manager must also himself be involved in direct output. Thus, a sales manager delegates a group of clients to a subordinate, and expects that subordinate to get on with his work of selling – the direct output activity. But periodically – say once or twice a year – the sales manager must himself visit some, if not all, of the clients to deal at a higher level in the client organization than his sales subordinate can; for example, to meet the managing director, where the salesman is dealing only with the chief buyer subordinate to the managing director. The sales manager is thus able to settle a range of sales policies, including, say, pricing policy, minimum quantities to be taken, special design or other services to be supplied, policies within which his sales subordinate can then carry out his on-going sales activity with the client's chief buyer.

In these circumstances the manager is primarily engaged in delegating direct output to the sales subordinate, but from time to time must engage in direct output work in support of his subordinate's activity. We shall refer to this model as *direct output support* – the **DOS** model.

Differences in Managerial Situation

Certain critical differences may be noted in the manager-subordinate relationship for each of these models. They call for differences in managerial activity, not as a matter of difference in style but as a matter of the requirements of the three objective variations in the manager-subordinate role relationship.

In the DDO situation the manager spends all of his time in planning and managing DDO. The Str-2 manager must ensure that he keeps abreast of how his subordinates are faring – whether they are up to the tasks to be done, how well they are performing, whether they need training or retraining – his total orientation is managerial. This managerial outlook also informs the role of the Str-3 manager, for he is managing direct output in turn through managers. He must assess his immediate subordinates in terms of how well they are managing to obtain direct output from his subordinates-once-removed.

The central point to note in the DDO situation is that in no case is the manager actually sharing a direct output with his subordinate in the sense of working together on it with him. The manager must manage from a distance, without direct interaction on the task. He must assess subordinate activity mainly in terms of review of results, with only occasional opportunity for direct observation of the quality of his subordinate's work while he is working. The manager does not even see all the direct output. He is able only to sample it by walking about. For the rest the output leaves the department unseen by the manager, and comes to him mainly in the form of paper records of number of clients seen, number of complaints, amount of production output, with the number of good parts produced, the number which had to be rejected because of poor quality, the numbers of tools and other expendables used, etc. Indeed, the subordinate feels that too much direct supervision impoverishes his role by reducing freedom of action – role impoverishment in contrast to role enrichment.

In the ADO situation, the manager is continually in contact with his subordinate aide or assistant. In fact it is incorrect to use the title 'manager' for him. The proper and usual title is the activity or professional title; namely, research investigator, social worker, designer, layout engineer, dietician. In these situations – most if not all professional employment roles would be included – the managerial component of the role is almost automatic and needs little focusing. The 'manager' is inevitably directly assessing the quality of the subordinate's work, since he gets the results back to himself in order to be able to do his own direct output work.

Thus, for example, the research investigator uses his laboratory assistant to carry out special tests or examinations for him, the results of which he uses in his research, or has his assistant help him to assemble equipment or to run complex experiments requiring more than one person to carry out; the social worker uses her aide to obtain information for her, or to see a client to ensure that certain procedures are being carried out, so that the social worker can carry out her own casework more effectively; the designer uses a draughtsman assistant to do detail drawings within a master plan, which will become parts of the designer's full-scale drawings.

It is necessary under ADO conditions for the superior to become explicitly a manager only from time to time – when a new aide is to be appointed, when performance assessment must be recorded for salary review purposes, when the subordinate wants a career discussion. But otherwise, 'managing' is going on implicitly all the time, the superior being directly aware by on-going direct review whether or not he is satisfied with his subordinate's work. To emphasize the managerial content of such roles, and to give the superior management training in accord with the DDO model, is to reduce his effectiveness in direct output work. What so often happens is that as the research investigators, social workers, designers, etc., become better and better DDO-type managers they delegate more and more of the direct output activity, engage less and less themselves in research, casework and design, and the quality of work falls because of its being too much delegated to too low a level. Requisite management style here is for the superior to be good at his own professional work and to be able to take his aide or assistant along with him.

The DOS situation lies somewhere in between DDO and ADO. The sales manager must be able to handle the DDO type of relationship with his subordinates, leaving them accountability for the clients and sales to the clients. But he has a special opportunity periodically to review the work of each of his subordinates directly, as well as to set the policy for that work. In his assessment of his subordinate's work he must be able to take account of the policy framework he has negotiated, and any performance targets he may set must be within that framework.

Another way of describing the DOS relationship would be that it is a DDO relationship, which periodically becomes an ADO relationship while the manager negotiates a new framework, and then returns to being a DDO relationship once again. The managerial style required is for the manager to be able to take over periodically and then to leave the subordinate to get on with his work.

We have brought this issue of the DDO, ADO, and DOS models of manager-subordinate relationships in at this point because, as will be apparent, one particular model is relevant to each of the three operational activities: the DDO model for M, the ADO model for D, and the DOS (sometimes the ADO) model for S. The consequences for managerial training have been pointed out.

In more general terms, the DDO model probably encompasses the largest number of roles with managerial content, since it covers almost all manufacturing work, and most office work of the invoicing, ledger-keeping, clerical type. It must be recognized, however, that the ADO model is also exceedingly important, especially because it encompasses nearly all so-called professional roles.

Professionalism and ADO Relationships

The recognition of the ADO type of relationship is important in the organization of professional work within bureaucracies. It is often argued that professionalism is inconsistent with bureaucratic organization. The reason for this view is the tendency to treat all roles at Str-2 and above as though they were in the DDO situation, with the consequence that their incumbents should have as many subordinates as possible to manage. Thus once the professionals – and this applies to groups as diverse as design engineers, nurses, architects, psychologists, social workers, statisticians, lawyers, therapists, technologists, scientists – are employed in bureaucratic hierarchies, the pressure builds up for them to become as competent as DDO managers; that is to say they are encouraged to spend more and more of their time managing others and less and less doing their own professional work. This pressure is reinforced by their getting paid more if they acquire more subordinates, recognition tending to be tied to their managerial duties. As a result the institution loses the advantage of their professional skills.

What is required in order to prevent such a development is to establish first of all the basic level at which professional work is required. The designer of bridges or of new cars, for example, may be required at Str-5, with a small team of just a few assistants at Str-4 and perhaps another handful at lower strata: but with the top-level designer himself engaged in design work assisted by his subordinates, to produce innovative and original work. The duties involved in social work, by contrast, may throw up a basic Stratum-2 level of work,[6] and so may district nursing or physiotherapy. Here again, the art of designing an organization is not to burden the research investigator, social worker, district nurse, designer or physiotherapist with a mass of subordinates; they should rather be left to

---

[6] See, for example, the description of the social worker role in *Social Services Departments*, Social Services Organization Research Unit of Brunel Institute of Organization and Social Studies (1974).

get on with their professional work and have opportunity for upgrading in their careers on the basis of professional merit without being forced to take on more subordinates in order to get ahead.

Satisfaction in work can be achieved so long as the professional is employed as professional and provided with such few assistants as may be required (ADO), and not tied down to becoming a DDO manager of professional aides. It is when the attempt is made through managerial training and other procedures to impose a DDO model on the bureaucratic organization of professional work that the professionals squirm and become uneasy. They rightly realize that they are becoming deprofessionalized in a situation which continues to call for a professional output at their own level. When incorrect emphasis on DDO managing takes over, the professional knows he is becoming an administrator instead of doing his professional work, at the expense of the quality of service. But he tends wrongly to conclude that this outcome is an inevitable consequence of the dehumanizing effects of bureaucracy, instead of realizing that it is a matter of the dehumanizing of the bureaucracy itself by using it incorrectly.

17
Horizontal Role Relationships and Degrees of Accountability and Authority

The literature on bureaucratic organization commonly provides for two sets of so-called formal role relationships – line and staff organization. Bureaucratic systems are in fact much more complex. In addition to the vertical manager-subordinate relationships, provision must be made for a range of lateral role relationships, varying in degree of intensity of accountability and authority. These gradations in intensity lay the basis for an ordinal scale for these two important dimensions of role relationships; and point in the direction of a possible equal-ratio scale measure.

The role relationships to be described include: prescribing, supervisory, attachment, staff specialist, monitoring and co-ordinating, quality inspection, advisory, collateral, conjoint, service-getting and scanning. Once these relationships are established it becomes possible rigorously to define those various types of laterally organized working groups which are usually referred to in such vaguely defined terms as 'teams' or 'matrix organization' or 'functionally autonomous work groups'.

Lateral Role Relationships

The analysis of bureaucratic systems in terms of 'formal' and 'informal' organization usually describes the formal in terms of one-way downwards-only autocratic manager-subordinate relationships.[1] It has been assumed that the formal organization of bureaucracy allows for nothing more than for managers to order their subordinates to do things. Anything more than this downwards communication of instructions (line) and some provision for staff roles, tends to be seen as a matter of so-called informal organization. This formulation is not sound. It takes the fact that managerial behaviour in bureaucracies is often autocratic, and concludes that unsanctioned one-way coercive power relationships are an integral property of all bureaucracies rather than a sign of pathology in some.

The actual structure of bureaucracies is far more complex. It has already been shown that the vertical dyadic manager-subordinate

---

[1] This view dominates the human relations school stemming from Elton Mayo and the Hawthorne Experiment. It is to be found in the majority of contemporary writers on organization.

relationship between manager and subordinate is not simply one-way downwards, but is in fact a two-way relationship, as indeed all role relationships must inevitably be. How far they function satisfactorily as two-way relationships will be determined by such factors as the degree of institutionalization of procedures through which subordinates may take part in sanctioning the authority of their managers; as in, for example, representative and appeals procedures, and ordinary two-way manager-subordinate consultation.

In addition, however, bureaucratic systems require a whole range of lateral relationships between roles in different managerial lines of command, which cannot be contained within the concept of staff. Nor can these relationships simply be dealt with by referring to them as informal.[2] They are an integral part of the functioning of the system, and need precise definition in terms of the accountability and authority in the relationships. These relationships may be simple dyads, or may be part of role nets involving three, and sometimes more interconnected roles. They form a network of cross-connections serving to support the functioning of the system as an integrated whole.

These support activities are essential. They are one of the main expressions of the division of labour, and grow up in response to many different demands: the need of managers for assistance in co-ordinating the work of subordinates; opportunities for providing specialized services on a centralized basis; organization-wide growth of the same professional or technical specialisms. But because they usually arise spontaneously they are not adequately catered for in terms of definition of their accountability and authority. This unclarity produces a fuzzing of accountability and of authority in the operational spine of the organization. The result is an all-round weakening of organization, personal frustration and decrease in efficiency.

The line and staff concepts generally used to try to overcome these well-known difficulties were adapted from military organization by Urwick.[3] These two concepts cannot, however, cope with the problem for two reasons: first, they are themselves not sufficiently defined for effective use; and, second, as there are more than just two role relationships involved, two concepts cannot by themselves bear all the traffic.

Field work at Glacier, and then in the complexities of health and social services and public administration has uncovered a dozen or more different role relationships which can be shown extantly to exist. As will be described, each of these relationships differs in significant respects from the others; significant in the sense that the differences in the degree of accoun-

---

[2] Or as has become popular today, by compressing them into the ill-defined concept of matrix organization.
[3] L. Urwick (1947), *Elements of Administration*.

tability and authority matter in no uncertain fashion to those involved in the relationships.

It is proposed, therefore, to review those support role relationships which have been teased out in the course of field work. The relationships described are not the only relationships possible: there are undoubtedly more to be discovered. But certainly the ones to be dealt with have been found essential to any understanding and specification of the functioning of hospitals, factories, offices, sales and research departments, governmental institutions, social services.

Failure to identify which of these relationships is needed in each circumstance, and to specify it, leads to endless trouble and complications. Wrong assumptions are made about who is accountable for what, and about the authority properly to be exercised. Legitimacy is undermined, and the expression of power becomes a matter of personal interactions inadequately framed and bounded by authority. Interpersonal suspicion and mistrust are stimulated. If the need to differentiate among some dozen or more distinct role relationships seems unnecessarily complex, it is well to remember that pathological complications arise not from complexity itself but from the failure to recognize complexity and the consequent tendency to treat the complex as though it were simple. It is when gallons of different role relationships are poured into the 'staff-line' pint pot that confusion, consternation and stress arise.

Degrees of Intensity of Accountability and Authority

It may be noted that the formulation proposed contains the concept of degrees of accountability and authority. This idea can be made explicit, and will suggest an ordinal scale for establishing greater and lesser amounts of accountability and authority. It has not been possible as yet to construct an equal-interval or equal-ratio scale of measurement, but an ordinal scale would prove an important step on the way.

Accountability and authority are commonly thought of as simple attributes: either a person is accountable by virtue of his role, or he is not; and similarly, either he has authority or he has none. Precisely the opposite, however, is the case. There is a scale of degrees of accountability and authority, some roles carrying more than others in descending order.

Let us consider the question of accountability first, limiting the discussion to accountability in bureaucratic systems. It may be noted that as we proceed from lower to higher levels in the hierarchy, the managers higher up are accountable for more than are their subordinates, for they are accountable for the performance of their subordinates as well as for their own. But it may also be demonstrated that managerial roles carry greater accountability for outcomes than do various other types of role concerned with assisting managers to carry out their work – whether in helping to supervise one section, or in staff officer roles concerned with one specialist aspect such as personnel activities, or in being accountable for various inspecting, monitoring or co-ordinative activities.

Corresponding to these gradations in accountability there are equivalent gradations of authority. Here the picture is more complex. Accountability has to do simply with outcomes. The authority which is needed to match accountability, however, has two main aspects, each of them complex: first, that aspect connected with the task; and second, that aspect connected with the sanctions, positive and negative, which the incumbent of one role can exercise towards the incumbent of a laterally connected role. Let us consider each in turn.

Authority concerned with the task has two elements: the initiation of the task; and the setting of limits within which the task is to be carried out. There are varying degrees of authority in initiating tasks. The strongest is to have authority to order another to carry out a task; and if the other does not do so he is guilty of negligence or gross misconduct. Less strong is the authority to try to advise and persuade another to carry out a task; but if the other is not persuaded then he need not do so. The weakest is to be authorized to request another to carry out a task; and if the other says he cannot do so the requester has to drop the matter as far as his relation with the other is concerned, without the authority even to try to persuade him.

With respect to the setting of limits there are two degrees of authority. The strongest is to have the authority to decide the limits within which another works. Less strong is to have authority to recommend given limits to another, but leaving it to the other to decide.

Authority concerned with *sanctions which can be exercised* towards another also has two elements: the appraisal of the competence of the other; and influencing the other's position and career in the system — his level of reward, his career movement, and indeed whether he continues to be employed in the system at all. Both these elements have two degrees of authority: to decide, or only to recommend for the other's manager to decide.

These various aspects of authority may be summarized thus:

Task-connected:	initiate tasks:	order / persuade / request
	set limits:	decide / recommend
Sanctions:	appraise competence:	decide / recommend (to other's manager)
	rewards:	decide / recommend (to other's manager)

It is essential that these gradations in accountability and authority be clearly understood and defined. It is an old managerial maxim that accountability and authority must match. That statement does not go far enough. The essential point is that the degree of authority defines extantly the degree of accountability it is reasonable to expect. Thus, for example, one person may be accountable for setting tasks for another. How much authority he will carry to do this, however, can be varied by varying the sanctions he is authorized to exercise. If he is to be able on his own behalf to order the other to act, he must be authorized to take some part in the appraisal of the other's performance and in deciding his reward and movement in role; if he is expected to do his best only to persuade the other to act, then he must be authorized only to report to the crossover point if he is unsuccessful; if he is expected only to request the other to act, then he ought requisitely to be authorized only to report to his own manager that he is unable to obtain a particular service.

The first of these relationships will be recognizable as a manager-subordinate relationship. The second and third will be referred to as monitoring and service-getting respectively. They are examples of the wider range of role relationships to be obtained through recognizing the possible variations in degree of accountability and authority. These relationships can be used to support the vertical manager-subordinate functions by building in a series of horizontal role relationships of different intensity, to co-ordinate activities, to exercise control of expenditure, quality and other features, to provide services, and to encourage co-operative action.

Table of Role Relationships

The general framework to be used is to proceed from the roles with greatest degree of accountability and authority to the roles with the least. The role relationships are summarized in the table opposite, and then described in the text.

The table is incomplete in the sense that it is possible to conceive of additional role relationships in the gaps between those listed. It is a kind of Mendeleev table. Thus, for example, there is room for a role relationship between the manager-subordinate relationship and the prescribing relationship, in which the person would have the authority to decide rather than to recommend the appraisal of another's personal competence. We have not so far, however, discovered any such role relationship in any of the social systems in which work has been done.

Prescribing Relationships

Next to the manager-subordinate relationship, the role relationship with the strongest accountability and authority so far found in work systems is

Type of Authority	Limit Setting	Appraisal of Conformity to Limits	Task Initiating	Appraisal of Personal Competence	Influencing Movement in Role	Reporting Results
Managerial	Decide	Decide	Order	Decide	Decide	Yes
Prescribing	Decide	Decide	Order	Recommend	Recommend	Yes
Supervisory	Recommend	Decide	Order	Recommend	Recommend	Yes
Attachment	Decide	Decide	Order	Limited Decision (1)	Limited Influence (2)	Yes Yes
Staff	Recommend	Decide	Order	0	0	Yes
Monitoring and Co-ordinating	Recommend	Decide	Persuade	0	0	Yes
Quality Inspection	Recommend	Decide	0	0	0	Yes
Advisory	0	0	Persuade	0	0	Yes
Collateral	0	0	Persuade	0	0	Yes
Conjoint	0	0	Persuade	0	0	Yes
Service-getting	0	0	Request	0	0	Yes
Scanning	0	0	0	0	0	Yes

(1) Person receiving attachment is limited to deciding only whether the attached person's performance is above or below the minimum required standard.

(2) If the person receiving attachment decides that the attached is below the minimum required standard, his influence is limited to having person's attachment to him discontinued.

that between doctors and the nursing and other hospital staff who must carry out their prescriptions for diagnosis or treatment.[4] Because the doctor is accountable for ensuring adequate quality of diagnosis and treatment for his patients, his prescriptions must carry considerable force.

In the prescribing relationship, the doctor can set limits within which others will deal with his patients and can monitor adherence to those limits. His prescriptions must be followed, and at the time he specifies. Indeed, it was the realization that prescriptions had to be carried out, and at the prescribed times, that first led[5] to the conclusion that the doctor-nurse role relationship was a much stronger one than was implied in our preliminary analysis in terms of service-getting. This latter formulation was quickly rejected by both doctors and nurses as too weak.

In order for the doctor to be able to be requisitely accountable for ensuring adequate diagnosis and treatment for his patient, he must be able to appraise the quality of any diagnostic or treatment procedures he prescribes. In doing so he is inevitably appraising the performance of the person whose actions he prescribes. Where this other person is someone with whom the doctor is regularly associated — for example a ward sister or

[4] See, for example, R. W. Rowbottom et al. (1970), *Hospital Organization*.
[5] The Brunel Health Service Organization Research Unit, as reported in R. W. Rowbottom et al., op. cit.

a particular physiotherapist treating his patients – then he will inevitably form an opinion of her personal competence, and will wish to express it – whether a positive appraisal for which he thinks she should be rewarded or a negative appraisal for which she should be penalized. Provision is thus made in the prescribing relationship to influence the appraisal of another's personal competence and to influence his career, by means of being able to make appropriate recommendations to his manager – leaving the decisions and final accountability for the other's performance in the role of that manager. If the prescriber were dissatisfied with the outcome, especially if he considered that the other was performing not just rather inadequately but below minimum acceptable standards, then he could take the matter further to the manager-once-removed and, if necessary, on up to the crossover point for resolution.

Supervisory Relationships

It may arise, as with the organization of office work or shop-floor production work, that it is useful to have a particular set of activities grouped under one manager, but that such a grouping leads to the manager's being unable both to cope with the work and at the same time to maintain a full-scale two-way manager-subordinate relationship with each of his immediate subordinates. This type of problem can often be overcome by providing the manager with one or more assistants to help him with his work but without taking over the managerial role and its accountability and authority in relation to subordinates. The role is here that of a supervisor, and, if there is more than one, each would be concerned with a separate section of his manager's total subordinate group.

A supervisor may assist his manager with the training, recruitment and assessment of the manager's subordinates, with the programming of tasks and with the methods they are using. He may oversee their work in the sense of ensuring that they are attending on time and occupying themselves reasonably diligently. He may help any one of them to overcome particularly difficult problems that may arise.

The supervisor can monitor the limits within which others work, but it is for the manager to set those limits: limit-setting effectively determines the level at which a person will work, and only the manager or someone accountable for ensuring certain minimal standards can requisitely do that. The supervisor may, however, make recommendations with respect to appraisal of competence and to rewards or penalties.

The supervisor does not carry managerial accountability or authority: that remains with the manager himself. The manager is assisted by his supervisor or supervisors but he must decide for himself the appraisal of the performance of his subordinates, and carry the full accountability of manager and the authority that goes with it, whatever recommendations he may receive from his supervisory assistant.

Conditions of reporting are similar to those for the prescribing relationship. A supervisor would normally not pursue a matter beyond his manager – unless he somehow felt that his recommendations were being treated in such a way as to constitute injustice or unfairness to himself, in which case he would appeal. It is for a supervisor to recommend – openly as far as those supervised are concerned – but for the manager to decide.

There is one other situation in which a supervisory relationship, as described, may arise. That is in the situation most commonly known as *secondment*. Secondment occurs where a subordinate is loaned for a limited period of time to work for another manager, under that manager's instruction and as a member of that manager's immediate subordinate team. The person's permanent manager remains his manager, receiving recommendations about him from the manager to whom he has been seconded. This latter manager has sufficient authority to get his work done in the temporary situation, by virtue of the supervisory authority vested in the role relationship.

Attachment (and Co-Management)

Attachment arises where it is desired to maintain a unified department of technical or professional practitioners, managed by a department head from that same occupation or profession, while at the same time the members of the department are assigned to work for other persons or departments. The attaching manager retains full managerial accountability and authority, and in addition is accountable for proposing and negotiating changes in policy and resources with those to whom staff are attached.

The member to whom the attachment is made is accountable for assigning work to attached members, or ensuring that appropriate work is being assigned by colleagues for whom he may be acting. He can take part in the procedure for appointment to the attaching role and can veto appointment of an individual who he feels would not provide a satisfactory service, and can seek the transfer of the attached member if the work done is below minimally acceptable standards. He can also monitor the activities of attached members to ensure that they conform to any policies which he is accountable for implementing.

Reporting in attachment is limited to reporting to the manager of the person attached that he is or is not above the minimum standard required in the role.

Attachment may be combined with other types of authority such as prescribing authority, supervisory authority or monitoring authority. It may also be combined under one special circumstance with managerial authority, giving an explicit 'two-boss' or co-managerial structure. This circumstance arises where the same specialism – say personnel, or programming, or production technology – occurs at two contiguous managerial levels.

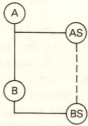

Figure 17.1

This co-managerial structure is achieved by having a specialist manager (AS) attach a subordinate specialist (BS) to an operational manager (B), and sharing with (B) the co-management of the subordinate specialist (BS). The specialist co-manager (AS) decides about the subordinate's technical competence; and the operational co-manager (B) decides about how useful he is in getting done the work he requires to be done. They can both share by this means in the selection and appraisal of the specialist subordinate (BS), jointly carrying out the functions of a single manager. Any difficulties must be sorted out by the crossover-point manager, A.

Staff Specialist Relationships

All work in executive hierarchies calls for: people working in an organized hierarchy of positions; in accord with a programme of resources employed through time; and using a specified technology. The co-ordination by a manager of the work of his subordinates requires attention to all three of these dimensions, which we shall designate P (personnel and organization), Pr (programming) and T (technology).[6]

The manager may require specialists in any or all of these three dimensions, to assist him in his own planning by advising him and to help to control the work of his operational subordinates. Where he wishes his specialist to help him with the control of the activities of his subordinates, he may requisitely assign him staff authority with respect to any one of the P, Pr or T dimensions.

The essence of the authority and accountability here is something less

---

[6] See W. Brown (1960), *Exploration in Management,* and Brown and Jaques (1965), *Glacier Project Papers.*

than in supervisory relationships. The staff specialist role, dealing only with one dimension of work, cannot be involved in performance appraisal even by recommendations, since performance in any one dimension cannot be divorced from being just one part of a whole. What can be created is a facilitating role. Each staff specialist can concentrate on his own field of specialization, assisting each of his manager's subordinates (his own colleagues), identifying common difficulties, formulating and recommending possible changes or developments in policies and methods which might avoid or prevent difficulties, but not getting involved in the selection and appraisal of his manager's subordinates. Thus it is that the staff specialist will confine his reporting to difficulties in the work, and will not report on the competencies of individuals. The staff specialist additionally carries the authority to interpret his manager's policies in his own specialist field and to issue instructions to the manager's subordinates on his behalf within the policies which he has set. The staff specialist's authority does not extend, however, to insisting upon his instructions being carried out. If his manager's subordinates do not agree with his staff instructions they can take the matter up with the manager to ensure that the staff specialist is in fact interpreting the manager's policies correctly.

It may be self-evident that it is essential that staff specialist roles be not established in the same work-stratum as that of the manager. If they are so established and successfully filled, the situation then is that the manager and the staff specialist become difficult to distinguish from each other. The subordinates will find it difficult not to treat the staff specialist as though he were a manager, for he in fact has the necessary work-capacity to be their manager and will perceive problems and solutions at the manager's level of abstraction. He will thus attract managerial authority without corresponding accountability. The manager's authority will be undermined and troubles will arise as a result.

In similar vein, if the staff specialist is in a work-stratum below that of his manager's subordinates, the staff authority will not be achieved. The staff specialist will be treated as a junior, as a personal assistant, carrying messages from the manager. He will not have the ability to operate at the same level of abstraction as the subordinates, and cannot therefore help them with their problems because he cannot analyse these problems at a level and in a way that would enable him to help.

Monitoring and Co-ordinating

A monitoring role arises where it is desired to ensure that the activities of members conform to adequate standards in some particular respect, and where a managerial, supervisory or staff relationship is impossible or needs supplementing. The field of performance being monitored might for exam-

ple be: adherence to the letter of contract of employment (such as atten-
dance, hours of work); adherence to the substance of contract of employment (quantity or quality of work produced); adherence to regulations;
safety; financial propriety; level of expenditure; technical standard of work;
progress on specific projects.

In order to carry out these activities a monitor must have authority to
obtain first-hand knowledge of the monitored person's activities and
problems concerning adherence to the limiting requirements. He must also
have the authority to persuade the person monitored to modify his performance, but not to instruct him.

It may be noted here that the authority is that of persuasion and not instruction. The monitor must use his best endeavours to get the person
being monitored to change what he is doing, if change is needed. But he
cannot insist. It is this fact which defines the nature of the reporting. If the
monitor is not satisfied with the outcome of his persuasive efforts, he must
report this to the manager of the person monitored, stating that he thinks
change is necessary, but that there is a disagreement. It is then for the
manager to go into the matter: that is why monitoring works most effectively when the immediate manager is at the crossover point for both the
monitor and the monitored.

Since the accountability of the monitor is limited to doing his best to persuade, he does not require authority to assess the personal competence of
those whom he monitors. A similar type of accountability and authority
occurs in the activity commonly referred to as *co-ordination* which may be
defined in the following manner.

A co-ordinating role arises where it is felt necessary to establish one person with the function of co-ordinating the work of a number of others in
certain respects, and where a managerial, supervisory, or staff relationship
is inappropriate. The activity to be co-ordinated might for example be: the
production of a report, estimate, plan or policy proposal; the implementation of an approved scheme or project; the overcoming of some unforeseen
problem affecting normal work.

In all cases the co-ordinator can only work within the framework of
some specific *task* whose definition is agreeable to all concerned.

Specifically, the person in a co-ordinating role is accountable in relation
to the task concerned for: negotiating co-ordinated work programmes;
arranging the allocation of existing resources or seeking additional
resources where necessary; monitoring actual progress; helping to overcome problems which may be encountered; reporting on progress to those
who established the co-ordinating role.

In carrying out these activities the co-ordinator has authority to make
firm proposals for action, to arrange meetings, to obtain first-hand
knowledge of progress, etc., and to decide what shall be done in situations

of uncertainty, but he has no authority in case of sustained disagreements to issue overriding instructions. Those co-ordinated have always the right of direct access to the higher authorities who are setting or sanctioning the tasks to be co-ordinated. As for monitoring, it is not part of the co-ordinator's role to make formal assessments of the general quality of the performance of those he co-ordinates.

Monitoring and co-ordination may be usefully employed in the situation where it is necessary for a manager on one geographical site to *outpost* subordinates to work on a separate site in order to be immediately in contact with work going on on that site; as in the case, for example, of an accountant needing to be immediately in contact with financial data, or a research investigator requiring direct contact with a particular process. It is possible for the manager to remain accountable for the work done, so long as there is a manager on the site to which the subordinate has been outposted who can be given monitoring authority to ensure that the subordinate conforms to the ordinary discipline of policies governing behaviour on that site.

Monitoring can also be used for the function of *inspection* to ensure that required standards are adhered to in the quality of goods and services. Recommendations are made with respect to the limits on quality standards in the light of client or customer requirement, and decisions are made about adherence to those standards. The authority to act is persuasive as in monitoring, but at a lesser degree in that the inspector is not involved in initiating the tasks which produce the outputs he inspects.

Advisory, Collateral, and Conjoint Relationships

There are three types of role relationships which carry about the same degree of accountability and authority but which are usefully distinguished in the organizational setting. The first arises when one member is accountable for giving advice to another on request or on his own initiative; the second when the work of two members interacts (as, for example, between two production managers, each accountable for part of a total production process) – a collateral relationship; and the third is a collateral type of relationship which always exists between staff specialists subordinate to the same manager (personnel (P), programming (Pr) and technology (T)) because each is concerned with one of three interlocking dimensions of his manager's work – a conjoint relationship.

These three relationships are similar. They are all limited to one person's trying to persuade another person to do something necessary for the discharge of the first person's duties. A *quid pro quo* exists, for each one will from time to time wish to seek some adjustment from the other. It is this mutuality of interest which stimulates co-operation, in a situation in which that co-operation is necessary for each one to carry out his own tasks. The essence of the relationship is that of persuasiveness in seeking mutual adjustments in the interest of objects which transcend both roles, even though it may make the work of one person or other more difficult in the immediate situation.

The regulation of advisory, collateral and conjoint relationships is always a tricky and difficult matter. In principle it is useful to keep interface work of this kind to a minimum. The difficulties arise because when two or more people are in such relationships, their crossover-point manager must, in judging outcomes, take into account his own personal judgment of each one compared with the other. Thus, if there is a good outcome, the manager must size up which one of the two he thinks might have contributed more; or if there is a bad outcome, he must decide who is the more culpable. It is a situation readily making for blame and mutual recrimination. Was the loss of a sale due to a production manager's failure to give a sales manager the help he needed with a customer? Or in the other direction, is a production manager's inefficiency due to a sales manager's unwillingness to alter his own sales scheduling sufficiently to work in with the production manager, and to enable him to overcome a scheduling problem arising from outside circumstances? Was an adviser's advice good or bad, or was it badly implemented? Or did all three staff specialists fail to adjust to one another's needs, or was one or the other more to blame?

Because of the overlap and mutuality in these role relationships, if the personal relationship between a manager and a subordinate is strained, then the subordinate will often tend to think he is being unfairly treated if he has to rely upon his collateral relationship with someone else in order to get his work done. For if something goes wrong, he will feel that the other person will be exonerated at his expense.

These kinds of situation show some of the subtleties which must enter into managerial judgments of subordinates. Not only must a manager judge the quality of a subordinate's performance, he must judge whether one subordinate was more co-operative than the other in, for example, a collateral interaction, or whether they both contributed more or less the same. Such judgments are not easy. But they must be made. One of the reasons why the existence of an institutionalized appeal system is so essential is to have a mechanism whereby potential feelings of unfair treatment in such situations can be aired.

Groups of members in advisory, collateral, or conjoint relations may sometimes meet regularly in an organized interface meeting to work out their mutual requirements. Such interaction between a number of colleagues can often be useful for planning how best to implement new policies. So long as each member of the advisory, collateral or conjoint group stays within his own manager's policy, courses of action can be decided which may involve all or most of them — and without having to refer back to any of their managers. Decisions taken in this way enhance the members' freedom of action.

Such groups are often thought of and referred to as functionally autonomous work groups or organizations, or committees, or teams. Such descriptions are misleading. The meetings are a simple matter of individuals in mutually adaptive role relationships, co-ordinating and adjusting their plans, within policy, so that each and all may be able to work more effectively. Each retains his own accountability. There is no voting. A majority cannot override a minority or indeed any single one of the members. Failure to agree on the sought-after mutual accommodation requires a reference back to the crossover-point manager for decision or for policy classification. There can be no functionally autonomous work groups and no true committee within bureaucratic systems, and the use of the term 'team' adds only to confusion because it is so ill-defined.

Service-getting and Scanning

Service-getting and scanning role relationships illustrate the extent to which the degree of accountability and authority can be reduced but still leave useful working role relationships.

In modern complex bureaucratic organizations nearly every employee will require to draw upon a variety of services in order to do his work. These services range over financial data, work study, stationery, typing, copying, tooling, millwrighting and maintenance, supplies and purchasing; the list goes on and on. Getting the authorized services on time and as required makes the difference between completing a task satisfactorily and on time and not being able to do so.

Service-giving requires a post carrying accountability for providing specified services to named authorized people. Authorized persons may request the services they need.

If the service provider cannot give the service required because of lack of resources, he must requisitely say so and indicate when he will be able to. Effectively he says 'I cannot', not 'I will not'. It is then for the service-seeker to decide whether to accept the situation or whether to take the matter further. If he decides on the latter, his authority is limited to reporting to his own manager, not on the competence of the service-giver but upon the lack of availability of the authorized service. It is then for the manager to decide whether to pursue the matter further or whether to leave it and note that his subordinate may be late in achieving his assigned tasks.

In the *scanning relationship* the degree of accountability and authority is reduced to nearly zero. These relationships are concerned solely with the gathering of prescribed information on results and the processing of data; for example, an accounts clerk getting out financial data; an office clerk processing production output figures. The authority is limited to reporting the presented information to a prescribed person or persons, without comment or interpretation.

Working Groups

The widespread desire somehow to get rid of the bureaucratic hierarchy because it is seen – incorrectly – as inevitably 'autocratic' to have managers, finds expression in the continual search for more 'democratic' or more 'organic' forms of work organization. Each new group structure – such as so-called functionally autonomous work groups, or matrix organization, or teams of various kinds – is hailed as a victory of cooperative groups over autocratic managers, and as the forerunner of the demise of hierarchy. In fact, they are simply various arrangements of laterally related roles into working groups – exceedingly important in their own right – which are essential components of effectively functioning bureaucratic systems.

So-called functionally autonomous work groups (as described by Emery, Thorsrud, Trist, and others) are simply Str-1 groups of hourly-rated operators or clerical staff subordinate to a Str-2 section manager, who are allowed and encouraged to work together in a collateral relationship, usually with someone selected from among themselves to co-ordinate them in deciding how best to plan and carry out their work. This arrangement gives increased opportunity for use of initiative and freedom in work, and usually gives each individual an increase in level of work as measured in time-span. It is thus possible to reduce or eliminate the usual panoply of Str-1 supervising roles (supervisors, charge-hands, petty officers, leading hands, corporals, etc.). But even though such groups may appear to be 'setting their own targets' or 'deciding their own methods', they are not in fact 'autonomous'. There is still an accountable manager who must oversee the work and judge whether the standards and methods are satisfactory, and if not, take steps to correct the situation.

Another important organizational situation arises where individuals have roles in more than one work group within the same bureaucratic system. The most common of these situations – and one which is of rapidly growing significance – is one where a person has a role in a professional, technical, or other specialized department, and at the same time exercises his specialist skills in a role in another department. Such situations are legion, and include, for example: a personnel specialist attached from a central personnel department to be personnel staff officer in a Str-3 manufacturing unit and co-managed by the unit manager and the personnel department manager; a hospital physiotherapist attached by her manager – the superintendent physiotherapist – to a consultant orthopaedic surgeon, managed by the superintendent and with her work activities co-ordinated by the surgeon; an accountant outposted from a headquarters finance department to provide services to a factory site in another city, who is managed by the chief accountant and monitored for adherence to site discipline by the site manager. In each of these cases the individual has a manager or co-manager within his technical department and a monitor or co-ordinator or co-manager in the department in which he does his daily work.

A more complex example is where teams or groups of such individuals are constructed for carrying out special projects; for example, a research project team made up of a statistician, a research chemist, a metallurgist, a physicist and a mechanical engineer, each with a home base and a manager in a department of his own discipline, and acting collaterally with the other members of the working team, and with one of them appointed as co-ordinator. This method is often called matrix organization.

Such work-groups are not somehow different from bureaucratic hierarchies. They are not democratic or co-operative or non-hierarchical. They are integral parts of the functioning of bureaucratic systems. The managers or co-managers remain accountable for the performance of their subordinates. This managerial accountability includes ensuring that their subordinates are co-operating effectively in the collateral groups or departments to which they have been assigned, and that the co-ordinative work is effectively carried out. Differences of opinion and the overall effectiveness of such groups must be assessed by the manager who is at the crossover point for all the functions which have been combined.

Whether such groupings of activity, such dual work-group memberships, such co-ordinated collateral teams, are referred to as matrix groups, or co-operative teams, or autonomous groups, is beside the point. What is required first is to recognize that bureaucratic organization is not and cannot be limited to the negativistic social science fantasy of a one-way downwards managerial autocracy with no upward or lateral connections. The construction and definition of lateral relationships is essential. So is the creation of various types of collateral working group, and provision for individuals to collaborate with one another and to have dual-role membership – in professional and technical departments on the one hand and in operational departments on the other hand. Each of these situations requires to be designed organizationally in relation to the demands of the work. The lateral role relationships described in this chapter have been found useful for this purpose.

Personal Consequences of Role Relationships

A number of dyadic and triadic role relationships have been described. The dyadic relationships range all the way from the strongest degrees of accountability and authority found in manager-subordinate role relationships, to the weakest found in the scanning relationship in which no judgments at all are made about the person, only reports about specified results.

Our analysis is incomplete. There are more gradations in accountability and authority to be found than have been used so far. They can be uncovered in the course of field research, More difficult, however, is the discovery of the underlying principle which could lead to the construction of an equal-ratio scale measuring instrument — a function or functions varying in concert with variations in accountability and authority and measurable against an objective scale of length. We have been unsuccessful so far in this search. We have been unsuccessful, by the same token, in deriving a rigorous operational definition either of degrees of accountability or of strength of authority.

What has been demonstrated, however, is that the range of different role relationships in bureaucracies is more extensive and complex than is usually assumed in organization theory. The differences emerging from our analysis may appear to be over-subtle, to have been over-elaborated, to be too finely drawn. Experience, however, suggests precisely the opposite conclusion. People are enormously sensitive to the precise degree of accountability and authority which exists in their role relationships. At stake are the expectations about the power to be exercised between people, and the mutual control of that power. It matters, and matters very much, to a person whether the other person in a relationship can make decisions about his progress, or merely recommend, or say nothing at all; or whether he can order him to do something, or try to persuade him, or only request him; or whether he can set boundaries within which he operates or merely recommend such boundaries, or whether they are both operating within the same boundaries set by someone else.

These distinctions in role relationships are associated with considerable differences in the quality of behaviour allowed and in the type of sub-identity expressed. The personal skills and competencies called for in persuading someone else to do something are very different from those called for in issuing instructions on a manager's behalf; making recommendations about someone else's competence is very different from having to refrain from doing so; having to rely upon someone else to fulfil a prescription, or being expected to fulfil it, calls forth different feelings from merely requesting a service or giving a service if possible, and creates different working relationships; and so on for each of the role relationships described. The more intense the accountability and authority in the role relationship, the greater the mobilization in the operating sub-identity of the deeper layers of the core of self-identity. And as the role relationships are more or less clearly and requisitely bounded, so changes in expressed sub-identity must occur.

In practice, in real life, with real human beings, in real bureaucracies, these distinctions loom very large in people's minds. To the extent that the distinctions are not clear, the working role relationships are open to constant personal manipulation. For the necessary definition of accountability and authority is a part of the construction of the institutional zone of the context of behaviour. The absence of adequate formulation of authority is nothing less than an inadequate legitimation of power in the relationship. An excess of unauthorized power must then be contained within the inter-subjective zone of the context of the social interaction – the two particular individuals involved must somehow balance out how much influence they will exert upon each other.

There is a two-fold effect of this inflow of institutionally unbounded power into the inter-subjective zone. First, it becomes impossible for others in the institution to decide who is accountable for which outcomes in the relationship between any two individuals; for the nature of each particular staff, or monitoring or prescribing or other role relationship, will be influenced beyond institutionally tolerable limits by the personalities and the expressed sub-identities of the particular individuals involved. Second, and even more striking, it is impossible to determine accountability even for any one particular pair of individuals, because the disposition of power between them will vary continuously, depending upon the vicarious ups and downs in their feelings and in the external circumstances in which they find themselves.

These differences in accountability and authority illustrate sharply the manner in which the amount of free-floating power in any social interaction is controlled by the nature and amount of legitimation of power through the sanctioning mechanisms of the cultural, legal and institutional zones of the context of behaviour. The less the externalization of the boundaries of power, the more the individuals are left to their own intuitive devices in mediating their inter-subjective relationships. The essence of the requisite definition of the institutional zone of role relationships in bureaucracies is precisely to enable each person to concentrate sufficiently upon the task in hand without having to be too distracted by a continuous inter-subjective struggle for power over others. At the same time it must allow sufficient scope for the fine adjustment of the play of power and of sub-identities between the particular individuals co-operating in work.

These possible difficulties, and hence an even stronger need for clear definition of the institutional zone of the behaviour context, may arise to a greater extent in the triadic role relationships described: in attachment, in outposting, in secondment, in supervisory relationships, in collateral relationships, and especially in the co-management situation of attachment combined with management. Here the power situation readily takes on the divide and conquer quality which Simmel described as pathognomonic of all triads. It is all too easy for the subordinate to play off one co-manager against another, a supervisor against a manager, a manager against a prescriber, and so on. And it is equally easy for each of the others to play off the third person in the relationship in the same way, to avoid accountability, to enhance personal power, to work out envy and jealousy.

The expression of personal unconscious or conscious motives is especially tendentious in three-person relationships. Some of the most primitive unconscious fantasies are stirred, relating to the earliest parental relationships. To the extent that social institutions such as bureaucracies fail to set requisite institutional boundaries governing triadic relationships, it is difficult for individuals to keep their more primitive unconscious intra-psychic conflicts from spilling into the inter-subjective field and colouring or dominating their working relationships. Social institutions break down when they become repositories into which each one may dump his inner problems. To the extent, however, that requisite institutional boundaries are set, each person must retain his intra-psychic conflicts as a personal responsibility for himself to resolve. Personal responsibility of that kind is one essential characteristic of citizens in a good society.

18
Grading, Career Progress, and Level of Aspiration

A major source of confusion in the design of organization for bureaucratic systems has arisen from the failure to recognize the need for two different systems of stratification each calling for separate treatment: first, the need for a system of work-strata within which work can be organized and delegated and the managerial and specialist systems organized; second, the need for a system of grading strata (grades) within which individuals can be paid and progressed – a means of providing for career progression and career planning in terms which individuals can understand and compare with their own levels of aspiration.

A system of work-strata has been described in previous chapters. In this chapter we turn our attention to grading. Some of the effects of the confusion between work and grading strata are described. There is presented a scheme for subdividing work-strata so as to gain a systematic set of grading strata related to work organization, a schema which can be applied in any bureaucratic system.

In considering grading matters it is useful to keep in mind the fact that people have strong feelings about the subject. Grading confers status. It helps to define a person's public identity and may be in accord with or in conflict with his sense of private identity. It establishes the boundaries of his current potential reward. It is a means of comparing the level of his role and that of others. It sets a major framework within which he formulates and pitches his immediate level of aspiration.

Confusion Between Work and Grading Strata

The lack of a systematic basis for grading systems can be seen in the enormously wide variations in practice in different bureaucratic systems. There is no detectable common framework of any kind. In the British Civil Service there are some 8,500 different grades with different titles: something like 1,400 occupational groups (classes), each class in turn divided into anywhere between 3 and 15 separate grades. In the National Health Service there are some 40 or 50 different grading schemes, one for each service – for example, 10 nursing grades, 15 clerical and administrative grades, 12 physiotherapy grades – and some grades are further divided into 'steps'. Most large employment systems have such grading schemes, and rarely only one set of grades – there are usually different schemes of grading for hourly-rated operators, for clerical and office staff, for senior staff, and there are usually the so-called management grades as well.

The one thing common to these grading schemes is that they are all used for conferring differential status, and they all have pay brackets associated with them, each grade having a related pay range. Even for these purposes, however, they tend to be incomplete. It is possible to identify which roles are of higher and which of lower status *within* the same occupational group; but it is not always easy to compare the relative status of roles in different occupational groups; for example, nurses as compared with administrators or physiotherapists. And with respect to pay brackets, sometimes the brackets are distinct – that is, each higher bracket begins above the top of the next lower bracket – and sometimes they overlap.

The question of how many grades there should be is always a difficult one. The British Civil Service in considering its organization in the 1960s was concerned to reduce the complexity of its grading scheme.[1] It examined the grading system of the United States Civil Service – a 23-grade scheme – but was unable to settle upon it because, among other reasons, it was thought that that number of grading levels was too many. Too many for what, it is difficult to say, but instead it was decided to merge three classes – clerical (three grades), executive (six grades) and administrative (six grades) – into one single administrative class with some 15 possible levels.

The main difficulty – and this is one of the reasons why the American 23-level system was felt to provide too many levels[2] – is that in the absence of any equally explicit systems of work-strata or levels, an explicit grading system tends to take over the function of a system of work organization as well. We described this phenomenon in Chapter 8 and showed how the Army ranking system, the Civil Service grading system, the industrial type of managerial, supervisory and charge-hand structure, are all grading schemes doubling up as managerial systems. The net effect is to proliferate far too many management levels – a sociological disease which is pandemic in all industrial nations.

The mechanism works as follows. A manager in grade M (say) has subordinates in grades K and J. These subordinates experience a missing promotion opportunity in grade L, and proceed to negotiate to have a role established there. If eventually they succeed, then one of them may get promoted. In the normal course of events, that person will be treated as an interposed manager, perhaps called deputy department head or some such title, and the new structure will appear as shown, with one additional

---

[1] Civil Service (1966/1968), *Committee on the Civil Service*, Vol. I.
[2] E. Jaques (1972), 'Grading and Management Organisation in the Civil Service'.

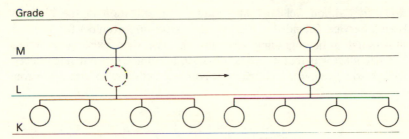

Figure 18.1

managerial level built in. In this way, it not uncommonly occurs that the roles at all levels in the grading system get filled, giving excessively long lines of command – a recipe for the creation of red tape.

An associated effect of this mixing of grading and work-strata is the introduction of an inflexibility in both organization and career progression. It may be noted from the foregoing illustration that for one of the subordinates to be upgraded from K to L required a reorganization of the managerial structure. Such a requirement makes upgrading a much more complex and difficult exercise. An example of a related difficulty is shown here. In order for subordinate R to be upgraded he must be promoted either to become a direct subordinate of P, his manager-once-removed, and hence to become a colleague of his former manager, or to become a subordinate of some other manager at the same level as his manager-once-removed. Some of these complexities are unnecessary if provision is made for several grades within each work-stratum.

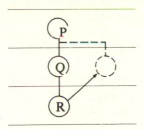

Figure 18.2

One of the minor tragedies of bureaucratic organization is that employees often believe that they can automatically enhance their career prospects by negotiating larger numbers of grading levels which then tend to double up as management levels. What so often happens, however, is that the new levels simply push the existing levels lower in status, in responsibility, and eventually in pay, thus worsening the situation for all. This commonly occurring effect can be illustrated by the implementation of the so-called Salmon Scheme[3] into nursing organization in the National Health Service. Intended to improve the career opportunities for nurses, it substituted a new grading structure for the then existing structure. The net effect was that matrons sought to become Chief Nursing Officers though some remained as Principal Nursing Officers. Assistant Matrons

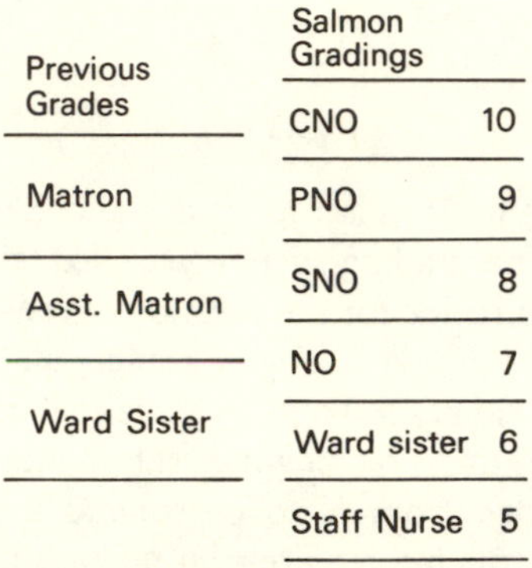

Previous Grades	Salmon Gradings	
	CNO	10
Matron	PNO	9
Asst. Matron	SNO	8
	NO	7
Ward Sister	Ward sister	6
	Staff Nurse	5

Figure 18.3

strove to become Principal Nursing Officers or at least Senior Nursing Officers. And the good experienced ward sisters sought upgrading to Grade 7 Nursing Officer in charge of two or three wards.

The result was that the best ward sisters tended to be creamed off the wards to be upgraded to become Nursing Officers (Grade 7). Because Grade 7 was considered to be managerially in charge of Grade 6, the Grade 7 Nursing Officers had too little to do and the ward sister roles tended to be submerged under the sheer mass of the four-level superstructure under which they now struggled. Within a few years the level of work of ward sisters was generally held to have decreased. Many experienced ward sisters were no longer on the wards; they had achieved promotion into what in many cases proved to be administrative dead-end posts, with little increase in reward and with decrease in career satisfaction and prospects.

Separation of Grading from Work-strata

A grade may be defined as a level-of-work band established for two purposes: first, to enable pay brackets to be established; and, second, to provide a system of bands within which individuals may organize their perceptions of their career progress in relation to their level of aspiration.

[3] Ministry of Health (1966), *Report of the Committee on Senior Nursing Staff Structure.*

What is required is for the ceiling of each band to be just the right distance from its floor and so to constitute a realistic level of aspiration for the individual and a sound framework for career planning by managers in conjunction with the individual.

The following experience in field work suggested that there might be a general principle to be discovered from which a uniform and systematic schema of grading would follow. The first significant finding emerged when the general system of work-strata was implemented as one development on the Glacier Project. It was recognized that common payment levels would have to be associated with the boundaries of each work-stratum, since there could be no sound argument for any differential payment between different roles at the same level in this work organization structure.

Appropriate pay levels were negotiated (using the equitable pay levels as a guide but not as an absolute arbiter). These pay levels manifested the following percentage increase bands from the bottom to the top of each work stratum:

Stratum-1 (up to 3-month time-span):	40%
Stratum-2 (3-month to 1-year time-span):	50%
Stratum-3 (1-year to 2-year time-span):	100%
Stratum-4 (2-year to 5-year time-span):	100%
Stratum-5 (5-year to 10-year time-span):	100%

Such a spread of payment seemed far too wide to all concerned. Examination of their existing structure of pay brackets, and that of a number of other bureaucratic systems, suggested that there was a fairly strong tendency towards actual pay brackets of about 7% to 10% in width around the Str-1 levels, increasing to about 15% to 17% around Str-2, and finally increasing to about 25% to 30% from Str-3 level upwards. Pay brackets of about this width seemed more comfortable: they seemed wide enough to give a person a sufficient sense of being able to make progress, and yet not so wide as to make the top of the bracket seem unachievable. They seemed to make it possible to set realistic levels of aspiration for the immediately planned rate of career progress.

Pay brackets of these empirically comfortable spans can be achieved by the simple step of dividing Stratum-1 into four grading and pay bands, and each of the other strata into three such bands. Such a structure is illustrated in Figure 18.4 on p. 282 and seems to work quite well in practice.[4]

Practical Implications of the Generalized Grading Schema

The width of the various grading bands described coincides with what is fairly common practice in pay administration and provides a psy-

[4] E. Jaques (1968), *Progression Handbook*.

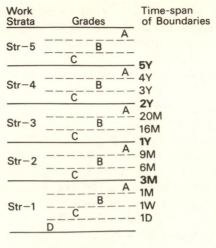

Grading schema

Figure 18.4

chologically comfortable fit. The schema, moreover, is applicable to any and all bureaucratic systems and to any and all departments or occupational groups within any bureaucracy. What would be optimum organizationally would be for a bureaucratic system to be organized in the first place into the work-strata which have here been set out as requisite. But the condition is not absolute. It is possible to apply the generalized grading schema by using the time-span definition of the grade boundaries, without necessarily implementing the system of requisite work-strata.

The combined use of requisite work-strata and the generalized grading schema, however, will give the firmest grip upon work organizational structure. Excess levels of work organization cannot proliferate, precisely because the work system is separated from the grading system. New work-strata need to be added only with significant stages in organization growth as will be outlined in the chapters in Part Six.

About three times as many grades as work levels are provided for. This fact means that it is possible for a manager to have subordinates in any of the three (or in the case of Str-1, the four) grades in the next lower work-stratum. Thus Figure 18.5 shows a manager in a Str-3B role with immediate subordinates in Str-2A, B, and C roles. In these circumstances the subordinate in the Str-2C role can be progressed not only within his grade, he can also be upgraded from 2C to 2B and to 2A if his personal capacity and work opportunity combine to make this possible, while still remaining subordinate to the same manager and without its being necessary to reorganize the work structure.

Only when a subordinate reaches the top of the highest grade in a

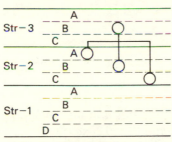

Figure 18.5

stratum do the more complex problems arise. That is the point at which promotion to the next higher stratum must be considered. If the subordinate is promoted he must at that stage move from the command of his immediate manager to that of a manager in a higher stratum. It is for this reason that it has proved so useful to have the upper boundary of the highest grade and the bottom boundary of the lowest grade in any given work-stratum coincide with the boundaries of the stratum itself. Promotion across the boundary from one stratum to the next can take place simultaneously with upgrading.

By providing for several grades in each work-stratum the generalized grading schema makes it possible, where necessary, for people to obtain recognized progression in work and status without necessarily having to take on managerial duties. In the case of the nursing organization described earlier, for example, it becomes possible to provide for ward sister roles to be established at three different grades – reflecting differences in level of work which may be caused by such factors as size of ward and technical difficulties in the work. Thus, as a ward sister (Salmon Grade 6) became more proficient she could be upgraded without having to take over the unsatisfactory pseudo-managerial responsibilities of a nursing officer (the Salmon Grade 7). She could remain on the ward, doing nursing work, but with adequate status and pay. If she became ready for promotion to a genuine managerial role in the next higher stratum, the schema would accommodate such a change – but it would be a realistic and serious move.

This solution to the nursing problem is relevant to innumerable situations in which professional staff are employed. It makes it possible for the individual to receive adequate advancement in terms of level of professional work and professional competence alone, without having to accept unsought administrative work so as to be able to collect the increasing number of subordinates needed to gain higher status. Too often 'head counting' becomes the major criterion for progression.

Finally, it may be noted that the generalized grading schema gives 22 grades for a Str-7 bureaucratic system. That is about the scale of organization of the new large British and American government departments. The schema may therefore make some sense of the US Civil Service grading structure. It would also suggest that the British Civil Service may have fallen between two stools in choosing to establish an administration class with fifteen grades: too many for work organization structure and too few for grading purposes.

Merit Progression, Upgrading and Promotion, and the Use of Time-span in Job Evaluation

It may be noted that we have distinguished from one another three types of progression of individuals.

The first is that of increases in payment and level of work within a grade. These increases may be automatic annual increments, as can be provided by grant-income institutions. Or they may be based on merit review, as must obtain in earned-income institutions. Such increases may be termed *merit progression*.

The second is the movement of an individual from one grade to a higher grade but within the same work-stratum. Reorganization is not necessarily involved. The individual is simply brought up to the next higher grade and continues to have the same manager, subordinates (if any) and colleagues. Such progress may be termed *upgrading*.

The third is the movement of an individual from one work-stratum to a higher one (and inevitably a higher grade). Such a move involves reorganization. The individual must have a new manager. If he had subordinates, they will have to be assigned to a new manager. Colleague relationships will change, with even the possibility, if the person is moved up to replace his own manager, that he will become the manager of his former colleagues. Such a change may be termed *promotion*.

Of the three changes defined, only promotion calls for evidence of emerging capacity in the individual at a new level of abstraction.

Use of these concepts requires that the role a person occupies must be capable of being evaluated for grading purposes. It is in this situation that time-span measurement comes into its own as a method of job evaluation. By means of time-span measurement any role can be allocated to a grade in the generalized grading schema presented. That allocation establishes the pay bracket for the role. The actual pay received by a person occupying the role would be determined by the merit progression through the grade.[5]

---

[5] A systematic progression and payment procedure using these concepts will be found in my (1961) *Equitable Payment*, Chapters 14 and 15. The supporting procedures are described in my (1964) *Time-Span Hanbook* and (1968) *Progression Handbook*.

Progression Characteristics of the Generalized Grading Schema

The width of grading bands must be a function of the rate of growth in work-capacity of individuals. Thus if a man were to increase in capacity by 10 per cent throughout his whole career, there would be no point in creating grades in which the top reflected a 50 per cent increase above the bottom. Such a man would be lost in such a grade: it would be far too wide. Similarly, if a man were to increase in capacity by 500 per cent throughout his career, he would feel constricted if he were put in a grading structure in which the top of each band was only 5 per cent above the bottom: such bands would be far too narrow and he would constantly be fighting for upgrading.

The foregoing can be translated into the more precise and quantitative language of time-span and equitable payment. If a man increasing from one-day up to one-week time-span throughout his career (a real equitable pay increase of about 10 per cent) were put into a grade running from one-day to two-month (a real equitable pay increase of about 50 per cent), he would feel lost. A man increasing from one-week up to two-year time-span through his career (a real equitable pay increase of about 500 per cent) would feel constricted in a series of brackets of, say, one-month time-span.

The possible significance of these assumptions may be seen if they are transferred to the capacity growth curves described in Chapter 10.

This grading schema provides the following patterns of progression. In Capacity Group I, progressing within Str-1, it takes from 5 years to 8 years to move through a grade in the early stages, and the progression then flattens off. In the intermediate and higher capacity groups, it takes from 3 years to 5 years to move through a grade in the early stages. Capacity Group II reaches stability between 35 and 40; Group III between 40 and 45; Group IV between 45 and 55; Group V between 55 and retirement; and Groups VI and VII can normally progress throughout their working life.

Whether or not there are any general principles of progression rates operating here is not clear. Research into level of aspiration has been concerned with the organization of aspiration in the person's immediate situation, and has not been connected with developmental processes. The capacity progression array must remain empirically derived conjectures, for the moment, with all the theoretical weaknesses that such a position entails.

Bureaucratic Organization and Level of Aspiration in Work and Pay

Even though our analysis has not been taken sufficiently far to explain the possible relationship between rate of movement in level of aspiration and rate of growth in capacity, it does point unequivocally to the necessity of separating a person's level of aspiration with respect to level of work from his level of aspiration with respect to pay. Aspirations with respect to level of work tend to be absolute: as a person's work-capacity develops he seeks an increasing level of work at time-spans consistent with his growing work-capacity. In contrast, his aspiration with respect to level of payment is relative: each one seeks to be paid in line with the current standards of differential equity, whatever those differential norms may be or however they may change.

The reason why the aspiration towards equilibrium between work-capacity and level of work is an absolute one and that towards an equilibrium between level of work and payment is relative, is not far to seek. In the case of pay, each person's aspirations appear to be geared to a sense of fairness in economic reward as compared with others. In the case of work, however, each person's level of aspiration is geared to his deepest feelings of reality and freedom.[6]

It should be made clear that we are referring to level of aspiration in the sense of a person's action – his behavioural flow – and not simply in terms of his possible responses in a questionnaire study, say, of what kind of occupation he might like to be in, or what status he dreams of. The two types of information may or may not coincide. We are here concerned with the first rather than the second.

Level of aspiration for a given level of work shows up a person's behaviour in bureaucratic systems in very definite ways. In particular it is reflected in stability in role. If a person is in a situation where his work-capacity is higher than the available level of work, or the level of work is well above his work-capacity, he will seek a change of role if opportunity arises: and indeed, in the second case, he will not be retained long in role because he will not be able to do the work required. In both cases, however, his level of aspiration will have undergone the sobering influence of reality testing – whatever the denials or evasions in which some may indulge.[7]

Moreover, if his level of work in time-span terms is shorter than his time-span capacity, his real freedom is being restricted. He is being deprived of that vital freedom to test his capacity at full stretch; that is to say, he is being deprived of the opportunity to maintain his relationship with reality over as wide a spectrum as possible. Part of his world will be missing.

If, contrariwise, his level of work in time-span terms is longer than his work-capacity, a person's freedom is being destroyed. His relationship to

---

[6] T. M. Newcomb (1950), *Social Psychology*, pp. 227–8; L. Festinger (1942), 'Wish, Expectation and Group Performance as Factors Affecting Level of Aspiration'.

[7] Thus, for example, Goldthorpe and Lockwood have described how workers will substitute an instrumental interest in pay to make up for frustration in work when their level-of-work aspiration cannot be fulfilled. (1968) *The Affluent Worker*, Vol I.

reality is being disorganized. This situation will tend to arouse the deepest-lying anxieties of persecution: in a real sense, it is persecution.

The construction of adequate grading and progression systems is an essential mechanism for making individual freedom real. In order to make this reality explicit in an organizational sense, it is necessary to locate clearly the point where decisions are to be made about the potential capacity of each employee. In *Equitable Payment* (Chapter 14) I argued that such decisions ought requisitely to be made by the manager-once-removed, and incorporated this conclusion in the Standard Payment and Progression Method which I described there. This conclusion can now be argued with greater force.

Every employee should be entitled to receive a periodic assessment of the adequacy of his performance – from his immediate manager. This procedure has been fully argued earlier in this book. But what of the assessment of his potential progress in the institution? What are his propects, given employment opportunity? Is he considered to have the potential capacity for upgrading? for promotion? for promotion across more than one work-stratum? How should he check his own assessment and level of aspiration against the views of those who know him and his work?

For the immediate manager to make such assessment of potential – Potential Progress Assessment or PPA as I have called it in *Equitable Payment* – is unsatisfactory. It is unsatisfactory because it calls for the manager to judge whether someone else is potentially competent to work at the manager's own current level of abstraction. Such judgments require to be made at least from the next higher level of abstraction if they are to be detached – in the full sense of that word as meaning a standing apart from. Such detachment is required also to give the subordinate a proper perspective on his own level of aspiration in the context of a competence which can fully encompass his own potential and aspirations.

Indeed, followed to its logical conclusion, this line of argument suggests that where it is likely that an employee's potential competence is to a work-stratum more-than-once-removed from his current stratum, the PPA should be finally checked and decided by a manager in a work-stratum one level higher still.

Their level of aspiration in work and pay is of great significance to people. They are entitled to know the degree of convergence or divergence of their aspirations as compared with the judgments of those in the employing institution who can determine how far those aspirations are likely to be realized in practice.

19

Elective Leadership and Managerial Leadership

There is a widely held belief that the structure of organization, the sanctioning of power, the specification of accountability and authority, would all be of much less significance if only there were a sufficient number of good leaders, leaders who were able to act decisively and to maintain good communications with their subordinates. From this point of view disruptive conflict and social breakdown are seen as a crisis of leadership; there is a consequent yearning after something called 'strong leadership' as the solution to the trouble.

It is not intended to diminish the importance of individuals and their personal qualities as factors making for the better or worse functioning of social institutions. Having the right individuals with the right qualities is manifestly essential. It is essential also to have individuals with qualities of leadership when they are in a leadership relationship with others. And the value of decisiveness and good communications cannot be denied. But it is equally certain that leadership in the abstract, as an indefinable quality, charisma, which a person either possesses or does not possess, cannot by itself resolve all difficulties. There is a magical quality to such demands for leadership, too much like seeking for the philosopher's stone. The functioning of social institutions depends upon more than having the right individuals: it depends to begin with upon having the right social structures.

As far as bureaucratic systems are concerned it is quite impossible to describe or to define what is meant by the right person, or by leadership, until the nature of the task has been defined, and organization designed and constructed to make it possible for the work to be done. Such a formulation would imply that there might be different kinds of quality involved in leadership in different situations. Precisely so. We have already indicated, for example, in Chapter 12 that the concepts of laissez-faire, autocratic and democratic leadership may have very different meanings with respect to the activities of members of an association as against the employees in a bureaucratic hierarchy: what would be democratic in the one would be laissez-faire in the other, and so on.

This analysis is now pursued in more detail by comparing the requirements of leadership in elective roles in associations with the requirements of leadership in appointed roles. (We shall not, however, treat of the more general question of political leadership and statesmanship, topics outside our present scope.) This comparison will highlight the two main types of leadership called for in bureaucratic systems: the leadership to be exercised by the elected representatives of employees in participating in the control of policy change; and the leadership to be exercised by the managers in the system.[1] In considering managerial leadership special reference will be made to the role of the chief executive, acting as manager in one role and as an agent of the governing body in another.

The Setting for Elective Leadership

Let us review certain familiar features of elective leadership in those associations formed by employees in order to take part in consultation; to negotiate; to participate in the control of policy change.

The first point to be noted is that there is no hierarchy within an association. All the members are equal. Every member is as valuable as every other member in the sense of having the same rights, although some may exercise more power because of their persuasiveness or reputation (or in the case of companies by virtue of shareholding). Each has one vote (except in companies, but even here no shareholder can give orders to any other shareholder). None is accountable for the activities of any of the others. None has the authority to instruct any of the others to do anything – even to be an active member of the association. In associations, each individual member is as active or inactive as he wishes to be. Each must of course obey the rules of the association – pay his dues if any, abide by its agreements – but so long as he stays within the rules there is nothing more he need do to forward the aims of the association. Most people leave that to those who like to act as representatives, or who are at least willing to be persuaded to do so.

A second point is that debate and persuasion are crucial for an association if the necessary consensus among its members is to be achieved. That consensus is usually expressed in majority voting, in accord with the view that the will of the majority is what must count. But that consensus requires not only a majority view but a minority willing to go along with

[1] R. F. Bales in his intensive researches into interaction in groups (*Interaction Process Analysis* (1950)) has observed the consistent emergence of two types of leader – the task leader and the social leader. It would appear that groups need to be able to coalesce around someone who is best at directing the task in hand, and at the same time to have someone who understands the common needs and aspirations of the group. These findings of Bales and his co-workers help to explain the importance of the separation of the executive system from the representative and legislative systems. The Bales distinction fits the distinction between managerial leadership on the one hand – Bales' task leaders – and representative leadership on the other hand – Bales' social leaders. It is one of the main requirements of managerial roles to provide task leadership. Equally, it is one of the main requirements of representative roles to be able to understand the common needs and aspirations of the constituents, and to help crystallize group consensus.

the majority, unless of course some sort of coercive power is to be exercised.

We are dealing here with power. Associations are power groups. Their members differentiate into power sub-groups for purposes of argument and debate. It is part of the art of leadership to facilitate this debate. Then when consensus has been achieved, it is the object of the association to act as a unified power group to seek to further the interests of its members by exercising power in relation to other power groups. The power of any association will depend in part upon the strength of consensus among its members, and the strength of their will to remain united around that consensus. The other part of its power derives from the importance of the association to the other power group or groups with which it is negotiating: the threat of withdrawal from the social or economic exchange relationship is in the final analysis one of the prime external sources of power of negotiating groups.

The significance of constitutional mechanisms is to provide a set of rules which set the limits within which power can be expressed. This constitutional framework applies to relationships within associations as well as to relationships between them.

A final point is that associations act through elected representatives. The elected representatives may or may not be the most competent members of the association. There may be others who could do better, but who do not choose to spend the necessary time or who for some reason do not come to be elected. These representatives are accountable to the association and to no-one else (apart from their accountability as citizens under the law). For example, a representative might be involved in negotiations with managers one of whom is his own immediate manager; in this negotiation, however, he is not accountable to that manager but only to his own elective association. This point is a matter of some importance in the analysis of communications.

Qualities of Elective Leadership

Against the background of these activities, then, what are some of the qualities called for in elected representative leadership? To begin with there is the sheer willingness to stand for election. The unwillingly drafted representative tends to act as a mere passenger in committees and at meetings. But willingness itself is not enough. The effective representative enjoys the expression of power. He gets satisfaction out of his own powers of persuasion and negotiation against the powers of others. He has a taste for exercising the powers conferred upon him by representing the consensus arrived at by his constituents.

In this enjoyment of power lies one of the seductive dangers in representative leadership. It is often easy for a representative to act on his own personal behalf or on behalf of a small clique. He can behave as though he were expressing the views of his constituents while in fact pursuing his own aims or those of his clique – perhaps political aims – which he believes his constituents ought to be pursuing. Adequate constitutional safeguards are essential to avoid the arrogation of undue power by individual representatives or cliques. These safeguards are missing from many representative bodies, such as, for example, some trade unions where representatives are elected by show of hands at meetings – sometimes sparsely attended – rather than by scrutineered secret ballot sent to all members. It is under such conditions that autocratic leadership has the fullest chance to flower.

The effective leader will understand the views of his constituents, and those are the views he will express. Indeed one of his main skills lies in his having the sense of the feelings of his members towards any particular issue. He will not be able to refer back to them on every issue, and must somehow absorb their outlook in the course of his ordinary daily contacts. This kind of intuitive sensitivity is crucial. It is not necessarily a conscious or calculated assessment, but rather an unconscious accumulating judgment. It is a sense for the needs of others, based upon subjective interaction. This sense is akin to the sense of the good entrepreneur for the needs of the market, or the sense of the professional for the needs of the client.

This last point about subjective interaction in sensing and understanding the needs of others points to the minimum level of capacity needed in the elected leader. It suggests a level of at least Str-2. This conclusion is consistent with the widespread experience that those who are elected representatives of Str-1 manual workers, office staff and technicians and who actually take the lead in defining goals, in negotiations, in reporting back, are in fact competent to take on managerial roles of Str-2 or above, but for a variety of reasons have remained or chosen to remain at work on the shop- or office-floor. The Str-1 capacity individual by contrast tends to provide what is best described as a messenger rather than a leader: his competence allows him to go no further than to express the views of his members in a mechanistic way, and to go back for further instructions when issues are not absolutely clear.

There is a problem in this conclusion: if elected representative leadership requires Str-2 capacity at minimum, then with greater social mobility in a society it becomes more difficult for shop- and office-floor workers at Str-1 to find adequate elected leaders from among their own numbers. To raise this problem, however, does not imply that social mobility is to this extent unfortunate – as Lipset and Bendix unhappily suggest in the course of their comprehensive treatise on mobility: 'it seems appropriate to question the frequent assumption that the removal of talent from the lower classes (through the upward mobility of individuals) is *prima facie* a good thing;

the gains arising from such mobility should be balanced, rather, against the detrimental effects of diminishing the stock of talent in the lower classes.'[2]

Two types of solution may be observed: the first is for leadership to be exercised by the very experienced older members at the Str-1/Str-2 boundary, combined with younger members of high potential capacity who accept representative leadership while still working at Str-1; the second is for leadership to be provided by full-time paid officials (employees) of the trade union or other association, who act on behalf of the members in a number of enterprises. The former process reinforces pluralism and face-to-face representation; the latter process runs counter to local on-site social interaction: it is a centralizing tendency, away from pluralism.

To say that representative leaders require the outlook of Group-2 level of abstraction is most decidedly not to say that this level of abstraction is necessary for anyone to have a view about the correctness of given policies. Policies are a matter of personal sense of the situation, and all individuals are equal when it comes to sensing what is right for people, where justice lies. That is why political democracy based on universal suffrage is possible, and why the jury process is possible.

The elected leader must finally be competent in dealing with his constituents in face-to-face relationships. It is useful if he can formulate issues, but that is not always necessary. The formulations of objectives will often be provided by paid officials of unions or other associations, or by proposals set out by management for consideration by employees, or by proposals fashioned in a council. But the elected leader must be able to explain to his constituents how they are affected by the issues involved, and to give the lead in proposing what attitude or course of action is in their best interests. It is at this stage that what is narrowly termed leadership comes in. The representative must assist his constituents to reach a consensus view, helping to iron out difficulties so that even if there are dissenting voices they will in the end find it possible to go along with the majority.

This reporting, debating, leading relationship with constituents must be accompanied in the representative by a sense of when it is necessary to refer back to them for further discussion, and when it is not necessary to do so because he feels he has a sufficient idea of what the consensus view would be. This kind of sensitivity is critical when the representative is involved in negotiation of policies. He must have the feel of how far he can go in shifting ground in response to proposed amendments put forward in the course of debate, or in putting forward new ideas of his own. He is an intermediary, expressing the consensus of constituents at the conference table and expressing the requirements of the conference table to his constituents.

[2] S. M. Lipset and R. Bendix (1959), *Social Mobility in Industrial Society*, p. 286.

In order to be able to give the lead described in debates on formulated proposals, the elected leader must have a strong feeling for the way things are done, for the myriad underlying customs, practices, mores, which must be taken for granted and intuitively understood. This social sensitivity is necessary in everyone who wants to adjust to his social milieu. But it is necessary in heightened degree in a representative. He must be able to judge when the desires of his constituents clash with existing customs and mores, and whether the desires should be pursued in the form of demands or whether they should be held in abeyance because of the fundamental nature of the customs and mores which would be under attack.

In short, the elected representative is engaged in the mediation of power-conflict relations. Power is the driving force of social relations: the human drive to get other human beings to co-operate in actions which will satisfy one's own needs and aspirations. Conflict is the expression of inevitable differences in needs and aspirations of individuals and groups. Representative leadership is the art of achieving a resultant of power forces which will satisfy the leader's own constituents while at the same time being not unacceptable to the needs of other power groups as expressed by their representatives. Sometimes the solution will be a simple resultant of forces, expressed in an all-round compromise. At other times new solutions will be found which replace all the proposals and resolve them at a different level.

The Object of Managerial Leadership

If we now turn to managerial leadership we come to a very different situation. The manager in a bureaucratic hierarchy is not an intermediating representative acting as spokesman for his subordinates with respect to policy and negotiating with managers higher up on their behalf. He is an appointed officer who must act within current customs and mores, and within whatever policies have been constitutionally adopted, to achieve the outputs he has been assigned. His leadership must be exercised towards other appointed members with whom he is in a manager-subordinate relationship. The leadership situation is thus the reverse of that of the representative: the representative leader is accountable to his 'followers'; the managerial leader's 'followers' are accountable to him.

If the managerial role has been requisitely established and filled, the managerial leader will be at least at Str-2, and whatever the level in the structure, will be one stratum higher in capacity than his immediate subordinate group, and more than one stratum higher in capacity than any subordinates which they in turn may have.

The question, however, is why any so-called leadership is required. If the manager has the higher capacity called for, and if he knows his job, why does he not just get on with it, tell his subordinates what to do and expect them to do it, or get rid of them if they cannot? The answer lies in the fact that manager-subordinate relationships establish the working situation for living human beings in social exchange contract. They are founded upon mutual dependence, and demand mutual understanding, mutual respect, mutual trust, and confidence. Without these qualities the sanctioning of managerial authority is undermined, and only coercive power remains – and managers will soon discover that coercion is a two-way process whether they like to admit it or not.

In hard reality, therefore, manager subordinate relationships are two-way reciprocal relationships and not just one-way downwards coercive relationships. The right of an employing association to employ members of the community to work for it is requisitely a social privilege and not an opportunity for autocracy. Each employed person is entitled to be able to rely upon his employment as his career opportunity, to be fulfilled in some bureaucratic system even if not the one in which he is currently employed. That ought to be in the employment contract, backed by the hard guarantee of abundant employment.

In unemployment conditions managerial behaviour tends inevitably towards the autocratic-coercive style, since gaining output becomes relatively more difficult than gaining satisfactory subordinates. Given abundant employment, however, managers must attend to the occupational needs of their subordinates. If they do not do so they will lose their subordinates, and will find them difficult to replace: that is the best guarantee of managerial concern for subordinates.

The issues here are similar to those which concerned Douglas McGregor[3] and his construction of his Theory X and Theory Y styles of management: the first, that subordinates are work-shy and need to be coerced; and the second that they are self-motivated and seek responsibility. My experience is in line with his Theory Y, and I have found that managerial leadership requires to facilitate this constructive motivation. There is nothing so effective as abundant employment to ensure a manager's paying attention to subordinates in the face of the constant reality of the continuous pressures upon him for output.

The need for managerial leadership is thus a reflection of the fact that the employment contract is not simply an economic exchange relationship, it is requisitely a social exchange relationship. It is not just a matter of the manager's saying 'Do this, it's what you're paid for!'; it is requisitely a matter of his saying, 'I want this task done and I am assigning it to you; I am accountable for assessing the outcome, and for keeping a running appraisal of your competence; if you do well, I shall arrange for you to be rewarded within the limits of the resources allocated to me, and I shall also

---

[3] D. McGregor (1960), *The Human Side of Enterprise*.

see to it that you are considered by those higher up for advancement; I believe that I will act justly towards you, but if you feel that I do not, then you have access to an appeal procedure in which you can cause any of my decisions about you to be reviewed by managers higher up the system; neither of us is infallible, and I expect you to do your best and I will do my best towards you. Thus, if you have any suggestions to make, let me have them; you must adhere to the rules and regulations which are binding upon us both; but within those prescribed limits you will have the freedom to exercise your own discretion in carrying out your tasks without undue interference from me; if there is anything you are not clear about, including the reasons for the particular tasks you are assigned and how they fit into the larger picture of the functioning of our enterprise, let me know.'

It is not of course implied that every manager will say all the foregoing every time he gives a subordinate something to do. But a statement to this effect is requisitely implicit in each and every managerial instruction. It gives the context of the relation between manager and subordinate within which the inter-subjective boundary zone for the subordinate's work is established. Any manager who is not willing or able to accept this type of relationship with subordinates ought not to be allowed to hold a managerial post. Competence in inter-subjectivity is the humanizing foundation of managerial leadership. Its absence gives an autocratic coercive feel to the relationship and is paranoiagenic.

Qualities of Managerial Leadership

Managerial leadership has a number of important characteristics. The manager must have the ability to set tasks or general responsibilities in a manner comprehensible to his subordinate. He must be able further to provide terms of reference which will set the context of direction and boundaries and enable the subordinate to understand what he has to do in connection with the wider setting to which the work is relevant. This setting of frameworks is sometimes best done with all his immediate subordinates together, and the manager will have to be proficient in conducting such meetings. They are not committee meetings and he is not the 'chairman'. They are consultation events in which he has the opportunity to set directions and to hear the views, reactions and suggestions of his subordinates in the light of their practical experience. The decisions at such meetings are his decisions. The act of leadership calls for a willingness on his part to allow his integrity and competence to be reviewed, and to make the decisions having heard and considered what his subordinates have had to say; it is not for him to abdicate by submerging his managerial identity in the group and taking part in so-called group decisions.[4]

A manager's decisions will not always be popular with all his subordinates. Nor will his subordinates necessarily agree that what he decides to do is the best decision. His leadership must be directed towards achieving consensus among them, but he does not necessarily have to have such consensus before he acts. He must be able to demonstrate that his decision is at least one of the reasonable possibilities, and that he has given serious attention to optimizing future employment opportunities. He must give the continual assurance that he accepts full accountability for what he is doing. For there can never be any final answer to which is the best course of action in given circumstances. It will be the manager's unformulated sense of the situation which will finally decide, and his sense ought to be the result of a wider grasp of the problem than any of his subordinates could possibly have. He must demonstrate his willingness to rely upon his judgment, to decide what to do, to scrutinize and evaluate his judgments in the light of experience, and to modify course when events dictate change.

By his manner, his tone, his inflection, his gestures, his comportment, the manager will convey a sense of his confidence or of his uncertainty in his decisions. He will also convey the extent of his sense of rapport with his subordinates, enthusing with them and winning their support or being left with their lukewarm acceptance. These non-verbal expressions of underlying attitudes and feelings will be as important as the verbal content of the debate.[5]

Furthermore along with the tasks he decides to assign to each subordinate, the immediate manager will be the most potent factor in determining whether each subordinate is able to achieve equilibrium between his work-capacity (C), level of work (W) and his payment (P). His credibility as a leader will depend upon his ability to assign tasks matching his subordinate's work-capacity. Here lies the core of his relationship with each of his subordinates. And it must be remembered that it is through each one individually that he will be able to get his work done. It is the manager's ability to put each subordinate at full stretch, to have each work at a time-span consistent with his work-capacity, which is the mark of sound leadership.

Along with providing a level of work which calls upon each subordinate's full ability, the manager must be able to assess whether the subordinate is giving of his best, and must provide progress in wage or salary

[4] A. Bavelas (1942), 'Morale and the Training of Leaders'; D. Cartwright (1965), 'Influence, Leadership and Control'; F. E. Fielder (1967), *Theory of Leadership Effectiveness*; and F. C. Mann (1965), 'Towards an Understanding of the Leadership Role in Formal Organisation'.

[5] It is precisely these behavioural communications and role-taking which sociologists and social psychologists like Birdwhistell, Goffman, Argyle, Ambrose and many others are investigating. See for example, R. L. Birdwhistell (1973), *Kinesics and Context*.

which matches the subordinate's progress in perfomance. He will be judged by all his subordinates in terms of his shrewdness in picking out those who are performing well and rewarding them; and his shrewdness in seeing through those who are putting up an apparently good show but not really performing well, and not rewarding them.

In the ADO (aided direct output) and DOS (direct output support) situations, the foregoing conditions are more readily achieved than in the DDO (delegated direct output) situations. The reason is that the manager works in direct contact with his subordinates. Indeed in the ADO relationship he has an almost continuous working relationship with them, observing directly their mode of work and receiving directly the outputs, as compared with the DDO relationship in which he can observe his subordinates at work only by making special tours of inspection from time to time.

Leadership by Manager-more-than-one-stratum Removed

The foregoing points all refer to leadership in the immediate manager-subordinate relationship. The notion of leadership is more often associated, however, with the higher manager in relation to his total command. It is most dramatically depicted in terms of the charismatic individual, the general who stands up in front of all his troops and exhorts them to greater effort, or else the senior officer or official who creates a dramatic or romantic picture of himself, one with which his subordinates can identify or which will at least impress them in such a way as to gain their loyalty and support.

The concept of charisma is psychologically interesting. But it is not a requisite feature of bureaucratic managerial leadership. It may be considered as a sometimes useful bonus. There are, however, several requisites. The manager-once-removed, for example, will contribute one of his most vital leadership acts by being aware of the potential of each and every one of his subordinates-once-removed for eventual progress and promotion. He will make sure that each one of them is aware of this judgment and of any changes in it. This judgment is the one more than any other which establishes where a person stands with respect to his present and future position in the particular bureaucracy in which he is employed.

The chief executive as well as the senior manager on each site will have to be able to exercise leadership in the negotiations with elected representatives of employees. That leadership will be expressed in a taste for debate, in a respect for the views expressed by representatives, in an acceptance of those views as representing the consensual outlook of the various significant power groups among the employees in his command, and in an expressed acceptance of the fact that one of the main sanctions for himself and his managerial subordinates as managers comes from his subordinates via their elected representatives.

Moreover, each manager at Str-3 and above will have to judge when to contract[6] his lines of communication. When what he has to say or to convey is the same for all his subordinates, then he should give the lead by speaking to them, writing to them, or otherwise communicating with them all directly and at once. It is an abdication of leadership, for example, to expect elected representatives to communicate management's views to their employees, or for a higher manager simply to use the managerial system as a kind of switchboard through which to pass messages.

Elective Leadership and Managerial Leadership Summarized

The characteristics of managerial leadership may thus be seen to be very different from those of elected representative leadership: the manager listens for suggestions and then decides and instructs – the representative advises and is instructed; the manager alone makes up his mind – the representative assists his constituents to make up theirs; the managerial process is an individual executive process – the representative process is a consensual one; the manager assesses and rewards his subordinates, and is accountable for their performance – the representative is accountable to his constituents and they for what he does on their behalf. It makes some sense to talk about democratic leadership style in relation to elected representatives; it makes no sense to do so in the case of managerial leadership, which requires to be authoritative and which can never be democratic other than in a broad and very general sense of being concerned about subordinates, and of being competent to provide for serious participative consultation.

This description of the requisite features of managerial leadership contains nothing more than an elaboration of what it is that a manager can do to ensure that the natural motivation of his subordinates is not inhibited: that is what managerial leadership is about. It is worth keeping in mind that managerial leadership is something that must go on day in and day out, year after year, throughout a manager's whole working life: and for months or most likely for years in relation to any given subordinate. We are considering enduring long-term relationships, of great significance to the life and career of each individual. That is why the whole question of managerial assessment and reward of subordinates is such a central feature of managerial leadership.

Decision-making in the Leadership Situation

The discussion of leadership flows inevitably into decision-making. The act of leadership calls for decisions which affect the 'followers', whether they

[6] This concept of contraction is fully developed in W. Brown (1971), *Organization*.

be electoral constituents or executive subordinates. The 'followers' are concerned about these decisions, and if not satisfied will argue about them. That is to say, leadership involves public decision-making in the sense that others have a felt interest in the decisions through being directly affected by them. This public feature of the decision brings out an important characteristic of decision-making. It has to do with the difference between the publicly formulatable framework within which a decision is taken, and the unconscious intuitive processes by which the person-in-action makes his decision but which he can never make explicit.

The reasons underlying the taking of any particular decision are always in the final analysis impossible to express. But managers and elected representatives are often made to feel foolish if they cannot give a reasonable argument in favour of their particular decisions. They try to do so, but all they can express are the explicit facts and data which constituted the context of the decision; the source of the decision lies imbedded in their intuitive behaviour flow. Then the trouble begins, for they find themselves bolstering up their case by producing rationalizations. Their constituents or their subordinates may then fasten on to the rationalizations, break them down, and apparently thereby expose the decision as foolhardy.

A similar situation may occur the other way around. A manager listens to a subordinate's argument in favour of a particular course of action; he challenges it and forces the subordinate to the wall. The subordinate then begins to produce arguments which are patent rationalizations; these are seized upon by the manager and the subordinate's case is demolished — particularly if the manager does not like the proposals in any case.

In all these instances, however, the outcome may be that the person whose case has been destroyed may nevertheless feel that he was right, and that if only he could have put his arguments better he might have convinced the others. Let me give two actual examples. A chief executive decides to recommend to the Board that a subsidiary manufacture and trading operation should be established in a particular country. He is strongly dissuaded by his chief accountant who has carried out a financial analysis which 'proves' that the operation would run at a loss; and by his sales manager whose data 'demonstrate' that the market would not be sufficient to justify the investment. The chief executive attempts to produce other figures which could outweigh those of the accountant and the sales manager: but they have access to more detailed data in their own special but limited fields, and can show to their own satisfaction that he is simply riding an ill-advised hobby horse.

In fact, the differences are not to be found in the data but in a variety of underlying assumptions about which there could be no data; for example, assumptions about the political future of the country in question, the likelihood that it would set up protectionist trade barriers and penalize im-

ports, the possible use of a new subsidiary as a launching pad for impingement on other markets in that part of the world, the advantage of being
able to provide an additional source of supply in a better labour market,
and so on. What is thought about these issues could be narrowed down by
some factual information, but finally a decision will have to be made on the
basis of hunch in a context of incomplete knowledge. The chief executive
decides to proceed, but there are hard feelings for some time between the
three: the chief executive feeling that his subordinates have tried to blind
him with 'facts', and the subordinates feeling aggrieved because they feel
their data founded in hard research have been treated in a cavalier manner.

Another example is that of an elected representative who considers that
a company's policies on overtime are unsatisfactory since they allow for
individual managers to decide when overtime should be worked, although
there are appropriate safeguards for individuals such as reasonable advance notice. The representative argues that managers should not have
such discretion, since representatives are just as interested as managers in
keeping overtime down and should be involved. This view is interpreted as
syndicalism or anarchy by the negotiating manager and by many of the
other representatives, the argument degenerating into a quarrel over
whether managers or representatives are to make the decisions about when
overtime is necessary.

This argument becomes very heated, lasting over many months, and
tempers are lost in very stormy meetings in which the manager and the
representative each think the other guilty of very bad leadership. It is finally resolved by an agreement that before a manager decides on overtime he
would contact the local representatives to find out whether they could help
to discover means of avoiding it. But this solution, felt to be an improvement by all concerned, does not emerge until the members of the Council
give up attacking each other's words and try to listen in such a way as to
get the sense of the other person's feelings about the problem.

Facts and Judgment in Decisive Leadership

Leadership and decision-making must be firmly based upon a person's intuitive feel of the situation. Leadership cannot be exercised by intellect
alone, any more than decisions can be made upon the formulated data
available. These statements do not imply that the intellect is not important
and that carefully researched data do not count. They have a quite important function in setting effective boundaries to the behavioural flux. But it is
out of the normal unconscious flow of mental functioning in which a person's experience is mulled over and brought to bear upon a problem that
the decision and the action emerge.

In decision-making associated with managerial leadership relations, it is useful if all concerned can be aware of the fact that the final reasons for a particular decision or a proposed decision can never be given. Good leadership requires an easy-going reliance by the manager upon his own judgment. He will judge how far to allow discussion to go before finally making up his mind what to do. Both he and his subordinates will recognize that it is a matter of judgment, and will the more readily sympathize with the outcomes.

He will want what he considers to be sufficient facts, neither too many nor too few. This recipe cannot be put into measurable terms. But it does point to the importance of having a person of the right capacity level in any given role. One of the signs of too low capacity for a role is that a person will seek more and more data, hoping that somehow a solution will come floating out through the facts. It never does. When the work-capacity of the manager matches the time-span of the role, the proper setting has been provided for balance in the play between the boundaries set by the facts and the flow of judgment channelled by those boundaries in decision-making.

There is yet another implication. The sound managerial leader must set an effective framework or terms of reference for his subordinates. What he is doing is setting the framework for the focusing of his subordinates' attention. In other words, the prescribed limits of a task set a channel within which a subordinate's thought processes will be expected to operate in exercising the discretion which constitutes his work.

In short, what is required in leadership and decision-making is not a seeking for more and more data, and the hope that computers can somehow do the job. There is certainly required a respect for data, for facts, and for the establishment of sound policies and other types of prescribed limit. But there is needed just as much a due respect for judgment, for discretion. Subordinates have no difficulty in sizing up when their manager is clutching at facts because his thought processes are not extensive enough to play over the whole of a problem, to bring a wider range of unformulated experiences to bear upon it than they themselves could. They are also aware when he is able to do so. Leadership is weakened in the former case and strengthened in the latter.

PART SIX

MODELS OF
BUREAUCRATIC ORGANIZATION

20

Growth of Bureaucratic Systems

This part turns from analysis of bureaucracy to synthesis. It looks at the way bureaucracies grow and develop, and considers the general patterns of organization of bureaucratic systems of different size ranging from Str-2 systems to Str-7 systems. Each organization pattern is described from two points of view: first, as though it constituted the total system with a chief executive in charge (for example, a Str-3 enterprise); second, as though it were one part of a larger system, with a manager in charge and with the chief executive somewhere higher up (for example, a Str-3 department in a Str-5 enterprise).

Organizational magnitude refers not to the number of people employed but to the level of work (measured in time-span) of the chief executive role in the case of a total enterprise, or of the top manager's role in the case of a department or section within a larger enterprise.

Pressures Towards Growth

Size of organization, related to scale of enterprise, tends commonly to be regarded as a function of such factors as size of market, the nature of the economy, scale of available investment, and type of technology. These factors provide the general setting and opportunities for bureaucratic growth. But they are not sufficient, either singly or in combination, to explain either the actual distribution of sizes of bureaucracy in a particular society or the pattern of growth of any single bureaucratic system.

The distribution of sizes of bureaucracy will be determined by the distribution in level of work-capacity of those available to manage the bureaucracies, and the growth in scale of any particular bureaucratic system will be determined by the growth in level of work-capacity of its chief executive. There is a kind of Archimedes principle at work by which bureaucratic systems grow to the level of work-capacity of their chief executives; and, conversely, chief executives stimulate bureaucratic systems to grow to that level consistent with their work-capacity. To say, however, that bureaucracy and work-capacity, like water, seek their own level, does not mean that markets, technology, capital, have no effect on growth. They facilitate or inhibit the movement to a given level, like dams and channels. But they do not determine the particular level towards which particular institutions will naturally seek to rise.

This argument leads to the conclusion described in Chapter 10, that if a higher proportion of the population of an industrialized nation were composed of Group-6, Group-7, and Group-8 individuals, then more of the bureaucratic hierarchies in the nation would be Str-6, Str-7, and Str-8 hierarchies. If there were a large and continuous supply of Group-9 individuals, there would come into existence a number of Str-9 institutions. This conclusion, of course, assumes a fully developed industrial economy, in which needs and markets may affect scale temporarily but would not do so permanently. When an enterprise saturates a given market, the governing body will have to pause in its development to discover new outlets, services and products. Development may then continue, but at a rate consonant with the growth in work-capacity of the individuals at the top. The extension of activities will show first of all in growth in turn-over or other criteria of work done. It may be accompanied by growth in number of employees. That is, the organization will grow by horizontal extension. When the chief executive reaches the boundary of the stratum he occupies and moves across that boundary in work-capacity to the next higher level, then, given the support of the governing body, growth by vertical extension will occur.

Growth by vertical extension requires the building of extra levels into the bureaucratic hierarchy. It calls for extensive reorganization each time a new level is added, revealing many of the most interesting features of bureaucratic systems and their design. Growth by vertical extension may also take place inside a bureaucratic system. It can occur at the point where an employee reaches the upper boundary of a stratum and his manager-once-removed decides that he wants to introduce at a higher level work of the kind which the employee is doing. The employee may be promoted to a newly created post and authorized to appoint someone as a subordinate to take over the post he has vacated.

The opposite of the processes described – namely, a contraction in bureaucratic systems – may occur with a downward movement in the work-capacity of a chief executive or any other manager, either because of deterioration in the manager's work-capacity or because of the replacement of one manager by another manager of lower work-capacity.

Organization Growth and the Division of Labour

A most significant feature of the process of growth of bureaucratic systems – and indeed of all social institutions – is that of the emergence of a wider and wider range of new types of role. This phenomenon has been commented upon by many authors. Aiken and Hage and their co-workers in America, and Hickson and Pugh and their co-workers in Britain, for example, have demonstrated systematically the universal occurrence of increasing complexity of function with growth in scale.[1] This increase in complexity is but one reflection of the role differentiation which occurs as bureaucratic systems grow.

In a sense it is true that new functions and complexities emerge with growth. It is useful to note, however, that in another sense it is not so much that new functions are emerging as that existing functions grow to the point where the amount of work involved requires a full-time role. At that point functions hitherto combined in one role are differentiated into separate roles, taking on a new scope, scale and complexity in the process. The following functions are always to be found in any enterprise of whatever scale:

1. Development (D) and provision (M) of goods or services, and maintenance of relationships with consumers or clients (S).
2. Maintenance of organization and personnel (P), of a programme (Pr), and of a technology (T).
3. Maintenance of financial resources and accounts.
4. Clerical and administrative work.
5. Inspection of quality.
6. Purchase and allocation of supplies and materials.
7. Procurement and maintenance of property and buildings.
8. Procurement and maintenance of equipment.
9. Coping with legal requirements.
10. Transport.

In small organizations only a few of these functions will be established in specialized full-time roles; that is to say in roles devoted exclusively to them. The rest will have to be carried out, but they are discontinuous, requiring to be done only from time to time. Some, like procurement of property or buildings, may arise only occasionally over periods of many years; and can be handled by obtaining the services of an agent, or a builder, for the particular project, without on-going commitment. Others, like accounts or a delivery service, may arise regularly but require resources and specialization beyond the scope of existing roles; these can be handled by retaining the services of professionals like accountants and solicitors or by sub-contracts, for example for delivery services. Still others, like inspection, secretarial work, cleaning, may arise regularly, and it may be possible to deal with them by combining them with other functions in existing roles or by having them done by part-time employment.

[1] J. Hage and M. Aiken (1967), 'Relationship of Centralisation to Other Structural Properties'; M. Aiken and J. Hage (1968), 'Organisational Interdependence and Intraorganisational Structure'; C. R. Hining and G. L. Lee (1971), 'Dimension of Organisation Structure and Their Context'; and D. S. Pugh, D. J. Hickson, C. R. Hining and C. Turner (1968), 'Dimensions of Organisation Structure'.

We are dealing here with the process of the division of labour, of specialization, in connection with growth and development. As each function grows in scale, it moves step by step along a path from the outside to the inside of the institution. To begin with, the function may be established completely outside, as part of a separate enterprise – a firm of solicitors, or accountants, or builders, or estate agents. These functions may be obtained on an *ad hoc* basis (the least connected) or on a retainer or regular contract basis (a slightly closer tie). Then as the need grows, the function may be bought in part-time, or assigned as part of an existing role, or combined with other part-time functions to constitute a new role. Then with still further development of need, a full-time role may be established for that particular function.

By this process, role differentiation and specialization occur within the institution. As enough work in, say, functions A and B becomes available to occupy one full role each, there is a tendency to place the whole of A into one role and the whole of B into another, rather than to have two roles each alternating half-and-half between A and B. It may be noted, however, that specialization is not absolutely inevitable: there is room for choice in organization – choice in the design of role content to meet the desires and interests of individuals along with the requirements of planning.

Role differentiation also occurs with further growth within functions once these become established. Thus, for example, an all-in personnel specialist role will eventually differentiate into a subordinate organization with separately institutionalized recruitment, selection, training, establishment, organization, and personnel research functions; accounting differentiates into financial accounting, budgeting, bought- and sales-ledgers, wage and salary payment, credit control, computer records; transport grows from a car or a van and driver to fleets of lorries and fleets of ships; production technology differentiates into methods development, time study, work study, tool design. Thus it is that with growth the area of accountability of the chief executive and his immediate subordinates widens in the sense of including a wider range of separately institutionalized activities.

21

Direct Command Systems: Two- and Three-Stratum Hierarchies

This chapter, in considering Str-2 and Str-3 bureaucratic systems, deals with the systems which are at the heart of the problem of building bureaucratic institutions without their becoming impersonal and anonymous. These are the two systems which are still small enough in size for *all* the members to be known to one another as real flesh-and-blood individuals. Reciprocal interaction and social exchange can occur in face-to-face relationship. Esteem and respect, hostility and rejection, trust and confidence, suspicion and mistrust, are felt towards a known person and can be checked within the realities of the other's immediate behaviour; they are not matters of detached and impersonal reputation at a distance.

The immediacy of relationship makes it possible for all employees to feel and indeed to be in contact with the objectives of the enterprise. The chief executive role (in a requisitely organized system) is either immediately superior or at most one stratum above that. The clients or customers can be seen by all, and may be dealt with directly by all. Every employee is in direct contact with the significance of his work for the whole. It is this awareness of the entrepreneurial activity, and the likelihood of involvement in it, which helps to give to such institutions the tone of quality which has led such writers as Miller and Swanson to refer to them as entrepreneurial systems, reserving the term bureaucracy to refer to larger-scale employment systems.

Moreover, as so many writers have recognized, the process of role differentiation has only just begun in these Str-2 and Str-3 systems. Everyone has plenty of opportunity to carry out several different functions in his role, and therefore the opportunity for change. Because of the smallness of scale and the face-to-face nature of all relationships, there is also likely to be maximum freedom to move physically about the place of work – freedom of spatial locomotion.

Stratum-2 Organization and the Supervisory Problem

The Str-2 enterprise is typically the small shop, restaurant, garage, farm or workshop, usually with an owner-manager employing a team of clerks, operators, labourers or other staff. If it is a registered enterprise it will have a simple board, most often comprising the proprietor, one or more members of his family, and the accountant retained by the business. The board will meet once a year to scrutinize and approve the accounts for tax purposes. Capital for development is provided by personal savings or by bank loan or overdraft. Such separately established small institutions will not be found in ordinary circumstances in the public and social service sector.

Inside larger enterprises, the Str-2 organization is the primary section level, with section managers in charge. It is the level of organization at which DDO work gets done, whether manual production work, or clerical work of the typing, invoicing, filing or business machine operating kind. In industry the people in managerial roles are most often referred to as foremen or assistant foremen; in offices – whether in industry, commerce, or Civil Service – they they tend to be referred to as office supervisors, executive officers, or administrative officers.

The contrast between work in small and large enterprises shows most strikingly in the comparison between work in the small Str-2 enterprise and in the Str-2 section within the large enterprise. It is the contrast between, on the one hand, the highest degree of spatial freedom and variation in activity available to employees in bureaucratic systems, and on the other hand, the most complete limitation imposed by standardization and the division of labour.

In the small Str-2 enterprise, the owner-manager will usually himself be directly involved in D, M, and S activities, working together with his subordinates to whom he will delegate M and S responsibilities. For the rest he will carry out all the P, Pr, and T, inspection and purchasing functions – which will be needed only intermittently – and will hire the maintenance, building and estate, accountancy and legal services required. The subordinates also will be involved in numbers of activities: serving customers; manual work; stock-taking; dusting goods; packing; taking cash; answering the telephone; running errands; etc., etc. But, as Rowbottom and Billis have shown,[1] the Str-1 subordinates will not be engaged in interpreting the needs of customers or of one another. That kind of judgment is for the Str-2 owner-manager to exercise – interpreting the needs of clients and customers as well as the needs of his subordinates.

In the Str-2 DDO section command within the larger enterprise, the section will usually be quite specialized: a milling or drilling or turning section; a wages section; a sales invoice section; a typing pool; a specialized administrative section; a section of counter clerks serving the public; the junior nursing staff on a hospital ward; and so on. There is usually less opportunity for changing roles or for variation in role, or for freedom of

[1] R. W. Rowbottom and D. Billis (to be published), 'The Stratification of Work and Organisational Design'.

spatial movement than there is in the small self-contained enterprise. Nevertheless, there can be just as full opportunity for the exercise of capacity as in the small enterprise, since the range of level of work is the same.

The Supervisory Role

It is exceptionally important that the managerial role in Str-2 sections be clearly identified, and that it should not be obscured and confused by intermediate supervisory-type roles vaguely positioned and with equally vague terms of reference. How this supervisory problem may arise can be demonstrated in the growing Str-2 setting. As the Str-2 enterprise or the Str-2 section grows from a small establishment of the owner-manager or section manager and three or four subordinates to one with fifteen to twenty employees, the manager may wish to leave one of them to supervise some or all of the rest, because he himself is heavily occupied as owner with selling, getting supplies, keeping records, assessing his stock, and so on, or as manager with attending meetings or co-ordinating his activities with colleagues. But in either case he remains the head, on the spot, managing his staff and his enterprise or section directly. He can manage very satisfactorily at the imaginal-concrete level, because everything is immediately to hand.

So long as every person he picks for supervisory duties is currently at Str-1 level of work-capacity (whatever their potential), the arrangement will work perfectly well. If, however, one of his supervisors is of Str-2 level of capacity, the owner-manager or section manager will soon begin to notice that the employees that the supervisor is looking after are treating him not as their supervisor but as their manager, and will find himself with a *de facto* manager in between himself and his subordinates. Unless he is ready to move up and create a Str-3 organization he is in some trouble. For after a period of time the supervisor begins to feel underpaid and the manager has been pushed out of immediate control. There is not enough work for another manager, and so organization crowding occurs.

This problem of supervisors inadvertently taking over managerial positions without explicit managerial accountability and authority is a common phenomenon both in Str-2 enterprises and in Str-2 section commands inside larger enterprises. The difficulty occurs insidiously as a result of the particular way in which most potential Str-2 individuals grow in capacity. Thus, for example, Figure 21.1 illustrates a typical case of a potential Str-2 member appointed a supervisor at the age of 34. He will reach the Str-1/Str-2 boundary in capacity about four to six years after he has been appointed. But he reaches this boundary slowly and imperceptibly. Another couple of years go by, and in capacity he has moved into

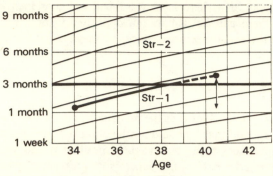

Figure 21.1

Str-2C about 5 per cent above the boundary. Changes occurring at such a slow pace are difficult to detect until symptoms begin to occur. These symptoms are characterized by pressures from supervisors for more recognition: they should have more pay; they should have more authority. If the demands are acceded to, the post of supervisor ceases to exist and is superseded by a non-requisite unrecognized managerial-type role.

This situation of supervisors of managerial capacity in anomalous positions somewhere between the manager and the subordinates is one of the main causes of the break at the bottom of the executive chain which we described some years ago.[2] It is a break occasioned by the fragmenting of the managerial relationships at this level. The result is that subordinates cannot and do not have an unequivocal manager immediately above them, nor does the manager have an unequivocal direct relationship with his subordinates. It is the situation *par excellence* of the 'middlemen' and the 'straw bosses'.

The solution to the problem is to maintain a requisite organization structure in which supervisory (and charge hand) roles are explicitly established as assistants to the manager and filled at Str-1A capacity level. If and when a supervisor in such a role is judged to have grown in capacity into the Str-2 level, then a change of role is required and must be sought. In larger enterprises the solution is to promote such 'supervisors' to managerial posts elsewhere in the organization as soon as possible. Too many such non-promoted and bottled-up supervisors in an office or a factory can cause extended and strong disaffection. Proper progression policies ought to skim off the potential managers as they reach Str-2 capacity, and so leave the supervisory roles intact.

This problem occurs much less often in the case of very high-potential individuals coming up from Str-1 through a supervisory promotion. They move very rapidly through the supervisory band without the imperceptibly

[2] See E. Jaques (1951), *The Changing Culture of a Factory*, pp. 293–7.

slow transition to section managerial level.

In the Str-2 enterprise which is not growing into Str-3, the requisite solution is a policy of facing the supervisor with the absence of any promotion prospects and with planned leaving. Abundant employment is essential to take the individual injustice out of such leaving by ensuring that other and more appropriate work is locally available.

Stratum-3 Units: Key to Requisite Organizations

The Stratum-3 unit is the key unit in the organization of all larger bureaucratic systems. Effective organization of Str-3 units is the necessary foundation for the design and construction of larger systems: if the Str-3-level organization is right, it is possible for the rest of the organization to be right; if the Str-3-level organization is wrong, then the rest of the organization will inevitably be wrong also. Consider its main features.

The Str-3 unit is the largest bureaucratic system in which mutual recognition can still be assured. It may have anywhere from just a few employees up to a maximum of two to three hundred under conditions of a normal-length working week. Mutual recognition allows people to be aware of one another as individuals, each one existing in his or her own individual way, each recognized by all the others – the opposite of anonymity. Requisitely organized (that is to say, without the interposition of badly structured supervisory, charge hand or other intermediate roles), there are but three organization levels – the office- or shop-floor, the Str-2 section managers, and the Str-3 unit manager. The manager of the Str-3 unit knows something about all his subordinates and a great deal about most of them, and can identify them all by sight. They in turn know him: they see him; they observe him in action because he is their manager-once-removed.

Although the unit is too large for the manager to know in detail what is going on everywhere, it is not too large for him to know what is going on in general, by scanning the total situation in his mind's eye. He can function by imaginal scanning. Direct command therefore remains possible.

The So-called One-man Business

As a separate business the Str-3 unit is the prototypical one-man business: for example, a shop with several departments; a petrol station under one manager, and a garage under a foreman, with the owner managing both and selling cars as well; a small hotel, with separately managed restaurant and rooms; a small printing works; a manufacturing workshop with a shop foreman, and with the owner engaged in selling; or any one of hundreds of other types of business in industry or commerce. Finance is still within the scale which can be coped with by personal investment and bank loans.

The operational differentiation is mainly into M and S; D most commonly remains undifferentiated from the chief executive role, but a separate D may sometimes be established. The organization will now require a book-keeper/accountant, perhaps with a typist-clerk. It may also require staff work – at this level most likely Pr. If there is a workshop, a maintenance engineer may be needed.

At its fullest growth by lateral extension the Str-3 enterprise will look something like:

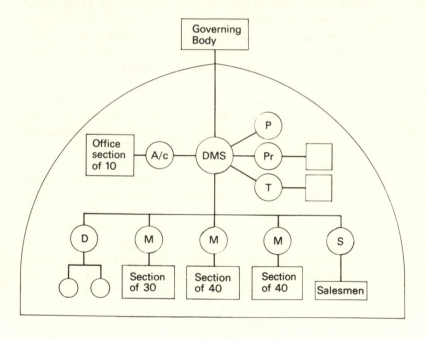

Figure 21.2

The governing body is an effective board, although small. Such enterprises are usually family businesses, the board being composed of the chief executive, the outside accountant, perhaps another member of the family, and perhaps one of the Str-2 managers who is interested in the business or another outside member. The board may meet quarterly to review plans and progress.

In running this enterprise the chief executive is now one removed from direct-output production. The management of most direct output is in the hands of subordinates. Moreover, he is no longer everywhere at once. He can keep in direct contact with everything by daily rounds of the total establishment. He can thus inspect the progress of work, stock levels, the quality of what is being done. He can also maintain direct contact with customers. To put all this information together, however, he must have the capacity for imaginal scanning, to be able to play it all over in his mind and decide what alternatives to make in methods, in priorities, in supplies, in layout, in service, in maintenance, in anything that needs doing to develop his business.

For purposes of forward planning he must meet regularly with his operational subordinate managers, his staff officer or officers, and his accountant. He must take them with him in the sense that his subordinates must accept his terms of reference sufficiently to apply them with understanding.

Stratum-3 Units Inside Larger Bureaucracies

The Str-3 unit inside the larger enterprise may be the larger type of DDO unit: a large income tax or employment or social security office managed by a chief executive officer, with Str-2 executive officers or higher executive officers; the manufacturing shop of 250; the large accounts office; the sectors of 200 to 300 operators on an assembly track of 800 men; the store with 120 employees in a chain of similar stores; a specialized sector of a large hospital with an assistant matron, six ward sisters, and 100 nursing staff.

Or the units may be smaller in size in the ADO situation where the direct output is specialized or professionalized and carried out mainly at Str-2: in a small to medium bank branch with a manager, a group of Str-2 cashiers and accountants, and a few Str-1 juniors; or a physiotherapy or social work unit with a Str-3 superintendent and Str-2 therapists or social workers, plus a few Str-1 aides; in a research or design unit with a Str-3 research programme head or chief designer, assisted by a few Str-3 research investigators or designers, with subordinate groups of laboratory assistants, technicians, or tracers; or in a personnel (or other specialist) department with a Str-3 personnel manager, Str-2 personnel and training officers, and Str-1 interviewing and clerical staff.

Similarly, the units will be smaller in a DOS type of sales department with a Str-3 sales manager supporting a group of Str-2 salesmen, and perhaps a small number of Str-1 clerks or sales technicians.

In the larger type of Str-3 unit the unit manager may require a full complement of staff officers attached from higher level – for example, a trouble-shooting technical staff officer, a progress chaser, and perhaps even a personnel officer if personnel and training issues present particularly difficult and continuing problems. He will also probably need a unit clerk, and possibly a store for stationery, tools, fixtures and other equipment.

Qualities of Stratum-3 Management

The essence of the small-scale ADO or DOS type of specialized or sales Str-3 unit is the possibility of intimacy in relationships between all three levels. Everyone can in a literal sense work together. Considerable freedom of spatial locomotion and of exchangeability and variability of role is available. The conditions are the closest to those for which the term 'entrepreneurial organization' is used. A competent manager ought to be able to cope easily without the need for sophisticated managerial aides.

The larger-sized DDO Str-3 units, however, whether independent enterprise or within a larger enterprise, throw up a different order of problem. Given, say, between 100 and 300 members, the manager will require to construct procedures and institutions to help him to cope. Let me illustrate the issues involved by reference to the largest type of unit, say of 300 people.

The Str-3 unit manager in these circumstances will require a small office staff, one or more specialist staff officers, possibly a store. He will be concerned with multifarious activities outside the unit – with customers and suppliers, with laterally related units, with general management higher up. He will be pulled in many directions.

At the same time he is the manager-once-removed of some 300 people. Here is a very special managerial task. At no other managerial level is a manager likely to be faced by such a large number of subordinates-once-removed. It is in the handling of this situation that the manager of the large Str-3 unit faces his greatest problems. All these subordinates are recognizable to him, and they all know him in turn. In exercising manager-once-removed leadership, however, he must be able to do more than merely recognize them all. He must know a large number of them personally – the outstanding performers, the problem cases, those ready for upgrading or promotion, the potential developers, those who have just joined, and so on – and he must have records of status and performance which allow him immediate access to information about the individuals and about differentials in status and pay.

In addition to the exercise of a proper manager-once-removed relationship with each individual, he must ensure that his Str-2 managers work fairly with the Str-1 sections and keep the general tone of reasonableness and firmness which is the necessary underpinning of social exchange relationships. One of his main tests of this tone – and a most important means of controlling it – is the appeals procedure. As the first level of manager-once-removed, his is the first level at which appeals can take place. Since he is on the spot in the direct command situation he ought to be able to deal fairly with all appeals and their aftermath: in the Str-3 unit within a larger enterprise, very few appeals should need to go higher than the unit manager if he is carrying his role competently.

Finally, the Str-3 manager will need to be able to interact with a representative system. The magnitude of organization has grown to the point where a certain amount of policy needs to be constitutionalized. In the case of the Str-3 enterprise, a full legislative system will be needed to allow for participation by the employees in the control of policy change. The same will usually be true of a Str-3 unit within a larger enterprise but located on its own geographically independent site. It is likely that the unit or sizeable sections of it will be trade-union organized, and this fact will have to be catered for in the representative system.

In the Str-3 unit which is within a larger enterprise and part of a larger geographical site, the unit manager will not be able to legislate policies, because any legislated policies will be a matter of differentials affecting the whole site. Appropriate unit practices can, however, be agreed within the legislated site policies, so long as they are not in conflict with those policies and have been agreed by the site manager and the site elected representatives so as not to raise consequential issues in other units on the site. Flexibility in local arrangements may thus be gained, enhancing the mutual recognition *gemeinschaft* feeling of the unit, and warding off the dead hand of excessively centralized bureaucracy.

A considerable amount of local autonomy can be built into Str-3 units, even on larger sites in larger enterprises. The personal feel is still there as the basis of organizational arrangements. Even in larger Str-3 units the personal quality can be retained by effective use of appeals procedures and representative and legislative systems.

As large-scale enterprises grow or are established, it is essential that they do so by establishing sound and strong Str-3 units. This principle holds equally true for Civil Service departments, industrial and commercial institutions, police, hospitals, schools, local government departments, and military organizations. The living face-to-face expression of a larger bureaucracy must be through its Str-3 unit managers. The living face-to-face contact of Str-1 employees with the larger bureaucracy is through their Str-3 unit manager: he is the immediate embodiment of the enterprise. Requisite Str-3 unit organization and proper filling of the direct-command managerial role are crucial factors in a healthy bureaucratic organization.

22

General Command Systems: Four- and Five-Stratum Hierarchies and Above

The move from Str-3 direct command systems to Str-4 and higher general command systems is one of the most important and dramatic steps in the growth of bureaucratic organizations. It is the step from work and management based upon concrete modes of thought to work and management based upon abstract modes of thought. No longer can the chief executive or manager perceptually encompass the whole of his task, even by imaginal scanning. He must be able to detach himself sufficiently from the concrete situation to be able to gain a rounded perspective and grasp it by means of conceptually formulated information.

The chief executive or manager must now be able to cope with the various aspects of his work separately from one another. While at any one moment he will be able to observe the effects of what he is doing upon some of the other things for which he is accountable, he will no longer have the reassurance of being able directly to scan the effects upon the whole of his field of accountability. The total field is available only in conceptual form — in statistics, records, inventories, drawings and other types of external conceptual model. He must have that sense of security in his abilities which will enable him to let go to some extent of the concrete outside world, and to rely upon an interplay between data of immediate experience and data culled from mental constructs.

Management in Abstracto

In descriptive managerial terms the problem is experienced as follows. The Str-3 chief executive, unit manager, administrator, battalion commander, designer, research investigator, has been used to working or to controlling and directing his command by being able himself to scan what is going on. He can be aware at first hand of all the main details of everything he is accountable for. If he is a manager, he is recognized by all his subordinates and in turn can recognize every one of them. He can feel secure with his direct and concrete control.

But suppose now that his work and organization grow to Str-4. Whatever work he is engaged in, he will almost certainly have subordinates some of whom may be managers each in turn in charge of managerial subordinates. His organization will most commonly have grown beyond mutual-recognition size. He will not be able to recognize everyone he employs. He begins to feel a stranger in his own enterprise. He no longer can be sure that he knows at first hand what is in his stores, or on the shelves, or in work-in-progress, nor what the terrain is like, nor how all the customers are faring, nor who all the suppliers are. And to the extent that he tries to hang on to direct command he runs into trouble.

This stage in development is familiar to business consultants as one of particular difficulty in business development. The chief executive has to be persuaded to let go and to be led into indirect management. This stage is expressed in military slang as 'becoming chairborne'. C. S. Forrester has described the process vividly in his novel *The General*. The theme is that of a very successful Lieutenant-Colonel battalion commander who gains rapid promotion to Lieutenant-General. It is only with the greatest reluctance that he learns not to try to lead his troops by direct first-hand command on horseback, but rather by sitting back in a tent, receiving information about this or that salient but never knowing the whole picture, giving leadership, as he contemptuously expostulates, 'from the end of a telephone'.

In short, what is required in general management at Str-4 and above is management by concepts, by data processing, by scrutinizing records and statistics, by analysis of client load and of community demand, by reference to supplies and stocks in financial terms, by appraisal of personnel numbers and categories. The manager or administrator must learn how to work from an office, not in complete detachment but with sufficiently frequent contact with the various parts of his domain to keep lively *examples* in mind of the activity of the situation he is dealing with *in abstracto*.

Investment Finance

A second outstanding characteristic of the transition from Str-3 systems to Str-4 and higher systems is that of going public. Nearly all Str-2 enterprises and Str-3 enterprises are private family enterprises. They obtain the finance they need from personal savings augmented by bank loans. By contrast, many Str-4 enterprises and most enterprises from Str-5 upwards are public enterprises. They require larger sums of capital and, most importantly, they require longer-term sums.

This change in the nature of capital finance shows in time-span terms. The Str-2 and Str-3 enterprises operating up to at most one year and two years forward, are readily financed within the normal terms of banking practice, depending upon the confidence of a bank manager. The Str-4 enterprise is the transition size, ranging from 2-year time-span to 5-year time-span. These enterprizes can get along with personal finance supplemented by bank loans in the early stages, but once they become involved in three- and four-year development projects requiring financial backing they will have trouble getting loan backing for such long periods. Certainly by the time they have reached the 5-year time-span Str-5 magnitude they can no longer rely on loan finance.

Capital for these enterprises which can no longer be financed by private owners either personally or with the help of loans, must be obtained from investors willing to put their money into the enterprise. The enterprise must therefore go public. To do so it must have a governing body and a chief executive who are not only competent in running an enterprise but have sufficient public recognition of their competence, to attract investors. These directors and chief executives are no longer private entrepreneurs; at least not in the sense of risking their own private capital. They, like other shareholders, risk only what they choose to invest in shareholding, the only legal requirement being that they hold at least one share.

Are we then no longer dealing with an entrepreneurial system run by entrepreneurs once an enterprise goes public? Have we entered the domain of the professional manager, the age of the managerial revolution heralded by James Burnham?[1] Such a view would be incorrect. It leaves out of account the fact that the primary feature of entrepreneurial work is not private investment but rather judging the needs of the clients or customers comprising a market, deciding how best to develop, produce and market the goods or services which will satisfy those needs, and managing to do so in such a manner as to cover all expenses, set some funds aside for replacements and development, and pay investors a reasonable dividend for the use of their capital.

If in addition the directors and chief executive do all these things on their own money, they are *private entrepreneurs*; in contrast to those entrepreneurs who work with capital provided either by government or by shareholding investors acting through a stock exchange, who might be termed *public entrepreneurs*. Both private and public entrepreneurial work are thus differentiated from public and social services provided by central or local governments, in which funds are provided by grant and there is no income to be earned or profitability at stake. The big distinction is thus between grant-income and earned-income bureaucracies. The latter are entrepreneurial regardless of scale, because a market is to be satisfied competitively as reflected in the willingness of client or customer to pay in full for the services or goods offered.

Stratum-4 Organization and the Establishment of Stratum-3 Units

The art of organization at Str-4 is to establish effective Str-3 operational units. For the Str-3 unit is the highest level of bureaucratic system at which

[1] J. Burnham (1960), *The Managerial Revolution*.

it is possible to keep in direct command or control of work. So long as general management can rely upon soundly organized direct control at Str-3 level and below, then it is free to carry on its longer-term strategic planning safe in the knowledge that there is a work system capable of putting the plans into practice. The enterprise will be able to retain a personal quality and avoid anonymity because of its foundation of Str-3 units.

When the enterprise as a whole has shifted from Str-3 to Str-4, further differentiation will have taken place, and the chief executive will find that he will have to add new functions. He will most likely have enough work for a differentiated D role. His premises and equipment will have extended and he will require full-time maintenance services. His chief accountant will have taken on responsibility for building up the annual accounts in preparation for the auditors. He will have to subordinate his Str-2 M and S subordinates to new intermediate Str-3 managers. He will require Personnel, Programming and Technical staff officers. An inspection organization will probably be necessary.

The organization at the transition from Str-3 may be employing anywhere from a few people to a maximum of 300 to 350 people. With successful development, the Str-4 system will grow to 1000 to 2000 by lateral extension. It will then have the general pattern illustrated. Here the feature to be noted is the construction of the Str-3 D, M, and S operational units, each unit manager having such staff as he may need – a point to which we shall return in a moment.

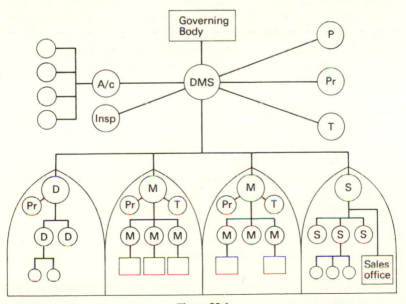

Figure 22.1

The Str-4 sub-systems within larger enterprises will themselves be specialized – operationally into D, M, or S – as, for example, in a Str-4 research department, or factory, or sales organization, or nursing organization in a large hospital, or army brigade, or area social services department. These Str-4 commands should themselves be divided into Str-3 units, just like the Str-3 units in the Str-4 enterprise.

Dual Control Systems

A second critical point may be noted in addition to the precipitation out of Str-3 operational units. That point has to do with the organization of specialist staff work in personnel (P), programming (Pr) and methods or technology (T), and of accounts. As organizations grow by vertical extension there is a strong tendency for already existing functions to float to the top or for new functions to be established there. The question is always what functions must requisitely be left behind at Str-3 level as well as what must be developed at the top.

Thus, for example, a Str-4 chief executive or manager may require his own programming staff to help him to plan his forward programme and to record and control the flow and stocking of material resources or to follow the pattern and amount of service provided. If he does need such staff, he must guard against the understandable tendency to draw together the whole programming function and to set it up subordinate to himself. A sizeable part of the activity of that department may be concerned directly with progression work inside the Str-3 production units. If then the total function has been centralized in one department at Str-4, the staff concerned with the units will be working from a central office outside the units, organizationally too far removed from the unit manager and the people in the unit whose work they are progressing.

The same can happen in the case of methods and technology. A centralized methods development, estimating and lay-out department is established, with time study, to carry out company-wide methods planning for the chief executive who requires this function. But so do the Str-3 production units require T work in trouble-shooting to overcome ongoing methods problems. Because of the centralization of function, however, the staff concerned with unit problems will be working from the central office outside the units.

In both cases it is often thought, and most often incorrectly, to be convenient, economic and efficient to have all programmers and all engineers together. Such thinking overlooks the critically important fact that if there is a full-time activity for a programmer or a methods specialist inside a Str-3 operational unit, it is essential to differentiate his function and establish his role there subordinate to the unit manager. The organizational mechanism of choice is that of attachment – a co-management arrangement in which the unit manager can have managerial control of deciding what activities he shall be assigned, while at the same time the staff specialist at the next higher level can be the co-manager accountable for his technical competence.[2]

Without attachment, the staff specialist occupies himself inside the Str-3 unit. He is a stranger there. The advantages of the mutual-recognition size unit are lost since he is organizationally an outsider. The Str-3 unit manager is bypassed and hears about trouble only by difficulties being reported upwards later. The Str-3 unit manager is to that extent not requisitely accountable for his command.

With attachment, the unit manager has his own specialist or specialists. He is not being bypassed. He can requisitely be accountable for his command. The advantages of the mutual-recognition unit are realized. His progress chasers and methods trouble-shooters are seen as inside the unit and not as strangers from outside: as 'one of us' rather than 'one of them'.

At the same time, by leaving in the Str-3 units such specialist staff as are needed by the unit managers, the chief executive at Str-4 has streamlined his own work because he now has subordinate to him only those aspects of the specialist activities that he requires in getting his own Str-4 work done.

One of the main reasons why the establishment of comprehensive and effective Str-3 unit commands is the *sine qua non* of the growth of efficient large-scale organization, is that the Str-4/Str-3 boundary is the boundary at which abstract policies are translated into getting things done in concrete and direct terms. Str-3 managers in charge of units must be self-contained in the sense that any activities concerned with co-ordinating and controlling the unit's work that require the full-time attention of one or more persons should be organized under staff established within the unit under the control of the unit head. Services may be obtained from elsewhere in the organization, but not staff work.

It will be seen to follow from the transition from direct to indirect command that appeals and legislative systems with explicitly formulated and organized procedures are requisite. They are necessary instruments to keep the chief executive in contact with the consensus of viewpoint of his employees and with any strong individual grievances they might have.

One final general point may be noted. The delegated D, M, and S activities are all at Str-3 level and below, and so are Personnel, Programming and Technical support activities. Any developmental work, therefore, carried out in their special fields by the chief executive's subordinates will be concretely orientated. New developments will be related to existing policies or products or services, will grow out of them, will evolve. The Str-

[2] As described in Chapter 17, and in more detail in W. Brown (1971), *Organization*.

4 detachment from the concrete will be lacking, so that only by accident will developments occur which are different in quality from what exists in the enterprise. Evolutionary rather than revolutionary D, M, and S development is the hallmark of the Str-4 enterprise. Revolutionary development will fall to the chief executive, and ought requisitely to be connected with the direction of the enterprise as a whole, rather than with D or M or S separately.

Stratum-5 Organization and the Transition to Large-scale Enterprise

When an enterprise has grown to the Str-5 level it has reached the point where its continued existence is becoming a matter of some importance to society at large. It may be employing as many as five or ten thousand people, although it may of course employ much smaller numbers. Its Board of Directors will have become a significant body in the sense of being involved continually in the policy development of the enterprise.

Effective Str-5 work cannot be done if it is combined with the management of direct command units. It requires more distance. That distance is obtained precisely by the establishment of an interposed Str-4 level of command, itself in charge of Str-3 units. The transition, therefore, is from the Str-4 chief executive with his unit managers to one of separation from the Str-3 units by consolidating them.

The schematic outline (Figure 22.2 on p. 325) illustrates the simplification of the chief executive's immediate operational command. He is able in principle to pattern his organization so as to give him Str-4 managers each of whom is in charge of a group of D or M or S units. He can also have a group of Str-4 staff officers, P, Pr and T, and a Str-4 chief accountant/company secretary.

It may be noted, therefore, that the chief executive may occupy himself heavily with the development of enterprise strategy, with interaction with the Board. He can be free to do so, since each of his immediate subordinates is capable of functioning *in abstracto*. Each in his own field is able to propose and to carry through qualitative shifts in policy; each is able to bring about revolutionary change when necessary, as against evolutionary modification.

The character of the work is that of the Str-5 under-secretary in the civil service, or of the divisional commander major-general in military organization. In local government we may be dealing with Str-5 directors of social services departments or directors of education, or chief architects, or borough engineers, each in charge of the development of major services for whole counties or large boroughs. It is the level of functioning where what is often referred to as strategic development has become possible.

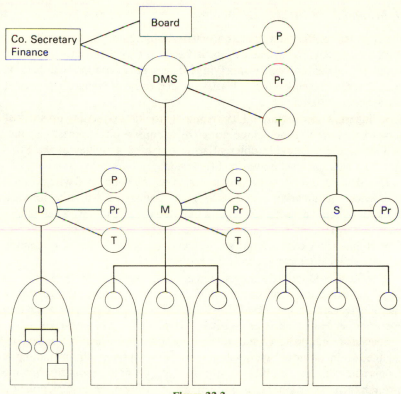

Figure 22.2

Rowbottom and Billis see the Str-5 organization as having a special importance in modern societies. They write: 'The Stratum-5 organization with its fully-realised capability for self-development emerges as the system of special interest. It appears to offer one concrete answer to the general problem posed by Schon[3] of how society is to produce organisations, both public and private, capable of coping with the demands of an increasingly unstable world. The increasing establishment of Stratum-5 organisations at the "periphery" (in Schon's term) seems to offer a means of getting away from a society dominated by the exclusive development of new ideas at the "centre", and their diffusion on a "centre periphery" model, with all the attendant problems he so ably identifies. It offers a means of retaining coherent organisational structure. At the same time it does not exclude the possibility of basic political and legal control from the centre.'[4]

---

[3] D. Schon (1971), *Beyond the Stable State*.
[4] R. W. Rowbottom and D. Billis (to be published), 'The Stratification of Work and Organisational Design'.

D, M, and S, in Stratum-5 Systems

Development of the enterprise as an institution requires first an explicated marketing policy. What market needs likely to exist five years and more ahead will the enterprise be satisfying? The selling function will need its market research section, or at least will need to be drawing upon market research consultants.

Selling may now require underwriting of stockists or setting up stockist networks; warehousing; appointing distributors or overseas agents; leading to a considerable differentiation out of S activities at the Str-3 direct operational level under the Str-4 head.

The Str-4 product development manager will be concerned with product or service modification and development connected with the forward marketing plan, and with influencing that marketing plan by development work and by recommending lines of development in the light of the interaction of his knowledge of the market and his knowledge of oncoming technical developments in the firm's business.

The Str-4 production manager is managing a series of Str-3 production units replacing the chief executive in his upward move. As growth by lateral extension occurs, new Str-4 production commands may come into operation as new markets are opened and new products marketed.

Specialist organization subordinate to the chief executive is heavily engaged in institutional maintenance and development. Programming is concerned with the totality of expense of physical resources flowing through the enterprise related to the income flowing back. Pricing policies, suppliers and supplies, balance of work load and priorities; these matters call for computerizable models of the organization's operation.

Personnel is concerned with the maintenance and development of the organizational structure and its manning. It will differentiate into organization analysis, recruitment programmes for management trainees and apprentices, management and supervisory training programmes, added to the recruitment, selection, organization and manning activities at Str-4 and Str-3 levels in the organization. Systematized recording and progression of individuals so that potential capacity is recognized and called forth is essential.

Technical specialist activities at chief executive level will now be concerned with developing the enterprise's capital planning in connection with production technology and with the technological consequences of new product and market plans. It may be necessary also to differentiate one or more teams composed of a Str-4 designer and a small group of high-level design staff to develop and bring into commission radical new developments in technology. When these developments are in production trim they can be handed over to a Str-4 production manager, and the design team can move on to its next project. By this means the Str-4 production managers can be accountable for ensuring that their own Str-3 designers keep up the pace of evolutionary modification within a one- to two- year development cycle, without the distraction of having to cope with the two- to five-year developments on techniques utterly different from those they are using currently.

Quality of Stratum-5 Work

Two organizational points may be noted which may illustrate the quality of work at Str-5. The first point is concerned with specialist work, and the second with the development of subsidiary enterprises.

Whereas staff authority and attachment seem relevant to the relationships between specialists and managers at Str-4 and Str-3 level, they do not appear to be so necessary in relationships between Str-5 and Str-4. A weaker monitoring and co-ordinative relationship appears to be sufficient. This shift is a reflection of the fact that the specialists and managers are functioning at a general level of abstraction. There is need for the Str-4 specialists to be able to sit back and reflect about their specialist work and its implementation in connection with strategic planning. There is time for the Str-5 chief executive to work out strategic practice with the Str-4 subordinates, the specialists assisting in the process and monitoring and co-ordinating implementation.

This situation contrasts with the Str-4 to Str-3 situation where direct operational work is being managed. Here staff authority enables work on direct output to be carried out in the framework set by the Str-4 manager. The staff officers must be able to help in this process, smoothing out problems for the Str-3 managers and ensuring that the on-going activity is in accord with the plans and goals set by the Str-4 head. The more active and direct authority of the staff relationship appears more apposite.

Second, in many Str-5 enterprises a tendency towards the precipitation out of separate Str-4 D-M-S subsidiaries may be noted. These subsidiaries may themselves be registered enterprises, and the Str-4 manager will have all the characteristics of the public entrepreneur. It is this setting up of new enterprises which emerges as an outstanding feature of Str-6 and larger enterprises.

Stratum-6, 7, and 8 Organization and the Creation of New Enterprises

I shall refer only briefly to the very large-scale enterprise whose top levels are at Str-6, Str-7 and Str-8. These enterprises are the giants. They may employ up to 125 000, 250 000, and one million people respectively. They are the nationalized industries of the United Kingdom – the Coal Board, the Railway Executive; the great industrial and commercial enterprises – General Motors, Unilever, Shell, ITT, Prudential Insurance; large civil service departments. These great institutions, nearly all of them international in activity and many of them multi-national, would require a separate treatise. Certain general features may, however, be noted.

One feature is that at Str-6 and above two main lines of organization development occur. In some cases the technology or problems require a unified D-M-S command, as in the case of large steel companies or civil service departments. In other cases the institution may begin to differentiate a series of full-scale D-M-S subsidiaries as independent bureaucratic systems one level below the chief executive. And even in the first case there is a tendency for such institutions to precipitate out bureaucratic subsystems. Certainly nearly all Str-7 and all Str-8 enterprises will be engaged in establishing full-scale D-M-S bureaucracies at lower levels. In short, one of the characteristics of institutions of this kind is that they are engaged in begetting other institutions. If they are public enterprises they not only seek investors of capital, but they themselves become investors.

Such enterprises will ordinarily have large property holdings, requiring a full-time estate management function. Similarly, the complex legal issues involved in mergers, licences, patents, international tax problems, the establishment of new enterprises, will call for a full-time legal department.

The time-span of operation of these institutions will run to ten or twenty years and more. It calls for extensive capital for projects whose full course will outrun the individuals who work on them. The time-scale is also noticeably longer than the time-scale which can be used by governments themselves in national planning, the very long-range programmes such as TVA in the United States being exceptional.

The decentralization of such enterprises is also of the greatest importance, especially in the respects which I have described: clear site management, with on-site representation of employees and policy legislation; the establishment and maintenance of clear-cut Str-3 operational units throughout the enterprise; the use of monitoring and co-ordinative authority by specialists at higher levels, rather than the stronger staff authority, allowing for maximum autonomy and involvement in policy-making.

It may also be apparent that systematic and agreed payment systems and uniform grading systems are essential: it is these which are the necessary foundation for negotiation and policy-making at the periphery on local site issues. They are necessary, moreover, to ensure that these giant enterprises, with their monopolistic potential, do not exist at the expense of unfair treatment of their employees. It is when the big bureaucracies are allowed to exploit their employees because of the absence of adequate instruments and controls to ensure equity and justice, that social and economic stress are induced in the community, and bureaucracy itself – whether free enterprise or governmental – rightly earns an evil reputation.

Political Significance of the Giant Bureaucracies

The general point which emerges is the obvious point, and a politically sensitive one, that these large-scale enterprises are functioning at the level of government itself. Their successful functioning becomes a matter of national importance, for reasons of employment, of international trade, and of national productivity. As Galbraith points out, they inevitably become part of national economic planning rather than part of the area of free competition.

There must, therefore, be strong assurance that top executives of the necessary calibre will be selected for the top posts. Nothing is quite so debilitating to a society as to have too many of its large-scale enterprises – whether in civil service, or social services, or industry or commerce – with top managers below the high levels of work-capacity required. Such institutions become flabby, unhappy places in which to work. The long time-spans of their operations make it possible for them to go on for years in an ailing state, contributing meanwhile to poor morale and frustration among their staff.

One of the ways in which such assurance about adequate top level talent seems to be established is in the tendency for the Board to become made up wholly or nearly wholly of full-time executive members, or for the setting up of a full-time executive Board. These Boards may operate in one of two ways. First, they may be simple two-level structures made up of a chief executive and his subordinates. But, second, if say on the retirement of the chief executive there is no one of sufficient calibre to fill his position, then *pro tem* it is possible to appoint one of the executive Board members to act in a chairman role, as a *primus inter pares*, and for the executive Board to take over the chief executive function as a group. Given an enterprise which has been functioning successfully for some time, it is possible for this second arrangement to hold the situation for some years because of the momentum and long time-scale of the activities.

Group leadership at the top cannot, however carry through forever. A Str-7 bureaucracy, for example, requires a Str-7 capacity individual at its head if it is not eventually to begin to slide. This point becomes exceedingly important nationally – for to maintain adequate succession of leadership at these levels becomes difficult, particularly if there are too many such large-scale enterprises competing for too small a supply of talent. Inadequate filling of these top roles can have serious consequences for national economies, affecting as it may do so many subsidiary institutions. But I shall treat of this theme in the next chapter.

PART SEVEN

PRELIMINARY SKETCH OF THE CONTRIBUTION OF CONSTITUTIONAL BUREAUCRACY TO INDIVIDUAL LIBERTY IN INDUSTRIAL SOCIETIES

23

Constitutional Bureaucracy, Alienation, and Community

In this final part of the book we shall examine some of the more general implications of our analysis of bureaucracy. They are in the form of a preliminary sketch, of ideas in development, of notions stimulated by experience.

Before setting out these tentative ideas, some of the main findings from the foregoing chapters will be pulled together in the form of a review of the conditions necessary to provide a sound constitutional basis for bureaucratic systems. The term 'constitutional' is used in the sense of the dictionary definition of constitution: 'the system or body of fundamental principles according to which a body politic is constituted and governed ... principles, any fundamental breach of which would involve either tyranny or anarchy' (OED).

But even if bureaucratic systems were all constitutionally organized, there still remain many questions about the type of social setting which would best support their operation. In particular, it may be asked under what kind of political economy is requisite bureaucracy most likely to thrive – free enterprise, socialist, mixed economy, or other? This question calls for a look at the more fundamental question of the nature of economic competition.

Both capitalist and socialist thought fail to recognize the difference between competition in a free market to supply consumer needs, and competition to get the cheapest labour in a labour market. The former may be termed *service-providing competition*; and the latter, *labour-exploitive competition*.

Service-providing competition is manifestly in the interest of society; labour-exploitive competition is not. Free enterprise systems, by retaining both types of competition, undermine themselves politically through the inhumanity and inequities of the labour market. Socialist systems, in trying to get rid of labour-exploitation, throw away all competitive market forces and lose the essential service-providing competition.

Our analysis of bureaucracy suggests that these difficulties could be overcome if the labour market were replaced by a national system of relating pay differentials to responsibility carried. One possible system is described. It would humanize the work situation and leave room for service-providing competition without exploitation of labour.

We shall then turn to some general questions of the relationship of bureaucracy to social stratification and social status, equality and inequality, relative deprivation and privilege, social class and class conflict, and social justice. These questions will take us into some of the fundamental relationships between bureaucracy and the core identity and self-esteem of the individuals employed in them.

There is a need for bureaucracy to provide for two hard-core conditions: the opportunity for everyone to work at a level of work corresponding to his work-capacity (a C-W equilibrium); and equally necessary, a sense of equity and hence of equilibrium in the work-payment (W-P) relationship. Failure to provide these hard-core conditions may help to explain some aspects of social conflict, including class conflict, with which bureaucracy − especially industrial bureaucracy − has been traditionally associated. Contrariwise, constitutional bureaucracy, by providing these conditions, may contribute to individual freedom in an open society.

Outline of Conditions for Constitutional Bureaucracy

Let me draw together the main strands of this account and set out the necessary conditions for the requisite organization of bureaucratic systems with constitutionally mediated role relationships. There are two sets of criteria by which requisiteness may be judged: the first is whether the structure of the organization enables its work to be carried out effectively; the second is whether the structure of role relationships will enhance the quality of trust and confidence in personal interaction and reduce paranoiagenesis − to provide a social setting consistent with the wider value of societal survival, or, in Alan Fox's terms, to be conducive to a 'high trust society'.[1]

These two sets of criteria are fundamental. They treat of the two main elements of man's relations with his environment: his relations with his physical world and with his social world.[2] In our analysis, however, we shall deal primarily with the social world. If trust-inducing institutions are developed, then they will give some assurance that the operational tasks will be effectively carried out, or at least not impeded, whether those tasks are directed towards production of goods or the provision of services or controls in the social world. The point is that the opposite does not hold true: just because a given institutional form proves efficient *pro tem* in terms of output, it does not necessarily mean that it is trust-inducing or that it can succeed in the long run.

---

[1] A. Fox (1974), *Beyond Contract: Work, Power and Trust Relations.*

[2] It is this double interaction, with the physical and social worlds, that is the central theme of the method of socio-technical analysis of Trist, Emery, Bamforth *et al.*

The following is a summary of the necessary conditions. This summary is set out for a particular reason. None of the conditions is sufficient by itself to produce much change in the absence of the others. A total shift is required from the dominance of interactive and mutually reinforcing paranoiagenic conditions in the bureaucratic sector, to a system of interactive trust-supporting conditions. In society we are dealing with fields of force and with open systems, not with independent and isolated variables. It is essential therefore to present the whole pattern before turning to consider any single part.

Internal Conditions

(a) requisite structuring of bureaucratic hierarchies so as to provide clear individual accountability and one-stratum distance manager-subordinate role relationships; with an appeals procedure for individual justice;

(b) filling of roles in such a manner (at C-W equilibrium) as to ensure especially that managers have the required level of capacity; and systems of selection, training and progression to provide individuals with the opportunity to seek advancement;

(c) the maintenance of mutual-recognition-size direct command Str-3 operational units, with representative systems, as the locally based foundation of the organizational structure of larger-scale bureaucracy;

(d) opportunity for employee participation, through elected representatives, in the control of policy change;

(e) a strengthening of community by grounding this participation in representative and legislative systems on each geographical site if a bureaucratic system is dispersed over two or more sites;

(f) providing for professional independence and the avoidance of excessive bureaucratization.

External Conditions

(a) existence of a pluralistic democratic political system;

(b) abundant employment distributed locally, with the opportunity for everyone to obtain work at a level consistent with his work-capacity and interests – that is to say, to obtain C-W equilibrium;

(c) equitable distribution of wages and salaries;

(d) the maintaining of fluidity in social stratification by means of open boundaries;

(e) consequent freedom of the person and of association within the limits of requisite law, that is to say of law that is supportive of trust and confidence in reciprocal social interaction.

The internal conditions will be considered in the rest of this chapter, and the external conditions in the final chapters.

Managerial Authority and One-stratum Distance

What are some of the special conditions within bureaucratic systems which are necessary if they are to function in a manner best calculated to strengthen a sense of community in the bureaucratic sector? The first condition is that the design of organization must provide a setting which facilitates sound manager-subordinate role relationships. A number of features must be included.

The first of these features is the fact of each person's accountability for his own performance – and in the case of managers, their accountability for the performance of their subordinates. It is this fact of individual accountability which allows each person to connect with the social system through his work. It exercises and stretches his sense of responsibility. It enables him to feel wanted. It allows him to rely upon his capacities, and to stretch those capacities to the full if his level of work (in effect, his level of accountability) is up to his level of capacity. Thus it can be one of the most constructive of human experiences.

Along with this accountability goes the balancing authority necessary for the accountability to be real: authority with respect to resources, and, additionally in the case of managers, the minimum requisite managerial authority. This balancing authority is sanctioned and delimited power: the authorized exercise of power related to the accountability in hand. Lord Acton's observation that all power corrupts and that absolute power corrupts absolutely applies only to unsanctioned power. Power transformed by being duly authorized through legitimation by adequate sanctioning processes not only does not corrupt but may have exactly the opposite effect. The exercise of power within the framework of proper authority in connection with the due discharge of contractual accountability enlarges a man: it makes him more of a social being; it increases his faith and confidence in himself and in his relationships with others.

Authority in this sense of the sanctioned and legitimate expression of power is the exact opposite of the corruptive autocracy of the dictator. It is of value to the subordinate and is not coercive. Requisite manager-subordinate role relationships are not autocratic, nor paternalistic; they are reciprocal, mutually interdependent, the success and achievement of the manager depending upon his subordinate, and the subordinate's achievement depending upon the competence of his manager. The operating of the relationship can strengthen the competence of both parties to participate in creative reciprocal interaction.

To be requisite there must be the one-stratum separation between manager and subordinate which has been elaborated in detail. It is that separation which is essential to the subordinate's freedom of movement in organizational space. Having a manager in the same stratum – that is to say one who is called a manager but who is extantly a supervisor or perhaps a staff officer – constricts the subordinate's freedom of movement as much as being machine-paced does.[3] Mutual lack of confidence is inevitable, and it readily grows into suspicious anxiety. But with sufficient distance the subordinate is free and can rely upon a manager who is big enough to be able to set terms of reference of the right width and to encompass and assess the subordinate's work confidently. The subordinate can rely upon his good performance being recognized and appreciated: and he can equally count upon being admonished for poor performance.

There must also be a final safeguard for the subordinate in the appeals procedure described. The subordinate's having the right to appeal against decisions by his manager which he feels affect him unfairly contributes an essential ingredient to the legitimation of managerial power. It is the ingredient which gives the final reality to the fact of upward as well as downward flow in manager-subordinate relationships.

People of the Necessary Level of Work-capacity

The importance has been emphasized of every citizen's having the opportunity, if he wishes to take it, of employment in the bureaucratic sector at a level which accords with his work-capacity. I shall have more to say about this issue in Chapter 25 in connection with social status. But it is of equal importance that employees should have the necessary work-capacity to fill the roles to which they have been appointed. The presence in a bureaucratic system of an individual who is below the work-capacity needed, is not only a diminution of the efficiency of the system. It is also a slight on the others who must work with him as subordinates, as managers, as colleagues.

In Chapter 11 we reviewed the symptoms in the individual who is under-employed or over-employed. Let me here indicate the effects upon others of the over-employed individual, the one who is not big enough in work-capacity for his role.

Such a person is a headache to his manager if that manager is forced to keep him against his judgment. In effect, the manager has to descend into a role at a lower level of abstraction than his own work-capacity, since he

---

[3] Freedom of movement, or autonomy, has at least three components: freedom in organizational space, as described here; freedom in psychological space, or the opportunity to have a level of work consistent with one's work capacity; and freedom in physical space, or the literal freedom to move about. Job enlargement and job enrichment programmes are aimed at the second and third of these components respectively.

must carry out the intermediate time-span planning; that is to say, he has to do the work that an intermediate manager would do. It is a strain emotionally, and very demanding in time to go into the detail necessary.

If the over-employed person is a manager, his subordinates are presented with the irritating difficulty of having a manager who cannot set an adequate framework and who descends to their own level of work. In so doing, he reduces their time-span and their opportunities, and squeezes their freedom of movement in organizational space. One or other of the subordinates is likely to be able to perform more effectively than the manager, and everyone somehow feels constrained.

Colleagues are subjected to annoyance and hold-ups. They cannot get the service they require. In meetings with their manager – if they are immediate colleagues – all will feel themselves being held up by their colleague because he is slower in understanding. They will find him too rigid and inflexible, or unrealistically accommodating and therefore unreliable.

This situation is like that mentioned in Chapter 9 in connection with the subordinates who were unable to keep up with the chief executive and with younger colleagues who were progressing across the boundary of a stratum while they were not. The overall effect is that of chronic anxiety all round.

And yet there is a strong tendency to avoid recognizing this situation. The decision that a manager is not up to his role – because he was badly selected, or beccause he has deteriorated, or because his role has developed beyond him – is one which most people would wish to avoid having to face. What is needed is greater recognition of the social consequences of failing to act – it is an assault upon society – and the acceptance of the need to provide for greater opportunities for sideways moves, the establishment of special roles, early retirement, and the acceptance of the financial cost of doing so.[4] The social costs of failing to act are far too great to be tolerated.

The most serious situation of all, however, arises when the chief executive himself is too small in capacity for his post. That is a tragedy all

---

[4] When the National Health Service reorganization was being prepared in 1972, the committee preparing the proposals for the reorganization attempted to face this problem and arrived at the following formulation: '. . . managers must be held accountable not only for their own work but also for the work of their subordinates. In order to carry this accountability, the authority of managers must be made clear and it must carry with it the right to have immediate subordinates who are capable of doing the work required. The manager must therefore be able to decide how he delegates the work; he must assess the performance of subordinates; and, to the extent that he is required to have or retain subordinates who cannot do what is necessary, he cannot be held fully accountable for their performance. Policies and procedures will therefore have to be developed for improving the opportunities for transfer of personnel into posts where they may make their best contribution.' (Department of Health and Social Security (1972), *Management Arrangements for the Reorganized National Health Service*, p. 17, para. 1. 28).

round. Everyone suffers, and at the worst will suffer very badly indeed. It is intolerable that the situation should be allowed to continue. Governing bodies have a profoundly important responsibility in ensuring that their appointed chief executives have the necessary talent and competence. Otherwise all talk about such matters as leadership is hollow.

This point about chief executives is of grave import in large-scale bureaucracy and needs explicit attention. If more and more bureaucracies of such magnitude are established there will come a point where the number of top-level positions will over-reach the number of top-level people available to man them. When that point is reached, the proliferation of additional large-scale bureaucracies will begin to sow the seeds of serious trouble. That is one of the reasons why centralization of bureaucracy *ad lib*, with the absorption of small-scale institutions, into a plethora of large ones will lead to ill-managed monoliths.

My hunch is that this stage may already have been reached in Great Britain.[5] And yet we are continuing to produce still more large-scale bureaucracies by mergers, by nationalization, by the creation of larger-scale governmental and social services departments. The result is that more and more of our largest bureaucracies may be being subjected to the stresses of a top leadership which cannot cope. Whether or not this particular diagnosis is correct, every fully developed industrial society is likely to reach the point where it can grow no more large-scale bureaucracies without over-reaching the work-capacity available in the population. It is essential that this point should be watched for. The healthy functioning of bureaucracy in society absolutely hinges upon it.

Gemeinschaft Qualities in Requisite Bureaucracy, and the Factor of Size

Requisite manager-subordinate role relationships may serve to overcome the corruptive paranoiagenic influences usually associated with power and subordination. Managers and subordinates are placed in a strong

[5] And possibly in other fully developed nations such as the USA, West Germany, Holland. I am in disagreement here with the view that seems to be so commonly held that there can never be a sufficient number of positions at the top for those who aspire to them and could cope with them. Thus, for example, Lipset and Bendix write as though it were a well-established fact that 'access to the limited number of top-elite positions should be distinguished from movement into and out of the more numerous middle class. Regardless of how open the top elite is in any country, the number of persons who can achieve positions in it is not large enough to make it a goal towards which men may realistically work.' S. M. Lipset and R. Bendix (1959), *Social Mobility in Industrial Society*, p. 278.

Might it not be just as possible that there are now more top elite positions than there are people with the ability to fill them? The question at least needs asking. In general terms the proportion of middle-class positions to top-elite positions is a reflection of the distribution of capacity in populations rather than of any inherent sociological fact.

reciprocal relationship, mutually reinforcing and stimulating the full use of skill and ability. Provision is made for equitable distribution of reward, and justice for the individual is safeguarded. The question we now reach is whether, in addition, bureaucratic systems can be constructed so as to give some of the social advantages of the tightly-knit *gemeinschaft* community.

The particular qualities include first the association of people of a wide range of ability and socio-economic status on one geographical site in a common activity. The village community has this intermixing. The urban industrial community, in contrast, is split up into districts composed of separate socio-economic groups, so that sharing in activities across class or status boundaries is almost impossible. The whole of life is impoverished as a result.

Second is the quality of working together on one geographical site, of sharing the same piece of the physical world, and of relying upon it for one's material sustenance. Concern for that site can be the result – just as well-designed housing can encourage its occupants to care for the immediate physical environment.[6] Working together on the same territory in a shared endeavour concerned with keeping alive connects human beings with one another in societal relationship having the substantial reality of being grounded in the physical world.

The third quality is that of being part of a mutual-recognition group, of being able to identify with specific other human beings in an on-going relationship. The mutual-recognition phenomenon is one of the keystones of social life. If society is to function, its members need mutual-recognition size units through which to connect: without such units isolation and alienation are reinforced. The existence of such units does not guarantee social connection, but it at least makes it possible – and it most certainly does not provoke alienation.

Bureaucratic systems can be organized so as to go some way towards providing the qualities outlined. The first and universal requirement is to ensure – as bureaucracies increase and reach Str-4 and higher in scale – that full-scale Str-3 units are retained as the foundation of the larger system. Soundly organized Str-3 units, on geographically independent sites if possible,[7] are the key to the sustaining of feelings of personal connectedness in the face of the seeming inevitability of individual descent into anonymity in the bureaucratic colossi which have been brought into existence by expansion, mergers and take-overs.

If Str-3 operational units are strictly maintained, the paranoiagenic anonymity of large-scale bureaucracy is avoided by giving every individual a latching-on focus in the mutual-recognition size unit. Everyone

---

[6] O. Newman (1973), *Defensible Space*.
[7] Or perhaps side by side with a few other units on an independent Str-4 site.

knows everyone else and is known by everyone else. And if the unit grows beyond the mutual-recognition size limit of, say 250 to 300 people, it can and should then be sub-divided into two units.

Having true Str-3 units not only provides the mutual-recognition quality, it also keeps all Str-1 personnel in contact at one remove with a Str-3 manager, with one single true Str-2 immediate managerial level in between. And just one level above that unit is the Str-4 level of innovative work. There is a potential closeness of contact between many levels of ability in working relationship.

The interactive connections can be further strengthened if the base of the representative system is established at Str-3. Representatives should be elected within the Str-3 unit, by the members at both Str-1 and Str-2, to meet with the Unit Manager so as to sort out local problems within the context of legislated policies fixed higher up.

Str-3 operational units so constructed can enable the members to develop a social cohesion and *esprit* which can meld into their relationships outside work. Much benefit can accrue to the participants, particularly if the unity of the Str-3 system is reinforced by local representation – for such representation brings the individual into mutual-recognition involvement in a representative system immediately at hand and intimately concerned with his interests.

The social cohesion of the Str-3 unit can, of course, be only a partial cohesion as compared with the organic life of a village or of family entrepreneurial activity. The operational unit, for instance, involves only the breadwinner and not the whole family. But the point is not that the Str-3 unit is just like a village or fully entrepreneurial activity. For it is not. But the unit has its own potentially constructive social characteristics, characteristics which arise out of the very nature of bureaucracy, and it is these particular qualities which need to be capitalized upon so long as we continue to make widespread use of bureaucratic institutions.

Site-based Participation

The social bonding qualities of the Str-3 unit can be further added to by the principle that when bureaucratic systems are broken up between two or more separate sites, there will be a policy-legislating council on each geographical site. The arrangements are usually made the other way round. Negotiations are carried out centrally – usually by national trade union officers and a central personnel department – and the local elected employee representatives are left on the sidelines. In consequence the special local needs – which can vary so much from site to site because of variations in conditions, customs and traditions – are lost sight of. Local confidence in such central negotiations is very fragile, employees readily becoming alienated from their own distant representatives as well as from the employing organization and the society in which it is placed.

The primacy of site negotiations and participation in policy control makes it possible to turn the whole process of negotiation to good effect for employers and employees equally. Employees are represented by their own directly elected representatives right there on the local site where they can be seen, and where they are directly connected with the representative system in each of the Str-3 operational units. Participation in policy-making locally in this way allows for all kinds of differences in arrangements to be catered for, including such things as differences in training, in induction and recruitment, in starting and finishing times, in shift arrangements, in holiday arrangements, in production organization, in developments affecting the particular site, in the organization of tasks in relation to the locally available range of employment opportunity, and so on.

Such local negotiation requires of course that there should be an overall policy framework, an umbrella policy, within which local arrangements can be made. But even these umbrella policies can be arrived at by agreement among all the site councils, meeting if necessary in conference. They do not require some sort of detached national negotiating body.

This analysis in terms of adding strength to the local on-site social groupings may be self-evidently associated with the organization of bureaucracy in support of pluralism as against centralism. But does it not have a potentially fragmenting effect upon national institutions such as, for example, the nationally organized trades unions? This question can be answered with an unequivocal 'no'. On-site negotiations plus national conferences fit readily into trade union organization. They place the appointed union officials in their proper role as support to the elected employee representatives rather than taking over from them; they allow for local differences in trade union affiliation where appropriate; and they allow for national trade union support when the negotiations involve national umbrella policies.

But most of all this kind of on-site arrangement gives every employee the opportunity for direct participation in a constitutional policy-controlling process. It enables each one to experience at first hand the nature, the significance and the human value of due constitutional process. It is through such experiences – and, indeed, mainly through such experiences – that individuals can gain confidence in the fact that sanctioned authoritative relationships are possible; in the fact that individual behaviour can be constructively controlled and directed within well-designed social institutions; and in the fact that mutual trust is realistic where the institutional framework of relationships and behaviour is constitutionally rooted in consensus.

It is this direct experience of the meaning of constitutionally agreed policies and procedures for the constructive delimitation and regulation of human behaviour in social interaction that must be one of the main goals of pluralism. It is an experience which periodic voting for central government cannot provide; such voting is too remote from the individual, and the consequences upon him cannot be readily perceived. But the local experience of participation can act as a most important bridge to grasping the meaning of democratic government. It is a bridge which, once crossed, can give a new sense to the meaning of individual freedom, of freedom with responsibility. This freedom is real and substantial precisely because it is set within the constraints necessary for reciprocal interaction to occur with sufficient confidence and trust between the participants. Moreover, the regulations and the freedom are directed towards the human activities by means of which society lives.

Professionalism and the Enhancement of Pluralism

The extension of professionalism both in private practice and in ADO[8] employment in bureaucracies as well as the extension of semi-professional technical work in bureaucracies, is one important way of increasing the number of higher-level non-managerial roles in society, both within bureaucratic systems and outside them. Society stands in need of the creation of many more roles of an independent or quasi-independent nature to be filled by people of high ability free to pursue the profession in which they are competent. To force them to use their talents through DDO managerial work alone is to deny them opportunity. Such a development is important for industrial society – or, as Daniel Bell has it, for post-industrial society.

The peculiar significance of professional work for the enhancement of pluralism in society is that the regulations and standards of the professional associations are binding not only upon the individual members but also upon associations who employ professionals in bureaucratic systems. In this way the bureaucratic systems themselves are influenced by one or more independent bodies professionally recognized by society, to whose standards they must conform and upon whose members they should be able to rely.

The most fully developed state of this professionalism is that of the doctor, the lawyer, the priest, with full professional autonomy. In these cases society vests extreme independence in the professional role, with no access by the bureaucratic manager to the relationship between the professional and the individual served, even for the purposes of assessing the quality of discretion exercised. Here are conditions which may begin to

[8] Aided Direct Output, as described in Chapter 16.

approximate to Durkheim's occupational association with high morality. Professional work is one of the strongest antidotes to bureaucratic impersonality.

The full-scale extension of professionalism to all occupational groups could contribute greatly to trust and confidence in the bureaucratic sector. It would mean that everyone, at every level, would be working within the constraints of the socially accepted ethical code of his profession. To this extent, occupational standards and morality would be internalized in each individual and would have to rely less upon managerial controls. The ethical standards of society would thus be strengthened through the strengthening of conscience and inner control in each person.

The Bureaucratization of Everything? Universities, Churches, and Hospitals Considered

Having considered some of the main internal factors necessary for constitutional bureaucracy, let us finish by referring to certain important conditions under which bureaucratic organization should at all costs be avoided. There is a strong tendency in industrial societies to bureaucratize everything, and we risk losing some institutions which are part of our most precious cultural heritage.

Bureaucratic organization is useful for the large-scale production and provision of goods and services. It is inimical, on the other hand, to the free development of ideas, to the expression of sacred belief, and to the intimacy of the confidential doctor-patient relationship. The reasons for this view – with particular reference to the tendency to impose bureaucratic organization upon our universities, our churches, and upon the doctors in our hospitals – can be outlined as follows.

Somewhere in every society institutions must be provided in which individuals are free to develop their own ideas, including a critical appraisal and evaluation of the society itself, without fear of negative sanctions should their ideas not appeal to the governing body or to the government. That function is – or should be – carried by academic freedom in our universities. For our universities to provide such academic freedom is, however, totally inconsistent with the organization of academic staff into bureaucratic systems based upon manager-subordinate accountability.

If the head of an academic department is manifestly described or thought of as its manager, then he begins to be accepted as accountable for the work of the members of the department, including their research and the ideas they might develop. Such a relationship of managerial control of idea development is death to academic freedom. It is steadily seeping into many areas of our universities.

What is required is the recognition that academic staff are not simply employees of the university but members of the university, members of the association. They require to be established with independence. The most common method is to give them life tenure (as described in Chapter 3) as members of the association (that is to say, as members of the university). By this means academic staff are given security of university membership for life, and are free to get on with their own critical work and research.

The necessary direction and control are readily achieved in these circumstances without managerial accountability and controls. That is what collegial functioning is about (see Chapter 4). Each academic department may require a chairman. The staff can determine general teaching and course requirements, and agree allocations of teaching duties – all, of course, within the general policies of the university. So long, then, as each academic staff member conforms to the collegially established limits, he is free to express his own ideas as part of his teaching and in his research. The department chairman requires only to have monitoring and co-ordinative authority, possibly combined with veto power on appointment of new staff.

These collegial arrangements are familiar in all true universities. They include the notion that every student is a free individual, accountable for the pursuit of his own education. In this industrial age, however, these ideas are likely to get submerged under the general tendency to think of all large-scale organizations in bureaucratic hierarchical terms – with the head of department as the 'boss', the academic staff as the subordinates, and the students as the customers to whom knowledge is being purveyed.[9]

A similar problem arises in the case of church organization; here again there is a tendency to think of the organization of the clergy in bureaucratic manager-subordinate terms.[10] This view fails to take into account that a church is an association and that the clergy are *members* of that association, *members* of the church, and not merely its employees. Once the clergy become regarded as employees within a manager-subordinate bureaucracy, the congregation come to be regarded as the customers. The sacred relationship between clergy and laity will be completely lost.

Most churches over the centuries have overcome this problem by providing effective life tenure for clergy, often underwritten by the local

[9] I should add here that bureaucratic organization is appropriate for educational institutions which are part of the service sector of the bureaucratic sector, and concerned with the purveying of existing knowledge rather than with the critical evaluation of that knowledge – as in primary and secondary education and in technical colleges. I am thus using the term university to refer to those special institutions of higher education which have the critical function I have emphasized.

[10] In one management consultancy report on the organization of a Church of England diocese, for example, the Archbishop is described as the Chairman of the Board, the Bishop as the Managing Director, the Rural Dean as the General Manager, and the Vicar as the Manager of the congregation!

parish. Under these conditions the sacred relationship between priest and parishioner can obtain, without managerial interference or control but within ecclesiastical policy and central monitoring. The organization is best thought of as horizontally differentiated (on a geographical basis) rather than in terms of a vertically differentiated hierarchy.

Indeed, it is useful to note that the term *hierarchy* derives from the early days of church organization and means sacred leadership (*hieros* – sacred, and *archon* – leadership), and not a vertical hierarchy as in its current usage. This sacred leadership is expressed in biblical references to shepherding rather than to anything resembling managerial authority. A person's relationship with the sacred, through the church, is a most private and intuitive matter, and impingement of a managerially organized institution can only disrupt it.

The confidential doctor-patient relationship is also an intimate personal relationship, one in which the patient can express his anxieties about his prognosis and about death, and seek counsel and reassurance from his doctor. It is a delicate and often poignant human relationship requiring great personal sensitivity on the part of the physician.

This quality in the doctor-patient relationship is undermined if doctors are organized in manager-subordinate relationships in bureaucracies, as is often the case nowadays in hospitals. In the first place, confidentiality cannot be preserved if whoever is the doctor's 'manager' is to be accountable, for he must be able to check upon what is being done. Once confidentiality is gone and the manager is free to look into what the doctor is doing, the immediate doctor-patient relationship becomes more of an economic transaction and loses the quality of being a complex social transaction.

These difficulties can be overcome by retaining clinical freedom for hospital doctors; that is to say, the freedom to use their clinical judgment in diagnosis and treatment *without managerial review* so long as they stay within the law, within professional regulations, and within the limits of sanity.[11]

The rest of the services in a hospital can readily be bureaucratically organized, however, including, for example, nursing, administration, the various therapies and the diagnostic and laboratory services. These services, mostly highly professional, do not carry the accountability for *deciding* the diagnosis and the general programme of therapy, nor for confidential discussions of the prognosis with the patient. They can be called upon by the accountable physician by prescription. They do not require

---

[11] For a fuller description of clinical autonomy see R. Rowbottom *et al.* (1973), *Hospital Organization*. Clinical autonomy does not preclude so-called peer group review to ensure that in general terms a doctor is staying within the boundaries of policy as set by colleagues or by higher authority – so long as no-one else can be held accountable for *particular* diagnoses made by the doctor or for treatments he decides to prescribe.

the clinical autonomy carried by the physician.

We may note, therefore, that bureaucratic organization is relevant and workable for the production and provision of all material goods and all services — including educational, diagnostic, and therapeutic services — where the content of the service is objectively definable. By the same token, we may note that when delicate, confidential, personal services are required, or when tricky questions of absolute freedom to think outside existing social frameworks arise, or when the inexpressible mysteries of the sacred are involved, bureaucratic organization is anti-requisite: manager-subordinate relationships interfere with the sensitive intuitive behavioural flow that is called for. It is such activities — all of great importance to pluralism in society — that are threatened by the bureaucratization of everything.

24

Economic Competition Without Labour Exploitation

In considering the external conditions likely to affect the functioning of bureaucracies, one of the immediate questions which arise is whether bureaucracy is likely to fare better under a capitalist, or socialist, or mixed economy. In particular, is private ownership consistent with requisite bureaucracy? Or are centralized governmental ownership and control necessary? Or is a mixed economic organization the most appropriate?

One of the difficulties has been that it has never been possible to ask these important questions other than in relation to non-requisitely organized bureaucratic systems. If our analysis is valid, there can be no satisfactory answer to such questions under these conditions. The questions take on an entirely different hue if we assume the existence of requisitely organized bureaucracy, for capitalist, socialist and mixed economies would all be significantly different in these circumstances.

One of the main reasons for the difference lies in the great change in the meaning of markets and of competition which occurs with the introduction of requisite bureaucracy. Given requisite constitutional bureaucracy, competition between different employing associations could no longer take place at the expense of their employees. The differential distribution of wages and salaries would be determined by constitutional means. Competition could exist only in appropriate commercial terms; that is to say, it would be limited to competition to provide better service to clients and consumers, without opportunity to carry on the competitive struggle in terms of employers outdoing one another in the exploitation of employees. A society with consumer service competition but without an exploiting competitive labour market is neither capitalist nor socialist. There is a strong case for its being requisite.

Bureaucracy in the Political Arena

Bureaucratic systems are open systems. They are in intimate interaction with their surrounding society. They are affected by that society; and they most assuredly have a profound impact upon it. The interplay between bureaucracy *per se* and its social surround occurs mainly in the socio-economic field: in industrial production; in commercial activities; in the provision of public services supporting the economic system; and in the determination of the differential allocation of wages and salaries and the attendant differential socio-economic status. And even more dramatically, bureaucracy is caught up in the maelstrom of the central political struggle of our time: the capitalist-socialist conflict expressed in terms of who should own the means of production and what should be the role of the market place and competition between production systems.

In relation to bureaucracy these two main questions become: first, should there be any place for private entrepreneurial employment of individuals in bureaucracies, or should all employment be in the hands of the state? Second, should service to clients and consumers be decided by competition between suppliers in the open market, or should competition be excluded and replaced by centralized planning and State monopoly?

Anyone who raises these issues is more than likely to be subjected to two strong and inconsistent criticisms. The first of these criticisms is made by those who believe that bureaucratic systems cannot possibly be requisitely organized and managed under private ownership. Is not private enterprise based upon capitalism by its very nature inevitably inimical to socially healthy or requisite bureaucracy? Is there not an irreconcilable conflict of interest between private entrepreneur and employed worker? And is not any argument which fails to say so firmly and unequivocally merely an apologia for capitalism, an anti-revolutionary liberal bourgeois rationalization and denial of absolute conflict between capitalist class and working class?

The second criticism is precisely the opposite of the first; it is made by those who believe that requisite bureaucratic systems could never be organized and managed under socialist state ownership and centralization. Is not state enterprise inimical to pluralist bureaucracy, equity and individual justice? And is not any argument which fails to say so firmly and unequivocally merely an apologia for socialism and an argument against competition in a free market – including a free labour market – in which supply and demand can regulate the price of labour and the individual can be free?

Our concern here, however, is neither with capitalist nor with socialist apologetics, nor with social democracy, nor indeed with any particular political or economic system. Our concern is with the common aspirations for the good society for mankind which seem to inform all such political ideologies, however the accompanying political systems may differ in the methods deemed necessary to achieve that good society. I would therefore seek the indulgence of the reader in my attempts to move for the time being outside the official arena of competing political systems. I do so in order to examine the possible implications for any of these systems of the foregoing analysis of the bureaucracies which are such a central feature of the socio-economic systems around which much of the ideological struggle revolves.

Competition, Free Enterprise, and State Control

The debate over private versus public ownership and the need for economic competition has been confused and impeded by the failure to distinguish sufficiently clearly between two very different areas of economic competition. The first area of competition is that directed towards the improvement of goods or services offered to the market,[1] or the discovery and development of new goods or services, or the discovery of improved means of providing those goods or services so that they are more readily available or available at a lowered price through improvement in methods of provision: such competition is concerned with providing an improved service, and may be termed *service-providing competition*.[2]

The second type of competition is that directed either towards getting labour to move from one place to another or towards reducing costs by getting labour as cheaply as possible by shrewd coercive bargaining, taking advantage of pockets of unemployment, or otherwise holding pay levels as low as possible. Here the theme is to avoid trade union organization, to find cheap sources of labour wherever possible, to avoid progressing employees unless it is desired to promote someone to a higher post which needs filling, to have recourse to bonus incentive schemes and productivity bargains, to meet power with power. Even where intentions are humanistic, it is necessary for employers to exploit their employees at least to the extent to which their competitors have succeeded in doing so. Such competition may be termed *labour-exploitive competition*.

A main element in the capitalist-socialist antinomy centres on the nature of economic competition: is there to be free enterprise or state planning and control? There is a common underlying conception in this argument: namely, that either there is free enterprise in every sense, that is to say, both service-providing competition and labour-exploitive competition, or that both types of competition should be abolished. The free-enterprise argument, of course, is that a free market – both commodity market and labour market – is necessary for individual freedom and socio-economic advance. The socialist argument for abolition is based on the view that the labour market is exploitive and wrecks individual freedom and that free enterprise economies inevitably contain such exploitation and preclude central planning.

Our analysis of bureaucracy points to the following route to a radical separation of these two types of market and competition, making it pos-

---

[1] I am using the concept of market to refer to all clients or customers receiving goods or services, whether from industry and commerce or from public or social services.

[2] This type of competition is often referred to in socialist countries as 'socialist competition'. The point is that service-providing competition is held to be essential in most political systems. The differences in ideology are concerned with how such competition is to be effected.

sible to have the advantage of service-providing competition without labour exploitation.

Service-providing Competition

Service-providing competition is manifestly in the interest of society. It is socially bonding in the sense that availability of choice gives a sense of freedom to consumers, as against the paranoiagenic restrictionism of a monopolistic situation, whether private or public. Moreover, competition of this kind requires those accountable for bureaucratic work and its output of goods and services to orientate themselves to understanding and fulfilling the human needs they are supposed to be satisfying.

It is in connection with this last point that competition emerges as one requisite feature of bureaucratic functioning. One of the main reasons for the development of the pejorative meaning of bureaucracy as red-tape bound monoliths is connected with those bureaucratic systems in which any possibility of competition from other bureaucratic systems is legally precluded, as, for example, in the case of most government departments and social services. In the absence of competition it is easy for standards to fall; or, conversely, it is difficult for standards to rise.

Service-providing competition, however arranged politically, is an essential factor in the development of standards of bureaucratic operation. There are no absolute standards of what may be achieved by people in bureaucracies with given resources, nor can there ever be. What can be known is the best that has been achieved at any given time. Standard setting is markedly improved, therefore, if different people have the freedom and the opportunity to show what they can do. Without such freedom to compete in effectiveness of service-provision – that is to say with private or state monopoly – complacency can readily set in. That outcome is especially true in the case of governmentally controlled monopolies, whether the government is socialist or capitalist.

The opportunity to compete contains a number of freedoms: first, the freedom to seek backing for better ways of doing things, or for the production of things which it is thought might satisfy needs not yet catered for, and to offer up the fruits of those efforts in the form of goods or services; second, the freedom of clients and consumers to choose the goods or services which are most attractive to them.

A main issue here is the judgment of human need. Who is to say how good are such judgments? In the long run, only the people whose needs are being served – or not served – can do so. But however well or badly served, who can say whether anything better could have been done by someone else? The simple answer is that no-one can ever say. No-one can ever know for sure whether something might have gone better if only such-and-such had been done, or if only so-and-so had been doing it. The important thing is to try to ensure that there are others actually competing to try to do better. The existence of competition is the sole means of giving an objective basis to judgment by providing comparisons.

In the absence of competitive comparison it is difficult to avoid some complacency. For it is these comparators which provide the information which is necessary for the reality-testing of subjective judgments about performance, made either by the producer or the consumer. With such comparative information, the reality principle stands a chance of operating. Without this information, unchecked judgments are inevitably to some extent at least affected by the producer's unconscious fantasies about his own competence and performance, and by the consumer's unconscious greed and envy.[3]

Labour-exploitive Competition and the Labour Market

The labour market, like the commodity market, is held to operate in terms of supply and demand. Even in Soviet Russia, without a free labour market, it is held to be necessary to relate the price of labour to the supply and demand situation in order to encourage the movement of labour where it is most needed. Our findings, however, suggest a very different picture, and lead to the following analysis.

Material goods and services have no inherent price. Their market price is determined by their relative value to particular groups of consumers at particular points in time: this market price will vary with changes in consumer need and fashion, and will run down to zero if there is no demand, regardless of the work and materials which may have been put into the production of the goods or services. The market price can, of course, be controlled by governmental decree or monopoly, but that is merely to subvert the consumer's freedom of choice with respect to the goods and services he desires.[4]

Human labour, however, is a very different proposition. There is an absolute differential value of human labour, regardless of any supply and demand situation, related to the differential work-capacity of individuals and

---

[3] See my (1970), 'Psycho-Analysis and the Current Economic Crisis' pp. 200–214.

[4] The Marxist analysis of surplus value of course assumes that material goods and services have an inherent value; namely, the value of the labour that goes into their production. It is therefore assumed that this value must be the major determinant of market value as stated in price. This view is the same as that which leads to all the errors of cost-plus pricing in capitalist systems. There is, in fact, no necessary relationship at all between the cost of producing material goods and services and their value to consumers. Market value, in the sense of price at which consumers will actually purchase something, is determined, and determined only, by the needs and attitudes of consumers, regardless of cost of production. (See, for example, the elaboration of this argument in W. Brown and E. Jaques (1964), *Product Analysis Pricing*.)

the level of work they are carrying out. We have demonstrated this inherent or natural differential structure in the price of labour in our findings that each person seeks a level of work consistent with his work-capacity, and a level of differential pay which is equitable for that work. Herein lies the great difference between the valuation of the work of human beings and the valuation of material goods and services.

The differences between human labour, on the one hand, and material goods and services on the other, can be pointed up once it is realized that neither cars, nor coal, nor cattle, have any feelings whatever about the price offered for them. Their price is negotiated or otherwise set by men. In the case of human labour, however, the object of the price is man himself, with his relative socio-economic status, prestige and self-esteem at stake, all related to his sense of his own work-capacity relative to others. If then a society values the work and creativeness of its people in relation to supply and demand in a market, in the same way as it values animals in a cattle market, there need be no surprise if people respond with consternation, confusion, apparent unreasonableness and greed, and eventually (perhaps over many decades) with hostile rejection of that society.

Thus it is that under capitalist free enterprise, labour-exploitive competition becomes virulently paranoiagenic. Marginal unemployment, freedom to shut down uneconomic plant, movement of companies to cheaper labour markets elsewhere in the world, and other phenomena stir the deepest anxieties in people. Collective bargaining can only temporarily alleviate the problem and eventually exacerbates it. Labour-exploitive competition is coercive on the surface and fosters violence in the depths. In due course this violence pervades collective bargaining and permeates society.

The Marxist analysis of capitalism and the development of a revolutionary working-class consciousness is directed against this labour-exploitive component of competition under capitalism. In seeking, however, to root out the cancer of labour exploitation, it indiscriminately removes the healthy organs of service-providing competition at the same time.

With the centralization of ownership and the control of all bureaucratic systems and the removal of an openly competitive labour market, the socialist State overcomes some of the worst difficulties of capitalist economies, in particular, unemployment and labour-exploitive competition between private entrepreneurs. But in other respects it replaces these difficulties by others which are just as paranoiagenic. First, by destroying service-providing competition and replacing it by cumbersome State monopoly, it makes it almost impossible to regulate and evaluate standards, and they inevitably deteriorate. Second, it merely shifts the coercive power field to the State itself: pay differentials are settled neither in terms of equity nor even in terms of the Marxist formulation of 'from each according to his ability and to each according to his needs'. They are settled by a State machinery which determines levels of pay in relation to current needs to persuade labour to shift to wherever the State considers necessary, with coercive direction available as a last resort, contained within closed national frontiers.

Moreover, socialist states will be inherently no better than capitalist ones when it comes to consultation with employees on payment, or indeed on other types of policy changes in bureaucratic systems. Once these systems are all State-controlled, all employees find themselves the servants of the nation. As we have tried to show, nations – democratic or otherwise – are not necessarily good employers. Leviathan, or Behemoth, the excesses committed in the name of the common will – be it the democratic will, the people, the proletarian dictatorship – are familiar enough.[5]

In short, inequitable rewards and coercion are characteristic of both the capitalist and communist organization of the bureaucratic employment sector of the economy. Both types of economic organization treat human labour in market supply and demand terms and are thereby dehumanizing. Both could be transformed if requisite organization of bureaucracy were introduced, so that arrangements for equitable and differential distribution of income were substituted for supply and demand valuation. Let me describe the possible outcomes.[6]

[5] That is why, on a much smaller scale, trade unions and co-operative societies are noticeably backward when it comes to giving opportunity for participation to their own employees – employees are expected to accept the consequences for themselves of anything the central committees might decide to do, since it is for the 'democratic' membership.

[6] I have only just been sent, through the courtesy of Alan Fox, a copy of the excellent review 'Alienation, Freedom and Economic Organization: A Review Note' (1974) by Felix R. FitzRoy of the Alfred-Weber-Institut at the University of Heidelberg. It is too late for me to incorporate his views in my manuscript but I must at the least add this last-minute footnote.

FitzRoy reviews the work of a wide range of social and economic writers who try to deal with the problem of achieving democracy and participation in industry as a central feature of the growth of democracy in industrial societies. In his wide-ranging review he cites timely references from Marx, Engels and Lenin, John Stuart Mill, Kropotkin (1910), and Bertrand Russell (1916), through to the current work of Adizes (1971), Ellerman (1972), Oberländer (1972), Heilbronner (1974), Gintis (1971), Horvat (1971), Melman (1970), Nutzinger (1974), Šik (1968), Vanek (1974), and others.

The gravamen of his argument is to demonstrate the inability of both capitalist and socialist industrial societies to provide adequate opportunity for the expression of the participatory and democratic aspirations of those employed in industry. The socialist nations have failed to overcome the problems of industrial capitalism; first, because they have merely replaced private ownership by heavily centralized state ownership which gives no greater opportunity for employees to participate in the control of policy in their own work organization; and, second, because of the failure to provide a democratic consumer market. The Yugoslav experiment also is beset by problems arising over the difficulties in separating employee control of local enterprise from the requirements of investment and national planning.

These views are not dissimilar from my own argument, but my analysis leads to rather different conclusions about what needs to be done.

Constitutional Setting of Income Differentials

If the bureaucratic sector is to stand a chance of being an overall social bonding influence in society, as against being a paranoiagenic influence, the labour-exploitive and coercive elements have to be removed. These elements constitute the ugly face of both capitalism and socialism. They can be eliminated, given the necessary political will. Where this political will is likely first to show itself would be difficult to say.

What is required is to recognize in the first place the inherent and differential value of individual work-capacity and of the contribution which individuals make to society through their work-capacities. If this were done, and if political mechanisms were provided for determining differential pay structures, then the labour market with its competitive and coercive price bargaining would be redundant and could simply disappear. Differential payment could become a matter of national consensus and not a matter of fragmented power bargaining, whether within one bureaucratic organization, or within one industry, or in relation to the members of one trade union. Now that the full writings of Marx are becoming available, it is clear that Marx himself laid great stress upon the importance of fairness in distribution of wealth and payment, although he had no satisfactory definition of what he meant by fairness.[7]

The question, however, is what constitutes a fair differential distribution of income in a nation: what should be the differential distribution of wages and salaries? and what should be the differential distribution of the total of wage and salary incomes as compared with incomes from rents, dividends, and entrepreneurial work? And, moreover, by what means can these distributions be constitutionally arranged?

In publishing our findings about the norms of felt-fair pay which accord with levels of work as measured in time-span, we have sometimes been understood to be proposing that this particular distribution of wages and salaries is *the* fair one and that it, and it alone, should be implemented. In fact it is not proposed that any particular differential distribution of wages and salaries is necessarily more fair than any others, or even more fair than doing away with differentials altogether. Our views can be summed up in two statements: first, it has been found that felt-fair pay does accord closely with measured time-span in a role; second, using time-span measurement it has been observed that there appear to be general norms of felt-fair pay differentials for employment work. It is not known yet whether the pattern of these differential norms has changed through time or whether it will change in the future. But it does seem to be the case that a strong pattern of felt-fair differentials does exist, for better or worse — and this

[7] D. McLellan (1975), *Karl Marx: His Life and Thought*.

pattern shows that there is widespread support for a system of differentials granting larger reward the higher the level of work.

In short, it would seem that relative inequality in economic status is the pattern society chooses for rewarding social worth as expressed in work. This pattern seems to have been universal at all times in history, except for some very few, very small-scale experimental societies in which equal sharing of income was established.[8] It still remains the pattern in all socialist and communist nations in terms of both income distribution and the distribution of benefits such as cars and housing.[9]

The main point, however, is not what the distribution of wages and salaries in the bureaucratic sector shall be, and how it shall be related to the scale of dividends, income from rents, prices, social security benefits of various kinds, pensions, and so on, but rather that some mechanism must be devised which allows a nation to decide the answers to these questions explicitly by constitutional political means. Such a constitutional mechanism which will enable everyone to be represented in the process of establishing the pattern of economic status, or at least of the income part of economic status, is an absolute requirement of industrial societies.

Just such a mechanism has been described in Chapter 14 in Wilfred Brown's proposals for a National Council for the Regulation of Differentials (NCRD). It could provide the means by which the labour market could be made redundant, in theory and in practice. The general principle in Wilfred Brown's proposed mechanism is a sound one: economic status in the bureaucratic sector relative to other sectors is set by governmental decision; it is then for the employee representatives of the bureaucratic sector to arrive at agreement upon the differential pattern of earnings. Such a notion brings the question of economic status into the forefront of social awareness and debate. It does so in broad terms affecting the whole of society, and not in fragmented negotiations affecting this group now, and that group next, and so on.

Time-span measurement could assist such a mechanism by making it possible to frame decisions about patterns of differential payment in terms of given levels of pay for given levels of work regardless of occupational title. But even without level-of-work measurement, practical results could be obtained just by the simple process of representatives looking at the differential pay problems as a whole — rather than having a situation in

---

[8] The kibbutzim in Israel, for example. My own guess would be that for such communities to succeed they require a fairly uniform level of capacity among their members, a condition which might conceivably be achieved by the careful selection process used by the kibbutzim in accepting new members. D. Billis (to be published), 'Differential Administrative Capacity and Organisational Development: A Kibbutz Case Study'.

[9] D. Granick (1954), *Management of the Industrial Firm* in the U.S.S.R.; and D. Lane (1971), *The End of Inequality? Stratification under State Socialism*.

which, because there is no mechanism at all for dealing with the problem, every individual feels that he has the right to complain.

Moreover, let me recall that the relationship between felt-fair pay and time-span measurement demonstrates the existence in society of the ability to form norms of economic equity and justice. The equitable-work-payment scale is a true depth structure. It is at this depth that the roots of social justice grow. The problem is to develop social institutions and procedures which allow the deep-lying norms of equity to be reflected at the surface of social relationships. The significance of the equitable-work-payment scale is likely to be as much in its demonstration of the existence of norms of economic equity as in the provision of any particular pattern of differential payment.

Inflation, Greed, and Fairness

If equitable pay distribution can be agreed, then the main source of the scourge of industrial societies in the 1960s and 1970s, namely wage-push inflation, will have been removed.[10] The critical stimulus to such inflation is the inexorable leap-frogging which is part of collective bargaining, to the slight advantage of the wage and salary sectors of the population but with little real gain for anyone. Consensus-based equity in income distribution can eliminate this restless and fruitless upward climb. Abundant employment can be the more easily maintained. And it becomes possible to have service-providing competition without any accompanying labour-exploitive competition.

The consequence of such an outcome would be to alter man's perception of himself in a dramatic way. It would become possible to recognize that the inordinate seeking after wage increases which has caused so much economic damage through inflation is not due primarily to the insatiable greed of individuals. People are much more complex than that: capable of feelings of love, equity, fairness, and concern for others, as much as of greedy self-seeking, egotism, and devil-take-the-hindmost unconcern for others, even in the economic sphere. Our present beliefs about the essence of human nature are dominated by our experience of people behaving in a social context of coercive power bargaining which leaves room for nothing but greedy self-seeking even to retain a reasonable relative position on the wage and salary income ladder. What we have not seen as yet, anywhere in the world, is the release of the constructive motivation in people, the sense of economic fairness and justice, which would be facilitated by the provision of explicit institutions for the consensual regulation of differential income distribution.[11]

[10] See E. Jaques (1969), 'Fair Pay: How to Achieve It'.
[11] A most revealing example of how we confuse and mislead ourselves with economic

Mixed Economy Plus Constitutional Bureaucracy

The elimination of labour exploitation is most likely to be met by a mixed economy with constitutionally operated bureaucracy. Such a mixed economy is more likely to be socially bonding than either a capitalist economy with its labour-exploitive market competition or a socialist economy with coercive State power and without service-providing competition.

A mixed economy with constitutional bureaucracy can provide certain gains. It allows for competitive individual ownership and entrepreneurship but without the labour-exploitive blight, and thus makes total centralization of control less necessary; it can help to prevent the indiscriminate bureaucratization of everything; it allows for service-providing competition within and between the public and private sectors.

The mixed economy provides for both State and private enterprise in competition with each other. Under the conditions outlined, private ownership could not be labour-exploitive, and State enterprise would not be monopolistic or monolithic. By this combination of private and public ownership the whole bureaucratic sector could be kept under constructive conflict and stress.[12]

It is important for an individual to have the choice between bureaucratic roles and private entrepreneurial roles[13] – whether in industrial or commer-

---

double-think is that of the so-called productivity bargaining policy in Great Britain during the late 1960s. Manifestly, the policy stated that in order to obtain an increase in pay, a collective bargaining group had to agree to contribute a compensating increase in productivity. Increases, so the economists argued, would thus be non-inflationary.

The reality, however, is that increases in productivity cannot come from people working harder unless they have been slacking hitherto. They come from investment in new methods and from the elimination of inefficient organization or of restrictive practices. The consequence is that the only way to get an increase under a productivity bargain policy is to have a restrictive practice to sell, or to threaten a restrictive practice such as a refusal to accept a new method, or to be doing less than a reasonable day's work.

The result was that for three years or more there was no way for a group to get an increase unless they had a restrictive practice, or were prepared to develop one, or went into collusion with management to pretend that some increase in productivity was being achieved by the super-human effort of those concerned. Those who were getting on with their work, or whose physical outputs could not be readily measured, got nothing. The so-called productivity policy led on the one hand to restrictionism, and on the other hand to the political radicalization of non-restrictionist groups such as teachers and nurses as they found themselves falling lower and lower on the incomes ladder.

[12] J. K. Galbraith's distinction between the small business market system of capitalist economies and the big business planned system, and the need to keep the competitive market system in a healthy state, underlines the argument I am pursuing here. J. K. Galbraith (1974), *Economics and the Public Purpose.*

[13] D. R. Miller and G. E. Swanson, among others, have shown the potentially deleterious impact upon personality development, family life and community life of the shift in a community from private entrepreneurship to bureaucracy as a result of the sudden taking-over of small private enterprises. Those who were in business on their own become employees, and the disturbance is intense. (1958) *The Changing American Parent.*

cial enterprises or in various types of professional role. Entrepreneurial activity can be enormously creative socially and individually, so long as the profitability of such enterprise is not and cannot be at the cost of differentially poor conditions for the employees – a possibility precluded by the requisite patterns described. For the entrepreneur must be willing to risk his own resources or at least his reputation, in backing both his judgment about social need (the market he proposes to satisfy) and his ability economically to fulfil that need. This personal risk is the best assurance that he will use all his sensitivities in judging the requirements of the people whose needs he hopes to satisfy while at the same time keeping his costs down. It thereby ensures his contribution to keeping the bureaucratic sector under the constructive stress of service-providing competition.[14]

The Employee's Side of the Freedom and Equity Bargain

What is required is the provision of working roles which preserve the individuality of the person in a setting of responsible social interaction; that is to say, a system of roles in which the expression of individuality adds to the strengthening of social interaction, of social bonds, of local community. The conditions outlined would have a fair chance of doing this: opportunity for entrepreneurial activity for those who wish to risk it, but without profiting at the expense of employees; opportunity for each employed person to use his abilities at full stretch and to have a fair socio-economic status; opportunity for the State to take part in competitive economic activity.

Given a situation of all-round economic justice, what are the accompanying duties of the individual? What is the price which must be paid in social obligation? The main price lies in the flexibility which would be required with respect to type of work. What the conditions outlined cater for is the opportunity for every individual to work, and to be able to do so at a level of work which matches his capacity, and by and large to have such work available in the community where he lives. What they cannot cater for is that this work should exactly match his current skill, experience and interest at any given time. As demands change, as technology and procedures change, so do the types of work and the methods used in work. The individual would be expected to adapt to such changes, taking advantage of opportunities for re-training.

Moreover, individuals employed in bureaucracies could not expect

---

[14] I have elaborated this theme of the potential creativity in entrepreneurial activity in (1970) 'Theses on Work'.

It has of course been argued in a substantial manner by liberal political economists such as M. Friedman (1962), *Capitalism and Freedom*, and F. A. Hayek (1960), *The Constitution of Liberty*.

automatically to be given just the role they sought merely for the asking. They would still have to be prepared to compete for the position with others, and to show their capabilities against the standards set by such competition. In addition they would have to accept that there would be no feather-bedding – no safeguarding of their particular roles against the realities of changes in consumer needs and in technology. Any such cushioning against change would be a negation of the reality-testing which requisitely organized work can provide.

Apart from this individual acceptance of flexibility, everyone would have to accede to the general functioning of bureaucracy – to carry his role or roles requisitely, to accept policies arrived at through the participation process, to accept risk if engaged in entrepreneurial activity, and to exert reasonable endeavour in work as the prime factor in gaining reasonable opportunity to be considered for progress. Such attitudes are an essential part of any co-operative and democratic society.

25

Status, Class, and the Open Society

This final chapter briefly sketches some preliminary ideas about the relevance of our theoretical notions to certain general social and philosophical questions: social status, social stratification, and class formation; social mobility and the avoidance of rigid and inflexible stratification; and the maintenance of individual freedom in an open society – all in the context of a requisitely organized bureaucratic sector.

These considerations may support the conclusion that questions of ethics and morality have to be analysed not only in terms of the intentions and behaviour of individuals, but also in terms of the social institutions within which individuals interact. Since the role relationships provided by social systems channel and set direction for individual behaviour, then social institutions themselves can be evaluated on moral and ethical grounds in terms of the behaviour which they point towards or allow, and that which they preclude.

Relative and Absolute Status, Needs, and Deprivation

Every person has a relative position or status on many different social scales, including, for example, economic or income status, occupational prestige status, educational status, honour, political status. These various statuses are of the deepest significance to the individual. They are the social counterpart of the underlying needs which they reflect. Taken together they give the pattern of a person's social recognition, his prestige, his public identity. In particular, they tell him how the world places him relative to other people – how valuable a person he is considered to be as compared with others.

In considering problems of status it is well to keep clearly in mind the enormous emotional power which can be attached to an individual's view of his status at any given time. Such feelings are especially powerful in the case of work. Nearly everyone, for example, will have had the experience of being passed over in connection with a promotion, and of seeing someone else get the advancement to which the person himself feels entitled. Such circumstances provoke intensely violent reactions: pain frustration, undermining of confidence, sense of injustice, diminishing in the eyes of others, shame and loss of self-respect, and above all a general sense of losing out, possibly for life. It is because the status issue is of such great human importance that systematic performance assessment and progress review procedures are so necessary, and that adequate grading structures are needed.

Whether or not a person will necessarily agree with the statuses conferred upon him is, of course, an open question. There may be very big discrepancies between his own self-esteem or self-evaluation and his statuses in society. Or there may be greater inconsistencies within the profile of his various statuses (status discrepancy as against status congruence) than his inner sense of integrity and identity can allow for. Such discrepancies imply a schism between the nature of his public indentity and of his self-identity. Such schisms are of great moment to the individual, for they disturb his attempts to maintain a coherent picture of himself and of how he is regarded by others, and may leave him resentful, uncertain or confused. In such circumstances feelings of deprivation and attendant anxieties will be aroused, and defences will be mobilized against both the anxiety and the public identity.

Because each of these statuses is the reflection of deeper-lying needs in the individual – for family, for the things money can buy, for power, for honour, for education, and in general for appropriate prestige or recognition – it is important that they should be based on criteria which seem realistic to people and which are generally acceptable. The difficulty, however, is that by and large these statuses are relative, and as such are variable, uncertain, built on shifting sand. They do not provide any objective basis upon which a person could agree that his various statuses were at least fair, whether or not he found them wholly acceptable. It would thus be a matter of some importance if any absolute and objectively assessable statuses could be established, to act as an anchor for the otherwise free-floating complex of statuses making up a person's identity.[1]

Most social scientists and philosophers, however, would deny the usefulness of the concept of absolute status, and of the related concepts of absolute need and absolute deprivation. Runciman, for example, uses John Rawls' theory of justice[2] to argue the case for eschewing the idea of absolute wants, or entitlements, or deprivations, an argument which he applies equally to status.[3] Runciman's point of view is realistic *within the limits of the status with which he is concerned*: inequalities in the disposi-

---

[1] As I indicated in Chapter 2, I find it useful to follow the current trend in sociological theory towards a multi-dimensional analysis of status, as against a uni-dimensional analysis which bundles all statuses together into a single generally ascribed social status. The uni-dimensional analysis over-simplifies and loses the important human complexity of degree of congruence or of discrepancy between a person's various statuses.

[2] J. Rawls (1972), *A Theory of Justice.*

[3] W. G. Runciman (1966), *Relative Deprivation and Social Justice,* and H. H. Hyman and E. Singer (1968), 'Problems of Research on Relative Deprivation'.

tion of wealth, of prestige, of power, of social status.[4] But there is one status which could be absolute; namely the status that would be conferred upon a person by the true level of work he carries out, if that level of work could be publicly manifested and known. We shall refer to it as *work-status* (in order to distinguish it sharply from occupational prestige – the prestige carried by occupational titles such as judge, nurse, miner, architect, car worker, etc., almost irrespective of the true level of work which might obtain in any particular role in any of these occupational categories).

If it can be established that work-status is an absolute status, then it could be not only an anchor to the relativity of other statuses but a peculiarly important and telling anchor, linked in a most powerful and direct way with the core identity of the individual. For, in the first place, a person's work-status would be the clearest public statement of his work-capacity, of his socio-economic worth, of his material contribution to society: it would show where he rates in this primary arena of reality. In the second place, his work-status, in setting his income, determines his relative economic status, and that is a powerful determinant of prestige and therefore a matter of grave concern in industrial societies. Taken together, work-status and economic status form the basis upon which a person's prestige depends in the sense of how big or competent a person he is reputed to be.

Level of Work (W) as an Absolute Status and Right

That a person's work-status is an absolute status can be readily enough established if it is accepted that there is one unique level of work at any particular time in his career which corresponds to his level of work-capacity at that time. Findings have been presented which argue in favour of the existence of this relationship. At any given time a person's level of work is either absolutely congruent with his level of work-capacity or is above or below that level. If his level of work is below his level of work-capacity he

---

[4] His argument is less convincing, however, than Dahrendorf's, which attempts to establish a distinction between absolute and relative deprivation as having different consequences with respect to violence as against intensity of class conflict. 'If the social condition of industrial workers, who are as such excluded from authority, falls below a physiological subsistence minimum or "poverty line", the effects of such deprivation are likely to be different in kind from those of relative deprivation. I would suggest that in this case, and in this case only, the superimposition of scales of status and the distribution of authority is likely to increase the violence of class conflict. This is a subtle and complex relation. So far as we know, oppression and deprivation may reach a point at which militant conflict motivation gives way to apathy and lethargy. Short of this point, however, there is reason to believe that absolute deprivation coupled with exclusion from authority makes for greater violence in conflict relations. Relative deprivation, on the other hand, tends to affect the intensity of conflict rather than its violence.' R. Dahrendorf (1959), *Class and Class Conflict in an Industrial Society*, pp. 217–18.

suffers not a relative deprivation but an absolute one. If his level of work is above his level of work-capacity he suffers an absolute superfluity.

As compared with the absolute status of level of work in relation to a person's work-capacity, his income status in wage or salary is a relative one. But it is a relative status of an interesting kind, in that it can be given a firm and objective basis through the equitable work-payment scale. Discrepancy or congruence of income status can thus be stated in near-absolute terms by comparison between actual payment and equitable payment – although the equitable work-payment scale is itself a relative scale of differentials which may vary from time to time.

In general terms, therefore, we are dealing with the question of congruence between a person's work-capacity (C), the level of work in his role (W), and his level of payment (P): the C-W-P equilibrium. This congruence is arguably the hard core of status congruence as a whole, linking as it does with the primary sense of reality as experienced through work. Work-capacity (C) is an attribute of the core region of a person's self-identity, touching in the very deepest sense upon what he is like as a result of his constitutional make-up moulded by interaction with his environment. W – the level of work in his employment role – links that role immediately to his core self-identity, and leaves him with the experience of being more or less in equilibrium or disequilibrium with his role and work environment. At the same time, W, if properly formulated, provides the crucial public evidence allowing for the establishment of a social evaluation of his objective public identity as far as his work is concerned. P – his level of pay for the work expected of him – establishes his economic status or ranking, thus linking the economic status component of his public identity through his level of work to his core self-identity.

C-W-P equilibrium thus implies an internal consistency between: work-capacity, part of the core region of self-identity; level of work, which is a central feature of role and of the core region of public identity; and differential pay, which sets the economic status which is such a fundamental feature of social status.To the extent that there is a discrepancy between work-capacity and level of work, or between level of work and pay, or between all three, then stress and conflict occur between the individual and society and within the individual. Core self-identity and the innermost regions of personality are disturbed, and self-esteem is threatened. It is this inner disturbance which may express itself in inhibition and self-destruction, or in smouldering resentment, anger and overt aggression against the immediate society.

Bureaucracy and the Provision of an Adequate Work- and Income Status

Suppose then that every person could be assured of a state of affairs in which he could gain a level of work (regardless of occupational title) which accorded with his work-capacity, and a level of pay that was equitable for that level of work: in short, suppose everyone could be assured of C-W-P equilibrium. And suppose further that there were some mode of publicly recognizing that level of work. At one go, a person might have the possibility not only of satisfaction in his work but also of a realistic social ranking in terms of work for the community and in that sense of personal worth, plus a congruent position in economic ranking. By this means the bureaucratic sector would provide a work system such that every person could have a role congruent with the central core of his identity, rather than there being conflict all round.

A properly managed bureaucratic sector would under these conditions play a major part in securing the appropriate social and economic status for the individual, at least as far as ranking in work and income were concerned. In so doing, it would be contributing a hard core to the multitude of social statuses a person might have and a solid foundation for his self-esteem, since the public marks of his level of work and his income status would point to his social competence as reflected in his work-capacity.

The means by which a requisitely organized bureaucratic sector would provide for C-W-P equilibrium have already been presented. The public recognition of level of work (W) would be achieved automatically by the implementation of the systematic scheme of bureaucratic work-strata. People in the same stratum are carrying similar levels of work. If and when such strata came into universal use, it would be possible for everyone to have a publicly identifiable level of work, regardless of occupation, which could be compared with any other person's level of work. One type of occupation might confer more prestige than another, but would not affect a person's level of work and income statuses.[5]

[5] One of the current difficulties both in sociological theory and in society at large is that at present the only generally available criterion for ascribing work-status is occupational prestige. The trouble is that the prestige of occupation refers only to occupational title – for example, secretary, bricklayer, doctor, manager, etc. – and that these titles do not necessarily tell very much about the real level at which any given person is actually working within the category covered by the title. Moreover, the prestige of given occupational titles is influenced by many factors such as current ideologies, and the relationship with real work levels is obscure. The use of occupational prestige as a status criterion, therefore, serves only to reinforce the current prejudices about responsibility in occupations, and can be seriously misleading as an indicator of true level of work-status. Even the sophisticated recent refinement of occupational prestige ranking carried out by J. H. Goldthorpe and K. Hope (1974, *The Social Grading of Occupations*) in no way overcomes the difficulties in the earlier studies by D. V. Glass, C. A. Moser and others (1954, *Social Mobility in Britain*), for there is no established relationship whatever between these rankings and level of work.

Equilibrium between work-capacity and level of work would be provided by the opportunities that would go with abundant employment as discussed in the previous chapter. Then given the implementation of procedures for agreeing equitable differential pay linked to differentials in level of work, equilibrium could be established between level of work and level of pay (W-P congruence).

Abundant employment is thus a necessary safeguard for C-W-P congruence and against abuses of bureaucratic employment. Everyone ought to be exposed to it. The healthiest situation would be one in which no-one had anyone but himself to blame if he did not have a level of work to match his abilities and a level of pay congruent with his level of work. In these circumstances bureaucratic organization can begin to come into its own as a trust-supporting social institution. It can be a focus of guarantee that the hard core of status congruence can be correctly established and that self-esteem will be satisfied because of the congruence of self-identity and public identity in work.

By these arrangements the bureaucratic sector could help to establish fairness and justice in the hard core of social and economic status for the 70–90 per cent of the population in industrial societies who are employed in bureaucracies. But what of the other 10–30 per cent of the working population – the entrepreneurs, politicians, judges, priests, university teachers, and independent professionals such as lawyers and doctors? How would they be assured of reasonable status in the scheme of things? The answer is that they could have no such assurance. For are these roles not individual entrepreneurial-type roles? Is not the essence of these roles that they leave a man free to find his own level in society – in prestige, in reputation, in economic status and success – without being dependent upon the judgment of a manager? It would be wrong to try to impose a blanket administrative tidiness upon such occupations and their social status. They give individual opportunity; they carry a corresponding individual risk.

Indeed, this question helps to point up the fact that the reason for trying to achieve some general framework of control for the requisite functioning of the bureaucratic sector is not for the purpose of imposing a status system upon society. It is rather the other way around. Some control is necessary, because without it there is too much risk of social pathology developing in the bureaucratic sector and spreading disruption and discord throughout the whole of society.

If the hard-core level-of-work and differential income statuses are satisfactorily dealt with, then status congruence in general becomes somewhat less of a problem. No difficulties need arise from the fact that statuses such as personal esteem and honour are free-floating. Occupational prestige as well could vary independently if members of a society deemed that there were particular features of self-denial and of service to the community – as in the case, perhaps, of such vocations as nurses, or teachers, or political leaders – which warranted special feelings of recognition. It is when the hard-core statuses are not catered for that society may well be concerned about all statuses and about status congruence. When there are no fixed points in social reality on which to focus, social status becomes an uncertain free-for-all in which everyone must grasp what he can.

It may finally be noted that there are other features of constitutional bureaucracy which strengthen feelings of self-respect. The mutual respect of a manager and subordinate for each other depends upon their being at one-stratum distance; this condition is not sufficient, but is certainly necessary. Opportunity for participation in the control of policy and of change, and opportunity for individual appeals, are in the same category. They enhance every person's sense of personal value and significance, and give to everyone the same status as citizens, despite the differences which may occur in work-status and other statuses. Indeed, one of the general characteristics of all constitutional arrangements is that the status of everyone is increased: constitutional bureaucracy is no exception.

Equality and Social Stratification

Turning from questions of status to questions of class and social stratification, here again it may be noted that bureaucratic systems have a bad reputation, being regarded – falsely – as inevitably bringing rigidity and inflexibility into industrial societies. Because they are hierarchies with superordination and subordination, they are therefore suspected of supporting the higher echelons against the lower. They tend to be seen as systems protective of elitism and ruling class interest. That elites and the ruling powers may use bureaucracies in this way must be accepted. But that fact is merely a statement about elites and ruling classes and about one of the steps they might take to retain power; it is not a description of any inherent property of the bureaucratic hierarchy. The question remains of whether and how bureaucracy might be used as a force in society against rigid stratification and against the formation of a closed system of social classes.[6]

The reason for raising these general questions lies in the fact that requisite organization and functioning of the bureaucratic zone demand an open society in which there is reasonable equality of opportunity for in-

---

[6] The concept of class will be used as defined in Chapter 2, in the Marxist sense of a bounded group with a common relationship to the means of production, and dynamic in the sense of being politically active. By contrast, the concepts of strata and stratification are used to refer simply to the existence of the horizontal differentiation of a society or a social institution into a hierarchical structure of bounded groups.

dividuals: equality of opportunity for progress – no matter which class the individual or his family belongs to. It is the equality of opportunity which is needed to enable everyone, if he wishes to strive to do so, to achieve and maintain a level of work (W) consistent with his work-capacity (C) and the attendant payment (P) upon which economic status depends – C-W-P equilibrium.

Given such equality of opportunity, there is then certainly no need for equality in what people are called upon to do or are enabled to do: full recognition can be given to differences in capacity and these can be utilized in a hierarchy of employment opportunity in bureaucracy. The issues have been well stated by Ralf Dahrendorf in his essay (1968) on 'Liberty and Equality': 'At the two extremes of the status hierarchy, we have found social equality (in the sense of the exclusion of extremes) and individual liberty (in the sense of the opportunity for self-fulfilment) to be clearly compatible; indeed, we have found equality a condition of the possibility of liberty. But the equality that our restrictions seek to guarantee is not equality of social status but equality of citizenship. In the vast domain between the ceiling and the floor of the status hierarchy, the domain in which equality of citizenship can be taken for granted, equality of social status is an enemy of liberty. As a stimulus, a medium, and a reward of personal self-development, social stratification is essential to human freedom. The more monolithic, the less differentiated a society is, the more it restricts its citizens' chances of liberty; the more pluralistic and differentiated a system of social stratification is, the more easily can it do justice to the citizens' multifarious individual needs and talents. Once equality of citizenship is assured, inequality of social status is necessary to the chance of liberty.'

In spite of any utopian aims – the value of which has in any case yet to be demonstrated – it is impossible to abolish inequalities in work and in socio-economic status without exercising a complete day-to-day control over the person. That these inequalities should not become unreasonable as far as wage and salary differentials are concerned could be assured by the means we have described for determining the general pattern of differentials. But the question would remain as to whether the continued existence of bureaucratic hierarchies with their inherent expression of human inequality would not lead inevitably to the rigid stratification of society, to the formation of social classes, and to dissensual class conflict.

Bureaucracy and the Emergence of Social Stratification

On considering the question of social stratification in connection with our analysis of bureaucracy, we are faced with another question. Might it not be that the multi-modality in the distribution of work-capacity which we have postulated as the underlying source of the depth structure of strata in bureaucracies, acts in the same way as a potent force towards stratification in society at large? If this idea were combined with reference group theory, it would lead to the postulate that people with a common picture of the world in terms of level of abstraction, who achieve a common level of work and a common socio-economic status deriving from that work, will tend to precipitate out loose common-interest reference groupings. Permeable boundaries would then form, in effect, at the 3-month, 1-year, 2-year, etc., time-span levels of work-capacity.[7] There would thus tend to be precipitated out a hierarchy of layers in society, corresponding to the hierarchy of levels of work-capacity and of work-strata which we have seen to be such an outstanding characteristic of people and of bureaucratic systems.

If this postulate is valid it would serve to explain the tendency in societies to form hierarchies of social stratification. Do we have here, then, a possible explanation of the precipitation out of a closed system of social classes as the end point of the process of social stratification reflecting the multi-modality of work-capacity in human populations? A moment's consideration, however, suggests that this explanation is simply not true. The likely nature of a system of stratification resulting from stratification in human capacity, is that it would be open and allow for social mobility and would not be a closed and rigid source of conflicting classes. The formation of social classes must come from other forces in society.

That the multi-modal distribution of work-capacity would induce only open stratification is self-evident. Such stratification would cut right through immediate family and wider kinship groupings, ethnic groups, and religious groups; it would cut right across colour, education, and sex barriers. For a person's level of abstraction and capacity growth are independent of all these memberships, except where hereditary factors cause a child to have the same level of abstraction as both parents. And even in the latter case, there is no predicting the level of capacity of the different children in the same family, except that they are quite likely to differ in this respect from one another and from each of their parents.

Thus if stratification based on common level of work-capacity resulting from common level of abstraction were to exist unimpeded, it would be a system of loose reference groupings, each joined by anyone progressing to that level, regardless of family, race, ethnic group, colour, sex, wealth. The

[7] It has already been suggested, for example, in Chapter 9 that there is some consistency between on the one hand the finding of a perceptual-tactile concreteness in Str-1 work and in the Capacity Group I, and on the other hand the physical-tactile mode of communication in working-class groups as described by Basil Bernstein and by Miller and Swanson. I would postulate that similar connections will be found between the various gradations of middle class (for example, lower and upper) and the Capacity Groups II and III, and so on.

boundaries between strata would be completely permeable to anyone of appropriate level of abstraction. Identification with a particular stratum would be of no significance whatever, other than as a projection of the existence of multi-modal distribution of work-capacity. It would confer no closed-club membership; there would be movement across boundaries *ad lib* as individuals grew in capacity; there would be no guarantee that children would be in the same stratum as parents, and hence no automatic elitism; and even the reflection in differential reward for work would be a matter of explicit consensus among the representatives of all groups at all levels.

If, then, the multi-modal distribution of work-capacity underlies social stratification but does not produce closed and rigid strata, what are the forces in a society which do produce rigid stratification leading eventually to conflicting social classes? It is surely such factors as family, ethnic group, sex, colour, caste, education, inherited wealth, which play their part in creating closed reference groups.[8] Members of these groups seek to maintain the same standards for one another, and tend in the direction of excluding others. Parents seek to ensure that children are in the same stratum as themselves – or higher – by passing on the accumulation of wealth independently of the work-capacity of the children. Members of the same race, religious grouping, caste, group together and seek to assist one another to achieve high status regardless of ability and to preclude others from out-groups from doing the same.

These other closed reference groups thus tend to wreck the natural structure of open permeable boundaries which form at the natural lines of horizontal cleavage in society. They clog the boundaries, making them dense and impermeable for members of other groups. At the same time they lift in-group members across boundaries which they could not traverse by their own competencies – giving them special education, nepotistic appointments, gifts of wealth, special modes of speech and behaviour, name, and all the other trappings of public identity connected with a particular social class.

The net effect is towards the development of a rigid and complex hierarchy of social strata based upon everything and anything except individual ability: feudal or caste families; white Anglo-Saxon protestantism; political party elitism; tribal affiliation; colonial power. In these circumstances high-level capacity is held down in lower-level strata; and low-level capacity is buoyed up in higher-level strata. It is at this point that the necessary forces for class formation and class conflict are generated.[9]

---

[8] H. H. Kelley (1955), 'Saliency of Membership and Resistance to Change of Group-Anchored Attitudes'; and T. M. Newcomb (1962), 'Persistence and Regression of Changed Attitudes'.

[9] The working class described by Engels in (1958) *The Condition of the Working Class*

Social mobility – both upwards and downwards – has been brought to a halt. Society becomes closed. The higher-level dispossessed become the inevitable initiators and leaders of the forces of change – forces which will be potentially explosive to the degree that the boundaries of stratification are closed and to the extent of the overall amount of discrepancy between work-capacity and opportunity in the suppressed population.

Work-capacity seeks its own level of work. Dam up work-capacity and it will exercise force against the dam. If the dammed-up capacity increases it may overflow into manifestations of dissatisfaction if the dam is not too high, or it may simply burst the dam and wash it away if the height of the dam is increased to stem the tide.

Bureaucracy and Freedom

If our argument is valid, then the natural stratification of society and the natural stratification of bureaucratic hierarchies occur at the same levels and are manifestations of the same characteristics of human nature. It would follow from this argument that constitutional bureaucracy, far from being a cause of rigid stratification, would act as an antidote to it. It could not entirely resolve the problem of how a society is to gain sufficient opportunity for mobility, but it could help greatly. For if the bureaucratic work system in a society is set up as a system enabling individuals to reach and to work at their full capacity regardless of race, creed, colour, mode of speech, school, family, then fossilization of the structure of stratification is less likely to occur – and it is fossilization of strata which is the scourge of a society, begetting social classes with closed boundaries, dissensual conflict, and violence.

We may then define social mobility not simply in terms of the number of people actually moving from one stratum to another, but rather in terms of the proportion of people who are moving into the level of work and the socio-economic status appropriate to their abilities. A one-hundred per cent open or mobile society would not be one in which every individual was on the move, but one in which everyone had the opportunity to achieve C-W-P equilibrium regardless of background. And it would imply 'downward' as well as 'upward' mobility, in the sense that sons and daughters would not necessarily have positions as high as their parents. Levelling-up processes would have to be allowed full expression, for it is

---

in England in 1844 had a high proportion of individuals of high capacity held down by class boundaries made impermeable by artifacts of kinship and race. Add to this condition of frustration and alienation the further injustices of unemployment and of inequity based upon exploitation of those who do work by cutting their differential conditions of work, and a socially explosive mixture is induced. Predictably, the explosion will be led by the suppressed high-capacity groups.

these processes which compensate for the relative but not necessarily absolute downward positioning of those who do not move. The sociological requirement would thus be in favour of steady controlled economic inflation in society, in the course of which the essential levelling-up process could occur by some people not receiving increases in payment.[10]

The argument thus leads to a constructive social paradox. It may be that the identification and explicit recognition of multi-modality in the distribution of abilities in the members of a society, and the establishment of a rational hierarchical structure with true boundaries in its bureaucratic sector, may provide conditions which would help to prevent the formation of impermeable class boundaries with their gross inequality of effect upon individuals. It is when social stratification becomes detached from its roots in the differentiation of individual capacities and is absorbed on an irrational basis into class structures, that the strata become closed up and a social menace. Given mobility in the bureaucratic sector of an industrial society, that society will be less likely to crystalize into fixed social classes.

Time-span and Free Will

Requisite bureaucracy is thus a potentially powerful force in the direction of freedom and justice in industrial society, by acting to ensure openness and social mobility. It is also potentially more than that. It is potentially the purveyor of the setting for a crucial experience of maximum free will for the individual in his prime relationship with reality – namely in his work.

In *Time and Free Will* (1910), Bergson has shown that the concept of free will is relevant only to the world of durée. In the conceptual abstraction of a mechanical physical world of static serial clock time, all is deterministic cause-and-effect, and everything is predetermined to the exclusion of free will. But in the real human world in which time is continuous flow and duration, all is free will, albeit not under the conscious control of the individual. In terms of our current analysis, the flow of behaviour simply is. In that sense it is free. It cannot be analysed in terms of cause-and-effect points in clock time, since these constructs destroy the flow.

The freedom of the behavioural flux does, however, have constraints. It is bounded. It occurs in a framework. It has direction. It can be constrained by the individual, or by the context set for the individual from outside. In

---

[10] I am referring here to annual inflation rates of the order of three to four per cent, and not the galloping inflation of 10 per cent, 20 per cent, 30 per cent and more which has been the scourge of much of the world economy recently. As mentioned earlier in the text, bureaucracy with equitable pay differentials determined by due constitutional process, would be a powerful force towards the rational control of inflation, by removing the wage- and salary-push component of inflation.

bureaucratic systems these contexts are set in terms of the boundaries of role relationships and the assignment of tasks which establish goals and direction.

We may now note a peculiar conjunction between the individual, his work, and freedom or free will. If the time-span of his role is shorter than his work-capacity, he is over-constrained and his freedom is impaired; that is to say, too short a time-span set in clock time interferes with the scale of a person's patterning and ordering of his individual flow of discretion in durée. Similarly, if the time-span is longer than his capacity, he is exposed to disorganization of his flow of discretion in durée, and his free will is disrupted through excess.

The situation of maximum freedom is that in which a person's time-span in clock time just matches his work-capacity as expressed in the scale of intuitive 'future' with which he patterns and orders his flow of discretion in durée; that is to say in a match between scale of work and scale of individual life-space. It is in this setting that the individual can exercise free will in a genuine way – genuine because it is limited. The maximization of the freedom comes not from any limitation, but from that special and particular limitation in which durée meets clock time in the reality of the match between the work-capacity of the individual and the demands of the external world of work reality.

Requisite Organization and the Genesis of Confidence

We now come full circle to the central issue which we left open at the beginning of the book – that of the definition of requisiteness in connection with social institutions. We left this issue to one side, saying that the book itself would unfold the definition. We can now complete the task.

In general terms requisite organization is that which enables work to get done as effectively as possible. In more specifically human terms however, it is that pattern of organization which provides a context which enhances social interaction between those occupying roles in a social system, and facilitates their co-operation in a manner consistent with effective interaction with the wider community in which they are placed. This definition of requisiteness thus includes relationships across social systems, the enhancement of social interaction all round being the object, and not just effective interaction within in-groups and exclusion or rejection of out-groups.

Requisiteness has at least two major components: structural soundness, and the induction of faith or confidence in working relationships. Structural soundness refers to the need to have a structure in which authority and accountability are matched, in which it is possible to get the right number of people in the right tasks at the right time, and so on. The induction of faith or confidence may usefully be the subject of a final comment.

It may have become apparent that, underlying our whole analysis, there emerges a dominant theme, that of enabling people to relate to one another with confidence and to root out suspicion and mistrust. For the Kantian moral imperative 'act as if the maxim from which you act were to become through your will a universal law of nature', we may substitute the principle of acting in such a way as to increase, by however little, the amount of faith and confidence which people may have in one another.

People are enormously sensitive to these features of behaviour. Melanie Klein has shown, for example, just how alert babies are from earliest infancy to whether the mother is to be relied upon, loved, trusted, or whether she is suspect and disturbing, a source of persecutory anxiety. The former reponse arises out of a relationship with a secure loving mother; the latter out of a relationship with an emotionally disturbed and anxious mother.

Adults respond just as sensitively. There are a thousand and one nonverbal cues, as well as verbal ones, which trigger off feelings as to whether the other person can be relied upon – a flicker of the eyes or a straightforward gaze, sudden hesitations or a dry throat or an easy relaxed flow of speech, awkward shifting of arms or shoulders or a quiet assured posture. The reactions are immediate and powerful: on the one hand feelings of relaxation, warm sympathy, and co-operativeness, of ease of relationship and interaction; and on the other hand, anything from slight discomfort and unease and a holding back from full interaction, to uncertainty about the other's motives, wariness, doubt, suspicion and downright mistrust, all interfering to some degree with mutual understanding, and in extremis leading to hostile rejection and violence.

It is not sufficient, however, to rely upon individual exhortation and admonition to get confidence-inducing – pistogenic – behaviour on the one hand and to reduce paranoiagenic behaviour on the other. Individual goodwill must be supported and encouraged by social mechanisms and institutions which channel and direct behaviour within confidence-inducing limits. Thus, for example, if the social systems within which individuals interact are composed of insufficiently specified or contradictory roles, individuals are thrown back upon 'personalities' with uncertainty and fears of coercion or of unfair use of status; or if the social structure sets paranoiagenic limits by allowing only for coercion or dissembling or tricky behaviours, then it is not surprising if suspicion and mistrust become rife.

An institution or pattern of organization may thus be defined as requisite to the extent that it reinforces the expression of behaviours supportive of confidence and trust in human interactions, and reduces suspicion and mistrust. Given public institutionalized reason for confidence in others, individuals may be better enabled to live together in co-operation, with justice, and with mutual understanding, sympathy, and goodwill. That, simply, is what requisiteness of social institutions is about.

Our discussion leads to the view, therefore, that social institutions can be looked at in terms of the moral, the reasonable, the just, the normal, the good. They can be considered in these terms because of the constraints and direction they set upon the behaviour of their individual members. Thus, for example, bureaucratic systems which have procedures which are designed to arrange for C-W-P equilibrium for employees are to that extent good or moral institutions. They are good or moral because they set boundaries and goals which are in line with individual freedom and which reinforce confidence and social bonding in the institution and in society, and are thus pistogenic. Contrariwise, bureaucratic systems which do not function in this manner are bad, irrational, abnormal, anti-moral, in that they frustrate the normal flow of behaviour and are paranoiagenic.

In the same way, the features we have outlined as composing requisite constitutional bureaucracy can be claimed to be socially and morally good. They are socially bonding and mitigate paranoiagenesis and its socially fragmenting effects. They are consistent with normal behaviour in the sense of normality which I set out in the Prolegomenon.

Morality and the problem of values, then, are not just affairs of the individual. They are concerned with the individual in his social relationships as those relationships are bounded within the framework of social institutions. For example, how are we to categorize the behaviour of an individual who seeks to get what he can regardless of what happens to others? Is that ethically good behaviour? Is it abnormal in the sense of being selfish and greedy? Unless the social situation is known it is impossible to say. If a person is a member of a trade union engaged in collective bargaining, his behaviour must be seen as ethically good because he is co-operating with his fellow workers, even though the bargaining might disregard the interests of other groups; his personal behaviour is as socially bonding as the situation will allow. If, however, he behaves in a similar manner in his friendships, his behaviour will have an entirely different moral and ethical connotation.

The fact that the evaluation of the morality of individual behaviour must be carried out in relation to the social setting in which the behaviour occurs, has of course been argued commonly enough. What has been less remarked upon, however, is that the same argument implies an ethical evaluation of the social setting itself. Thus, if collective bargaining directs behaviour towards unconcern for the status and welfare of out-groups, whereas friendship does not necessarily do so, then friendship as an institution can be seen to be potentially more socially bonding and less paranoiagenic than collective bargaining.

If this example seems over-simple, that would merely be to argue that it is not necessarily all that difficult to assess the pistogenic – confidence-inducing – or the paranoiagenic qualities of small-scale institutions. The difficulties arise at the macro-level, as in, for example, comparisons between the requisiteness of democratic as against single-party rule in developing nations. That is why analysis at the micro-level of the requisiteness of sub-institutions is so important. A growing understanding of what is socially bonding in these sub-institutions can be used in the construction of larger-scale institutions – or as Karl Popper has pointed out, what we require is step-by-step small-scale social engineering and less of the preoccupation with idealistic grand social designs.

It is important that these assessments of institutions should be made in terms of their likely social bonding (or pistogenic) effects, or their likely paranoiagenic effects. When a system of social relationships is itself fragmenting and organized for conflict, it need occasion no suprise if the behaviour of the ordinary constructive person given no choice but to live in the system turns out to be constructive towards the in-group and disruptive or destructive to others.

We have pointed to many examples of paranoiagenic situations in connection with bureaucracy: not only collective bargaining, but also failure to define managerial accountability and authority; confusion of grading and work-strata; failure to provide for participation, equity, and individual justice; lack of conditions to ensure C-W-P equilibrium; an exploitive labour market. We have also pointed to more requisite institutions to replace the pathological ones, and in consequence to replace paranoiagenesis, alienation, dissensus, and the wastage of human lives and creativeness, by trust and confidence, social bonding, consensus, pistogenesis.

Thus, for example, in connection with the effects of bureaucracy upon those employed within them, it may be useful to emphasize once again that they are social institutions which call for the public acceptance of individual accountability. The individual cannot conceal his personal responsibility in the group. Any social institution which is so deeply rooted in public personal responsibility has a good start in the direction of social health, morality, requisiteness. The immediate task is the construction of requisite superstructures upon this wholesome foundation.

The design of social institutions is thus crucial for the good society. These institutions set the limits which determine just how far it will be possible for people to live together, to work together, to be together, in socially good, ethical, moral terms – to be human. A humanitarian society depends upon the humanity of its social institutions. Bureaucracy is the inevitable handmaiden of large-scale technology, and it is unlikely that post-industrial society will do other than magnify the bureaucratic phenomenon. The attainment of requisitely humanitarian bureaucratic systems is essential, therefore, for human progress in industrial societies, regardless of the political or economic systems in which they are placed. It is essential, moreover, if mankind is to discover its better self.

Bibliography

ABRAMS, Mark
  1968 'Some Measurement of Social Stratification in Britain'. In Jackson, J. A. (ed.), *Social Stratification*: Cambridge University Press, 1968.
ACKOFF, Russell L. and EMERY, Fred E.
  1972 *On Purposeful Systems: An Interdisciplinary Analysis of Individual and Social Behaviour as a System of Purposeful Events:* London, Tavistock Publications.
ADAMS, J. S.
  1963 'Wage Inequities, Productivity and Work Equality': *Industr. Relat.,* 3, pp. 9–16.
  1963 'Toward an Understanding of Inequity': *J. Abnorm. Soc. Psychol.,* Vol. 67, pp. 442–6.
  1965 'Inequity in Social Exchange'. In Berkowitz, L. (ed.), *Advances in Experimental Social Psychology*, Vol. 2: New York, Academic Press.
ADIZES, Ichak
  1971 *Industrial Democracy. Yugoslav Style*: New York, Free Press.
AIKEN, M. and HAGE, J.
  1968 'Organisational Interdependence and Intraorganisational Structure': *American J. of Sociology*, Vol. 33, No. 6, pp. 912–13.
ARGYRIS, Chris
  1957 *Personality and the Organisation*: New York, Harper & Rowe.
  1960 *Understanding Organizational Behaviour*: London, Tavistock Publications.
BALES, Robert F.
  1950 *Interaction Process Analysis*: Cambridge, Mass., Addison-Wesley.
BARKER, R., DEMBO, T., and LEWIN, K.
  1945 'Frustration and Regression': In 'Studies of Topological and Vector Psychology', *University of Iowa Studies in Child Welfare*, XVII, No. 2.
BAVELAS, Alexander
  1942 'Morale and the Training of Leaders'. In Watson, G. (ed.), *Civilian Morale*: Boston, Houghton Mifflin.

BELL, Daniel
1974   *The Coming of Post-Industrial Society*: London, Heinemann.
BENNIS, Warren G.
1966   *Changing Organizations*: New York, McGraw Hill.
BERGSON, Henri
1910   *Time and Free Will*: London, George Allen and Unwin, 1971.
1911   *Matter and Memory*: London, George Allen and Unwin.
1911   *Creative Evolution*: London, Macmillan & Co.
BERNSTEIN, Basil
1971   *Class, Codes and Control*, Vol. 1: London, Routledge and Kegan Paul.
BILLIS, David
1971   *Process of Planning in the Kibbutz*: Unpublished doctoral thesis, London University.
1977   'Differential Administrative Capacity and Organisational Development: A Kibutz Case Study'. To be published in *Human Relations*.
BION, W. R.
1962   *Learning from Experience*: London, William Heinemann Medical Books Ltd.
BIRDWHISTELL, Ray L.
1973   *Kinesics and Context*: Harmondsworth, Penguin Books.
BLAU, Peter M.
1955   *The Dynamics of Bureaucracy*: Chicago University Press.
1964   *Exchange and Power in Social Life*: New York, John Wiley.
BLAU, Peter M. and SCOTT, Richard
1960   *Formal Organizations*: London, Routledge and Kegan Paul.
BLAUNER, R.
1964   *Alienation and Freedom*: Chicago University Press.
BLUMBERG, P.
1968   *Industrial Democracy: The Sociology of Participation*: London, Constable.
BRIDGMAN, P. W.
1927   *The Logic of Modern Physics*: New York, Macmillan.
BRIM, O. G.
1960   'Personality Development as Role Learning.' In Iscoe, I. and Stevenson, H. (eds.), *Personality Development in Children*: Austin, Texas, University of Texas Press.
BROWN, Wilfred
1960   *Exploration in Management*: London, Heinemann Educational Books Ltd.
1962   *Piecework Abandoned*: London, Heinemann Educational Books Ltd.
1971   *Organization*: London, Heinemann Educational Books Ltd.

1973   *The Earnings Conflict*: London, Heinemann Educational Books Ltd.

BROWN, Wilfred and JAQUES, Elliott
1964   *Product Analysis Pricing*: London, Heinemann Educational Books Ltd.
1965   *Glacier Project Papers*: London, Heinemann Educational Books Ltd.

BURNHAM, James
1960   *The Managerial Revolution*: Bloomington, Ind., Indiana U. P.

BURNS, T. and STALKER, G. M.
1961   *The Management of Innovation*: London, Tavistock Publications.

CARTWRIGHT, D.
1965   'Influence, Leadership and Control'. In March, James G. (ed.), *Handbook of Organisations*: Chicago, Rand McNally.

CICOUREL, Aaron V.
1973   *Cognitive Sociology*: Harmondsworth, Penguin Education.

CHERRY, C.
1957   *On Human Communication*: New York, John Wiley.

CIVIL SERVICE
1966/1968   *Committee on the Civil Service, Vol. 1*: London, HMSO.

COCH, L. and FRENCH, J. P. R.
1948   'Overcoming Resistance to Change': *Hum. Rel.* Vol. 1, pp. 512–32.

COLLYEAR, J. G.
1975   *Management Precepts*: Bradford, MCB Books.

CROZIER, M.
1965   *The Bureaucratic Phenomenon*: London, Tavistock Publications.

DAHRENDORF, Ralf
1963   *Class and Class Conflict in an Industrial Society*: London, Routledge and Kegan Paul.
1968   'Values and Social Science'. In Dahrendorf, R., *Essays in the Theory of Society*: London, Routledge and Kegan Paul.
1968   'Liberty and Equality'. In Dahrendorf, R., *Essays in the Theory of Society*: London, Routledge and Kegan Paul.

DAVIS, Kingsley
1949   *Human Society*: New York, Macmillan.

DEPARTMENT OF EMPLOYMENT
——   Felt Fair Pay: Research Monograph (to be published by the Department).

DEPARTMENT OF HEALTH AND SOCIAL SECURITY
1972   *Management Arrangements for the Reorganised National Health Service*: London, HMSO.

DEWEY, John
1922   *Human Nature and Conduct*: New York, Henry Holt.
DIMOND, S.
1972   *The Double Brain*: Edinburgh, Churchill Livingstone.
DUGUID, Andrew and JAQUES, Elliott
1971   *Case Studies in Export Organisation*: London, HMSO.
DURKHEIM, Emile
1952   *Suicide*: London, Routledge and Kegan Paul.
1961   *Moral Education*: New York, Free Press.
1964   'The Determination of Moral Facts'. In Durkheim, E., *The Rules of Sociological Methods*: Glencoe, Ill., Free Press.
ELIOT, T. S.
1951   'Ben Jonson'. In Eliot, T. S., *Selected Essays*: London, Faber and Faber.
ELLERMAN, David
1973   On Property and Contract in Political Economy: Manuscript, Dept. of Economics, University of Boston.
EMERY, F. E. and THORSRUD, E.
1969   *Form and Content in Industrial Democracy*: London, Tavistock Publications.
EMERY, F. E. and TRIST, E. L.
1965   'The Causal Texture of Organisational Environment': *Hum. Rel.*, 18, pp. 21–32.
ENGELS, Friedrich
1958   *The Condition of the Working Class in England in 1844*: London, Blackwell.
ETZIONI, Amitai
1964   *Modern Organizations*: Englewood Cliffs, N. J., Prentice-Hall.
EVANS, J. S.
1970   'Time-span: The Neglected Tool': *Personnel Management*, February 1970; and *The Professional Engineer*, Vol. 15, No. 2.
1970   'Tracing Salary Patterns': *Personnel Management*, December 1970.
1971   'Salary Patterns and the Language of Responsibility': *Personnel Management*, May 1971.
1971   'Contrasting Task Analysis Procedures in Consultancy-based and Survey-based Research': *Hum. Rel.*, Vol. 24, No. 2, pp. 139–48.
1971   'Responsibility: Can We Talk It?': *New Society*, 23rd July 1971.
1976   *Management of Human Capacity*. (To be published)
FARBER, M. L.
1944   'Suffering and Time Perspective of the Prisoner'. In *University of Iowa Studies in Child Welfare*, Vol. 20, pp. 155–227.

FESTINGER, Leon
    1942   'Wish, Expectation and Group Performance as Factors Affec-
            ting Level of Aspiration': *J. Abnorm. & Soc. Psychol.* (1942), 37,
            pp. 184–200.
    1954   'A Theory of Social Comparison Processes: *Hum. Rel.*, 7, pp.
            117–40.
FIEDLER, F. E.
    1967   *Theory of Leadership Effectiveness*: New York, McGraw Hill.
FITZROY, Felix R.
    1972   'Foundations of Political Economy'. Discussion Paper 19,
            Fachgruppe Wirtschaftswissenschaften, Universität
            Heidelberg. Published in *Participation and Self-management*,
            Vol. 5 (Proc. 1st Int. Soc. Conf. on Participation and Self-
            Management, Dubrovnik, Dec. 1972) Zabreb, 1974.
    1973   'Economic Organization and Human Capital': Discussion
            Paper 32, Fachgruppe Wirtschaftswissenschaften, Universität
            Heidelberg.
    1974   'Alienation, Freedom, and Economic Organization: A Review
            Note': memorandum of the Alfred-Weber-Institut, Universität
            Heidelberg.
FOX, Alan
    1974   *Beyond Contract: Work, Power and Trust Relations*: London,
            Faber and Faber.
FRENCH Jr., John R. P. and SNYDER, Richard
    1959   'Leadership and Interpersonal Power'. In Cartwright, D. (ed.),
            Studies in Social Power: Ann Arbor, University of Michigan,
            Institute of Social Research.
FREUD, Sigmund
    1923   *The Ego and the Id*. Standard ed., Vol. XIX: London, Hogarth
            Press, 1961.
FRIEDMAN, M.
    1962   *Capitalism and Freedom*: Chicago University Press.
GALBRAITH, J. K.
    1957   *American Capitalism: The Concept of Countervailing Power*:
            London, Hamish Hamilton.
    1974   *Economics and the Public Purpose*: London, Deutsch.
GARFINKEL, Harold
    1967   *Studies in Ethnomethodology*: Englewood Cliffs, N. J., Prentice-
            Hall.
GINTIS, Herbert
    1972   'Alienation in Capitalist Society'. In R. C. Edwards, M. Reich,
            T. E. Weisskopf (eds.), *The Capitalist System*: Engelwood Cliffs,
            N. J., Prentice-Hall.

GLACIER METAL COMPANY LIMITED
London Factories Standing Orders
Policy Document

GLASS, D. V., MOSER, C. A., *et al.*
1954 *Social Mobility in Britain*: London, Routledge and Kegan Paul.

GOFFMAN, Erving
1961 *Encounters*: Indianapolis, Bobbs-Merrill.
1970 *Strategic Interaction*: Oxford, Blackwell.

GOLDSTEIN, Kurt
1948 *Language and Language Disturbances*: New York, Grune & Stratton.

GOLDSTEIN, Kurt, and SHEERER, G.
1939 *The Organism*: New York, American Book Co.

GOLDTHORPE, John H., and HOPE, Keith
1974 *The Social Grading of Occupations: A New Approach and Scale*: Oxford, Clarendon Press.

GOLDTHORPE, John H., and LOCKWOOD, D.
1968 *The Affluent Worker: Vol. 1, Industrial Attitudes and Behaviour*: Cambridge University Press.

GOODMAN, Paul S.
1967 'An Empirical Examination of Elliott Jaques' Concept of Time-Span': *Hum. Rel.*, Vol. 20, No. 2, pp. 155–70.

GRAICUNAS, V. A.
1937 'Relationship in Organisation'. In Gulick, L. and Urwick, L., *Papers on the Science of Administration*: New York Institute of Public Administration.

GRANICK, David
1954 *Management of the Industrial Firm in the U.S.S.R. (A Study in Soviet Economic Planning)*: New York, Columbia University Press.

HAGE, J. and AIKEN, M.
1967 'Relationship of Centralisation to Other Structural Properties': *Admin. Sci. Quart.*, 12, pp. 72–92.

HANSARD
1969 *House of Lords Official Report*: 19th November 1969.

HANSEN, D. R.
1973 'Some Results of a Test at Canadian Forces Base Uplands of a Measure of Work and Responsibility': *DRAE Memorandum M. 45*: Department of National Defence, Ottawa, Canada.
1974 'Results of a Test at a Land Base of a Measure of Work & Responsibility': *ORAE Memorandum M.60*: Department of National Defence, Ottawa, Canada.

1975   'Tests of a Measure of Work and Responsibility in Some Naval
        Units of the Canadian Forces': *ORAE Memorandum M.66*:
        Department of National Defence, Ottawa, Canada.
HARVEY, O. J., HUNT, D. E. and SCHRODER, H. M.
1961   *Conceptual Systems and Personality Organisation*: New York,
        John Wiley.
HAYEK, F. A.
1960   *The Constitution of Liberty*: London, Routledge and Kegan
        Paul.
HAZEKAMP, F. C.
1966   'Werk, Capaciteit en Beloning in het "Glacier Project" ':
        Polytechnisch Tidschrift, 6.7.66.
HEALTH SERVICES ORGANIZATION RESEARCH UNIT, BRUNEL UNIVERSITY
1973   *Working Papers on the Reorganisation of the National Health
        Service.*
HEBB, D. O.
1972   *Texbook of Psychology*: London, W. B. Saunders & Co.
HEILBRONNER, Robert
1972   *The Worldly Philosophers*: New York, Simon und Schuster.
1974   *An Inquiry into the Human Prospect*: New York, Norton.
HILL, J. M. M. H.
1951   'A Consideration of Labour Turnover as a Resultant of a Quasi-
        Stationary Process': *Hum. Rel.*, 4, 1951. pp. 255–64.
HINING, C. R. and LEE, G. L.
1971   'Dimensions of Organisation Structure and Their Context': *J.
        Brit. Soc. Assn.*, 1971, 5, pp. 83–93.
HOBBES, Thomas
1962   *Leviathan*: London, Fontana Library. Abridged edition with
        introduction by John Plamenatz.
HOMA, Edna B.
1967   'The Inter-Relationship Among Work, Payment and Capacity';
        Unpublished doctoral dissertation, Harvard Business School.
HOMANS, George C.
1951   *The Human Group*: London, Routledge and Kegan Paul.
1961   *Social Behaviour: Its Elementary Forms*: London, Routledge
        and Kegan Paul.
HORVAT, Branko
1968   'An Integrated System of Social Accounts for an Economy of
        Yugoslavian Type'. In: *Review of Income and Wealth*, 14.
1969   *Essay on Yugoslav Society*: White Plains, N. Y., International
        Arts and Sciences Press.
1971   'Yugoslav Economic Policy in the Post War Period: Problems,
        Ideas, Institutional Developments'. In *AER*, 61, Supplement.

HOWE, Christopher
   1973   'Labour Organization and Incentives in Industry, Before and
           After the Cultural Revolution'. In Schram, Stuart R. (ed.),
           Authority Participation and Cultural Change in China: Cam-
           bridge University Press.
HYMAN, H. H.
   1942   'The Psychology of Status'. *Archives of Psychology*, No. 269.
HYMAN, H. H. and SINGER, E.
   1968   *Readings in Reference Group Theory and Research*: New York,
           Free Press.
   1968   'Problems of Research on Relative Deprivation'. In *Readings in
           Reference Group Theory and Research*: New York, Free Press.
ISAAC, D. J. and O'CONNOR, B. M.
   1969   'Experimental Treatment of a Discontinuity Theory of
           Psychological Development': *Hum. Rel.*, Vol. 22, 5, pp. 427–55.
   1973   'Use of Loss of Skill under Stress to Test a Theory of
           Psychological Development': *Hum. Rel.*, Vol. 26, 4, p. 488.
JAMES, L. R. and JONES, A. P.
   1974   'Organizational Climate: A Review of Theory and Research':
           Admin. Sci. Quart.
JAQUES, Elliott
   1951   *The Changing Culture of a Factory*: London, Tavistock
           Publications.
   1956   *Measurement of Responsibility:* London, Tavistock
           Publications.
   1961   *Equitable Payment*: London, Heinemann Educational Books
           Ltd.
   1964   *Time-Span Handbook*: London, Heinemann Educational
           Books Ltd.
   1965   'Social-Analysis and the Glacier Project'. In Brown, W., and
           Jaques E, *Glacier Project Papers*: London, Heinemann
           Educational Books Ltd.
   1968   *Progression Handbook*: London, Heinemann Educational
           Books Ltd.
   1969   'Fair Pay: How to Achieve It'. *New Society,* 27th November
           1969.
   1970   'Disturbances in the Capacity to Work'. In *Work, Creativity
           and Social Justice*: London, Heinemann Educational Books
           Ltd.
   1970   'The Human Consequences of Industrialization'. In *Work,
           Creativity and Social Justice*: London, Heinemann Educational
           Books Ltd.

1970   'Time and the Measurement of Human Attributes'. In *Work, Creativity and Social Justice*: London, Heinemann Educational Books Ltd.

1970   'Psycho-Analysis and the Current Economic Crisis In *Work, Creativity and Social Justice*: London, Heinemann Educational Books Ltd.

1970   'Theses on Work'. In *Work, Creativity and Social Justice*: London, Heinemann Educational Books Ltd.

1972   'What is the Normal Personality?': Unpublished article, *Scientific Bulletin of the British Psycho-Analytical Society*, No. 63.

1972   'Grading and Management Organization in the Civil Service: *O. & M. Bulletin* (Civil Service Department), Vol. 27, No. 3.

KAHN, Robert L. and KATZ, Daniel

1953   'Leadership Practices in Relation to Productivity and Morale'. In Cartwright, D. and Zander, A. (eds.) *Group Dynamics*: Evanston, Ill., Row, Peterson.

KATZ, Daniel and KAHN, Robert L.

1966   *The Social Psychology of Organisations*: New York, John Wiley.

KATZ, D., MACOBBY, N., and MORSE, N. C.

1950   *Productivity, Supervision and Morale in an Office Situation*: Ann Arbor, University of Michigan Institute of Social Research.

KELLEY, H. H.

1955   'Saliency of Membership and Resistance to Change of Group-Anchored Attitudes'. *Hum. Rel.*, 1955, No. 3, pp. 275–89.

KEYNES, J. M.

1936   *The General Theory of Employment, Interest and Money*: London, Macmillan.

KLEIN, Melanie

1948   *Contributions to Psycho-Analysis*. In Klein, M., *Collected Writings*: London, Hogarth Press, 1975.

1946   'Notes on Some Schizoid Mechanisms'. In Klein, M., *Collected Writings*: London, Hogarth Press, 1975.

1957   *Envy and Gratitude*. In Klein, M., *Collected Writings*: London, Hogarth Press, 1975.

KOGAN, Maurice, CANG, Stephen, DIXON, Maureen, TOLLIDAY, Heather

1971   *Working Relationships Within the British Hospital Service*: London, Bookstall Publications.

KOGAN, M. and PACKWOOD, G. F.

1974   *Advisory Councils and Committees in Education*: London, Routledge and Kegan Paul.

KRIMPAS, G. E.

1975   *Labour Input and the Theory of the Labour Market*: London, Duckworth.

KROEBER, Alfred L.
1944   *Configurations of Culture Growth*: Berkeley, University of California Press.
KROPOTKIN, Peter, A.
1910   'Anarchism'. In: *Encyclopaedia Britannica*. 11. edn., New York.
LANE, David
1971   *The End of Inequality? Stratification under State Socialism*: London, Penguin Books.
LAWRENCE, Paul
1958   *The Changing of Organizational Behaviour Patterns*: Boston, Graduate School of Business Administration, Harvard University.
LÉVI-STRAUSS, Claude
1968   *Structural Anthropology*: London, Allen Lane Penguin Press.
LEVINSON, Harry
1972   *Organizational Diagnosis*: Cambridge, Mass., Harvard University Press.
LEWIN, Kurt
1936   *Principles of Topological Psychology*: New York and London, McGraw Hill.
1942   'Time Perspective and Morale'. In his *Resolving Social Conflicts*: New York, Harper Row, 1948.
1952   'Frontiers in Group Dynamics'. In Cartwright, D. (ed.), *Field Theory and Social Science*: London, Tavistock Publications.
1952   'Regression, Retrogression and Development'. In Cartwright, D. (ed.) *Field Theory and Social Science*: London, Tavistock Publications.
LIKERT, R.
1961   *New Patterns of Management*: New York, McGraw Hill.
LIPPITT, Ronald *et al.*
1952   'The Dynamics of Power': *Hum. Rel.*, 5, pp. 37–64.
LIPPITT, Ronald and WHITE, R. K.
1947   'Experimental Study of Leadership and Group Life'. In Newcomb, T. M. and Hartley, E. L., *Readings in Social Psychology*: New York, Holt, Rinehart and Winston.
LIPSET, Seymour M. and BENDIX, Reinhard
1951   'Social Status and Social Structure: A Re-examination of Data and Interpretations, I and II'. *British Journal of Sociology*, II (June and September 1951).
1959   *Social Mobility in Industrial Society*: London, Heinemann.
LOW, Albert
1976   *Zen and Creative Management*: New York, Doubleday.

388   A GENERAL THEORY OF BUREAUCRACY

MACCOBY, E. E., NEWCOMB, T. M. and HARTLEY, E. L.
  1958   *Readings in Social Psychology*: New York Holt, Rinehart and Winston.
McGREGOR, D.
  1960   *The Human Side of Enterprise*: New York, McGraw Hill.
MacIVER, R. M. and PAGE, C. H.
  1960   *Society: An Introductory Analysis*: London, Macmillan.
McLELLAN, David
  1973   *Karl Marx: His Life and Thought*: London, Macmillan.
McLELLAND, D.
  1973   'Testing for Competence Rather than "Intelligence".': *American Psychologist* (January).
MANN, F. C.
  1965   'Towards an Understanding of the Leadership Role in Formal Organisation': In Dubin, R., Homans, G. C., Mann, F. C. and Miller, D. C., *Leadership and Productivity*: San Francisco, Chandler Publishing Co.
MARX, Karl and ENGELS, Friedrich
  1939   *The German Ideology: Early Writings*: New York, International Publ.
MEAD, G. H.
  1932   *The Philosophy of the Present*: Chicago University Press.
  1934   *Mind, Self and Society*: Chicago University Press.
  1938   *The Philosophy of the Act*: Chicago University Press.
  1956   *The Social Psychology of George Herbert Mead*: Chicago University Press.
MELMAN, Seymour
  1970   'Industrial Efficiency under Managerial versus Cooperative Decision Making'. In: *Review of Radical Political Economics, 2*.
MERLEAU-PONTY, Maurice
  1974   *Phenomenology, Language and Sociology*: London, Heinemann.
MERTON, Robert K.
  1957   'Bureaucratic Structure and Personality'. In his *Social Theory and Social Structure*: Glencoe, Ill., Free Press.
MICHELS, Robert
  1949   *Political Parties*: New York, Free Press.
MILL, John Stuart
  1861   *Representative Government*: Reprinted in *Three Essays,* with introduction by Richard Wollheim: Oxford, Oxford University Press, 1975.
MILLER, Daniel R.
  1963   'The Study of Social Relationships: Situation, Indentity and

Social Interaction'. In Koch, S. (ed.), *Psychology: A Study of a Science*, Vol. 5: McGraw Hill.

MILLER, Daniel R. and SWANSON, Guy E.
1958 *The Changing American Parent*: New York, John Wiley.

MILLER, James
1960 'Input Overload and Psychopathology': *Amer. J. Psychiat.*, Vol. 116, pp. 321–32.

MINISTRY OF HEALTH, SCOTTISH HOME AND HEALTH DEPARTMENT
1966 *Report of the Committee on Senior Nursing Staff Structure*: HMSO, London.

MOORE, Wilbert E.
1963 *Social Change*: Englewood Cliffs, N. J., Prentice Hall.
1966 'Changes in Occupational Structures'. In Smelser, N. J. and Lipset, S. M. (eds.), *Social Structure and Mobility in Economic Development*: London, Routledge and Kegan Paul.

MOUNTCASTLE, V. B. (ed.)
1962 *Interhemispheric Relations and Cerebral Dominance*: Baltimore, Johns Hopkins Press.

MOUZELIS, N.
1967 *Organization and Bureaucracy*: London, Routledge and Kegan Paul.

NEWCOMB, T. M.
1950 *Social Psychology*: New York, Dryden Press.
1962 'Persistence and Regression of Changed Attitudes': *J. Soc. Issues*, 19, pp. 3–13.

NEWMAN, A. D. and ROWBOTTOM, R. W.
1968 *Organization Analysis*: London, Heinemann Educational Books Ltd.

NEWMAN, Oscar
1973 *Defensible Space*: London, Architectural Press.

NISBET, R. A.
1966 *The Sociological Tradition*: New York, Basic Books.

NUTZINGER, Hans G.
1974 *Die Stellung des Betriebes in der sozialistischen Wirtschaft. Allokationsmodelle zum Verhältnis von betrieblicher Entscheidung und gesamtwirtschaftlicher Abstimmung*: Frankfurt/M. (Herder und Herder).

OBERLÄNDER, Erwin
1972 'Einleitung'. In: E. Oberländer (ed.), *Anarchismus*: Olten, Walter.

ORNSTEIN, R.
1973 *The Nature of Human Consciousness*: San Francisco, W. H. Freeman.

ORTEGA Y GASSET, J.
1932   *The Revolt of the Masses*: London, Unwin Books, 1961.
PARSONS, Talcott
1949   *Essays in Sociological Theory Pure and Applied*: New York, Free Press of Glencoe.
PASCAL, Blaise
1941   *Pensées and Provincial Letters*: abridged edition, New York, Modern Library.
PEPPER, Stephen C.
1970   'Survival Value'. In Laszlo, E. and Wilbur, J. B. (eds.), *Human Values and Natural Science*: New York, Gordon and Breach Science Publishers.
PIAGET, J.
1953   *Origin of Intelligence in the Child*: London, Routledge and Kegan Paul.
1971   *Structuralism*: London, Routledge and Kegan Paul.
POPPER, K. R.
1972   'On the Theory of the Objective Mind'. In his *Objective Knowledge*: Oxford, Clarendon Press.
PUGH, D. S., HICKSON, D. J., HINING, C. R. and TURNER, C.
1968   'Dimensions of Organisation Structure': *Admin. Sci. Quart.*, 13, pp. 65–105.
RAWLS, John
1972   *A Theory of Justice*: Oxford, Clarendon Press.
RICE, A. K.
1963   *The Enterprise and its Envirnment*: London, Tavistock Publications.
RICHARDSON, Roy
1971   *Fair Pay and Work*: London, Heinemann Educational Books Ltd.
ROBINSON, Joan
1933   *The Economics of Imperfect Competition*: London, Macmillan.
ROGERS, Kenn
1963   *Managers: Personality and Performance*: London, Tavistock Publications.
ROMMETVEIT, R.
1955   *Social Norms and Roles*: Minneapolis, University of Minnesota.
ROWBOTTOM, R. W., and BILLIS, D.
1976   'The Stratification of Work and Organisational Design': *Hum. Rel.*
ROWBOTTOM, R. W., *et al.*
1973   *Hospital Organization*: London, Heinemann Educational Books Ltd.

RUNCIMAN, W. G.
  1966   *Relative Deprivation and Social Justice*: London, Routledge and Kegan Paul.
RUSSELL, Bertrand
  1916   *Principles of Social Reconstruction*: London, Allen and Unwin.
SAINT AUGUSTINE.
  1961   *Confessions*: tr. by R. S. Pine-Coffin, Harmondsworth, Penguin Books.
SAMUELSON, Paul A.
  1964   *Economics*: New York, McGraw Hill.
SCHACHTEL, Ernest G.
  1963   *Metamorphosis*: London, Routledge and Kegan Paul.
SCHLEMENSON, Aldo Eduardo
  1971   'Professional Work in Organisations with Special Reference to Partnership as a Model of Organisation': Unpublished M. Tech. thesis, Brunel University.
SCHLICK, Moritz
  1962   *Problems of Ethics*: tr. P. Rynin, New York, Dover Books.
SCHON, Donald
  1971   *Beyond the Stable State*: London, Temple Smith.
SCHUTZ, Alfred
  1967   *Collected Papers I: The Problem of Social Reality*: The Hague, Martinus Nijhoff.
  1972   *The Phenomenology of the Social World*: London, Heinemann Educational Books Ltd.
SHILS, E.
  1968   'Deference'. In Jackson, J. A. (ed.), *Social Stratification*: Cambridge University Press.
ŠIK, Ota
  1971   *Czechoslovakia: The Bureaucratic Economy*: White Plains, International Arts and Science Press.
SIMMEL, Georg
  1950   *The Sociology of Georg Simmel*: Glencoe, Free Press.
  1950   'Secrecy'. In *The Sociology of Georg Simmel*: Glencoe, Free Press.
  1950   'Superordination and Subordination'. In *The Sociology of Georg Simmel*: Glencoe, Free Press.
SIMON, Herbert
  1957   *Administrative Behaviour*: New York, Macmillan.
SOCIAL SERVICES ORGANIZATION RESEARCH UNIT, Brunel University
  1974   *Social Services Departments: Developing Patterns of Work and Organization*: London, Heinemann.

SPERRY, R. W.
   1966   'Brain Bisection and Mechanisms of Consciousness'. In Eccles,
          J. C. (ed.), *Brain and Conscious Experience*. New York,
          Springer Verlag.
STAMP, Gillian
   1974   'Mental Functioning in Human Capacity': Unpublished
          memorandum, Brunel Institute of Organisation and Social
          Studies.
STENHOUSE, David
   1974   *The Evolution of Intelligence*: London, George Allen and
          Unwin.
SUMNER, W. G.
   1959   *Folkways:* New York, Dover Books.
TAGIURI, R. and LITWIN, G. H. (eds.)
   1968   *Organizational Climate*: Harvard University, Graduate School
          of Business.
THORNDIKE, R. L.
   1938   'On What Type of Task will a Group do Well?' *J. Abnorm. and
          Soc. Psych.*, 33, pp. 409–13.
THORSRUD, E. and EMERY, F. E.
   1970   'Industrial Democracy in Norway': *Industrial Relations*, pp.
          187–96.
TOCQUEVILLE, A. de
   1952   *Democracy in America*: reprinted, London, Oxford University
          Press.
TUMIN, M. M.
   1967   *Social Stratification*: Englewood Cliffs, N. J., Prentice-Hall.
URWICK, Lyndall
   1947   *Elements of Administration*: London, Pitman.
VANEK, Jaroslav
   1970   *The General Theory of Labor Managed Market Economies*:
          Ithaca, Cornell University Press.
   1971   *The Participatory Economy*: Ithaca, Cornell University Press.
   1972   'The Yugoslav Economy viewed through the Theory of Labor
          Management'. Working Paper 36, Dept. of Economics, Cornell
          University.
VOEGELIN, Eric
   1952   *The New Science of Politics*: Chicago University Press.
VROOM, V. H.
   1964   *Work and Motivation*: New York, John Wiley.
WEBER, Max
   1918   'Science as Vocation'. In Gerth, H. H. and Mills, C. W. (eds.),
          From Max Weber: London, Routledge and Kegan Paul.

1947 *The Theory of Social and Economic Organisation*: Glencoe, Ill., Free Press.

WESTLEY, W. A.
1971 *The Emerging Worker*: Montreal, McGill Queens Press.
1972 'An Evaluation Model for Worker Participation in Management': Paper prepared for the First International Sociological Conference on Worker Participation and Self-Management, Yugoslavia, December 1972.

WESTLEY, W. A. and KOLAGA, J.
1965 *Workers' Councils – The Yugoslav Experiment*: London, Tavistock Publications.

WORTHY, James
1950 'Organisational Structure and Employee Morale': *Amer. Soc. Rev.*, 15, p. 178.

ZUCKERKANDL, Victor
1956 *Sound and Symbol: Music and the External World*: New York, Pantheon Books Inc.

Index